COLLABORATIONS AND PARTNERSHIPS IN USER EXPERIENCE

Foundations and Innovations in Technical and Professional Communication

Series Editor: Lisa Melançon
Series Associate Editor: Sherena Huntsman

The Foundations and Innovations in Technical and Professional Communication series publishes work that is necessary as a base for the field of technical and professional communication (TPC), addresses areas of central importance within the field, and engages with innovative ideas and approaches to TPC. The series focuses on presenting the intersection of theory and application/practice within TPC and is intended to include both monographs and co-authored works, edited collections, digitally enhanced work, and innovative works that may not fit traditional formats (such as works that are longer than a journal article but shorter than a book).

The WAC Clearinghouse and University Press of Colorado are collaborating so that these books will be widely available through free digital distribution and low-cost print editions. The publishers and the series editors are committed to the principle that knowledge should freely circulate and have embraced the use of technology to support open access to scholarly work.

Other Books in the Series

Lora Anderson (Ed.), *Rewriting Work* (2023)
Stephen Carradini and Jason Swarts, *Text at Scale: Corpus Analysis in Technical Communication* (2023)
Han Yu and Jonathan Buehl (Eds.), *Keywords in Technical and Professional Communication* (2023)
Jason C. K. Tham (Ed.), *Keywords in Design Thinking: A Lexical Primer for Technical Communicators & Designers* (2022)
Kate Crane and Kelli Cargile Cook (Eds.), *User Experience as Innovative Academic Practice* (2022)
Joanna Schreiber and Lisa Melançon (Eds.), *Assembling Critical Components: A Framework for Sustaining Technical and Professional Communication* (2022)
Michael J. Klein (Ed.), *Effective Teaching of Technical Communication: Theory, Practice, and Application* (2021).

COLLABORATIONS AND PARTNERSHIPS IN USER EXPERIENCE

Edited by Joy Robinson and Ryan Weber

The WAC Clearinghouse
wac.colostate.edu
Fort Collins, Colorado

University Press of Colorado
upcolorado.com
Denver, Colorado

The WAC Clearinghouse, Fort Collins, Colorado 80524

University Press of Colorado, Denver, Colorado 80203

© 2025 by Joy Robinson and Ryan Weber. This work is licensed under a Creative Commons Attribution-NonCommercial-NoDerivatives 4.0 International license.

ISBN 978-1-64215-251-7 (PDF) | 978-1-64215-252-4 (ePub) | 978-1-64642-736-9 (pbk.)

DOI 10.37514/TPC-B.2025.2517

Produced in the United States of America

Library of Congress Cataloging-in-Publication Data

Names: Robinson, Joy, 1965– editor | Weber, Ryan P. editor
Title: Collaborations and partnerships in user experience / edited by Joy Robinson and Ryan Weber.
Description: Fort Collins, Colorado : The WAC Clearinghouse, [2025] | Series: Foundations and innovations in technical and professional communication | Includes bibliographical references.
Identifiers: LCCN 2025016628 (print) | LCCN 2025016629 (ebook) | ISBN 9781646427369 paperback | ISBN 9781642152517 adobe pdf | ISBN 9781642152524 epub
Subjects: LCSH: Customer services | Customer relations | Strategic alliances (Business)
Classification: LCC HF5415.5 .C6148 2025 (print) | LCC HF5415.5 (ebook) | DDC 658.8/12—dc23/eng/20250903
LC record available at https://lccn.loc.gov/2025016628
LC ebook record available at https://lccn.loc.gov/2025016629

Copyeditor: Don Donahue
Designer: Mike Palmquist
Series Editor: Lisa Melonçon
Series Associate Editor: Sherena Huntsman

The WAC Clearinghouse supports teachers of writing across the disciplines. Hosted by Colorado State University, it brings together scholarly journals and book series as well as resources for teachers who use writing in their courses. This book is available in digital formats for free download at wac.colostate.edu.

Founded in 1965, the University Press of Colorado is a nonprofit cooperative publishing enterprise supported, in part, by Adams State University, Colorado School of Mines, Colorado State University, Fort Lewis College, Metropolitan State University of Denver, University of Alaska Fairbanks, University of Colorado, University of Denver, University of Northern Colorado, University of Wyoming, Utah State University, and Western Colorado University. For more information, visit upcolorado.com.

Citation Information: Robinson, Joy & Ryan Weber (Eds.). (2025). *Collaborations and Partnerships in User Experience*. The WAC Clearinghouse; University Press of Colorado. https://doi.org/1010.37514/PER-B.2025.2517

Land Acknowledgment. The Colorado State University Land Acknowledgment can be found at https://landacknowledgment.colostate.edu.

Contents

Acknowledgments..vii

Introduction 3
    Joy Robinson and Ryan Weber

PART ONE. COLLABORATIONS IN INDUSTRY AND THE ACADEMY

Chapter 1. Building Relationships Across Professional Spheres in Academic-Industry Collaborations: A Cross-case Synthesis 23
    Benjamin Lauren, Casey McArdle, Jennifer Ismirle, and Keith Instone

Chapter 2. "We need to figure out how to do better!": Opportunities for UX Professionals in Project-based Organizations—An Activity Theory Analysis of a Technical Design Project....................47
    Richard Douglas Divine and Mark Zachry

Chapter 3. Working with Ladies in UX: Building Academic/Industry Partnerships for User Research Projects............................75
    Heather Noel Turner, Laura Gonzáles, and Liza Potts

Chapter 4. A Case for (Re)Envisioning Academic UX Spaces: Lessons Learned at a Polytechnic University..............................85
    John M. Spartz

PART TWO. COLLABORATIONS IN COMMUNITIES

Chapter 5. Voice of a Community Partner: Challenges and Benefits of Novice Students Conducting Onsite Usability Tests 97
    Billy Kangas and Chalice Randazzo

Chapter 6. Designing Virtual Reality User Experiences for a Nonprofit Organization: Perspectives from Engineering Graduate Students and Community Partners 121
    Missie Smith and Felicia Chong

Chapter 7. Reflections on a Graduate-Level Engineering Service-Learning Project in a Virtual Reality and User Experience Course 149
    Missie Smith and Felicia Chong

Chapter 8. Critical Success Factors for Teaching an Accessible User Experience Project Across National Borders and Disciplinary Boundaries 155
    Sushil K. Oswal, Zsuzsanna B. Palmer, and Rita Koris

Chapter 9. Sustainability-Driven User Experience: A Strategic Approach to Interdisciplinary Collaboration............................... 173
    Tatiana Batova

Chapter 10. How Long Have We Been Doing This Again? Establishing a Long-Term Interdepartmental UX Collaboration on Campus......... 183
    Ashley Patriarca and Kristin Williams

Chapter 11. Forming and Sustaining One Collaborative Service-Learning Partnership Around UX...................................... 195
    Joseph W. Robertshaw

PART THREE. COLLABORATING WITH USERS

Chapter 12. Twitch and Livestreaming as User Experience Platforms...... 207
    Amelia Chesley and Cody Reimer

Chapter 13. Collaborating on the Interface: Rhetorical and Hermeneutic Theory for User Experience Design 233
    Eric J. York

Chapter 14. Achieving Veteran-Centered Design: Case Study of the Human-Centered Design Process Used During the Vets.gov Project 255
    Jeffrey M. Gerding

Chapter 15. Collaborating Through Usability in Health and Medical Contexts 283
    Kirk St.Amant

Chapter 16. Feature Flow Analysis: Collaborate More Deliberately with Your Users.. 305
    Lane T Lynn, Matthew R Miller, Holly Lussenden, and Joy Robinson

Chapter 17. Empathy, Access, and Engineering: Empathy Maps in a Disability Studies Course for STEM Students 311
    Sarah Summers and Renee D. Rogge

Chapter 18. Crafting the Story: Engaging Stakeholders in UX Research ... 317
    Ginnifer Mastarone

Contributors 323

Acknowledgments

Joy Robinson: I am eternally grateful to Kevin G. Davis-Smith and Lisa Dusenberry for their inspiration and unwavering support. To my partner—John—thank you for putting up with my endless projects and late nights. I couldn't have done this without your patience and love. To Ryan (coeditor) who made this entire project come together. We all owe him a debt of gratitude for pulling this together and providing us a glimpse into this important field.

Ryan Weber: Huge thank you to Lisa Melonçon for incredible guidance and support putting this collection together. We also appreciate all the work and assistance from Mike Palmquist at the WAC Clearinghouse, as well as the anonymous peer reviewers for their productive feedback and insight. Thank you to Kirk St.Amant and the Louisiana Tech Usability Studies Symposium for helping publicize the CFP for this collection. Thank you to Katherine MacGilvray and Kalyn Jones for excellent editing and formatting work on drafts of this collection. Thanks to my awesome coeditor Joy Robinson for her tremendous work on this collection.

COLLABORATIONS AND PARTNERSHIPS IN USER EXPERIENCE

Introduction

Joy Robinson
GOOGLE

Ryan Weber
THE UNIVERSITY OF ALABAMA IN HUNTSVILLE

UX Needs Better Collaboration

User experience (UX) is a team sport; no one expert or discipline can do UX alone. UX work requires collaboration because of its sweeping scope and interdisciplinary approach. If you follow one classic definition of UX from the Nielsen Norman Group that "'User experience' encompasses all aspects of the end-user's interaction with the company, its services, and its products" (Norman & Nielsen, n.d.), then UX involves a huge range of experiences and knowledge from many academic disciplines, industries, experts, government agencies, community organizations, and users themselves. User experience work demands a more sustained effort at collaboration—a process through which individuals work together to accomplish a shared goal, and in doing so "they create something (e.g., knowledge, expertise, ideals) that did not exist individually" (Robinson & Dusenbery, 2020, p. 210). Organizations want collaboration because it works toward a shared vision of creating powerful and sustainable results. The shared vision of UX is products, services, and experiences that actually help people, that actually meet their needs, that actually make their lives better. UX cannot fulfill its promise or function without collaboration. Notably, the ability to collaborate and work in teams is frequently cited as one of the most important UX skills (Rosala & Krause, 2020; Rose, Putnam & McDonald, 2020). While collaboration takes time, energy, compromise, and commitment to a shared vision, people can achieve more through collaboration than they can alone.

Collaboration can take many forms. In industry, UX collaboration might involve several specialists in a company—programmers, software engineers, UX and interaction designers, researchers, graphic designers, information architects, product managers, technical communicators, marketing personnel, quality assurance experts, and others—coming together to ensure that products truly meet user needs. In academia, collaboration might involve faculty from multiple departments and colleges joining forces to create programs that help students prepare for the interdisciplinary nature of UX work. In communities and governments, collaboration might involve representatives of organizations working directly with members of the public to ensure that programs and services truly help people.

But these idealistic, hypothetical collaboration scenarios may not play out in reality. Many issues may prevent UX professionals from working together and sharing knowledge. Within universities and companies, experts might remain siloed in their own disciplines. Scholars in academia and practitioners in industry may not share their insights and best practices with one another. On a deeper level, people may not even agree on what UX means. As Kou and colleagues (2018) write, "Due to the emergent and evolutionary nature of this new inter- and transdisciplinary space, ideas and opinions in the UX field are contested, often lacking even a consensus over the definition of UX" (p. 2069). Differing definitions, vocabularies, incentives, priorities, organizational structures, and time commitments can drive apart people who should be working together.

■ We Echo Longstanding Calls for Collaboration

We are not the first to call for better UX collaboration. Twenty years ago, Richard Anderson and colleagues (2005) argued for collaboration among UX professionals:

> WHO OWNS USER EXPERIENCE (UX)? This is the wrong question to ask. We don't believe that any single group can own UX.
>
> What's the alternative? In our view, a useful focus is collaboration, not ownership. The best successes come from collaboration. Whatever type of product, service, or document you are creating, whether it's a Web site, an application program, an MP3 player, or a financial form, user experience encompasses so many diverse aspects of your product that "ownership" just isn't a useful perspective. (p. 40)

That same year, Keith Instone (2005) argued for user experience as an umbrella topic that unites various professionals. With the goal of creating meetings where anyone "interested in standing on this common ground was welcome" (p. 1087), Instone identified many different professional organizations related to UX, including the Association for Computing Machinery (ACM) and its SIGGRAPH special interest group, Society for Technical Communication (STC), the International Institute for Information Design (IIID), IEEE Computer Society, Human Factors and Ergonomics Society (HFES), American Institute of Graphic Arts (AIGA), and The Industrial Designers Society of America (IDSA). Jonathan Follett (2008) calls this proliferation of UX groups "Alphabet Soup" and suggested that there might be an overabundance of organizations: "All of these organizations compete with each other—whether directly or indirectly—for the attention, volunteer time, and resources UX professionals have to offer. If you're actively involved in the UX community, it's easy to feel pulled in too many directions at once" (para. 5). At the same conference where Instone presented (CHI 2005), Whitney Quesenbery and colleagues (2005) discussed their vision for UXnet, a networking organization intended to "provide a 'home' for the big picture or strategic discussions that, by their very nature, require cross-disciplinary communications" (p. 1098).

Unfortunately, UXnet disbanded in 2010. Many of the disparate societies identified by Instone and Follett still operate, are still interested in UX, and are still largely siloed in their independent disciplines. UX does have one overarching disciplinary association, the User Experience Professionals Association ("About UXPA"), founded in 1991, which had nearly 2,400 members and 59 local chapters and serves over 60 countries as of 2024. The organization publishes both The Journal of Usability Studies and User Experience Magazine, and UXPA is the most prominent interdisciplinary UX organization bringing diverse professionals together under the umbrella of UX. However, data from Yavuz Inal and colleagues (2020) suggests that most UX professionals are not members of any professional communities, so even the wide reach of the UXPA might not incorporate the full range of UX professionals.

Different Approaches and Language Make Working Together Difficult

As a collection coming out of technical and professional communication (TPC) and attempting to engage UX practitioners in several fields, we note that TPC has a long tradition of engaging with usability and user experience. Summarizing several decades of research and disciplinary work, Paul Thompson Hunter (2023) writes that "TPC can be considered a keystone discipline for contemporary UX research and design" (p. 2). Like UX, TPC heavily prioritizes users, including their needs, emotions, abilities, and contexts. According to Ginny Redish (2010), "Technical communicators are by training and necessity user-centered. Their focus is always the audience, the people who will use whatever they are creating. Their goal is to make even complex interactions understandable and usable" (p. 91). Many of the skills between TPC and UX overlap as well (Redish, 2010). In their analysis of 502 UX job postings, Claire Lauer and Eva Brumberger (2016) argue that TPC and user experience share many core competencies and that technical communication could "in fact, play a central role in UX" (p. 248). TPC and UX make for natural allies.

Despite promising overlap between TPC and UX, Emma Rose and Joanna Schreiber (2021) warn that "these connections may be waning" (p. 345). As evidence, they cite research by Erin Friess and Ryan K. Boettger (2021) finding that UX was a primary topic in only 30 of 672 articles published in flagship technical communication journals between 1996–2017. Similarly, Felicia Chong (2016) found that technical communication textbooks give "meager attention" (p. 12) to usability. In fact, Geoffrey Sauer (2018) concludes that, when it comes to the relationship between usability/UX and TPC, "the discipline has some work to do before we can consider them integral to our theory, our practice, and our scholarly production/assessment" (p. 370). For Rose and Heather Turner (2023), part of the problem is that TPC has not moved from a limited notion of usability to a holistic notion of user experience. They write,

> it feels like other fields and industry have progressed beyond and more fully embraced a broader notion of UX. We believe now more than ever that this is an opportunity for the field of TPC to carve out its unique approach to UX, one rooted in social justice, rhetorical in nature, and highlights reflection as a key practice. (p. 10)

Challenges to UX collaboration in TPC also create widespread issues across the many disciplines and industries engaged in UX. Disparate vocabularies, approaches, methods, and communication styles often keep user experience professionals siloed and separated (Hassenzahl, 2018, Vermeeren et. al., 2010). Collaborations require participants taking on what Robert R. Johnson (1998) calls "the burden of comprehension," which involves "the responsibility of understanding the ideologies, contexts, values, and histories of those disciplines from which we borrow before we begin using their methods and research findings" (p. 75). The multiple disciplines and perspectives of UX make this burden of comprehension especially difficult. In a call for radical interdisciplinarity within UX, Peter Wright and colleagues (2006) argue for a "liberal arts" approach that engages many types of design experts in dialogue. However, they acknowledge that such dialogue is not without its challenges:

> A fundamental problem is having sufficient knowledge of another's language, practice, perspective and ways of looking to begin to engage empathetically in dialogue. A tendency in this situation is to reduce the other's perspective to one's own. That is to do a kind of translation process which can undermine the uniqueness of that perspective (p. 9).

Lachner et. al. (2016) argue that existing UX approaches "rarely cope with the required degree of interdisciplinarity to reflect the different angles of e.g., engineering, design, marketing, or psychology" (p. 2). In the introduction to a special issue on collaboration published by *User Experience Magazine*, Mindy Maxwell (2013) plainly states that "Working across disciplines requires understanding others." (para. 7)

In academia, the sheer number of fields involved in UX adds extra challenges to collaboration. Research by Laura Luther and colleagues (2020) found that the top five fields for UX research were psychology, computer science, business economics, engineering, and information science/library science, leading them to describe the UX research field as "complex and scattered" (p. 1). Still, the researchers find a strong interdisciplinary bent to UX, as many journals publishing UX research span two or more disciplines. Joy Robinson and colleagues (2017) offer similar findings. Among the top fields producing UX research are computer and information science, engineering, health, performing arts, library and information science, psychology, and education. However, the greatest number of publications were interdisciplinary, though most of these studies came out of fields related to HCI. Even with this interdisciplinary bent, it is clear that the vast and disparate fields conducting UX research make it difficult for researchers to cross disciplinary bounds. While it is possible for faculty in, say, engineering, art, and psychology to collaborate on a research project (and certainly some do), this type of work requires extra effort and initiative. These scholars employ different concepts and vocabulary, use different research sources and citation methods, and labor under different promotion and tenure guidelines. They also use different research methods. For instance, research in user experience design, healthcare, market research, and social media strategy uses "inconsistent and unsystematic" methods to create personas (Guan et al., 2021, p. 4446), and these differences emerge based on the methods and goals of the different fields.

UX professionals in industry face similar challenges to collaboration due to confusing, sometimes competing, job titles, responsibilities, and professional identities. The field still "lack[s] clear boundaries and [has] yet to develop into a profession with a specified, coherent body of knowledge" (Kou & Gray, 2018, p. 322). The state of UX is in flux. Some companies have just realized they need to incorporate UX, but don't understand what it means or how UX would integrate into their operations (Kou & Gray, 2018). Other companies have had people performing UX tasks for years without recognizing that work in their job titles or descriptions; findings from a 2019 Nielsen Norman survey on the UX profession found that some companies "didn't have carved-out UX roles; instead, people working in design, engineering, or product became responsible for UX" (Rosala & Krause, 2020, p. 15). Still other companies may hire for positions that put UX in the title but involve little meaningful UX work. For instance, Michael Thompson (2018) analyzed 287 customer experience (CX) job ads and found 46 percent were CX jobs in name only, while another 20 percent just added a few CX activities to more traditional job roles. Thompson argues that successful companies need clear job descriptions, partially because consistently "defined roles help teams collaborate" (p. 74). People struggle to work together when they do not have a clear understanding of their own or their colleagues' functions in the workplace and when they lack the responsibility to perform the functions their job titles suggest.

The collaboration problems created by unclear job titles are exacerbated by a proliferation of job titles related to UX. The profusion of UX in various companies and fields over the past decade has resulted in the differentiation of roles inside the field. These roles and their titles are slowly gaining traction in the industry even as companies struggle to define, promote, and integrate UX as a whole. UX duties and responsibilities have been differentiated into distinct areas including UX designer, UX researcher, UX developer/engineer, UX writer, UX architect, or UX generalist, and so on. Many companies use different titles for similar jobs, which can lead to confusion about what people do. For instance, the 2018 UXPA salary survey (2018) allowed respondents to choose from 18 different job titles, and eight job titles received at least 18 percent of respondents indicating that the titles described their roles. While 56 percent of participants indicated "User Researcher" as their title, several also indicated that their titles are User Experience Architect/Engineer, Interaction Designer, Interface Designer, Usability Practitioner, Information Architect, Graphic/Visual Designer, or Manager. A Nielsen Norman survey (Rosala & Krause, 2020) found that while UX Designer and UX Researcher were the most common job titles, participants gave 134 unique titles for jobs, with many people holding more than one title. A similar problem plagues TPC, where job postings exhibit "enormous variety in position titles" (Lauer & Brumberger, 2016, p. 224).

In 2021, we released a short, IRB-approved survey for local UX professionals that asked respondents about their titles, their UX roles, the time they spent performing UX duties (as opposed to other duties), and the skills they needed to perform them. The survey results (n=115) found that professionals identified predominantly as generalists, researchers, designers, developers, and tech writers. Even though most participants spent the majority of their time on UX activities, no one in the study had official UX titles. Instead, participants held as many as 10 different titles including Software Engineer, Web Software Developer, Website Designer, Cyber Systems Engineer, Human Factors Engineer, Multimedia Designer, and System Software Analyst, which is not uncommon (Rosala & Krause, 2020). Additionally, most study participants (30%) revealed they functioned as a UX Generalist, indicating they wear multiple hats in performing their work. The next most popular roles were UX Designer (22%) and UX Researcher (18%). Overall, UX professionals spent 65 percent of their time working on UX activities while generalists quite a bit more (76%) and researchers spent somewhat less (only 53%).

The alignment or creation of new titles in a company is complex—a process that is carefully weighed and considered. Modern working environments demand job titles that reflect emerging work trends; for example, new fields such as artificial intelligence (AI) or machine learning (ML) have newly created titles such as AI Application Engineer or ML Engineer. New job titles are created due to shifting needs of the company, efforts to remain competitive, and/or a need to be "more descriptive in order to accurately reflect new positions and functions" (Hayward, 2019, p. 2). Titles and position descriptions should also clarify not only different UX roles and responsibilities in an organization, but also issues of promotion and advancement by elaborating the various responsibilities of junior and senior positions, or delineating the responsibilities of UX managers. Companies struggle with where to place "technical experts," and these struggles make it harder for UX professionals to collaborate with one another as well as others inside and beyond their companies. As such, clearer UX job titles would provide professionals with more accurate information about the work done in these roles, provide clarity around work responsibilities, expectations, and necessary skills, and indicate pathways for improved collaborative experiences.

Beyond navigating unclear and inconsistent job titles and responsibilities, employees and companies also struggle to unify a mishmash of frameworks and methodologies that emerged from UX's varied theoretical roots. For example, one thread of UX features human-factors engineering (HFE), most often associated with hardware, devices, or systems in relationship to humans, typically related to human safety. The human-computer interaction (HCI) field focuses on human engagement with computers and the interface between human and machine. Yet, clearly HFE, HCI, and UX share similar concerns: the interface of a product and its ultimate and sustained impact on the human user. All these fields utilize some, if not all, of the same methods, and often borrow from the same sets of analytical research-based processes, such as surveys, interviews, and observations. Professionals from each of these fields might work at the same companies in the same teams or even share the same projects. Their work, that is the work of all of these human specialists, decidedly depends on the users they examine and the environments where users work.

For example, given the same project—improve the Sikorsky X_2 helicopter cockpit interface—an HFE specialist might ensure that the locations of the various switches and indicators are compliant with specifications and meet all safety requirements such that humans can comfortably, effectively, and safely operate them. The HCI researcher might use eye tracking of pilots to understand where best to place important indicators and switches. The UX professional might seek to simplify overly complex workflows in the cockpit and better integrate the entire environment: switches, indicators, and screens to improve the pilot's overall experience. Unfortunately, these opportunity slices in the overall problem space often result in specialists working independently of one another even though the range of expertise for these professionals might overlap. These artificially created silos result in problems not just for the users who ultimately benefit (or don't) from holistic solutions, but also for the stakeholders, who finance and support these projects. Without working together within similar fields, projects often take longer, solutions are less complete, and processes are out of sync.

UX is already an uncomfortable fit into modern production processes. Project managers and other professionals who deliver work products typically function on a product life cycle cadence, which includes periods designated to complete the work and then milestones designated for releases of the completed work. Designers, engineers, programmers, writers and other professionals' work, for example, often fits seamlessly into this cadence. However, UX, with its holistic, user-centered process and deliverables, cannot always have a 1–1 flow with production (Lárusdóttir et al., 2012). Consider this scenario for the update of legacy web application interfaces. Production might require front- and backend development programmers complete 15 features by a specific milestone date. System engineers would ensure that planned hardware upgrades and security protocols will be in place to support the new software and integrate with existing network infrastructure. Technical writers work with the programmers to develop the appropriate documentation, ideally during but sometimes after the product development (and many technical writers have advocated for greater involvement in more tasks throughout product development processes due to their own abilities to facilitate communication and represent user perspectives, as Robinson (1994), Hillary Hart and James Conklin (2006), Aijaz Fatima (2018) report). However, UX work done well covers the entire lifecycle of product development instead of fitting neatly into one phase. UX professionals rely on user research to inform any work product or UX deliverables. At minimum, this requirement adds one extra step to the UX professional's to-do list before any deliverables or products can be completed. However, user testing might uncover that the entire 15 planned features are not desired by the users, potentially derailing the entire plan of work. Obviously, the team might view UX professionals and the voice of the users like the famed sword of Damocles—constantly hanging precariously over the production schedule. The challenges of incorporating UX and user perspectives into development products with already strained timelines and budgets may help explain why many companies still neglect and downplay UX (Ardito et al., 2014; Kuusinen, 2015).

■ We Can Make Collaboration Better

Despite concerns and challenges about how well various UX scholars and practitioners can work together, great research exists about how to conduct collaborative work in UX. Educators have determined how to involve users in the classroom (Scammell et al., 2015). Scholars like Peter Beresford and Fran Branfield (2006) and Hannu Torvinen and Pauliina Ulkuniemi (2016) describe how users can collaborate with governmental and public organizations to develop better services and policies. Emphasis on community in user experience helps researchers develop participatory projects that explore issues like the usability of health insurance information for immigrants (Rose et. al., 2017) or crowdsourcing systems that curate indigenous knowledge (Alfaridzi & Yulianti, 2020; Cabrero et al., 2016). Educators have determined how to involve users in the physical and online classroom (Mtebe, 2020; Scammell et al., 2015;) and prepare designers for teamwork (Kiernan et al., 2017). Case studies show how collaboration occurs in industries like video gaming (McAllister & White, 2015), commerce (Heximer et. al., 2002), virtual reality (Hrimech et al., 2011; Kohler et. al., 2011) and healthcare (Bate & Robert, 2007). Research has begun to examine the user experience involved in collaborations between humans and AI (Pohlt et al., 2018). Several scholars describe how collaborations with users can improve information access, translation quality, and social justice (Gonzáles & Turner, 2017; Rose et. al., 2017; Suojanen et al., 2014; Walls, 2016). Research also discusses how organizations partner with specific types of users, such as mental health service users (Campbell-Hall et. al, 2010; Trivedi & Wykes, 2002), and how researchers work successfully (Acharya, 2018; Poudyal, 2020) or unsuccessfully (Cabrero et. al., 2016) with underserved communities. And of course, UX scholarship often focuses on how designers and users can collaborate in product development (Akinola et al., 2019; Frison et al., 2019; Lachner et al., 2018; Pallot et al., 2010; Patchen et al., 2020). Others call for historically marginalized populations to not just participate in but take the lead on design projects (Peters et al., 2018).

Industry experts have also written about their work in collaboration. Designers tested collaboration personas that help creators design products and experiences for teams by providing "empirically derived descriptions of hypothetical groups of people with specific qualities, goals, and needs realized through collaborations with each other" (Matthews et al., 2012, p. 1997). Google employees (Kayacik et al., 2019) described how UX and machine learning research scientists collaborated to create a machine learning interface and offered tips on how to foster better cross-functional partnerships. Similarly, Fabien Girardin and Neal Lathia argue "that designers and data scientists must immerse themselves in the other's approaches to build a common rhythm" (2017, p. 5). To accomplish this task, they suggest participants from both disciplines work together to develop a vision, assess assumptions, ensure both sides of the team are asking the same questions, and clarify success metrics.

Many product development models have also suggested how collaborative frameworks can best integrate UX (Kuusinen, 2014). For example, Agile management framework supports three different models for collaboration with UX teams:

1. integrate more fully into production by determining product features only after users have been involved (Continuous delivery UX),
2. work on faster, smaller, shorter research cycles fitting into the existing production timeline (LeanUX), and
3. operate slightly ahead of production to ensure research is done prior to production needing the information (Dual Track Agile).

While it can be easily argued that each Agile model has different affordances and applicability, based on work context, business maturity model, and other factors, the theme that runs through each of the models is tight collaboration with UX. Thus, the Agile management framework supports collaboration with UX professionals working in small teams among engineers, programmers, writers, managers, and other specialists, and UX research and outreach to users is scaffolded under this framework. However, in companies housing entire departments of UXers, or employing multiple teams/projects with many UX professionals, a different approach may be required. Therefore, to leverage the value of UX—often equated to return on investment (ROI)—scaling UX appropriately is a necessity.

One recent model of scaled UX is called DesignOperations or DesignOps. The DesignOPs framework is designed to support UX professionals across a company, enabling them to maintain and deliver both quality and consistency by sharing resources, leveraging knowledge, and most importantly, collaborating with each other. DesignOps works by addressing the synergies between three core areas (Kaplan, 2019),

1. How teams collaborate and work together to organize and align around shared responsibilities, establish effective measures for collaboration, and enable employee development.
2. How teams work to use processes to achieve consistent design quality, establish repositories for knowledge sharing and efficiencies, and effectively prioritize projects.
3. How teams create impact including measure design work, share and reward team success, and enable others—even those outside of the team—to learn and use design and research activities.

DesignOps traction has been slow even with the rapid growth in UX over the last few years (Nielsen, 2017). A survey (n=557) by NN/g reported that only 22 percent of respondents used DesignOps focused activities (Kaplan, 2020). When asked about collaboration activities, only 18 percent of respondents reported having activities focused on team collaboration. Given that the UX field is expected to grow from 1.5 million professionals to 100 million in the next 30+ years (Nielsen, 2017), collaboration at scale will be critical to our success moving forward.

While UX has some time to grow into embracing the concept of DesignOps and collaboration at scale, the time is now to embrace the importance of collaboration. Collaboration is not only one of the key intersections between TPC and UX (Redish & Barnum, 2011). "Collaboration" is not just the buzzword of today, but likely an overarching concept that will define our times. The last few decades have provided us with a host of unprecedented technology tools that have enabled us to communicate like never before. But through this communication, we have been connecting, we have been sharing, we have been collaborating? It is through collaboration we learn and grow. We began this piece by making the bold statement that no one expert can do UX alone. But, perhaps we should say instead, no one UX expert can learn alone. After all, the human experience is a collaborative one: to UX is human.

Good and Frustrating Collaborations Inspired this Collection

We first decided to put this collection together based on our own experiences working in TPC, building academic UX programs, teaching students, talking with members of our local UX community, and in Joy's case, straddling the academy/industry divide; after working as an assistant professor of English at The University of Alabama in Huntsville, she took a position as a UX project manager for a large company. Creating UX programs brought on, at least for us, unparalleled challenges and opportunities. Contributing to UX programs in the English department (where technical writing is housed) involves working with colleagues from multiple fields such as psychology, communication arts, art, business, computer science, and elsewhere to give our programs breadth while emphasizing the humanistic core of UX. Modern UX students need a host of skills and abilities: user research, prototyping, project management, graphic design, coding, software skills, statistical knowledge, web design, report writing, presentation skills, and countless others. Our colleagues from many disciplines are enthusiastic about UX and have taught and championed UX from various approaches for years. However, we sometimes found that institutional and bureaucratic hurdles thwarted our attempts at interdisciplinary program development. Everyone wants to work well together, but course prerequisites, major and minor requirements, faculty teaching schedules, scarcity of new faculty lines, course rotations, competition for students and resources, differing department and college priorities, and other institutional factors sometimes make collaboration difficult.

Our technical communication and UX partners in local industry told similar stories. Many worked on small UX teams that struggled for budgets, resources, and recognition. They wanted to work more closely with the engineers, developers, and designers at their companies, but found themselves having to define and evangelize UX to get involved in the early aspects of product development, where they could truly advocate for and implement user-centered design. Like academics, these professionals had lists of "dream projects" that they did not have time, resources, or mental energy to tackle. Other professionals told stories about companies that were enthusiastic about UX but did not know how to define or implement it. Some companies did UX without realizing it. The ambiguity of UX presented both problems and opportunities for these professionals.

Amidst these frustrations, we also saw the wonderful outcomes of partnerships that stretched boundaries. Our classes produced terrific projects for clients. Students got great jobs and internships. Guest speakers and workshops brought diverse knowledge and perspectives. Our program received insightful feedback from UX professionals on how to develop sophisticated, relevant curriculum. We conducted a research project with friends from industry to collect data on personas that we could all use. We heard inspiring stories about UX teams improving products and their users' lives.

The 18 pieces in this collection offer similar accounts of both the frustrations and joys of collaboration. Some of these pieces offer theoretical or empirical approaches to collaboration to help us reconceive it. Others offer narratives on collaboration; some are success stories, some are cautionary tales, and some involve both the ups and downs of people working together. These pieces identify productive sites for collaboration, including the classroom, community organizations, corporate projects, and the streaming platform Twitch. Not surprisingly, many of the best collaborations come from interacting directly with users, and several of the contributors describe these kinds of partnerships, such as an in-depth case study on the VA's approach to the Vets.gov website redesign and a student project that involved interviewing users to create empathy maps that improve accessibility. To model collaboration, we wanted to bring in authors from beyond technical communication. We also wanted to print collaboratively authored pieces, especially those that involve partners reflecting and dialoguing on their collaborative experiences. And to capture a wider variety of stories from a wider variety of authors, we solicited three types of peer-reviewed submissions for this collection. We wanted traditional academic chapters that offer perspectives on research, theory, and praxis. But we also wanted shorter case studies pieces that used about 2,500 words to describe a specific collaborative experience or project that does not require the detail of a full academic chapter. Furthermore, we requested lessons learned pieces that offer specific, actionable insights on how to improve collaboration.

Our contributors bring a wide range of perspectives to collaboration, but central themes emerge throughout their work. Good collaborations take time and sustained energy, often more energy than busy people can muster. Technology can both facilitate and hamper collaboration, so it must be used strategically. Varying institutional structures, missions, and incentives present challenges to working together, so partners must ensure that they really understand (and appreciate) the people they work with. Even successful partnerships involve frustration, and success often looks different than participants initially envisioned it. For collaborations to work, all partners must buy in and experience benefits. And ultimately, collaborations are an essential part of UX.

We hope that this collection contributes to ongoing calls for better UX collaboration. Starting with the basics of why we collaborate helps to remind us of why we are here; to build relationships with our users. We conceived of this text not just for UX or technical writing professionals but for all the stakeholders and future collaborators across the spectrum of UX in academia, industry, communities, government, and user groups. Taken together, these chapters represent efforts to connect professionals both within and beyond TPC as they explore the field of UX. We see these conversations not as the final word on collaboration but as continued moves in an ongoing discussion. We need more of these conversations if TPC is going to fully embrace UX and if UX is going to fully embrace collaboration.

■ References

About UXPA. (2021). In uxpa.org. https://uxpa.org/about-uxpa-international/.
Acharya, K. R. (2018). User empowerment: Promoting social justice and human rights through localized UX design. *SIGDOC '18*: Proceedings of the 36th ACM Interna-

tional Conference on the Design of Communication, 6, 1–7. https://doi.org/10.1145/3233756.3233960.

Akinola, M., Herbert, L. E., Hill, B. J., Quinn, M., Holl, J. L., Whitaked, A. K. & Gilliam, M. L. (2019). Development of a mobile app on contraceptive options for young African American and Latina women. *Health Education and Behavior*, 46.1, 89–96. https://doi.org/10.1177/1090198118775476.

Alfaridzi, M. D. & Yulianti, L. P. (2020). UI-UX design and analysis of local medicine and medication mobile-based apps using task-centered design process. *2020 International Conference on Information Technology Systems and Innovation (ICITSI)*, 443–450. https://doi.org/10.1109/ICITSI50517.2020.9264947.

Anderson, R., Instone, K., Knemeyer, D., Mazur, B. & Quesenbury, W. (2005). User experience network: A passion for collaboration. *Interactions*, 12(3), 40–41.

Ardito, C., Buono, P., Caivano, D., Costabile, M. F. & Lanzilotti, R. (2014). Investigating and promoting UX practice in industry: An experimental study. *International Journal of Human-Computer Stu*dies, 72, 542–551. https://doi.org/10.1016/j.ijhcs.2013.10.004.

Bate, P. & Robert, G. (2007). *Bringing user experience to healthcare improvement: The concepts, methods, and practices of experience-based design*. Radcliffe Publishing.

Beresford, P. & Branfield, F. (2006). Developing inclusive partnerships: User-defined outcomes, networking, and knowledge—A case study. *Health and Social Care in the Community*, 14(5), 436–444. https://doi.org/10.1111/j.1365-2524.2006.00654.x.

Cabrero, D. G., Kapuire, G. K., Winschiers-Theophilus, H., Stanley, C. & Abdelnour-Nocera, J. (2016, April 13). A UX and usability expression of Pastoral OvaHimba: Personas in the making and doing. *CHIuXiD '16: Proceedings of the 2nd* International al Conference in HCI and UX Indonesia 2016, 89–92. https://doi.org/10.1145/2898459.2898473.

Cabrero, D. G., Kapuire, G. K., Winschiers-Theophilus, H., Stanley. C., Rodil, K. & Abdelnour-Nocera, J. (2015). Reflecting user-created persona in Indigenous Namibia—What NOT to do when working in foreign land. In G. Avram, F. de Cindio & V. Pipek (Eds.), *International Reports on Socio-Informatics (IRSI), Proceedings of the Work-In-Progress Track of the 7th International Conference on Communities and Technologies* 12(1), 53–62.

Campbell-Hall, V., Petersen, I., Bhana, A., Mjadu, S., Hosegood, V. & Flisher, A. J. (2010). Collaboration between traditional practitioners and primary health care staff in South Africa: Developing a workable partnership for community mental health services. *Transcultural Psychiatry*, 47(4), 610–628. https://doi.org/10.1177/1363461510383459.

Chong, F. (2016). The pedagogy of usability: An analysis of technical communication textbooks, anthologies, and course syllabi and descriptions. *Technical Communication Quarterly*, 25(1), 12–28. https://doi.org/10.1080/10572252.2016.1113073.

Fatima, A. (2018, October 8). Technical writing: More than a support function. *UX Matters*. https://www.uxmatters.com/mt/archives/2018/10/technical-writing-more-than-a-support-function.php.

Follett, J. (2008, June 23). The state of the UX community. *UX Matters*. https://www.uxmatters.com/mt/archives/2008/06/the-state-of-the-ux-community.php.

Friess, E. & Boettger, R. K. (2021). Identifying commonalities and divergences between technical communication scholarly and trade publications (1996–2017). *Journal of Business and Technical Communication*, 35(4), 407–432. https://doi.org/10.1177/10506519211021468.

Frison, A., Wintersberger, P. & Reiner, A. (2019). Resurrecting the ghost in the shell: A need-centered development approach for optimizing user experience in highly automated vehicles. *Transportation Research Part F*, 65, 439–456. https://doi.org/10.1016/j.trf.2019.08.001.

Girardin, F. & Lathia, N. (2017). When user experience designers partner with data scientists. *AAI Spring Symposia*, 1–6. https://aaai.org/papers/15364-15364-when-user-experience-designers-partner-with-data-scientists/.

Gonzáles, L. & Turner, H. N. (2017). Converging fields, expanding outcomes: Technical communication, translation, and design at a non-profit organization. *Technical Communication*, 64(2), 126–140.

Guan, K. W., Salminen, J., Lene, N., Jung, S. & Jansen, B. J. (2021). Information design for personas in four professional domains of user experience design, healthcare, market research, and social strategy. *Proceedings of the 54th Hawaii International Conference on System Sciences*, 4446–4455.

Hart, H. & Conklin, J. (2006). Toward a meaningful model of technical communication. *Technical Communication*, 53(4), 395–415.

Hassenzahl, M. (2018). The thing and I: Understanding the relationship between user the product. In M. Blythe & A. Monk (Eds.) *Funology 2. Human-Computer Interaction Series (pp. 303–313)*. Springer, Cham. https://doi.org/10.1007/978-3-319-68213-6_19.

Hayward, C. (2019, September 27). How can changing job titles benefit your company? *Forbes*. https://www.forbes.com/sites/forbeshumanresourcescouncil/2019/07/18/how-can-changing-job-titles-benefit-your-company/?sh=7f59d3486e56.

Heximer, E. E., Markova, U., Wu, L. & Yoon, J. (2002, October 20). A multidisciplinary approach to improving the user experience—Information development, test, and user experience design teams working together. *SIGDOC '02: Proceedings of the 20th Annual International Conference on Computer Documentation*, 72–78. https://doi.org/10.1145/584955.584966.

Hrimech, H., Alem, L. & Merienne, F. (2011). How 3D interaction metaphors affect user experience in collaborative virtual environment. *Advances in Human-Computer Interaction*, 2011, 1–12. https://doi.org/10.1155/2011/172318.

Hunter, P. T. (2023). Toward TPC-UX: UX topics in TPC journals 2013–2022. *Journal of Technical Writing and Communication*, 54(3), 1–33. https://doi.org/10.1177/00472816231191998.

Inal, Y., Clemmensen, T., Rajanen, D., Iivari, N., Rizvanoglu, K. & Ashok, S. (2020). Positive developments but challenges still ahead: A survey study on UX professionals' work practice. Journal of Usability Studies, 15(4), 210–246.

Instone, K. (2005). User experience: An umbrella topic. *CHI '05: CHI '05 Extended Abstracts on Human Factors in Computing Systems*, 1087–1088. https://doi.org/10.1145/1056808.1056824.

Johnson, R. R. (1998). *User-centered technology*. State University of New York Press.

Kaplan, K. (2019). DesignOps 101. *Nielsen Norman Group*. https://www.nngroup.com/articles/design-operations-101/.

Kaplan, K. (2020). DesignOps maturity: Low in most organizations. *Nielsen Norman Group*. https://www.nngroup.com/articles/designops-maturity-low/.

Kayacik, C., Chen, S., Noerly, S., Holbrook, J., Roberts, A. & Eck, D. (2019). Identifying the intersections: User experience + research scientist collaboration in a generative

Robinson, J. & Dusenberry, L. (2020). Building psychological safety through training interventions: Manage the team, not just the project. *IEEE: Transactions on Professional Communication*, 63(3), 207–226. https://doi.org/10.1109/TPC.2020.3014483.

Robinson, J. & Lanius, C. (2018). A geographic and disciplinary examination of UX empirical research since 2000. *SIGDOC '18: Proceedings of the 36th ACM International. Conference on the Design of Communication*, 8, 1–9. https://doi.org/10.1145/3233756.3233930.

Robinson, W. (1994). Writers as key members of product development teams. *IPCC 94 Proceedings. Scaling New Heights in Technical Communication, 382–385*. https://doi.org/10.1109/IPCC.1994.347494.

Rosala, M. & Krause, R. (2020). *User experience careers: What a career in UX looks like today* (2nd ed.). Nielsen Norman Group.

Rose, E. J., Putnam, C. & MacDonald, C. M. (2020, October 3). Preparing future UX professionals: Human skills, technical skills, and dispositions. *Proceedings of the 38th ACM International Conference on Design of Communication*, 34, 1–8. https://doi.org/10.1145/3380851.3416774.

Rose, E. J., Racadio, R., Wong, K., Nguyen, S., Kim, J. & Zahley, A. (2017). Community-based user experience: Evaluating the usability of health information with immigrant patients. *IEEE: Transactions on Professional Communication*, 60(2), 214–231. https://doi.org/10.1109/TPC.2017.2656698.

Rose, E. J. & Schreiber, J. (2021). User experience and technical communication: Beyond intertwining. *Journal of Technical Writing and Communication*, 51(4), 343–349. https://doi.org/10.1177/00472816211044497.

Rose, E. J. & Turner, H. N. (2023). The paradigm shift to UX and the durability of usability in TPC. *Technical Communication Quarterly*, 1–12. https://doi.org/10.1080/10572252.2023.2274067.

Sauer, G. (2018). Applying usability and user experience within academic contexts: Why progress remains slow. *Technical Communication Quarterly*, 27(4), 362–371. https://doi.org/10.1080/10572252.2018.1521637.

Scammell, J., Heaslip, V. & Crowley, E. (2015). Service user involvement in preregistration general nurse education: A systematic review. *Journal of Clinical Nursing*, 25, 53–69. https://doi.org/10.1111/jocn.13068.

Shivers-McNair, A. (2017). Localizing communities, goals, communication, and inclusion: A collaborative approach. *Technical Communication*, 64(2), 97–112.

Suojanen, T., Koskinen, K. & Tuominen, T. (2014). *User-centered translation*. Routledge.

Thompson, M. (2018). The CX tower of Babel: What CX job descriptions tell us about corporate CX initiatives. *Interactions*, 25(3), 74–77. https://doi.org/10.1145/3197575.

Torvinen, H. & Ulkuniemi, P. (2016). End-user engagement within innovative public procurement practices: A case study on public-private partnership procurement. *Industrial Marketing Management*, 58, 58–68. https://doi.org/10.1016/j.indmarman.2016.05.015.

Trivedi, P. & Wykes, T. (2002). From passive subjects to equal partners: Qualitative review of user involvement in research. *British Journal of Psychiatry*, 181, 468–472. https://doi.org/10.1192/bjp.181.6.468.

UXPA International. (2018, August). 2018 UX salary survey. 2016 UX Salary Survey (uxpa.org). https://uxpa.org/wp-content/uploads/sites/9/2017/10/UXPA_Salary Survey_2018v4.pdf.

Vermeeren, A. P. O. S., Law, E. L., Roto, V., Obrist, M., Hoonhout, J., Väänänen-Vainio-Mattila, K. (2010, October 16). User experience evaluation methods: Current state and development needs. *Proceedings of the 6th Nordic Conference on Human-Computer Interaction 2010*, 521–530. https://doi.org/10.1145/1868914.1868973.

Walls, D. M. (2016, September 23). User experience in social justice contexts. In *SIGDOC '16: Proceedings of the 34th ACM International Conference on the Design of Communication, 9*, 1–6. https://doi.org/10.1145/2987592.2987604.

Walton, R., Moore, K. R. & Jones, N. N. (2019). *Technical communication after the social justice turn: Building coalitions for action*. Routledge.

Wright, P., Blythe, M. & McCarthy, J. (2006). User experience and the idea of design. In S. W. Gilroy & M. D. Harrison (Eds.), Interactive systems. design, specification, and verification. DSV-IS 2005. Lecture notes in computer science, 3941 (pp. 1–14). Springer. https://doi.org/10.1007/11752707_1.

Youngblood, N. E. & Mackiewicz, J. (2012). A usability analysis of government website home pages in Alabama. *Government Information Quarterly, 29*(4), 582–588. https://doi.org/10.1016/j.giq.2011.12.010.

Youngblood, S. A. & Mackiewicz, J. (2013). Lessons in service learning: Developing the service learning opportunities in technical communication (SLOT-C) database. *Technical Communication Quarterly, 22*(3), 260–283. https://doi.org/10.1080/10572252.2013.775542.

Part One: Collaborations in Industry and the Academy

1. Building Relationships Across Professional Spheres in Academic-Industry Collaborations: A Cross-case Synthesis

Benjamin Lauren
University of Miami

Casey McArdle
Michigan State University

Jennifer Ismirle
Unaffiliated

Keith Instone
Unaffiliated

Abstract. This chapter presents an examination of eight individuals who have worked on industry-academic collaborations, specifically in user experience (UX). By analyzing experiences and approaching industry-academic collaborations in UX, we compare commonalities and differences, and present a synthesis that puts each case in conversation. To collect experiences, we interviewed eight UX professionals who have collaborated across academic and industry spheres on projects. We coded our findings to find connections between their experiences. We created experience maps from their collaboration stories, processes, and timelines, and then used the experience maps to assemble a broad view of the cases. Our data shows that collaborators often engage in similar recursive activities, such as building and investing in relationships, locating problems to solve, and discovering mutual benefits. While some of these projects can present unique challenges that are contextual to workplaces, such as differences in language/what constitutes research, priorities/mindsets/interests/goals, project scope or loss of interest, concurrence/divergence of the work, international education differences/cultural differences, they are valuable projects that inform academic and practitioner spaces. By providing useful cases and analysis, the chapter presents common pathways for readers to consider.

When we started the research for this chapter, the main challenge we faced as collaborators was not interpersonal.[1] Keith and Ben had been working on projects

---

1. We would like to thank our collaborators Eric Rodriguez, Dawn Opel, and Emily

DOI: https://doi.org/10.37514/TPC-B.2025.2517.2.01

related to industry-academic collaboration for the last three years.² Meanwhile, Jen and Casey had recently collaborated on a professional development workshop for the experience architecture program at Michigan State. We generally got along well and enjoyed interacting with each other. Our main challenge was learning *how* to best collaborate across different professional spheres, professionalization goals, and reward systems. Quite literally, our jobs paid each of us to do different things and fulfill different roles, and that is a powerful motivating force and an equally hefty deterrent. We also realized that these very challenges could be a useful lens for a research project meant to help others consider some best practices for collaborating across industry and academic spheres. As a result of this realization, we began working together through a series of inquiry activities that asked questions about how to ethically and effectively start and sustain successful industry-academic collaborations. Ultimately, these questions emerged in an IRB-approved study that produced the data we report on in this chapter.³ In this chapter, we present the full findings from our research collaboration as a cross-case synthesis, exploring and validating how user experience (UX) professionals—some in industry and others in academia—learned to effectively collaborate across disciplines and professional spheres. The eight professionals we interviewed for our research have worked either as academics and as industry practitioners, and in some cases have been in both roles. Each participant provides insight into building and sustaining relationships associated with UX research and education, including the work that goes into expanding the field for the future.

What follows in this chapter is a discussion of our research *and* our work together on how to best start and sustain industry-academic collaborations. The chapter begins with a brief literature review that focuses on how those working in UX and the closely related field of technical communication have discussed best practices in previous work. The chapter continues by offering a description of our methods and analytical procedures. Next, the chapter reports on the results of our case study, exploring and validating shared collaboration approaches that emerge in each case. The results note that practitioners and academics view their collaborations as a win-win scenario in terms of community partners, supporting students, and building better and more concrete bridges between both spheres. After the chapter discusses the results, it presents the implications of what was learned from the research. The chapter ends by arguing UX professionals to approach

---

Bowman for early support of this project. Thank you, also, to our participants for the valuable feedback.

2. Unfortunately, some of our research collaborators were not available to co-author this chapter, but deserve credit for contributing to the project. Much deserved credit goes to Eric Rodriguez, Dawn Opel, and Emily Bowman, each of whom helped intellectually shaped the work.

3. Also, in 2017 we presented at the User Experience Professionals Association conference in Toronto, Canada to solicit feedback on our work, and later followed up that presentation with an article in *User Experience* magazine (see Instone, et al., 2017).

collaborative work as a process of intentionally developing values that synthesize ideas, skill sets, and professional spheres.

What is Industry? Rethinking Professional and Cultural Contexts

In 1998 George Hayhoe called in people working in industry and academia to address the growing divide between professional spheres. Hayhoe (1998) explained, "Without cross-fertilization, both academe and industry face the prospect of sterility" (par. 16). To combat this sterility, Hayhoe argued industry practitioners and academics needed to be willing to learn from each other and find value in doing so. Hayhoe's urgent call to address the growing industry-academic divide has been echoed in technical communication (TC) and user experience (UX) scholarship over the years (e.g., Dicks, 2002), and the outcome of this call can be seen in edited collections by a variety of scholars, such as Barbara Mirel and Rachel Spilka (2002) and Tracy Bridgeford and Kirk St.Amant (2015), respectively.

An important theme emerging from the scholarship are the power relationships that are created between academics and practitioners. A good example of the power dynamics is discussed in Anthony Paré's (2002) account of working with Intuit social workers to define problems together, rather than the inverse, where a researcher or research team working alone defines problems for their participants. The latter approach not only unnecessarily created power distance, but it also assumed roles that foolishly relegated participants to expert or novice. Defining how collaboration could occur so strictly seemed an awkward approach, as Paré noted, because the outcome of the work made very little change at the workplace due to the absence of a meaningful collaboration occurring. There have been additional calls for academics to change their mindset when approaching collaborations with industry. For example, Deborah Bosley (2002) explained that academics "tend to separate themselves from practitioners in unproductive ways" (p. 27). Rather, Bosley would like to see "short-term" approaches adopted, wherein smaller projects could be started en route to more robust collaborations in the future. In this approach, large-scale collaboration is something a team could build toward.

In addition to discussions of cultural differences between industry and academia, published scholarship importantly pushes at the boundaries of what professional contexts can be defined as "industry." For example, scholars like Jeffrey Grabill (2007) have a history of work that focuses on intersections between computing technology, infrastructure development, and community change. Industry practitioners like Keith Instone (2005) have also been doing similar community building work in professional spaces by encouraging professionals to come together under the umbrella term UX regardless of workplace context. Even more recently, John Spartz and Ryan Weber (2015) argued that TC defines industry too narrowly. As a result, the authors claim the field often overlooks too many professional contexts, such as entrepreneurial ventures. In the same collection, James Dubinsky (2015) made a similar argument explaining that industry should also include community engagement, which is a key feature and expectation of land grant institutions.

The experience of marginalized people and identities have also been discussed as essential to understand when imagining how collaborations are designed and who they are designed to include. For example, Laura Gonzáles and Heather Turner (2019) explained that women and people of color experience a different set of challenges when working to start and sustain industry collaborations. They highlight the importance of communicating ethically, including listening and practicing empathy, as one way to learn about, encounter, and overcome such issues. Additionally, they explain that collaborations must work to understand the amount of labor and obstacles people from historically marginalized populations face when choosing to engage a project across professional spheres. Much of the labor women and people of color do was invisible, the authors explained, and was deeply influenced by the weight of embedded systems of oppression, such as colonialism, which were not always visible to fellow collaborators. Rebecca Walton and colleagues (2019) further help to position technical communication, and thereby UX, as deeply tied to the work of social justice. They demonstrate how coalitional approaches are needed to sustain change in communities and organizations, and that we must take on this work intentionally and by reflecting and working to understand what they refer to as the 3Ps, or how power, positionality, and privilege function in the work we do. While our chapter does not directly address marginalized people and identities, we wish to highlight these discussions as essential as context for our findings about building productive and reciprocal relationships across professional spheres.

Finally, the scholarship argues for the importance of building relationships as a ubiquitous element of successful collaboration. For instance, Instone and colleagues (2017) discussed how collaborators have to be open to learning each other's language and trying out different kinds of informal collaborations (such as guest lecturing in a classroom or running a professional development workshop). In this work, the emphasis was on interested individuals showing up to places where they don't usually go, like conferences or meet-ups. Similar sentiments were expressed in Jason Palmeri and Paul Tuten's (2005) description of their collaborative work together, where they observed their own commonalities and differences and worked to stay in dialogue about them throughout a project. Their work included paying attention to emergence and its relationship to difference, and to be intentional about responding to it. Still others discussed how relationships can lead to professionalization, internships, and mentoring relationships across professional spheres (Gonzáles, et al., 2017; Katz, 2015; Smith, 2015).

■ Research Questions

When we first began to work together in 2017, we started by posing questions similar to Palmeri and Tuten (2005) about our own collaborative approaches and how to best sustain them in reciprocal ways. Instead of documenting interactions with each other, however, we began to ask how other UX professionals worked together effectively and what that could teach us about how to best work together. We approached our interviews with research questions like:

- What would a broader look across multiple professionals show us about how to successfully start and sustain industry-academic collaborations in UX?
- What are some of the commonalities and differences across experiences?

To answer these questions, we developed a research study to collect experiences through semi-structured interviews with individuals who had participated in industry-academic collaborations.

Collaborating on Methods, Data Collection, and Analysis

Designing Procedures

We began collaborating on our interview instrument (see Appendix A) using iterative design approaches. We worked through questions together in several drafts, and then ultimately developed our ideas into an interview instrument. When submitting a proposal to the IRB, some of our collaborators were required by our institution as community members on a research team to complete research ethics training prior to initiating the study.

Participants

To locate participants, we used a convenience sample to make sure to capture rich experiences from those who we knew had sincerely engaged in industry-academic project work. Our eight participants were all at different stages of their careers and had engaged in different projects that we categorized by smaller one-offs (i.e., a guest lecture) all the way to larger, sustained projects (i.e., running a usability lab at a university). Also, we sought participants who worked both in universities and in industry contexts and could speak to working in both intellectual spaces. Notably, the participants often blurred the lines between these contexts in their professional lives, frequently working with/in both spheres.

Interview Procedures

Co-authors Keith and Ben conducted the interviews together. Each interview was audio recorded to create transcriptions and facilitate coding the results. Some participants offered interview answers by filling out our interview instrument and also participating in an interview. One participant chose to provide responses only in writing and chose not to participate in an interview. Since our interview protocol was written for this type of response, we felt the interview was still quite comprehensive and enriched our findings.

Data Analysis Procedures

First, we coded our findings to understand what Robert Yin (2013) called logic models (i.e., "The logic model deliberately stipulates a complex chain of events over an extended period of time."). Then, following the work of Jennifer Ismirle (2018), we assembled our interview data into experience maps (i.e., stages of a time-bound experience with a system, product, or service) that represented the collaboration experience of each participant. We chose experience maps because they help to identify moments of opportunity and pain points for engaging in a particular activity. In this way, it allowed us to better understand how each participant experienced academic-industry collaborations so that we could focus on further modeling the results beyond the themes. To make the experience maps uniform, we started with a template that could be altered to fit the interview results ethically and appropriately, and to account for a range of emergent experiences (see Nguyen et al., 2018). The experience maps helped us visualize the interview data to assemble our cross-case synthesis and consider the individual experiences as part of a larger dataset.

Cross-case Synthesis Procedures

To present our cross-case synthesis (i.e., an analysis and synthesis of multiple case studies to provide a better understanding of a broad system), we took each of the eight visualizations we assembled and combined them into a single table that represented a collective experience of all eight participants. Because of the immense amount of data we had to grapple with, we broke up each stage of the experience map into smaller tables (see Tables 1.1–1.6). To curate each table effectively and to honor the variety of experiences, we removed repeated ideas as we synthesized what we learned. Finally, while assembling each table of the overall experience map, we continued to work to sort and organize findings to make sure we were collectively synthesizing ideas presented by each interview. What we present in the next section of this text shows details about each participant prior to discussing what we learned from them.

Participants, Contexts, and Activities

In this section, we provide an overview of our participants and a summary of their individual contexts and engagement with industry-academic collaborations. The information in this section is helpful as a primer for understanding the cross-case synthesis presented in the following part.

Table 1.1. Participants Summary

	Job	Connections	Benefits	Importance
P1	Corporate manager	Bridging industry and academia	Everyone involved	Industry needs can supercede all other needs
P2	HCI researcher at a university	Share research with industry for collaboration	Brings academics and practitioners together	Understanding between both spheres
P3	Professor at a university	Attends events to understand current trends in industry	Publications and conference talks	Collaboration across the university and industry
P4	Consultant and adjunct professor	Connect academics and students with industry	Networking and problem solving	Inspire rather than just distribute knowledge
P5	Professor and UX researcher	Find similar personalities for collaboration	Leads to passion projects	Build trust in relationships between academia and industry
P6	Consultant	Share UX research with practitioners	"do science right"	Paths to specific solutions
P7	University lab director	Lab clients and graduate students	Deliverables for clients; work for graduate students	Consistent support between academia and industry
P8	Corporate UX manager	Curriculum educates students and informs community	Recruit talent	Synthesize the best of academia and industry

Participant 1 (P1) was a corporate manager who had recently started working for a university in an instructional role (see Table 1.1). On the interview instrument, P1 wrote about the importance of win-win value propositions as a way to fund and guide industry-academic research that had the potential to transform technologies and markets. P1 gave several examples of large-scale projects and collaborations, including some at corporations like Amazon and innovation centers like Bell Labs. In these projects, the goal was to bring some sort of technological innovation to market, and to work across industry and academic contexts to do so. In other words, the point of collaborating in this way was to find people interested in doing transformational work and who could persist through several rounds of ideation that would begin with workshops and move on to seeking funding. Then, the team would do the work and bring it to market.

When doing this sort of work, P1 described the importance of transactional interactions and relationships aimed at creating future opportunities for everyone involved. If there was an aligning principle of each team, it was this: to transform technologies while maximizing the unique benefits to everyone involved. However, P1 also reflected that, when it came to issues of power or timeline, business needs would take precedence over individual or academic needs. In other words, the transformational project work was of most importance, while the benefits to each individual collaborator was a close second. Even so, P1 seemed to believe it was important to assemble a team that was dedicated to supporting individual benefits as its central mindset because of issues of reciprocity and maintaining relationships in the future.

Participant 2 (P2) was an HCI (human computer interaction) researcher at a university who described collaborations in the context of observing industry practitioners to learn about their practice (e.g., using the organization as a field site), and this type of collaboration could involve some free consulting or data collection as a starting point in hopes for collaborations or partnerships in the future (see Table 1.2). In terms of finding connections, P2 attended events and gave talks (conferences, meet-ups, etc.), and utilized established university connections/networks to interact with practitioners to understand their interests and what's "new and exciting." When building relationships, P2 described focusing on the importance and challenge of finding a shared topic of interest for both sides. They also focused on working with larger organizations for stability and capacity and middle-level practitioners who had time for collaborating, and they found it helpful to work with practitioners who had some form of academic research background and appreciate the academic perspective and mindset.

To get collaborative projects started, P2 would share their research with industry practitioners to help bridge the divide. They also mentioned being involved with starting a conference focused on bringing academics and practitioners together and considering how to appeal and support both spheres. With this in mind, P2 also described a number of challenges to consider: how to bring academics and practitioners together at the same events; how to align interests and find mutual benefits with different mindsets; how to overcome differences in language; how to manage motivating factors (e.g., publications); and, how to manage time scale and long-term value (e.g., no immediate benefits or results).

Participant 3 (P3) was a professor at a European university who had transitioned from being a practitioner earlier in their career (see Table 1.3). P3 had been involved with a variety of university research projects for industry with a design result as the end goal and thought their previous experience as a practitioner helps them connect with industry practitioners as well as bringing in their academic perspective to projects. For these projects, the benefits were in the form of reports and publications, talks at conferences, and serving as a bridge between academia and practitioners. P3 also described collaborations in the sense of universities, such as teaching students about methods and tools as well as an overall strategic perspective, and involving students in industry projects for them to gain practical real-world experience and get critique from practitioners when trying to use what they have learned.

To facilitate collaborations, they attended events (conferences, workshops, etc.) and would meet with practitioners to connect and advocate for collaborations, and they were interested in finding out what is going on in industry. P3 also described a number of challenges and frustrations when engaging with practitioners or when working on projects even when the desire for collaboration and engagement is present, such as business goals and academic goals not aligning easily, and timing and benefit issues (e.g., being brought in on projects too late to be meaningful, constraints of role to feedback too late to be considered for industry timeline, etc.). In addition, P3 described considering ideas for collaborations across university departments/disciplines and developing innovations within the university, such as the creation of a lab/studio, although this involved considering challenges beyond simply deciding on a space and acquiring equipment/technology.

Participant 4 (P4) was a consultant and adjunct professor who spent time working in both industry and academia at different times and purposes (see Table 1.4). As a result, P4 seemed to have an important understanding of individual needs of each work context. In the interview, P4 discussed the importance of serendipity in industry and academic collaborations. At the same time, serendipity was something that grew from intentional interactions at conferences and other professional gatherings. P4 relied on host organizations, like conferences, to help locate potential collaborations. Creating the space for discussion allowed serendipity to occur, and for partnerships to form. When discussing engagement, P4 talked about a framework that focused on "lighting a fire" rather than "filling a bucket." In other words, inspire people to work on projects that compel them rather than trying to fill them up with knowledge or opportunity that won't necessarily help them.

Once a partnership was formed, P4 discussed the importance of talking through mutual benefits and seeking funding, including for students. Professional gatherings were important to P4 because they created opportunities for networking and to learn about problems, such as broad-scale technology issues or smaller-scale collaborations like assembling a space for conversations. In this latter scenario, funders can be the very professional communities that host conversations meant to lead to collaborations and the problem they are trying to solve is the lack of industry-academic collaborations in their professional community. Understanding the different kinds of problems could lead to finding people who want to work on these issues and/or have the bandwidth to do so.

Participant 5 (P5) was a professor who had experience teaching and researching UX (see Table 1.5). P5 focused on collaboration and building relationships as key components to expanding research, making connections, and supporting projects. In the interview, P5 stressed the need to find personalities that match for successful collaboration, but with an understanding that everyone will eventually find and develop their roles within the team. While some team dynamics might not be perfect, and while some projects might not be perfect, P5 believed that such interactions are a way to eventually locate projects individuals are passionate about.

As these passion projects become more apparent, P5 did not see a lack of funding as a roadblock. Such issues can find workarounds like finding necessary hardware and software to do transformational work. Essentially, if someone cares about a certain project or topic, they can find like-minded people they had worked with in the past, or find new ones, who would help or be interested in working together. This approach supported the balance between practitioner and academic as an iterative process that can be refined during each new project approach, including how to find collaborators. P5 continually stressed the importance of collaboration and the need to build trust in relationships in academia and industry.

Participant 6 (P6) was a consultant who specialized in synthesizing academic research related to user experience (like cognitive psychology) and sharing it with practitioners (see Table 1.6). P6's consulting engagements were driven by clients who wanted more scientific rigor, such as doing quantitative user research without as many shortcuts that are common in industry. P6 saw it as part of their mission to debunk "bad science" that had proliferated as UX practice has grown.

P6's collaborations across academia and industry had been centered around the ability to translate between and operate in both worlds simultaneously. At the heart of the collaborations was a shared desire and ability to "do science right". One of the key criteria for collaboration was finding clients who want to invest time and money to gain broad insights on the path to specific solutions.

Participant 7 (P7) was a university lab director with unique experience as a practitioner, educator, administrator, and mentor (see Table 1.7). P7 was balanced between running a lab that would take on clients, while also employing practitioners and graduate students to work for the lab and take classes in the program. In the interview, P7 stressed the importance of this balance and the responsibility to clients, grad students, the program, and practitioners. The systems in place to support such interactions were complicated, but simple in execution. Many interactions between clients and grad students supported the eventual hiring of graduate students after they left the lab and the program.

The lab structure generated a collaborative mentoring architecture that built on consistent support between academia and industry. P7 explained that it also balanced the need for self sufficient funding via clients and supported graduate students. Running the lab could be complicated at times given that some clients seek out the college atmosphere and the chance to connect with academia, while others are not interested in such connections and prefer a less traditional university experience (i.e., some students prefer lab and professional development work). P7 found this balance challenging, but also rewarding as it gave the lab a chance to be a bridge between industry and academia.

Participant 8 (P8) was a UX manager at a company who also taught boot camps because they were passionate about project-based education in a job-like setting (see Table 1.8). P8 developed bootcamp curricula and taught in order to give back to the community. Additionally, P8's employer supported their teaching "on the side" because it gave the company access to the best talent for recruitment purposes.

In our discussion with P8, they explored how to effectively collaborate with higher education institutions to synthesize the best of both worlds. That is, to establish the credibility, consistency, and long-term value of a university degree and the flexibility, immediacy, and applicability of industry training.

The Five Stages of Experiencing Industry-Academic Collaborations

Experience maps are often used as a method for visualizing a customer's experience with a product or service. When assembling experience maps, user researchers tend to focus on five stages, each with its own goal: doing, thinking, feeling, experience, and opportunities (see Kalmbach, 2016). The "doing" stage consists of actions our participants recounted to us, while the "thinking" stage included their rationale for doing that activity. The "feeling" stage of an experience map documents how participants responded emotionally while they were completing an activity. The first three terms are verbs, whereas the last two terms are summative: the "experience" category is how to describe or categorize the work done by users under the doing, thinking, and feeling stages, and the "opportunities" category focuses on the kinds of interventions that might occur or the kinds of next actions that are possible.

For the purposes of the experience maps presented in this section of our chapter, each stage catalogs the actions participants took throughout a collaborative lifecycle. That is, our interview protocol asked questions about getting started, sustaining and maintaining, and outcomes of engaging in industry-academic collaborations. In positioning each stage as a series of goal-oriented moves that occur on a timeline, we assembled representative examples from each section to help readers see how different pathways for collaboration can converge. In other words, what we present is meant to show how different experiences lead to a cohesive whole.

Table 1.2 represents the "doing stage" or what participants shared they did to begin a collaboration. For example, an individual might begin a collaboration by hosting or attending a workshop or discussion. Then, as they work to find a collaboration, they look for the right space or moment to begin discussions. During those moments, their next step is to find shared interests until they can find a project to pilot together. Sometimes the projects are large-scale that involve grants and/or corporate funders, and other times they are smaller-scale, such as guest lectures or presentations. The last stage is sharing the information learned from the collaboration in some way—through implementing or changing new products to publishing and/or presenting work at a conference or in a journal.

Table 1.2. Doing Stage of Experience Map

Foundation	Finding	Relationship	Collaborating	Maintaining
P1: Host workshops or discussions.	P4: Create space for collaborations to occur.	P2: Find shared interests.	P8: Pilot something together.	P3: Share work together in some way.

Table 1.3 represents the "thinking stage" or what participants did in terms of contemplation related to goals, connections, work, and collaboration. The Thinking Stage is particularly important because it demonstrates values and perceptions of the circumstances surrounding collaborative activities. In Table 1.3, collaborators begin by defining how the project can contribute to larger individual and organizational goals. Then, they try to find any groups of people who have already begun doing the work. As they work to build relationships, they try to make sure the timeline works for everyone. As the work gets done, collaborators start looking for outcomes that solve problems for people. Finally, as they finish a collaboration, a goal is to find new opportunities emerging from the work that was done together.

Table 1.3. Thinking Stage of Experience Map

Foundation	Finding	Relationship	Collaborating	Maintaining
P5: Define value adds to legitimize the project.	P2: Locate established relationships or networks.	P6: Learn if timing for project work is shared by all.	P4: Try to solve some kind of a problem for people.	P1: Find the opportunities emerging from the collaboration for next steps.

Table 1.4 represents the "feeling stage" and provides a sense of what participants were feeling as they began and engaged in collaborations. We found that some participants didn't really talk much about how they were feeling as engaging in the work. This may be because there wasn't an exact prompt in our interview protocol asking about emotional response, but also, we found some participants naturally talked about how they were feeling in the data. In this way, Table 1.3 is representative of the participants who discussed how they were feeling during collaborations. The timeline we assembled begins with Participant 4, who notes feeling that interests and values have to be shared as foundational to their work on collaborations. When finding a collaboration, Participant 7 noted having to downplay the role of their university, as it can be read positively or negatively. In building relationships during a collaboration, the idea of getting along well surfaced, as did feeling like small-scale collaboration is useful when/if it brings about funding for research that can be highly impactful. Finally, when a collaboration concludes, Participant 8 notes the importance of feeling like they must continue to learn—to not depend on the collaboration to do that work for them.

Table 1.4. Feeling Stage of Experience Map

Foundation	Finding	Relationship	Collaborating	Maintaining
P4: Interests in content creation & knowledge generation has to be shared.	P7: Downplay the university's role, depending on the client.	P5: Ask questions like, do you really want to work with this person?	P6: Have to find funding to do the "real" research.	P8: Keep learning after the collaboration is completed.

Table 1.5 represents the "experience stage" and provides insight into how experiences were recorded by those impacted by them personally. While this may appear redundant at first, the experience stage is how the data explained what it was like for participants to engage in collaborative work. In this way, we chose to highlight discussions that summarized experiences in particular ways. The foundational element of industry-academic collaborative experiences for P6, for example, was to locate the balance between scientific rigor and operational research. What P1 found was that the experience of a collaboration is highly dependent on who is in the lead. As well, P4 notes that relationships are formed when people are already intrinsically motivated to do so, while P7 notes that publishing often requires permission of funders and collaborators. Finally, P2 explains their experience as staying involved in conversations as a way to collaborate when it makes sense.

Table 1.5. Experience Stage of Experience Map

Foundation	Finding	Relationship	Collaborating	Maintaining
P6: There has to be a balance between scientific rigor and research that is operational.	P1: Depends on who is in the lead.	P4: People come together from different sectors because they want to.	P7: Publishing results often needs permission.	P2: Keep up conversations & consider potential collaborations.

Table 1.6 represents the "opportunities of collaboration" stage where the opportunities, presented through collaboration, are explored by the participants. In this table, we summarize the opportunities our participants perceived as they moved through a project. As with the other maps, the opportunities presented themselves uniquely depending on circumstance, work context, and individual motivations. We chose to focus this sample on talent acquisition and development. For instance, P7 explained one important aspect of collaborating was to "steal talent." Each participant discussed how important it is to shape collaborations in ways that help bring talent together, or to mentor students towards future careers and successes. Focusing collaboration on professional development activities seems to be a viable "win-win" for many working in user experience in particular.

Table 1.6. Opportunities of Collaboration

Foundation	Finding	Relationship	Collaborating	Maintaining
P7: It's okay to steal talent—the field is built that way.	P1: Win-win opportunities to build relationships with students & help educate them. It also creates a talent pipeline.	P8: Grow your team (pick from the best).	P4: Professional development & individual success is an important motivation for industry collaborators.	P5: Passion for projects beyond what is in it for you.

Table 1.7 represents the "challenges of collaborations" stage and explains the perceived challenges of collaborating that participants experienced in their spheres. The results in this section particularly demonstrate how, once again, values, relationships, and work contexts are at the center of effective collaborations. P2's comment that we have to find mutual benefits and combine people in convenient and unusual ways demonstrates a value for reciprocal relationships between individuals while P3's comment about showing academia what it should pay attention to demonstrates a focus on the workplace as a sorting mechanism. While many of these challenges seem predictable, the reality is that different organizations reward employees in increasingly different ways. While the opportunities seem to supersede the challenges, it is worth noting that the labor of grassroots engagement falls almost exclusively to the collaborators, and not on the organization or institution.

Table 1.7. Challenges of Collaborations

Foundation	Finding	Relationship	Collaborating	Maintaining
P3: Trying to show academia that they need to pay attention to what the practice is doing. Business & academic goals don't always align, so a chance for the right project may never come.	P2: It can be difficult to get higher profile talk opportunities to reach practitioners at their events & academic conferences may not be easily accessible to practitioners.	P3: Bureaucratic pitfalls & timing. You may start on industry projects too late for them to be meaningful.	P2: Practitioners may not be interested in potential disruption of the main business of their day-to-day work. While academics may be able to give insights into this work, there are often no immediate benefits for either.	P3: Higher education administrators may need to buy things to create a studio space, but the design of space and maintaining it is beyond typical university goals & research support.

What Did We Learn? Themes Presented Across the Tables

We started off this chapter asking two research questions:

- What would a broader look across multiple professionals show us about how to successfully start and sustain industry-academic collaborations in UX?
- What are some of the commonalities and differences across experiences?

In the below section, we share summaries of what our cross-case synthesis taught us as a collaborative team. We share these considerations as common elements of the collaborations we learned about through our interviews. Additionally, these considerations offer readers multiple perspectives on where to start and what to pay attention to when working on a collaboration across professional spaces. We find it particularly important to think about how values traverse these considerations.

Win-Win Scenarios

Our cross-case synthesis helps us see that significant parallels exist between academic and practitioner professional spaces, including a focus on how to negotiate a win-win scenario for everyone involved. For example, P7 saw distinct win-win scenarios as clients were able to get excellent support and research from well-trained graduate students and practitioners, while graduate students were able to get real-world experience by working with clients, receiving feedback, and networking with industry practitioners in a way that generated a possible line on employment after graduation. P1 also felt relationships with students were important and worked hard to help educate them to develop a sustainable talent pipeline. In doing so, these professional pipelines could create more opportunities for everyone involved. Such collaboration worked well when the goals and subsequent motivations of teams were compatible and on the same page.

Transforming Knowledge Is the Goal

Other parallels presented themselves within both professional spheres, such as transformation (of knowledge or technology) as a motivation. For example, P6 viewed themselves as a bridge between academia and industry. P6 found that clients would seek a better and more informed sense of UX research than the "bad science" that is currently out there. P6 also saw such interactions as a chance to transform UX research and ground it in methodologies that ensure scientific rigor. Meanwhile, P8 believed there were better ways to bridge curriculum between industry and academia, such as practitioners and academics co-teaching and sharing knowledge in other professional spaces, which can lead to a transformation for what it means to teach UX by finding a balance between the practical and theoretical. This balance can also lead to benefits for local communities and industry by developing talent pipelines. In this way, new educational approaches can transform more traditional academic spaces that focus on critique with practical applications.

Reciprocity and Future Action

The data also showed that, as collaborations emerge between industry and academia, interactions must be centered on reciprocity and future opportunities for the broader UX community. For instance, P3 stressed the importance of keeping open connections and conversations between practitioners and academics. P3 also noted that attending conferences, networking, and staying informed about what is happening in industry can help guide academic programs with issues currently being investigated by industry. As well, P2 also articulated the importance of such networking as it provided an opportunity to learn from different spaces. P2 further acknowledged that it can be difficult to get high profile presentation opportunities to reach practitioners at their events because of a disconnect of language ("academic speak"). At the same time, academic conferences may not be easily accessible to practitioners for the same reason.

Individuals and Relationships

One of the ways to create a sustainable space for collaboration across industry and academia was to invest in individuals and relationships. P6, as a single-person consultant, cultivated complex and essential relationships with strategic partners who understood the work they were doing. Part of this work centered on translating academic research into insights for practitioners to better explain the benefits of such rigorous scientific research. As well, P7 was invested heavily in relationships with clients and students. By securing clients who understood and appreciated their lab model, they were able to charge an amount to sustain the lab and recruit excellent graduate students. By supporting, hiring, and training excellent grad students, the lab is able to reinforce their reputation and secure clients willing to pay for their work. As a result, sponsorship and support were a viable way to fund different initiatives and investments in programs. P2 found it important to make connections at conferences, workshops, talks, and meet-ups. P2 did their best to find out what was exciting for professionals, what they were interested in, and how these projects benefit industry and academia in a way that gets buy-in from both sides. This type of buy-in could lead to funding streams outside of the usual academic models. For instance, P8 designed a system where bootcamps were funded.

Collaboration Across Professional Spaces

As was expected, collaboration between practitioners and academics was an essential feature of UX as a field. As noted in the previous paragraph, P8 explained that collaboration can be grounded in education and teaching, and as a result, P8 offered bootcamps as a means to explore a passion for project-based education in a job-like setting. Also, running the bootcamps were a chance to collaborate with those willing to learn more while also generating a possible talent pipeline for P8's business. P3 stressed the importance to meet with industry to discuss and advocate for collaborations that can combine the academic perspective with practitioner experience. These types of collaborations could be informative in terms of better understanding overlaps, but they could also lead to possible funding for projects both academics and practitioners find beneficial. P5 conducted extensive research, but found that the most rewarding research centered on projects they worked with others who had similar passions and interests. The idea of first building collaboration and then securing funding was important to each participant, but manifested itself in different ways.

Consider Funding

The need for funding was found to either play a heavy role, a limited role, or no role at all in the spaces of the participants. Funding for P7 was crucial in that without it, they could see possible intrusion from upper administrators focused on making changes. So, by being self-funded, they could control their own labs, who they hired, the clients they would take on, and so on. Any money offered or supplied by outside forces would come with possible demands for change from those outside forces. Funding, for P7, appeared to mean independence. For P5, funding was not as important as the passion for the project work. Funding served as an opportunity to secure a passion project and the chance to work with someone who might have the same passion *and* an ability to locate for funding for the work. P3 mentioned funding in a limited capacity. The end goal of building relationships between practitioners and academics was to make connections with industry and bring an academic perspective to industry projects. Similarly, P1 discussed the complexities of collaboration and that while important and beneficial in some capacity, businesses were the ones who benefit from the intellectual property (IP) generated from such collaboration. P1 also acknowledged that business needs would often take precedence over individual or academic needs. As a result, meeting the project outcomes was most important, and the benefits to each individual collaborator would always be a secondary concern.

Discuss Who Owns Intellectual Property

Knowledge outcomes were at the center of many collaborations, but each collaboration varied by who owns the outcomes and intellectual property. P4 noted that business needs tended to outweigh academic needs and that innovation can be stifled in such circumstances, but all work should have an end goal where everyone benefits. P7 conducted extensive research in their lab, and while the collaboration was productive between the clients and the lab, it was negotiated via financial compensation. Thus, as clients pay for the work to be done, all work and outcomes would be owned by the clients who paid for it. For others like P2 and P3, collaboration outcomes were not so much about ownership as they were about finding ways for everyone to benefit from the work.

■ Conclusion: Transformational Collaboration Awaits You

What this research project ultimately taught us is that Instone's (2005) invitation to practitioners and academics to come together under the umbrella term UX is indeed coming to fruition, but that reciprocal and respectful relationships must continue to be developed outside of individual professional spheres. As noted in our literature review, scholarship on industry-academic collaboration called on us to work together—to collaborate toward more just futures, products, and services. In other words, the call was to work together across workplace contexts to make the world a better place. The research in this chapter explains the experiences of making that sort of collaboration happen across a range of professional environments by people who intentionally work in both industry and academia. We also believe our work demonstrates that those of us working in UX must develop a better sense of our values for collaborating, to what ends and purposes, and to continue to find ways of engaging critically and effectively. As a research team, we practiced the development of our own values by asking questions about how to be better collaborators. We didn't rely on our own experiences and values to lead us to these answers, but intentionally designed a study to help us make sense of and question our own individual practices and theories.

We don't advocate for others working in UX to necessarily take the same approach as we did here, as we recognize the very real constraints people face when working to collaborate in the kinds of precarity many UX professionals experience today. However, we do suggest that we continue to formulate coalitional approaches across academic and industry intellectual spaces to *synthesize* unique contexts, values, constraints, and beliefs. Furthermore, we believe, as Walton and colleagues (2019) explain, that we must work to build and maintain such coalitions over the long-term in mutually beneficial ways. Our work teaches us we may not reach a consensus of ideas, but perhaps we can reach a synthesis of them. A synthesis points us towards futures and collaborations where ideas are iterative: recombined, reevaluated, and reimagined. In this way, our idea to conduct a cross-case synthesis to analyze collaborative work in different professional spheres as timely for us not as practitioners or academics, but as people who want to make the world a better place under the umbrella of UX. We cannot hold steady to professional spheres and identities to do this sort of broad-scale, large impact work, but we know this already. In fact, one way we've managed to do this work is through collaborating on the XA major at Michigan State University. In the end, we don't compel readers of this chapter with a call to action; rather, we compel you toward synthesis. Respectfully synthesize your knowledge, skill sets, and experiences with those whom you do not normally work with. Meanwhile, waiting somewhere, is a coalition who could use your help.

■ References

Bosely, D. S. (2002). Jumping off the ivory tower: Changing the academic perspective. In B. Mirel & R. Spilka (Eds.), *Reshaping technical communication: New directions and challenges for the 21st century* (pp. 27–40). Lawrence Erlbaum Associates.

Bridgeford, T. & St.Amant, K. (2015). *Academic-industry relationships and partnerships.* Baywood.

Dicks, S. (2002). Cultural impediments to understanding: Are they surmountable? In B. Mirel & R. Spilka (Eds.), *Reshaping technical communication: New directions and challenges for the 21st century* (pp. 13–26). Lawrence Erlbaum Associates.

Dubinsky, J. (2015). Making space for community voices: Rhetoric, engagement, and the possibilities for partnerships. In T. Bridgeford & K. St.Amant (Eds.), *Academic-industry relationships and partnerships* (179–196). Baywood.

Gonzáles, L., Potts, L., Turner, H. & Brentnell, L. (2017, August 11). Working with ladies that UX: building academic/industry partnerships for user research projects. SIGDOC '17: *Proceedings of the 35th ACM International Conference on the Design of Communication*, 29, 1–4 https://doi.org/10.1145/3121113.3121217.

Gonzáles, L. & Turner, H. (2019, October 4). Challenges and insights for fostering academic-industry collaborations in UX. SIGDOC '19: Proceedings of the 37th ACM International Conference on the Design of Communication, 21, 1–6. https://doi.org/10.1145/3328020.3353921.

Grabill, J. (2007). *Writing community change: Designing technologies for citizen action.* Hampton Press.

Hayhoe, G. (1998,). The academe-industry partnership: what's in it for all of us? Technical Communication, 45(1), 19–20.

Instone, K. (2005). User experience: An umbrella topic. CHI EA '05 Extended Abstracts on Human Factors in Computing Systems, 1087–1088. Association for Computing Machinery. https://dl.acm.org/doi/pdf/10.1145/1056808.1056824

Instone, K., Bowman, E., Lauren, B. & Opel, D. (2017). Industry-academic collaborations: Fostering a UX talent pipeline and discovering win-win opportunities. User Experience Magazine, 17(4). https://uxpamagazine.org/industry-academic-collaborations/

Ismirle, J. (2018, August 3). Using experience maps to consider individual stories. SIGDOC '18: Proceedings of the 35th ACM International Conference on the Design of Communication, 18, 1–6. https://doi.org/10.1145/3233756.3233954.

Kalmbach, J. (2016). Mapping experiences. O'Reilly Media.

Katz, S. (2015). Creating bridges with internships. In T. Bridgeford & K. St.Amant (Eds.), *Academic-industry relationships and partnerships* (pp. 77–96). Baywood.

Mirel, B. & Spilka, R. (2002). *Reshaping technical communication: New directions and challenges for the 21st century.* Lawrence Erlbaum Associates.

Nguyen, M., Turner, H. & Lauren, B. (2018). Disjuncture, difference, and representation in experience mapping. In R. Rice & K. St.Amant (Eds.), *Thinking globally, composing locally: Rethinking online writing in the age of the global internet.* Utah State University Press.

Palmeri, J. & Tuten, P. (2005). Dialogic negotiations: a reflective tale of collaboration across the academic-practitioner divide. *IEEE Transactions on Professional Communication, 48*(3), 313–323. https://doi.org/10.1109/TPC.2005.853939.

Paré, A. (2002). Keeping writing in its place: A participatory action approach to workplace communication. In B. Mirel & R. Spilka (Eds.), *Reshaping technical communication: New directions and challenges for the 21st century* (pp. 57–80). Lawrence Erlbaum Associates.

Smith, H. J. (2015). Collaborating with industry using mentoring programs and internships. In T. Bridgeford & K. St.Amant (Eds.), *Academic-industry relationships and partnerships* (pp. 97–116). Baywood.

Spartz, J. & Weber, R. (2015). A technical communication venture in building academic-entrepreneur relations and partnerships. In T. Bridgeford & K. St.Amant (Eds.), *Academic-industry relationships and partnerships (pp. 31–54).* Baywood.

Walton, R., Moore, K., Jones, N. (2019). *Technical communication after the social justice turn: Building coalitions for action.* Routledge.

Yin, R. (2013). *Case study research: Design and methods.* Sage.

Appendix A: Interview Protocol

These are questions we would like you to answer for our research in academic-practitioner collaboration in the context of user experience. You can glance over the questions to help you prepare for our discussion, or you can type your answers into this document and email it back to us. There are lots of questions, and some are somewhat redundant, so feel free to skip some questions if you think you have already answered them.

1. General stories of your collaborations
   A. What kinds of collaborations have you been a part of which have involved both academic faculty and UX practitioners? How would you classify these academic-practitioner collaborations?
   B. What motivated the collaborations? Were the collaborations always intentional or was there sometimes an element of serendipity?
   C. In general, who was involved in the collaborations? What fields or areas of practice? How would you describe the roles of people and/or organizations in the collaborations?
   D. How did the collaborations evolve over time? What factors influenced that evolution?
2. Summarize a few of your collaborations

   We know that you may have participated in several collaborations that were partnerships among academics and UX practitioners, but we would like you to focus on just a few of them for the next sets of questions.

Table 1.8. Collaboration Descriptions

	Collaboration #1	Collaboration #2	Collaboration #3
Name & short description			
Category/type			
Motivation			
Your role			
Roles by others involved			
Evolution over time			

3. Tools, assets & resources to support the collaborations

Tell us about the various tools, assets, and resources you used to make the collaborations happen. Examples might be grant funding, communication technologies, information resources, and meeting spaces.

Table 1.9. Collaboration Details

	Collaboration #1	Collaboration #2	Collaboration #3
Funding			
Technologies			
Information sources			
Meeting spaces			
Additional examples			
What you provided			
What others provided			
Most essential one & why			

4. Activities & processes to support the collaborations

Tell us about how these collaborations came to be and how they were carried out.

Table 1.10. Collaboration Implementation

	Collaboration #1	Collaboration #2	Collaboration #3
What was the genesis of the collaboration and how was it established?			
How did you get buy-in from the various stakeholders?			
Who was the lead on the collaboration and how was it managed once it began?			
What were the steps in the process, at a high level?			
How did you know when it was finished?			

5. Outcomes and benefits of the collaborations

Next, think about the outcomes and benefits of each of the collaborations.

Table 1.11. Collaboration Benefits

	Collaboration #1	Collaboration #2	Collaboration #3
What were the most important outcomes?			
What were the benefits for your organization?			
What were the benefits for you personally?			
What were the benefits for students?			
What were the benefits for other stakeholders?			
What was the most difficult challenge that had to be overcome?			
What is the most important lesson you learned?			

6. Overall reflections

   Finally, let's return to the big picture of academic-practice collaborations in UX.
   A. In the end, were your collaborations worth it? Why or why not?
   B. If you wanted to try to convince other people to create their own collaborations, what would you tell them? Why should they do it?
   C. What is the biggest challenge that people should expect if they attempt their own collaborations?
   D. What is your one "secret weapon" that has been the most useful for you in your collaborations?
   E. What sort of situations, contexts, qualities, or projects would trigger you to consider another academic-practitioner collaboration? How do you know when a collaboration is worth pursuing?
   F. Feel free to add in any other comments that come to mind about UX academic-practitioner collaborations.

One last question! Select one:

☐ I choose to remain anonymous: do not use my name when reporting results
☐ You can use my name when reporting results of the research

Thanks! If you are filling this out on your own, please email this to _____. If you want to do phone/online chat interview, send _____ some of your preferred meeting times.

2. "We need to figure out how to do better!": Opportunities for UX Professionals in Project-based Organizations—An Activity Theory Analysis of a Technical Design Project

Richard Douglas Divine and Mark Zachry
University of Washington

Abstract. The discipline of UX is most often explored through the usability of products designed to reach a consumer or end user. Less attention has been dedicated to understanding the contextual and situational advancements of the tools and methods that enable project-based design teams to achieve their design objectives most effectively. Our research uses an activity theory approach to model and embed reflective methods and tools as part of the project management lifecycle so that project workers might identify areas of contradiction or tension during the project and pivot to rapidly improve them.

The case study presented in this chapter examines a project-based organization (PBO) responsible for the design of a new commercial client website integrated with a back-end content management system (CMS). We conduct several data extraction methods using an activity theory approach, including a new method of analyzing a project worker's email and attachments. This new method aims to highlight potential areas of contradiction that might emerge through communications and artifacts used across the five process areas of project management, defined in the Project Management Body of Knowledge (PMBOK). Although our case study is historical in nature, our approach provides an application of multiple data extraction methods for in-project reflection and demonstrates the reflective assistance that a UX professional could bring to both the lifecycle and results of a design project.

Imagine Sebastian works as a UX researcher for a midsize technical consultancy. He is routinely engaged in multi-organizational project work meant to help clients develop custom software applications. Sebastian's role involves conducting user research for his team as they look to bring a new product to market. Every project that Sebastian joins is a unique configuration of workers that must collaborate for a finite amount of time on a joint objective. Many of the people he works with at his consultancy are routinely deployed on the

DOI: https://doi.org/10.37514/TPC-B.2025.2517.2.02

same projects, but varying client demands make it nearly impossible to offer the same team configuration for every project. As a UX researcher, Sebastian is trained in methods of observation and analysis. He has noticed that each project engagement involves two, if not more, organizations having to bridge work cultures, methods, and tools to effectively collaborate on their joint objective. Over time, he has begun to perceive patterns in the selection of tools and templates that are deployed across projects. Sometimes the projects are successful and sometimes they are not. Sebastian often wonders whether his training in UX could help make these patterns of project work more visible. In doing so, he might be able to find ways of analyzing episodic work to help determine if modifications to certain project mediators could make a difference in the success of future projects.

The role of the UX professional is typically focused on commercial products, with research and design initiatives targeting the needs of end users. The role is less commonly associated with efforts to research and adapt internal tools and methods used by project professionals during the development of those commercial products. Our research focuses on UX in work practices. We specifically focus on project-based organizations (PBOs) that navigate the episodic work associated with product design (Hobday, 2000). We demonstrate through our research that a role exists for the UX professional to assess and improve the internal tools and methods that are routinely adopted and adapted to meet the situated needs of collaborative project work. Although we focus on the role of a UX professional, we acknowledge the longstanding interplay between UX and technical communication (Redish & Barnum, 2011). Our focus on the UX professional does not exclude similar contributions that could be made by technical communicators in the workplace, as the theoretical and methodological underpinnings of this work are common to both disciplines. Our primary objective is to demonstrate the importance and efficiencies of integrating a role with a strong background in activity-based observations, artifact assessment, communication analysis, and user-centered collaboration with the more defined practices of the project management lifecycle used to deliver new products. We utilize the UX researcher role as a focal point because it is a role that is recognizable within the workplaces that comprise our case study.

Teams require tools and workflows to deliver new products to market. The efficiencies and usability of those tools and workflows require the same level of attention that a UX professional might commit to commercial product designs. Our research uses an activity theory approach to model and embed reflective methods and tools as part of the project management lifecycle. Finding ways to surface, analyze and optimize how tools and procedures are used by a unique configuration of project workers is a UX challenge, one that if met, could have a cascading effect on the downstream usability of project designs. As a window into our work, we present a case study of a project-based organization tasked with the design of a CMS integrated website for a commercial client. We introduce a multi-method, activity-based approach to the analysis of this project. Triangulating modeled results from three different data extraction methods, we demonstrate how the identification of key contradictions between the expected features of a project and the observed features of a project, can surface recommendations for improving the flow of project activities. Although our study is reflective in nature, our approach provides a method for in-project reflection and demonstrates that reflective assistance by UX professionals during the lifecycle of a project has the potential to not only improve a specific project's design, but can also help identify systemic issues persisting throughout the entire project ecosystem. The process of identifying and understanding project-based contradictions, we contend, promotes an opportunity for UX professionals to get more involved in the evaluation of internal tools and processes at the center of episodic design projects or similar project-based work.

▌ Background

UX researchers like Sebastian are emerging throughout industry with varying skills and being asked to perform a variety of roles. Given the vast range of opportunities and the skills needed to fill them, the role of the UX professional has been the subject of research attempting to better align academic approaches to teaching UX with the skills being demanded in the workplace. UX professionals can have a varied career involving skills that include but are not limited to usability testing, content strategy, information architecture, user research, interaction design, and UI design (Getto & Beecher, 2016). Ongoing research is dedicated to finding efficient ways to sequence UX methods and activities to align more effectively with project management, especially agile methodologies (Kuusinen 2015; Kuusinen & Väänänen-Vainio-Mattila, 2012;). The primary focus of both academic and professional research agendas, however, seems to focus on the skills needed to improve consumer-based products for end users. Little, if any, exploration of the UX role in improving internal work practices has been conducted. This is especially true in the work of software development projects that employ UX professionals.

Research related to project management tools sheds some insight on the reasons why UX professionals are needed to evaluate and improve internal project work. A study by Muhmamed Sajad and colleagues (2016), compared seven popular project management applications against IEEE Standard 16326–2009, which outlines specifications for project management plans covering software projects. The authors found that only 63 percent of the features outlined in the IEEE standard for software development projects were in fact met by the project management tools analyzed. This means that 37 percent of the features outlined by the standard are not covered by project management tools commonly used in industry. These absent features are routinely accommodated by project tools created specifically to fill an operational or communication gap within a project. Further, many tools are routinely recycled from project to project to address systemic deficiencies. As new tools are created or appropriated, their use within the project management lifecycle can introduce several contradictions (Engeström, 2000) to the preferred flow of work. UX professionals are uniquely qualified to identify and mitigate these contradictions.

Our research leverages activity theory because it provides an orienting framework and modeling method capable of coordinating, collecting, assembling, reflecting, and learning from work-related activities and the communication artifacts that memorialize them over time. This theory has shown value in assessing engineering systems (Collins et al., 2002), fixing communication flows (Spinuzzi, 2013) and analyzing interconnected workflows like those found in healthcare settings (Engeström, 2000). Beyond this, activity theory has been proposed as a productive framework for understanding team interactions in project-based work (Zahedi et al., 2017). Aligned with this proposal, Benjamin Lauren (2018) has demonstrated how activity theory can be used to analyze the management of team change in a technical firm. Lauren's work bridges the field of project management to that of technical communication, which has a long history of exploring work practices using activity theory (see, for example, McNely et al., 2015, and Spinuzzi & Guile, 2019).

Our research specifically leverages Yrjö Engeström's (1987) activity theory method for modeling activity systems, which has been instrumental in reflecting on, modeling, and improving complex configurations of work. His methods of data collection includes interviews, document analysis, and direct observations of routine workplace activity. Like Engeström, we utilize interviews and document analysis as part of our project-based investigation. Direct observation of episodic work, however, is challenging since the motivated activities are temporary, persisting only long enough to complete the deliverable at hand. Our methodological modification therefore calls for the empirical assessment of episodic project-based work as memorialized in email to compensate for the inability to directly observe the work being analyzed. Leveraging workplace email as an archived source of project communications, activities, and tools, we use the modeling capacity of activity theory to make hidden work visible. Making such work visible, UX professionals are presented with the opportunity to assist project professionals in modifying project tools and workflow to increase efficiency. Our activity system modeling effort restricts the subject to a single entity, the project worker, and limits the modeling to a single activity system. This choice is not meant to suggest that multi-motivated systems are not worth exploring in project work; instead, we choose to restrict our modeling because we are interested in helping individual project workers reflect on their own work. Our approach also addresses limited access to other project subjects residing in partner organizations or subjects that are no longer available due to the episodic nature of the work itself.

Case Study: CollabCorp's Interactive Wireframe Design Project

The subject of our case study is a seasoned project manager employed by a small technical design company near Seattle, WA. Conditions of the project worker's participation required complete anonymization of all names and organizations discussed and observed within the study. Once the study was completed and the resulting narrative developed, we anonymized all names to the satisfaction of the participant and their employer. The primary organization of our study involves CollabCorp, a small but growing project-based organization, employing about 700 employees. The company focuses on projects and engagements that assist clients with process improvements through digital transformations. Our case study details a specific project that CollabCorp was hired to manage for a regional company that we will call ClientOrg. We will refer to this project as ProjectWeb. ClientOrg was engaged in a companywide branding campaign that would require a significant redesign to their corporate website. ClientOrg wanted a new online marketing experience that utilized dynamic content from a backend content management system (CMS). Through an open bid process, the contract to design the interactive wireframes and manage the overall project for the new website was awarded to CollabCorp. The back-end development of the CMS, however, was awarded to a third company that we will call DevTech. This case offers a unique opportunity to study the execution of a single project with work being coordinated across three different companies for the single purpose of delivering a digital tool to be used by consumers.

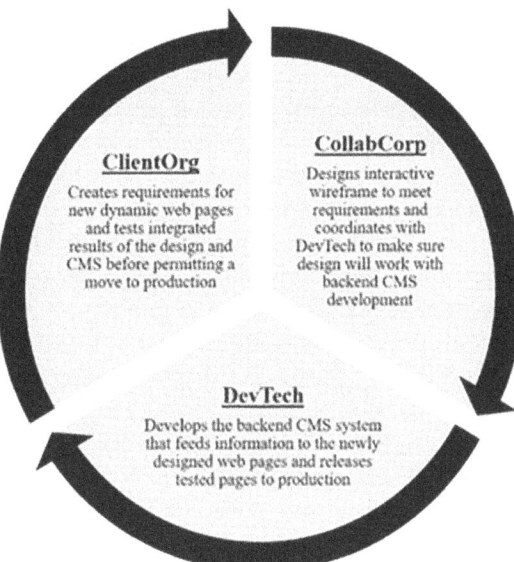

Figure 2.1. Collaboration configuration for ProjectWeb.

Both ClientOrg's marketing department and CollabCorp's design team had spent time and resources on UX inspired requirement efforts for the website; however, few resources were dedicated to ensuring the tools and processes adapted for this project were in fact optimized for the task at hand. We claim that dedicating UX resources to better understand internal work, especially episodic project work, can increase awareness of constraints surrounding the situated use of tools and highlight systemic social patterns that, if left unattended and unaddressed, might impact future projects.

■ Methods

Conducting an activity system analysis involves several qualitative methods aimed at acquiring a rich descriptive data set that can be interpreted and modeled. The most widely used methods in activity system analysis include interviews, document or artifact analysis, and direct observations (Yamagata-Lynch, 2010). Our case study uses all three methods of data extraction. To demonstrate the unique contributions each method makes within our case study, we deliver a resulting activity system model for each extraction method and discuss its value in making work visible. As each of the three models are developed, we compare them to identify contradictions. Resolving such contradictions, we contend, makes possible the learning and improvement needed to advance the work of the organization.

Our first data extraction method uses a semi-structured interview of a project professional with general reflective questions about the subject's professional background in project-based work. Questions aimed at understanding their familiarity with the five process groups outlined in the Project Management Body of Knowledge (Rose, 2013), questions meant to ensure that the subject is familiar with terms consistent with activity theory, and specific project questions guided by the activity system modeling structure are included. The resulting activity model represents the more salient features of the project as remembered by the project professional.

To meet the demands of a document or artifact analysis, we search for a central project document like a project charter or statement of work that outlines the key aspects of the project. Objectives, timelines, the community of participants and their roles, project rules dictating workflows, decision paths, and hierarchies are just a few examples of key project indicators traditionally found in the planning documents of a project that are easily mapped to an activity system model to represent the ideal version of the project as it was conceived during planning phases. Discovering such ideal versions of a project are useful for understanding the difference between planned work and realized work.

As an alternative to direct observations, which are impossible after episodic project work has been completed, we employ an assessment methodology that uses the project worker's email to model activity systems of specific phases of work based on the Project Management Body of Knowledge's five process areas (Divine & Zachry, 2018). Transforming key components of email into activity-centric models, we leverage workplace communications as empirical traces of work providing rich insights into past work events. Triangulating the data modeled from the empirical assessment of emailed project communications with a reflective interview of the project worker and the data modeled from the project's planning document or charter, it becomes possible to identify key contradictions between the models. These identified contradictions serve as the basis for new insights related to the social dynamics involved with the project and its supporting organizations. Efforts to resolve these contradictions can not only improve social awareness but also provide the very evidence UX researchers need to improve the efficiency of the project tools themselves.

Activity System Modeling

As data is collected via interviews, document analysis, and email analysis, each data set is thematically grouped to fit the structure of the activity system model. The activity system model represents the interconnections between the *subject* or person conducting the activity, the *object*, or motivated purpose for the activity, and the mediating *tools* used to achieve the desired *outcome* of the activity's objective. The model also represents the entire *community* involved in the activity, a mediating *division of labor* which articulates the role each community member plays in the activity, and finally a set of formal and informal *rules* that mediate a successful relationship between the subject and the activity's community. When the components of the activity are brought together in the model, a single unit of analysis emerges highlighting the influence that each node in the model exerts on the outcome of the activity. In our analysis of each data collection method, the subject and the object remain consistent; however, the other nodes of community, rules, tools, and division of labor, show unique differences between the models. These differences are identified as contradictions (Engeström, 2000) and it is through reflections on, and the resolution of, the contradictions that learning occurs and opportunity for improvement emerges.

The Subject (Gabe B.)

Following our methodological approach, the human *subject* of the activity system is a single individual. Our case study focuses on the subject Gabe B., the Lead Project Coordinator for CollabCorp. Gabe B. took over responsibility for the oversight of the execution phase of ProjectWeb four months into the project because timelines were being missed and communication issues between the partner organizations were starting to derail the project.

The Object (Execution Process Group—ProjectWeb)

Gabe's primary objective and desired outcome during the execution phase of ProjectWeb was to oversee the delivery of interactive wireframes meeting ClientOrg's marketing requirements, while simultaneously meeting the integration requirements of an associated CMS system being developed by DevTech. To achieve this objective, the activity would require significant coordination and collaboration between all three organizations.

Data Extraction Method for Reflective Interviews

To demonstrate the value each data collection method contributes to the study, we present them one at a time and offer a representative activity system model for discussion. The three activity system models are compared to one another as we progress through our analysis. To begin we present the analysis associated with our reflective interview. Participating in a semi-structured interview protocol, Gabe B spent nearly two hours providing background information on his career in project work, his company CollabCorp, and reflecting on the execution phase of ProjectWeb. The semi-structured interview contained key questions adapted from Daisy Mwanza's Eight Step Model (2002), which provides structured guidance to activity system modeling. This method facilitated guided reflection on the project phase being discussed, allowing the project worker to remember salient aspects of the project based on their memory alone. We thematically analyzed the answers and modeled them by applying an activity system analysis.

Interview Finding: The Mediating Tools

We asked Gabe during our interview about the tools required to facilitate work on the project. He responded as follows.

> So, it was the mocks and the interactive wireframes and that was about it I would say. We use some project tracking tools—I'm forgetting the name of the tool that they used; it was kind of like Basecamp and whatnot—in order to pass tasks back and forth since the web design or the web development aspect of the project was done from the third party who's also doing the CMS. So, we'd have to find some way to facilitate, and those guys were all offshore. Lot of email communication. I mean, daily standups were a big thing as to how we facilitated everything. But for the most part, Tracking Tool worked relatively well when we started putting some rigor into it. In the early stages it was just, "Oh, it's just [task] level." Very choppy stuff, so . . . I will add the caveat of if you have a project tracking tool and people use email around that, the email becomes distracting. Yeah. Why have the project tracking tool, which is what happens in most cases?

Gabe identified key tools used during the execution of ProjectWeb. Consistent with the desired outcome of this phase of the project, mock-ups and interactive wireframes were two of the main tools used to iterate on design requirements and assure compatibility with the backend CMS system. The requirements developed by ClientOrg's marketing department were stored and managed in a project requirement application that Gabe recalled as being something like Basecamp. The multi-organizational project team depended heavily on email to facilitate communication and work across organizational boundaries, and it became clear that Gabe was frustrated with requirements and decisions getting lost in email when they should have been updated in the tracking tool. The project team depended on regular stand-up meetings conducted virtually and via the phone to coordinate and progress their work. Given Gabe's senior position, contracts and financial documents were also standard tools that required referencing and amending during the execution of ProjectWeb.

Interview Findings: The Community and the Mediating Division of Labor

Gabe revealed three companies and at least eight individuals involved in ProjectWeb when prompted to describe his project community.

> Yeah, so when I first started engaging on this there was [Todd] and [Mary]. [Todd] was our PM, [Mary] was our designer. Then we had [Sam], who was the client. Then we had [Jasper], who was the third-party vendor. And then we had a bunch of [Sam's] people who were marketing-based, mainly marketing and finance. We had some people who did operational-type work over there. So, there was another [person, Kent], who was kind of our BA-type role. Basically, [Kent] would do all the navigation of the work aside from finance and marketing. Marketing had [Lonni] at the table and on the finance side. So yeah, I would say that that was kind of our core team. And then we had, obviously, third-party developers off to the side and whatnot, so.

CollabCorp was resourced with three individuals, Gabe, Todd, and Mary. The customer, ClientOrg, had three main participants, Kent, Sam, and Lonni. Finally, the CMS developer DevTech had a single contact named Jasper who worked remote from Michigan but managed development resources in India. The community for ProjectWeb involves a complex configuration of organizations each with its own positions of power and responsibility within the project. ClientOrg was the main customer paying both CollabCorp and DevTech for their services on the project. ClientOrg's main role in ProjectWeb was to facilitate requirements for the new site that impacted both the content design and the CMS design. They utilized resources in project management, business analysis, marketing, and finance. CollabCorp, the company that Gabe worked for, was responsible for the delivery of interactive wireframes that met the marketing requirements outlined by ClientOrg and accommodated dynamic content delivered by the evolving backend CMS. DevTech, led by Jasper, was responsible for delivering the CMS and configuring its code to work with the emerging designs provided by CollabCorp. Jasper coordinated offshore resources to deliver the CMS configurations needed to support the interactive wireframes.

Interview Findings: The Mediating Rules

Our analysis to this point has yielded few notable contradictions based on the interview data collected from Gabe. The activity model, thus far, seems to be providing a consistent representation of the execution phase of ProjectWeb. With any activity there are a set of rules, both implicit and explicit, that mediate the relationship between the subject and community and their ability to coordinate effectively in pursuit of the activity's objective. When asked about rules of engagement on the project Gabe offered the following information.

> It was interesting. First communication I had with [Jasper], the leader of the outsourced developers, I'm like, "[Jasper], what are you doing, man? Because you should be dropping code like every couple weeks for us to do testing on and figure out." . . . seemed like a nice enough guy but just didn't really understand how to accelerate what needed to be done nor did he have the power to pivot the team that he was working with on the other side of India . . . a lot of the things that he would say to us were, "Oh, well, that sounds like a change order," or, "Oh, I got to get it into those guys queue and see what we can do." And he's just like, "Well, our program really doesn't do that, that's custom dev." So those are kind of the things, the roadblocks, that he would throw at our way. And I would be like, "Oh my God. Just too much, bud, too much. *We need to figure out how to do better!*" And I just don't think he was empowered to be able to do better . . . I would come to them and they'd be like, "No. You're not our budget holder. Sorry, man. We don't report to you." Lots of that kind of stuff. Never fun.

Gabe's interview led to several key contradictions in this node of the activity model. First, Gabe complained that Jasper's approach to project work resulted in direct delays to project deliverables. These delays created conflict between ClientOrg and CollabCorp. CollabCorp was responsible for the overall delivery of the design which was realized when design requirements passed user testing in a fully integrated testing environment. To achieve testing, the interactive wireframes had to be successfully married to dynamic content supported by the CMS. CollabCorp was completely dependent on DevTech's timeline and delivery of the CMS components to successfully iterate and deliver functional web designs. Since ClientOrg hired CollabCorp to deliver interactive wireframes, and those wireframes were dependent on the CMS code being configured by Jasper and the offshore DevTech team, any delay on behalf of DevTech resulted in ClientOrg blaming CollabCorp.

The dependencies between the organizations involved did not seem to be managed by appropriate rules of engagement and responsibility. DevTech was directly hired by ClientOrg, so CollabCorp had very little power to influence the company's working behavior and timeliness. Since CollabCorp was responsible for the successful delivery of the newly designed pages, and the design was dependent on the CMS system, any delays by DevTech resulted in delays for the designs, which resulted in ClientOrg blaming CollabCorp for missing agreed upon timelines. It was also clear that CollabCorp and DevTech were not able to negotiate rules around methodology since CollabCorp was operating in an agile project environment and the DevTech developers were used to working in a waterfall environment. Although Jasper participated in the agile workstreams and standups, his development resources were delivering code on a timeline that did not work well with short sprints. Evidenced in Gabe's quote about Jasper, there also seemed to be a lack of rules governing a change management process as Jasper would use scope creep or changing requirements as a reason for missed dates. Without defined rules that govern iterative change requests, a formal definition of change goes undefined, leaving change as a safe excuse to justify poor performance.

The Activity System Model Based on the Reflective Interview

The interview with Gabe, lead program manager for CollabCorp, resulted in a succinct activity system model of the execution phase of ProjectWeb based solely on guided reflection. The modeled activity system is presented in Figure 2.2.

Key contradictions identified in the activity system (indicated by a lightning bolt icon) point to a lack of explicit rules that helped coordinate workflow, expectations, and results between the three organizations involved. According to Engeström (2000), these would be considered third level contradictions which occur between the existing form of an activity system and its potential to deliver a more advanced or desired outcome. In our analysis, we could not identify any tools that either helped mediate the lack of rules or provided implicit support to the rules of engagement. The lack of rules binding the multi-organizational configuration led to a secondary contradiction (occurring between the nodes of an activity system) in the activity related to DevTech's role in the division of labor, impacting the desired outcome of the project. Left unattended, these contradictions resulted in a meandering scope of work and missed deadlines. The impact of these contradictions resulted in CollabCorp assigning Gabe to the project in July 2018 to help get things back on track. Unfortunately, Gabe was unable to save the project and ClientOrg was removed from the project in December by which time they had delivered most of the interactive wireframes. The end results, however, did not flow and integrate effectively with the CMS. ClientOrg leveraged the designs delivered by CollabCorp and continued working directly with DevTech until they completed the project, nearly two years behind schedule.

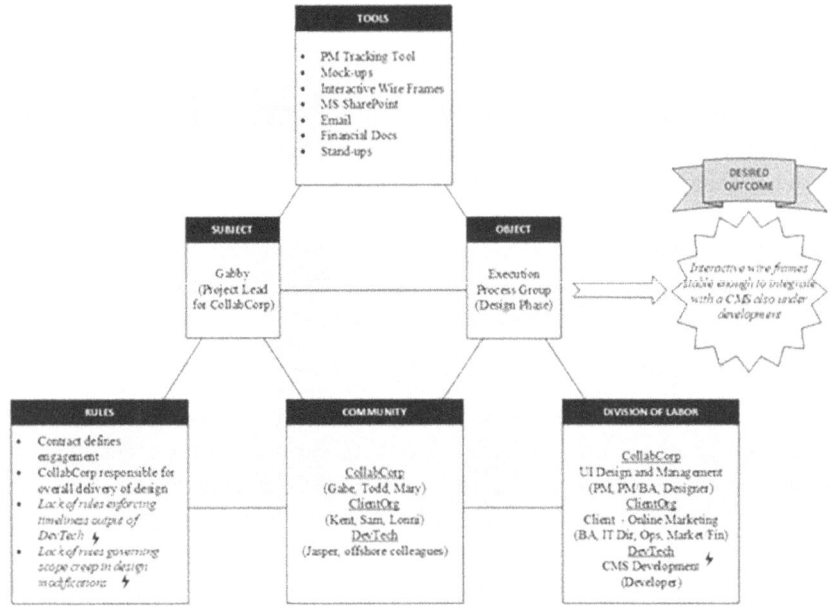

Figure 2.2. Activity system analysis of reflective interview with Gabe B.

■ Data Extraction Method for Document Analysis

Document analysis is another method of data extraction commonly used to inform an activity system analysis. When researching project work, we recommend identifying a central document that details the project's purpose, plan, and resources such as a project charter, project brief, or statement of work. These central documents align naturally with activity system models as they typically define the *objective* of the project, the members or *community* of the project, the role or *division of labor* each member performs, key *tools* and resources that will be used throughout the project and the various *rules* and guidelines that should be adhered to when engaged in the project. When modeled in an activity system format, the central project document reveals the original, "ideal" plan for the project phase and provides a model against which memories or actual empirical evidence of project activities can be compared. Comparing models helps identify areas of compatibility, indicating that things occurred according to expectation. Where the models diverge or are in contradiction with each other, one finds opportunity to learn and improve. CollabCorp typically issued a statement of work that outlined the key deliverables for their projects as well as associated financial instruments detailing the allocation and cost of their resources. A statement of work for this specific project could not be located by Gabe at the time that he took over the project in July of 2018. It remained unavailable when we conducted our interview. We were able to locate a document called PMTransitionDoc authored by Todd, the original PM from CollabCorp. This document, created to support Gabe's transition to replace Todd on the project, provided a single comprehensive reference identifying the people, processes, and tools associated with ProjectWeb.

Document Analysis Findings: The Mediating Tools

The transition document provided us with links to 10 key tools critical to ProjectWeb. Five of the tools referenced in the document would have been developed during the *Planning* phase. They were created to orient project members to certain engagement rules related to work sequencing and timelines but were continually used as reference tools during the *Execution* phase of the project. These included a site map of ClientOrg's website, a go-no go schedule, a pre-production release plan establishing rules for user acceptance testing and training, a production review process that provided rules of reviewing final content between DevTech and ClientOrg, and a workflow for ClientOrg's marketing department to approve designs. The other five tools detailed in the transition document were all actively used during the *Execution* phase of ProjectWeb and included email, the Wrike system for requirement management, InVision software for design review and markups, an executive level status report, and a SharePoint library for project documents.

When we compared the activity model we generated from Gabe's reflective interview, interesting primary contradictions (tensions occurring within a single node of the activity system) began to emerge. We began to see acknowledgments of key physical computing tools used to manage various aspects of the project that were not mentioned in the reflective interview with Gabe. Gabe mentioned a requirement system like Basecamp, but we learn through this document that the requirement system was called "Wrike" and it was owned and operated by DevTech. This system was the trusted source for all requirements and their status. We also learned about a system called InVision that served as a collaboration tool for review and markup of the interactive wireframes produced by CollabCorp. Both systems are important because they factor into workflow rules detailing how the three companies were expected to sequence their work. The final primary contradiction related to tools involves a tool named the Exec Level % Complete Report. The report was an excel file pulled directly from the Wrike requirement system and circulated via email for status updates. This contradiction is important because the verbiage in the central reset document indicates that this specific report must be kept current for regular status updates indicating its importance in conveying progress to project personnel and project stakeholders.

Document Analysis Findings: The Community and the Mediating Division of Labor

The central document analysis revealed three companies and six individuals involved in ProjectWeb. Though all three companies were represented across the two activity models, there were notable primary contradictions in the make-up of both CollabCorp and ClientOrg and the roles they represented. DevTech remained consistently represented with Jasper leading offshore development efforts. In CollabCorp, only the designer Mary G. was listed, highlighting CollabCorp's primary responsibility of design during the project. Neither project manager at CollabCorp, Gabe nor Tom, were mentioned in the project reset document. This may be a result of Todd transitioning away from the project when the document was created and Gabe having yet to be identified as the replacement. ClientOrg was noted as having four resources, Kent, Amy, Daniel, and Lonnie while Gabe's interview only identified Kent (BA) and Lonni (Marketing) in common. Amy and Daniel identified through the reset document were both Technical Operations resources for ClientOrg. Gabe's interview identified Sam, ClientOrg's IT director as a resource; however, Todd's document does not discuss Sam's role. This difference was due in large part because Gabe's position at CollabCorp gave him increased power to negotiate with a higher-level position within ClientOrg. Where Todd was working primarily with Kent and Lonni at ClientOrg, Gabe worked with their superior, the IT Director of ClientOrg.

Document Analysis Findings: The Mediating Rules

Several artifacts provide details on rules that should have been followed when engaging in ProjectWeb processes. These rules surface key primary contradictions when compared to the lack of rules described during our interview with Gabe. First and foremost, the process tools identified by the central project document define clear rules related to the sequencing of work and the roles each company and contact plays in that sequence. These rules were not mentioned by Gabe during the interview. The *approval flow for interactive wireframe designs* was a specific document that clearly outlined the status points in the approval process and the expected sequence of events needed to transition from one status to the next. However, consistent with Gabe's assessment that the project lacked proper rules enforcing DevTech's timeliness, or rules governing scope creep in design modifications, none of the process documents offer any affordances to keep these two issues in check. This finding, however, identifies specific tools that could be altered to prevent the two main issues raised during Gabe's interview. Additional status definitions or workflow sequences could have been added to the *approval flow for interactive wireframe designs,* assuring DevTech's specific contributions to the collaborative process were made more visible. Highlighting CollabCorp's dependence on DevTech's output and officially holding DevTech equally responsible for missed timelines might have eliminated the very problems that plagued Gabe's predecessor and may have salvaged the project from its ultimate demise.

The Activity System Model Based on a Central Project Document

To recap, we have assembled two unique activity system models for the execution phase of ProjectWeb. The first model was derived through thematic analysis of an interview with CollabCorp's lead program manager Gabe. The second model, presented in Figure 2.3, was derived through a thematic analysis of a central project document, in this case a project transition document created for Gabe by the exiting project manager, Todd. By comparing these two models we were able to identify key primary contradictions between the project that Gabe remembered through guided reflection and the same project memorialized in a transition document. Reflecting on such contradictions enables a project worker to identify tools, rules, and roles that could be adjusted to make the project more efficient.

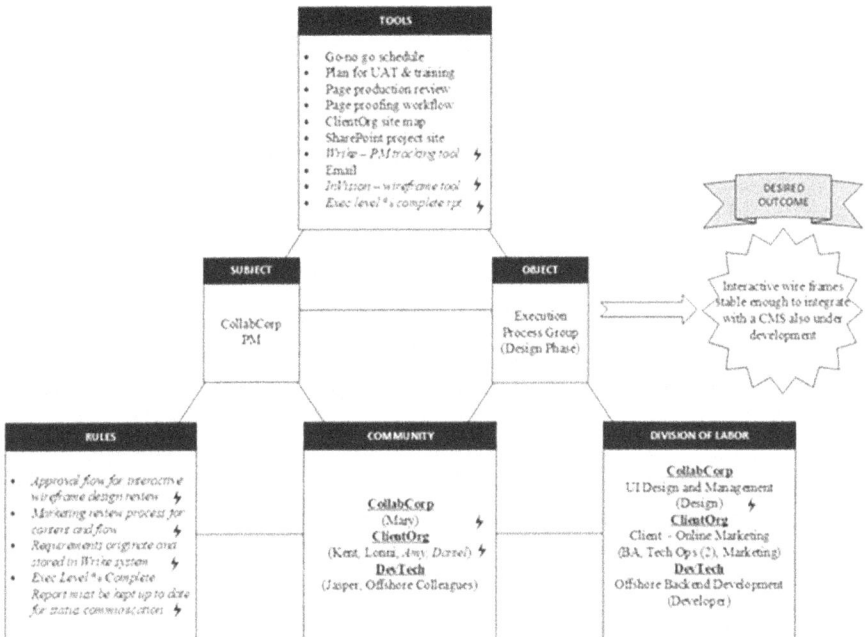

Figure 2.3. Activity system model of a central document for ProjectWeb.

A UX researcher like Sebastian, equipped with skills in interviews and document analysis could easily apply activity system modeling to identify improvement opportunities, not only from a usability perspective, but also from a perspective of flow and governance. These two data extraction methods alone produce interesting findings, but the lack of direct observation of the work being studied still leaves many open questions. As mentioned, project work is difficult to observe when compared to more sustained and systemic work practices associated with knowledge work. If UX researchers were assigned to monitor a project in process, direct observation could yield rich results. In the case of our study, the project finished, and the companies are no longer associated. The project professionals of CollabCorp, however, take on new clients daily and recycle many of the project tools and resources we have reviewed in our study. Without an agenda to constantly reflect on the mediators of projects (tools, rules, and roles) project professionals like those in CollabCorp run the risk of recycling failed mediators in future projects.

Data Extraction Method for Email Analysis

We now turn our attention to a data extraction method meant to allow empirical analysis of work activity even after the work has been completed. By accessing a project worker's email, framed to include only SENT email associated with a specific PMBOK process group, one can access memorialized workplace communications and acts of collaboration for a past project. Binding the object to one of the five PMBOK process groups (initiating, planning, executing, monitoring, and closing) allows all project professionals to use a consistent orientation for this type of analysis, regardless of the project management methodology they employ. Waterfall managed projects and agile managed projects each have their own unique aspects within project phasing, but the PMBOK process group is generic enough to apply to all types of projects and is typically identifiable by project professionals. Email was selected as an empirical source for work analysis because its use in project-based organizations is nearly ubiquitous. Other project management tools currently on the market like Slack, Trello, Jira, Wrike, Teams, etc., could serve in place of email; however, few of those tools are designed to carry communication across organizational boundaries. They are great resources for internal teams of an organization but once a project team is comprised of multiple companies, those products present challenges to uniform access, security, and retention configurations. Email is a consistent and reliable method of communicating and sharing project artifacts across communities of practice and organizational divides.

Our analysis of Gabe's SENT email folder was limited to the date range of the execution process group for ProjectWeb. The distinct date range was July 1, 2018 to March 1, 2019 reflecting the time frame that Gabe joined the project until ClientOrg removed CollabCorp from the project and began working directly with DevTech to complete delivery. The email collection included in the date range was filtered further to remove any emails not associated with ProjectWeb. Although Gabe's dataset was easy to obtain because he organized his work email using project folders, many project professionals do not bother sorting their email by project. In cases such as these, project specific email can be identified using key word searches against the email subject line or leveraging the email distribution header (To, CC, BCC) to identify key project members.

Gabe's final Outlook dataset consisted of 121 emails that he personally sent or forwarded about ProjectWeb excluding emails that communicated project-based calendar entries. Once the frame was obtained, a thematic analysis was conducted to translate key components of email into an activity system model. Gabe, of course, remains the subject of the activity, and the object is bounded by the chosen PMBOK process group. In this case, the Execution process group involving the design of interactive wireframes was chosen. The distribution headers (To, CC, BCC) reveal the total community membership receiving project specific messages. Anyone receiving a message is considered an interested member of the project community. Attachments found in email are operationalized as being direct tools in service of the project. Of Gabe's 121 SENT emails, 13 of them had attachments, and each email with an attachment had only one artifact attached. The two nodes of the activity model that are not easily derived directly from email are Rules and the Division of Labor. Many times, the attachments will reference documents generated during the *Planning* process group of a project and can be referenced for rules of engagement and sequencing flows, much like we saw when we modeled the components of the central transition document for ProjectWeb. Email signatures can be leveraged to determine roles or a division of labor of individual community members, but the results should be confirmed with the project professional participating in the analysis since the responsibilities of a role can be misleading when comparing common position titles across organizational cultures. The derived activity system for Gabe's SENT email pertaining to ProjectWeb is modeled in Figure 2.4. At first glance one can see how robust the results from an empirical analysis of email can be. Next, we triangulate this model with the two models derived previously to identify additional contradictions that enrich Gabe's growing assessment of ProjectWeb.

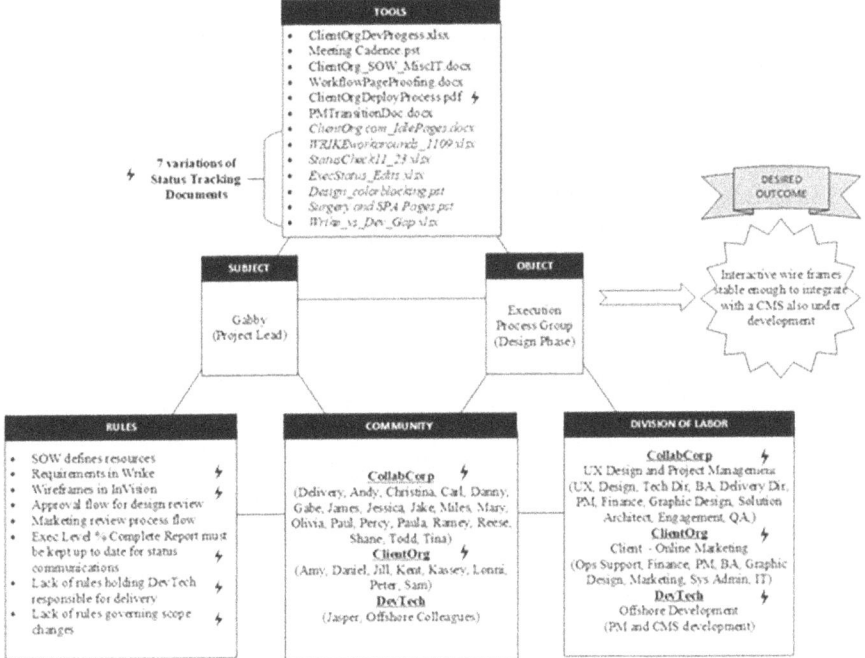

Figure 2.4. Activity system model of Gabe's SENT emails for ProjectWeb.

Email Analysis Findings: The Mediating Tools

When using the email analytic method for activity system modeling, the SENT email frame should be filtered for attachments to identify a portfolio of tools that were intentionally used during the phase of the project being analyzed. We take email as a given tool used to intentionally communicate and distribute project artifacts to the project team and stakeholders. Other project tools, of course, are also at play in the activity being modeled besides those identified via the email analytic methodology. We have seen several of those tools included in our analytical work using other data extraction methods, namely design software, project management applications, and stand-ups. Unfortunately, it is not always possible to access direct assessment of these tools in a manner that is consistent with their use on a project. By focusing on the attachments in email an analyst can obtain an empirical dataset that includes tools specifically situated to meet the demands of the project. In fact, because they are identified in the SENT folder, they represent tools specifically used by the sender to mediate their project objective. In addition, when attached to email, the tool is often accompanied by text in the body of the email that provides contextual background related to the tools' role in mediating the object of the project.

In our case study, Gabe's SENT folder contained 13 unique attachments representing tools that he intentionally used or shared during the execution phase of ProjectWeb. In total there were six variations of MS Excel spreadsheets, three examples of MS Outlook files referencing old emails, three MS Word files, and one PDF document. When grouped by their functional role in ProjectWeb, one attachment related to a resource contract and statement of work, four represented workflow rules, and eight represented some variation on statuses related to design requests. The contract document merely provided costing expectations for a temporary resource to be added to ProjectWeb. Two of the four workflow documents have already been discussed as they included the central project transition document modeled earlier and the page proofing workflow artifact that the transition document referenced. The third document was a proposal for a new meeting cadence that presented interesting data related to the division of labor that we will discuss later. The fourth artifact representing workflow was the emergence of a tool called ClientOrgDeployProcess.pdf. This artifact offered a workflow diagram detailing the collaboration flow between the three organizations, sequencing each organizations' step in the design process and the dependencies that existed between them. This artifact was a joint creation negotiated by CollabCorp's Gabe and DevTech's Jasper. This artifact represented a primary contradiction in the role of a critical tool, highlighting the fact that the rules of this phase of the project were lacking an explicit structure to mediate the most efficient collaboration strategy between the organizations involved. This artifact seemed to be a direct attempt to mitigate the lack of rules that Gabe mentioned during his interview, a situation that ultimately led to the project's demise. The fact that the workflow diagram was missing the needed rules, and it was not recognized as a fatal problem, is the basis for the contradiction.

"We need to figure out how to do better!" 65

The more important finding related to the tools identified in the email analysis for ProjectWeb centers on the seven variations of status documents circulating in Gabe's SENT mail alone. This indicates a significant primary contradiction in the role of status documents throughout the project. Although several of the artifacts appear to have originated in alignment with, if not directly from, the Wrike requirements system, none of the documents had consistent titles, nor did they contain any form of uniformity across the status structure. Some documents could be tracked back to an originating ticket in Wrike, but in many cases the notes, statuses, and details were orphaned completely from the source system, requiring significant effort to marry the appended information back to the original source. We were unable to identify indicators that also tied the requirements to the InVision system used for interactive wireframe development. This variability in the status and requirement sharing tools is a strong indication that the scope of the project, and the evolving design changes, were not properly controlled. This is consistent with the major issues Gabe revealed in his interview. Because the status tools did not properly control the flow of work against the requirements, many of the unique artifacts found in Gabe's SENT folder were created to help take an inventory of the work completed to date and establish a new baseline of work for resetting the project. For example, Wrike_vs_Dev_Gap.xlsx was an inventory created to compare all the design requests in Wrike against the actual production website to determine what work had been completed and what work remained. Had the requirements been controlled properly from the beginning of the project, this tool would not have needed to be created.

Email Analysis Findings: The Community and the Mediating Division of Labor

One of the more telling aspects of the activity system modeled from the email analytic is the vast size of the community recorded when modeling all distribution information related to Gabe's SENT messages. The details can be found in Figure 2.5. The total frame revealed 29 unique individuals, 17 of whom were not included in either the reflective interview or central project document models. This primary contradiction found between the community profiles of each model suggests that stakeholders to the project were not generally acknowledged as key community members when thinking about or documenting the project. Gabe's company alone has 14 project community members who were not mentioned in the other data collection activities. This highlights two key concepts. First, Gabe's email suggests a much larger communication pattern with other members of CollabCorp not directly associated with the Execution phase of ProjectWeb. This has much to do with Gabe's lead role within the company and suggests that he had an opportunity or responsibility to leverage other lead members in his company as he navigated the reset of ProjectWeb. For a company that makes revenue off project resources, the involvement of so many additional individuals should be analyzed further to understand the true impacts of the project's cost.

Company Name	Employee Name	Employee Role Based on Title	Identified in Reflective Interview	Identified in the Central Project Document	Identified in Email Analytic
DevTech	Jasper M	PM Lead	YES	YES	YES
ClientOrg	Kent J	BA	YES	YES	YES
ClientOrg	Lonni B	Marketing / Finance	YES	YES	YES
ClientOrg	Sam B	Director of IT	YES	NO	YES
ClientOrg	Amy W	Operations Support - Tech Lead	NO	YES	YES
ClientOrg	Daniel B	Finance Director	NO	YES	YES
ClientOrg	Jill M	Program Lead	NO	NO	YES
ClientOrg	Kassey S	Graphic Design	NO	NO	YES
ClientOrg	Peter S	System Admin	NO	NO	YES
CollabCorp	Mary G	Designer	YES	YES	YES
CollabCorp	Andy M	UX Designer and QA	YES	NO	YES
CollabCorp	Delivery Team	Project Managers	YES	NO	YES
CollabCorp	Carl F	BA / Tester	YES	NO	YES
CollabCorp	Gabe B	PM Lead	YES	NO	YES
CollabCorp	Todd G	PM Original	YES	NO	YES
CollabCorp	Christina C	Managing Director of Tech	NO	NO	YES
CollabCorp	Danny F	Managing Director of Delivery	NO	NO	YES
CollabCorp	James K	Finance	NO	NO	YES
CollabCorp	Jessica V	Designer	NO	NO	YES
CollabCorp	Jake C	Solution Architect	NO	NO	YES
CollabCorp	Miles C	Engagement Manager	NO	NO	YES
CollabCorp	Olivia K	QA	NO	NO	YES
CollabCorp	Paul T	Engagement Manager	NO	NO	YES
CollabCorp	Percy C	UX Engineer	NO	NO	YES
CollabCorp	Paula B	Software Engineer	NO	NO	YES
CollabCorp	Ramey L	Product Architect	NO	NO	YES
CollabCorp	Reese H	Tech Ops Lead	NO	NO	YES
CollabCorp	Shane B	Director Solutions Delivery	NO	NO	YES
CollabCorp	Trina H	Director Client Dev	NO	NO	YES

Figure 2.5. A comparison of community members by data extraction method.

We noted a significant secondary contradiction (a contradiction occurring between two nodes of the activity system) when reviewing the MS Outlook file attached to one of Gabe's SENT emails. This file outlined a new meeting cadence that was being established as the original project manager Todd was leaving the project and Gabe was onboarding. The MS Outlook file was a message thread between Lonni, ClientOrg's key marketing contact and the departing project manager from CollabCorp, Todd. Lonni indicates in that thread that although Gabe was joining the project to replace Todd, many of the tasks that Todd was facilitating in his division of labor would in fact be assigned to Lonni as the transition was implemented. As Gabe took over as the lead project manager for CollabCorp, he thought it more appropriate that the lead marketing resource at ClientOrg should handle key coordination duties between the organizations. Although Gabe and Jill's titles and roles remained the same, the labor associated with the roles changed significantly during the reset. These changes, however, were not officially documented in any of the legacy project documents. Such a transition in the division of labor can have substantial impacts on all mediating nodes of the activity system. A single change in project personnel can impact the rules the original team follow as well as the tools situated to specific project flows, especially if the division of labor varies significantly from the person's title and the perceived responsibilities that follow that title.

Email Analysis Findings: The Mediating Rules

Another significant secondary contradiction between the nodes of mediating tools and mediating rules centered on the Exec Level % Complete Report. This report was identified in the central project document analysis as a required report that must be updated regularly. Gabe's email offers a variation to the report called ExecStatus_Edits.xlsx. Gabe insisted that the original report lacked the structure necessary to accurately reflect the completion of work. Requirements had varying degrees of percent complete, and it was near impossible for Gabe to determine how to interpret percent complete in terms of time remaining. One requirement that was 43 percent complete might take five days to finish, whereas another requirement at 78 percent complete might take an hour to finish. Gabe offered a replacement model that tracked completion based on the phase of production the requirement was in during the time of status. A requirement in design would be 25 percent complete, a requirement in UAT would be 75 percent, and so on. This recommendation would allow for a more accurate reflection of the status of a requirement and tie it back to an area of responsibility. Had this modification been adopted by the project community as a revised tool and a revised rule for the project community it may have helped mitigate the growing confusion between the collaborating organizations.

■ Reflecting on the Three Activity System Models

As we look across all three activity system models and the contradictions they surface, we can identify specific themes for improvement. These themes, rooted in the Execution phase of ProjectWeb, can be considered for future projects within the organization since the project analyzed is no longer operational. The tools and the people that were part of this temporary engagement will go on to perform in other episodic engagements. Learning how specific mediators impact an activity system can at the very least encourage project professionals to reflect on those mediators when encountered in future work.

Reflective Insights from a Focus on Tools

In the area of tools, a key recommendation would be to eliminate multiple sources for status control and status communication when engaging in future projects. When presented with the activity system from the email analysis that showed seven different formats used to convey status updates Gabe laughed saying, "I knew it was bad, but I didn't realize it was that bad." Gabe acknowledged his attempts to alter the Executive % Complete Report that was routinely circulated insisting that the format was useful. When asked why he thought there were so many status documents being circulated he replied,

> It is very representative of the chaos experienced during the project. When I joined the project, we had to dig into everything to find the status of work. Everyone was on different pages. Just looking at the name of the documents it brings back all these side projects I asked people to do just to surface the current state of requirements. The requirement system and the development site were completely out of sync and we needed a baseline to figure out how much work was actually left.

We advised Gabe that in the future he might attempt to identify a single communication tool that pulled information directly from the requirement system and allowed updates. He could then devise a routing strategy that allowed updates to be married back to the source system on a regular cadence. Further, this single tool should deliver a status that is both informative and actionable. Gabe recalled his attempts to change the Executive % Complete Report to make it more actionable, but that at the late stage of the project his request was not a priority. He acknowledged that if he had access to specific examples of status documents like those presented in the activity system derived from email that he might have been able to convince others, and to some extent himself, that the multiple status documents were hurting the situation instead of helping. He indicated that he would pay more attention to this on future projects.

Reflective Insights from a Focus on Rules

In the category of rules, where some are explicit and others implicit, we recommend that more focus be applied to explicitly stating rules and making them visible throughout the life of the project. Rules are often dictated through tool design and it is important to understand this relationship. As a tool is altered it is important to be mindful of how that alteration can undermine or completely change rules of engagement. When reviewing the workflow documents highlighted by the central project document activity system, Gabe recognized them but stated,

> Yeah, I knew that Todd (the original PM for CollabCorp) had worked with [ClientOrg] to figure out all those workflows, but I assumed when I joined the project that everyone was aware of those flows. I didn't think I needed to rehash that work. Maybe that was a mistake. Given the time constraints and our attempt to save the project we were moving quickly so it probably wasn't the best time pick at people for not following a workflow created so early in the project.

Gabe acknowledged that he routinely works through flows that define rules of engagement during the planning stages of a project, but rarely revisits those rules and documents on a regular basis. This is something that he will consider in future work, finding a way to build in a systematic reorientation to project workflows.

Reflective Insights from a Focus on Community

Finally, in the categories of community and division of labor we suggest explicitly redocumenting any changes in the actual work responsibilities when project team members enter or exit the project. This effort will help eliminate confusion between actual responsibilities and the perceived responsibilities associated with title or position. Gabe acknowledged that during the reset of the project they did not take the time needed to adequately redefine the division of labor. Gabe confirmed that when he joined the project to replace Todd, the original PM, that he was contributing labor that was not being billed to the client. Given his role in the company and the fact that CollabCorp was not billing ClientOrg for his services, he felt justified in transitioning certain responsibilities away from his PM role and placing the burden back to the client. When asked about how this was communicated, Gabe stated, "Honestly, I took it as a given. The original PM didn't work out. He was let go. I was focused on higher level tasks to get the project back on the rails. I was not there to handle the day to day. That was something that [ClientOrg] should have been handling anyway."

When asked whether this assessment would have helped them identify specific ways to help people work together Gabe indicated that if time were not such a pressing concern, they all could have done a better job resetting the project and communicating new expectations.

> I would definitely, definitely, definitely agree with that. I don't think we ever reset appropriately. And I think that there were so many people involved, who had their belief of how things were working. And there was no governance over that. I mean the client stakeholder went to his management numerous times, and just basically bitched about his own staff and is like, I can't get these guys to function appropriately to get things done. So, it was hard. Just a mess, just a mess.

When demonstrating the vast difference between the community members identified across the activity systems and noting how many more individuals were found through the email derived analysis, Gabe was not terribly shocked but found it very interesting.

> Well, it makes sense to me that I would have emailed so many people within my own company given the effort to get this thing

back on track, but you raise a great point about costs. My efforts were not being billed to the client. None of these people's time was billed.

Highlighting this data really made an impression on Gabe. He even indicated that this was one area that he thinks management would be really interested in analyzing further. How much time is management engaged in online communication that is not billable?

The Reflective Value of Activity System Modeling

Gabe provided general impressions about the value of activity system modeling using email based on our case study experience. He indicated throughout our reflection that the findings were very representative of his experiences and that having specific examples organized in activity systems would have really helped make a case for specific changes. Although there were several lessons learned that he noted he will carry with him in future planning sessions, he acknowledged that given the time pressure he would not have had the luxury to execute this kind of research in real time to be effective. When asked if he thought whether this work would be beneficial if they had a dedicated researcher constantly looking at this type of information, he replied,

> Oh, absolutely. Yeah. No, no, absolutely. I think this is highly helpful and it's what we saw throughout the process. But I think it came back down to just the [Sam] guy not being empowered and not having the right ability to push and make things go well. Like just too many people running. This is a massive project that crossed all [ClientOrg]. And basically, you know, how do you herd the cats at that level? No one was listening, so . . . you know . . . they didn't make it urgent enough because the ownership of [ClientOrg] doesn't understand technology, doesn't understand the heavy lifting that needs to be done in order to pull something like this off.

Despite the aid that the activity systems provided for reflection there seemed to be certain things that were not represented that Gabe still believed to be root problems, such as the client's ability to understand the nature of such a robust technical project. Even if empirical examples could be found in email that supports Gabe's notion of ClientOrg's inability to comprehend the project, certain points may be more inflammatory than helpful when tensions are as high.

Conclusion

The method we designed to extract data from email and thematically model it using an activity system analysis shows great promise for surfacing empirical evidence of episodic work. Making work visible through activity system models allows UX researchers to not only triangulate multiple data collection methods, but, in the process, surface key contradictions to highlight opportunities for improvement.

Focusing on SENT mail keeps all work directly related to the subject of the analysis and assures that their individual perspective and involvement offers personal growth opportunity. If this analysis were conducted for all members of a project community, and the results were aggregated, a more complete picture of the activity system would emerge. Activity system models could highlight emerging contradiction during the project lifecycle and even bring structure to project retrospectives and postmortems, allowing project members to compare and discuss specifics of the project, complete with empirical examples to support their claims.

The effort required to manually model activity systems using metadata from email is significant. As Gabe mentioned during his reflective session, he would have a hard time conducting this type of analysis when dealing with the pressure of a project that has gone off the rails. This insight reinforces the notion expressed throughout this paper that a research role dedicated to internal UX discovery is warranted. A tool is also needed to bring some level of expediency to the process. To advance this capability we plan to leverage the information learned through our research to develop a data transformation protocol aimed at making email metadata easier to visualize on a more rapid scale.

This work offers a whole new frontier for UX researchers like Sebastian, the UX researcher introduced at the beginning of our study. Training in methods like activity theory that help surface the dynamic interplay of humans, the tools they use, and the social contexts in which they work, will open opportunities beyond the traditional focus on consumer products. This approach is well aligned with Torkil Clemmensen and colleagues' suggestion (2016) that activity theory can provide an enhanced understanding of user experiences that have broader social relevance than simple interaction studies. We contend that a comprehensive way to view work is needed to truly appreciate the interdependencies involved as tools are dynamically created, altered, and abandoned to meet the demands of episodic project work. Had Sebastian been a UX researcher dedicated to internal work analysis during ProjectWeb, he may have been able to use the results of such an analysis in real time to substantiate and socialize some of the key instincts that Gabe had to save the project. He may have suggested modifications to status documents and the workflow rules that generate them. He could have modeled potential impacts of altering the division of labor. He could have even surfaced key usability improvements in the primary source systems like Wrike and InVision that could likely improve cross-organizational use. Even if Sebastian had conducted a historical analysis as represented by our case study, he would still provide workers like Gabe with thematic improvements to consider when recycling tools, rules, and divisions of labor for future projects.

References

Clemmensen, T., Kaptelinin, V. & Nardi, B. (2016). Making HCI theory work: An analysis of the use of activity theory in HCI research. *Behaviour & Information Technology*, 35(8), 608–627. https://doi.org/10.1080/0144929X.2016.1175507.

Collins, P., Shukla, S. & Redmiles, D. (2002). Activity theory and system design: A View from the trenches. *Computer Supported Cooperative Work*, 11(1–2), 55–80.

Divine, R. & Zachry, M. (2018) Project management, contradictions, and textualized activity: Supporting reflection in project-based organizations. *Technical Communication*, 65(2) 194–209.

Engeström, Y. (1987). *Learning by expanding: An activity theoretical approach to developmental research*. Orienta-Konsultit Oy.

Engeström, Y. (2000). Activity theory as a framework for analyzing and redesigning work. *Ergonomics*, 43(7), 960–974. https://doi.org/10.1080/001401300409143.

Getto, G. & Beecher, F. (2016). Toward a model of UX education: Training UX designers within the academy. *IEEE Transactions on Professional Communication*, 59(2), 153–164. https://doi.org/10.1109/TPC.2016.2561139.

Hobday, M. (2000). The project-based organisation: an ideal form for managing complex products and systems? *Research Policy*, 29(7), 871–893. https://doi.org/10.1016/S0048-7333(00)00110-4.

Kuusinen, K. (2015). Task allocation between UX specialists and developers in agile software development projects. In J. Abascal, S. Barbosa, M. Fetter, T. Gross, P. Palanque & M. Winckler, M. (Eds.), *IFIP Conference on Human-Computer Interaction* (pp. 27–44). Springer, Cham. https://doi.org/10.1007/978-3-319-22698-9_3.

Kuusinen, K. & Väänänen-Vainio-Mattila, K. (2012, October 14). How to make agile UX work more efficient: Management and sales perspectives. NordiCHI '12: *Proceedings of the 7th Nordic Conference on Human-Computer Interaction: Making Sense Through Design*, 139–148. https://doi.org/10.1145/2399016.2399037.

Lauren, B. (2018). *Communicating project management: A participatory rhetoric for development teams*. Routledge.

McNely, B., Spinuzzi, C. & Teston, C. (2015). Contemporary research methodologies in technical communication. *Technical Communication Quarterly*, 24(1), 1–13. https://doi.org/10.1080/10572252.2015.975958.

Mwanza, D. (2002). *Towards an activity-oriented design method for HCI research and practice*. The Open University.

Redish, J. & Barnum, C. (2011). Overlap, influence, intertwining: The interplay of UX and technical communication. *Journal of Usability Studies*, 6(3), 90–101.

Rose, K. H. (2013). A Guide to the Project Management Body of Knowledge (PMBOK® Guide) (5th ed.). *Project Management Journal*, 44: e1. https://doi.org/10.1002/pmj.21345.

Sajad, M., Sadiq, M., Naveed, K. & Iqbal, M. S. (2016). Software project management: Tools assessment, comparison and suggestions for future development. *International Journal of Computer Science and Network Security* (IJCSNS), 16(1), 31.

Spinuzzi, C. (2013). *Topsight: A guide to studying, diagnosing, and fixing information flow in organizations*. CreateSpace Independent Publishing Platform.

Spinuzzi, C. & Guile, D. (2019, July). Fourth-generation activity theory: An integrative literature review and implications for professional communication. In *2019 IEEE In-*

ternational Professional Communication Conference (ProComm), 37–45. IEEE. https://doi.org/10.1109/ProComm.2019.00012.

Yamagata-Lynch, L. C. (2010). *Activity systems analysis methods: Understanding complex learning environments*. Springer Science & Business Media.

Zahedi, M., Tessier, V. & Hawey, D. (2017). Understanding collaborative design through activity theory. *The Design Journal*, 20(sup1), S4611–S4620. https://doi.org/10.1080/14606925.2017.1352958.

3. Working with Ladies in UX: Building Academic/Industry Partnerships for User Research Projects

Heather Noel Turner
SANTA CLARA UNIVERSITY

Laura Gonzáles
UNIVERSITY OF FLORIDA

Liza Potts
MICHIGAN STATE UNIVERSITY

Abstract. Research in technical communication and user-experience (UX) points to the value of building academic and industry collaborations and conversations (Browning, 2015; Cotugno & Hoffman, 2011; Gonzáles et al., 2017; Robinson et al., 2018). However, academic research is not as accessible to industry practitioners as it should be, and more conversations are needed to foster successful and sustainable academic-industry partnerships (Andersen & Hackos, 2018; Bosley, 2002). In this chapter, we share a brief case study that outlines a research partnership among various stakeholders within two organizations: the WIDE Center at Michigan State University and Ladies that UX (LTUX), a global organization to support women in UX. We share challenges and opportunities of collaborating with international organizations, including the need to coordinate across contexts and simultaneously prioritize both university and industry goals and objectives through collaboration (Gonzáles & Turner, 2019). We also highlight lessons learned from engaging in feminist-driven UX research methodologies (Gonzáles, et. al, 2017; Shivers-McNair et al., 2019). Through this discussion, we suggest that UX research and application should be developed from dialogue among researchers and practitioners (Albers, 2012). Together, women leaders at both organizations researched and instituted methods of communication and organizational structures that support the growth and development of women professionals both in industry and academia.

About Ladies that UX

The professional organization involved in this collaboration was Ladies that UX, a group developed in 2013 as a global support network for women in user-experience who may not have immediate contact with other women in this profession at their local workplace. LTUX was created by Georgie Bottomley and Lizzie Dyson, two UX professionals who "loved their jobs" but had "doubts about

DOI: https://doi.org/10.37514/TPC-B.2025.2517.2.03

where other women in the industry were" (Ladies that UX, 2024). Georgie and Lizzie wanted to establish a space for women UX researchers to connect.

The first meeting for this organization took place in Manchester, UK in 2013. Since then, Ladies that UX has expanded into a global network that includes sister branches in 53 cities spanning 25 countries. Each branch has a local group of leaders and organizers that build on Georgie and Lizzie's model. Local group leaders coordinate monthly meetups (F2F and remote), talks, presentations, and other events that allow UX professionals to come together and share ideas. The purpose of these meetups is to provide a low-stakes environment where women can ask questions, form collaborations, or simply be in the presence of other women in the profession without feeling pressured to speak up or perform (Ladies that UX, 2024).

■ About WIDE Research Center

In many ways, the structure of Ladies that UX echoes what is at the heart of the WIDE Research Center at Michigan State University. The WIDE Research Center focuses on researching and innovating experiences for emerging technologies in the digital humanities, including uses of social user experiences to solve social, cultural, and political problems; ways of constructing computational analytics for improving persuasive communication, and the need to create new forms of public engagement and democratic practice on a global scale. At the time of the initial LTUX collaboration, the three authors of this chapter worked at WIDE in different capacities. Liza is the director of WIDE, while Heather and Laura were graduate research assistants and are now both tenure-track professors and affiliate researchers with the center who have also established and lead UX projects and internship programs for students.

One of the WIDE's key aims is mentoring and collaborating with early career scholars at Michigan State University and across the field. Graduate and undergraduate researchers working at the lab have opportunities for collaborating with both academics and industry professionals. Sometimes this work includes conducting research, working on grants, developing and facilitating technology design camps with and for marginalized youth, and co-authoring papers; other times this work includes architecting, designing, and writing for digital humanities projects such as Sherlockian.net and various digital platforms.

■ Working with Ladies that UX

WIDE's collaboration with LTUX began in Fall 2015, when Georgie and Lizzie connected with Liza to request assistance understanding how the individual branches of their organization were working and how the organization as a whole could be more streamlined in working together. This initial email led to many more emails and Skype calls where the three of them talked about their professional careers and pathways as part of understanding each other's perspectives and backgrounds. During the calls in particular, Georgie and Lizzie shared information about their work in the UX field, their initial reasons for starting up their organization, and the rapid expansion of LTUX. At the same time, Liza explained her background in industry and academia, and related research being done on women-led organizations in academic, industry, and fandom communities (Potts et al., 2018; Sullivan et al., 2015).

It became clear that this project would connect well to this work, especially given the time and space during which similar women-led organizations were taking off. And Georgie and Lizzie had an urgent need to learn more about their growing membership. In just two years, LTUX had expanded across the globe. Georgie and Lizzie wanted to learn more about how each individual branch saw themselves as a community, how each group was coordinating events, and how they as organization leaders could better support the work of each local branch. Thus, WIDE and LTUX worked collaboratively using a "recursive participatory mentoring model," (Sullivan et al., 2015, p. 7), which foregrounds collaboration and co-development of research goals. We then collaboratively developed a study aimed at answering the following questions:

- How can local branches of LTUX be supported as they grow?
- Why are women professionals in user experience interested in joining local organizations?
- Why are women currently joining LTUX?
- What kinds of support are these women and their local leaders looking for as a group and from the global organization?
- What kinds of metrics for success can be used to measure organizational health at the local level?

Because the answers to all the questions are a part of an extended collaborative project, our brief case study here offers a limited snapshot.

A collaboration between WIDE and LTUX was critical in gathering the information necessary to answer these questions. As leaders of LTUX, Georgie and Lizzie hold valuable knowledge about their members and the values of the organization. WIDE, on the other hand, had the resources (including time, research assistants, and established research methods) necessary to design a research protocol that would provide valuable information for LTUX while also generating important research experiences for the WIDE researchers. Through collaborative discussions between WIDE and LTUX leadership, our team decided to co-design and conduct a 13-question survey via Typeform with LTUX leaders in 20 cities. Participants were recruited via a list of 113 local leaders compiled by the LTUX global leadership team and solicited via a notification in LTUX's monthly newsletter. The goal of the surveys was to learn how each unique LTUX branch functions—how their meetings were organized, who attended, and how each branch got funding. WIDE researchers then conducted follow-up interviews with 12 of these leaders, both in person within the state and online through a combination of video and voice calls. Since the participants of this study also functioned as co-designers of the study, the study was exempt from IRB. The questions asked during the interview included and expanded on the questions asked in the surveys:

- What is your LTUX local group role (and title)?
- How many people are managing the group? (If more than one, what are their roles?)
- How did you get started with your LTUX group?
- When did you hold your first LTUX meeting?
- Who attends your meetings? Professionals? Students? Can you tell me about the diversity of this group?
- How do you communicate with your LTUX group members?
- What does a typical LTUX meet-up look like for you? (theme, discussions, setup, attendees, locations)
- What are your thoughts on the financial viability of LTUX as an organization?
- Would you like to talk to other LTUX leaders? How would you want that to work? How would this be useful to you?
- How do you communicate now with LTUX global?
- What information did you receive to get started? Was this information useful?
- Are you a member of other UX or women-centered groups? Which ones?
- What is your occupation? (e.g., user experience, interaction designer, etc.)
- Could you describe your experience with LTUX in a sentence?
- How much time do you spend working on your local LTUX group?
- Any general thoughts or feedback about LTUX?

During these follow-up interviews, researchers asked closed and open-ended questions to learn more about how LTUX members felt about their organization, the types of support each branch had and the types of support they still needed. In essence, the survey was intended to help us build an inventory of organizational models, while the interviews were intended to help us better understand the relationships among members at the local and global levels. The collaboration between academic and industry researchers helped all parties to develop more effective methods and protocols for answering the research questions. In addition, learning about organizational models helped the WIDE researchers to develop their own approaches to organizational infrastructure that would then help them in their own academic administration and leadership roles.

The WIDE team worked collaboratively with LTUX to develop questions for both the survey and the interviews and to analyze the data that was gathered through each stage of the process. The team met through Google hangouts and coordinated meetings with interviewees via email and Slack. These platforms were already being used by both the WIDE researchers and by LTUX. Through discussions with Georgie and Lizzie, the WIDE researchers were able to get hands-on experience in negotiating researcher goals, objectives, and methods alongside an organization. While WIDE researchers had experience and training conducting field work, being in conversation and collaboration with LTUX leaders who were deeply invested in their organization and who wanted to get "big picture" feedback required the team to adjust their methods to fit both with best research practices and with a specific organization's goals.

After collecting both the survey and interview data, WIDE researchers developed a report that threaded patterns across all datasets, presenting this report and coordinating a follow-up conversation with the organization leaders Lizzie and Georgie. In these instances, we as WIDE researchers and colleagues presented our data through feminist frameworks that would both honor our participants' perspectives while respecting the work of our research collaborators. Following our debrief discussions, Lizzie and Georgie shared our collaborative results with members of the LTUX local branches, beginning the process of converting the results of the study into practical applications for LTUX.

▪ Findings

In general, we found that local LTUX chapters wanted more communication with the main LTUX leaders, and that women were joining LTUX to share strategies for gaining fair pay and employment, learn about different areas of UX that they may not be exposed to in their jobs, and network with other women in the field. This case study offers a limited snapshot into our broader research questions. Stemming from these findings, in this chapter, we share practical and methodological strategies for TPC researchers interested in making partnership with UX industry collaborators. As a result of our collaboration, our project helped identify challenges and opportunities within LTUX. Here, we will share lessons learned from exploring how women-centered professional organizations are established, expand, and sustain themselves.

Cross-Organizational Communication

Through our interviews with LTUX leaders, we answered research question, "How can local branches of LTUX be supported as they grow?" Specifically, we learned that the majority of the organizers were confident in the leadership from the main organization, and most branch leaders reported positively about their relationship with Georgie and Lizzie individually. Each individual branch leader had some suggestions for improving communication within their own branches, mentioning that digital platforms such as Twitter were most effective when communicating about events or sharing information and using MeetUp to communicate with members.

Communication within the larger organization—with leadership and across branches—was noted for being less robust. The interviews revealed that LTUX leaders were interested in connecting with each other, and many indicated that they would appreciate more interaction with other groups than was currently occurring. For example, one interview participant mentioned that more communication among the international chapters of LTUX would be helpful, stating, "Since I'm already in touch with everyone in North America, already exchanging ideas and listening to some pitfalls, it would be good to have more international connections. Some people are just not in touch at all." Gaining access to LTUX's shared Slack helped Liza better understand these communication concerns, as their channels were mostly quiet. Many of these branch leaders reported that their time was short due to the many obligations they had as professionals, caretakers, and organizers. That lack of time could explain the lack of chatter across Slack; however, as Shivers-McNair and colleagues (2019) found, intersectional technofeminist technology design needs to account for invisible labor (such as "finding child care, work replacements, travel funding, family support, and other necessities") invested into design processes in order to be sustainable (p. 52). Several interviewees referenced the labor needed to keep up the lines of communication between different LTUX chapters, with one interviewee referencing "the struggles of advancing your ideas in a collaborative environment when everyone is very busy."

Other suggestions shared by interview participants included creating more cross-branch meetups, hosting more frequent check-in calls with the organization leaders, and seeking sponsorship or other types of support to help arrange different events that would support members of their organization. Etienne Wenger (1999) argued that such communities of practice (like LTUX) need mutual engagement in addition to a shared repertoire in order to be successful. These ideas could connect them to larger networks and provide a greater sense of community across the organization. For example, one interviewee mentioned that she had been sponsoring LTUX meetups in her area, and that "we can't really do anything phenomenal without sponsorship support. I can't give that much of an investment." Learning about the communication breakdowns and successes within LTUX helped WIDE researchers to recognize the importance of consistent organizational communication across platforms.

Branch Organization and Taxonomy

Through our interviews with LTUX leaders, we also answered our research question, "What kinds of metrics for success can be used to measure organizational health at the local level?" Most LTUX branches operated as collectives rather than under hierarchical models with a single leader or director at the top. Leaders recognized and appreciated the roles of group members in organizing and forming directions for their groups and did not necessarily draw upon formal titles when discussing their roles. Many considered themselves organizers, noting that they were able to keep their community moving forward because of their organizational and communication skills. For example, one interviewee explained, "I call myself an organizer. Giving any other kind of title imposes a kind of hierarchy and I don't wanna do that." Participants also had various names for their members, such as advocates or coordinators, with many organizers pointing to these names as part of their group's ethos. Avery Edenfield (2019) articulated such differences between corporate businesses, conventional organizations, and cooperatives ("organizations owned and controlled by the people who use them") (p. 376), noting the need for rethinking methodologies and expanding sites of TPC research. Although LTUX does not identify as a cooperative, there is a "yet-to-be articulated praxis of UX in cooperative work" (Edenfield, 2019, p. 386). This in and of itself is noteworthy and could be a place for more research. Women across branches described this non-hierarchical model as the most effective for LTUX projects, and they pointed to the fact that more research is needed to both document and expand these feminist leadership practices. As one participant mentioned, "I don't wanna put myself in a sort of superior role. I'm just like, organizing this, and it's gonna be what it's gonna be. I don't wanna be like I'm imposing my vision on people."

Through conversations between WIDE and LTUX, the research team as a whole was able to develop questions for future research regarding feminist approaches to organizational infrastructure that can honor the labor of women leaders while also maintaining a non-hierarchical ethos in an organization (Shivers-McNair et al., 2019).

■ Outcomes for Academic Partners

The results of this collaboration brought benefits to various stakeholders, including LTUX and WIDE as an organization as well as to the individuals who participated in this project. The community itself was eager to engage during this research project and beyond. Senior UX women from multiple countries took time to mentor junior researchers as they also contributed to the research project.

Although this collaboration is in many ways a straightforward research project, the collaborative element and the connections between academia and industry fostered new and ongoing connections, collaborations, and considerations. For example, the WIDE graduate researchers got a chance to network with women in UX during the interview process. Structuring these kinds of networking opportunities and collaborations for students, especially female students on color, helps challenge ad hoc protégé models that rely on exclusive and invisible expectations about what kinds of mentorship paths are present and for whom (Gonzáles & Turner, 2019).

After reporting to Georgie and Lizzie that LTUX leaders wanted more opportunities for networking, WIDE helped organize a networking event across three cities in Michigan. Women who work in UX as academics and industry practitioners came together to share experiences and ideas. This event benefited the LTUX branches in Michigan (Detroit, Grand Rapids) looking to make connections and students at WIDE who wanted to connect with industry professionals. It provided a model for LTUX to think about cross-organizational events.

Furthering these partnerships, a leader of a local LTUX branch who was interviewed for this project later became a "Experience Architect in Residence" in the undergraduate degree program directed and designed by Liza. This collaboration led to other engagement and outreach programs sponsored by WIDE researchers Heather and Laura, when they were graduate students, which included a technology summer camp for Latinx and Indigenous girls that was implemented in following years. And, of course, there were outcomes relating to knowledge making and distribution in industry and academia. Through the data analysis and research report writing processes, junior researchers had the opportunity to present research to a professional organization—invaluable skills that would benefit future research projects. The project itself has been mentioned across several publications, and the authors are often asked to share ideas about industry/practitioner partnerships.

Implications for LTUX and Future Partnerships

LTUX also continued to evolve as an international organization and across local chapters. For example, chapters like LTUX Atlanta explicitly expanded their definitions of "ladies" to include "talented and intelligent women and non-binary individuals" (https://www.meetup.com/Ladies-That-UX-ATL/). LTUX Atlanta, Boston, Detroit, and others have opened their membership from current UX professionals to "anyone curious about UX," which could be a small, albeit indirect, step to mentor and support Black, Indigenous and People of Color (BIPOC) in UX. As the scarce representation and inclusion of women of color in UX and in the technology industry more broadly has been documented (Kapor, 2018), more intersectional approaches to feminist mentoring are deeply needed. As Heather and Laura have reported, explicitly scaffolding "get to know each other" time before (and during) engaging in specific UX activities" helps individuals share their experiences, hesitations, and positionalities in a way that builds empathetic collaborations and can lead to further inclusion and sustainability (Gonzáles & Turner, 2019). LTUX are currently working with an outside organization to manage people and processes.

Conclusion

This collaboration resulted in positive outcomes for each of our individual objectives, while also fostering relationships among the research group as a whole. While the logistics of a single research project are important, the most important takeaway for us is the networking that took place among various stakeholders involved in the project. As organizations shift both in industry and academia, connecting individual people along common interests and commitments can bring some stability in constantly fluctuating environments. Aside from helping with the development of a single technology or the protocol for a single project, academic and industry collaborations in UX can help all parties involved to combine resources and knowledge to continue supporting up-and-coming professionals.

■ References

Albers, M. J. (Ed.). (2012). *Human-Information interaction and technical communication: Concepts and frameworks.* IGI Global.

Andersen, R. & Hackos, J. (2018, August 3). Increasing the value and accessibility of academic research: Perspectives from industry. *SIGDOC '18: Proceedings of the 36th ACM International Conference on the Design of Communication, 5,* 1–6. https://doi.org/10.1145/3233756.3233959.

Bosley, D. (2002). Jumping off the ivory tower: Changing the academic perspective. In B. Mirel & R. Spilka (Eds.), *Reshaping technical communication: New directions and challenges for the 21st century* (pp. 27–39). Lawrence Erlbaum Associates.

Browning, E. (2015, October 1–3). What's in it for all of us: Critical reflections on and best practices for an academe-industry partnership in Florida's socio-political context [Presentation]. 2015 Conference of the Council for Programs in Technical and Scientific Communication (pp. 140). Utah State University, Logan, Utah.

Cotugno, M. & Hoffman, M. (2011). Seeking a direct pipeline to practice: Four guidelines for researchers and practitioners. *Journal of Business and Technical Communication, 25*(1), 95–105. https://doi.org/10.1177/1050651910380377.

Edenfield, A. (2019) Research in cooperatives: Developing a politically conscious research methodology, *Technical Communication Quarterly, 28*(4), 376–390. https://doi.org/10.1080/10572252.2019.1621388.

Gonzáles, L., Potts, L., Turner, H. N. & Brentnell, L. (2017, August 11). Working with ladies that UX: Building academic/industry partnerships for user research projects. Proceedings of the 35th ACM International Conference on the Design of Communication, 29, 1–4. https://doi.org/10.1145/3121113.3121217.

Gonzáles, L. & Turner, H. N. (2019, October 4). Challenges and insights for fostering academic-industry collaborations in UX. Proceedings of the 37th ACM International Conference on the Design of Communication, 21, 1–6. https://doi.org/10.1145/3328020.3353921.

Ladies that UX. (2024). About. Ladies that UX. https://ladiesthatux.com/about/.

McAlear, F., Scott, A., Scott, K. & Weiss, S. (2018). Data brief: Women of color in computing. Kapor Center/Center for Gender Equity in Science and Technology. https://www.kaporcenter.org/publication/data-brief-women-and-girls-of-color-in-computing/.

Potts, L., Beattie, M., Dallaire, E., Grimes, K. & Turner, K. (2018). *Participatory memory: Fandom experiences across time and space.* Enculturation Intermezzo.

Robinson, J., Lanius, C. & Weber, R. (2018). The past, present, and future of UX empirical research. *Communication Design Quarterly Review, 5*(3), 10–23. https://doi.org/10.1145/3188173.3188175.

Shivers-McNair, A., Gonzáles, L. & Zhyvotovska, T. (2019). An intersectional technofeminist framework for community-driven technology innovation. *Computers and Composition*, 51, 43–54. https://doi.org/10.1016/j.compcom.2018.11.005.

Sullivan, P., Simmons, M., Moore, K., Melonçon, L. & Potts, L. (2015, July 16). Intentionally recursive: A participatory model for mentoring. SIGDOC '15: Proceedings of the 33rd Annual International Conference on the Design of Communication, 1–10. https://doi.org/10.1145/2775441.2814672.

Wenger, E. (1999). *Communities of practice: Learning, meaning, and identity*. Cambridge University Press.

4. A Case for (Re)Envisioning Academic UX Spaces: Lessons Learned at a Polytechnic University

John M. Spartz
EDWARD JONES

Abstract: This chapter charts the rise and fall of a university UX lab. Though the lab started with great enthusiasm, it proved difficult to find paying clients outside of the university and to serve internal university clients who needed but could not pay for UX services. This chapter provides takeaways and reflections about why the lab failed and how it might have succeeded.

In another life, prior to my current position as a Senior UX Researcher at Edward Jones, I tried and ultimately failed to create and participate in a complex UX collaboration. This manuscript tells the story of that failure, not as a tale of woe, but as one from which others considering such an endeavor might learn. In the fall of 2014–2015, as a newly hired assistant professor at a comprehensive, regional polytechnic university in the Upper Midwest, I embarked upon a multifaceted collaboration to envision, establish, grow, and sustain an interdisciplinary and extra-institutional hub of UX activity—a university UX research center. Despite a concerted, five-year effort, this endeavor ultimately resulted in the center's decommissioning in the summer of 2019.

Given the center's eventual demise, perhaps it would have been wise to learn from Jakob Nielsen, who offers that he is "not sure that the answer [to a desire to improve product usability] is to build a usability lab right away" because "even though usability laboratories are great resources for usability engineering groups, it is possible to get started with simpler usability methods that can be used immediately" (Nielsen, 1994). Nonetheless, developing a lab remains as a topic of interest, and Jeff Sauro (2018) details the requirements of a successful UX lab, evaluating existing labs and considering the perspectives of both employees and clients of a potential, functioning lab. Still, creating a physical hub of UX and usability activity is complicated by the logistics of doing so and the development of methods and technologies to delimit its need. Jennifer Ismirle (2018), in her comprehensive literature review of mobile UX research (i.e., going into "the wild" and leaving the laboratory), concludes that doing UX and usability work in field settings, complemented by less restrictive mobile methods, allows for greater understanding of the UX and usability of an interface. Further, as noted, again by Nielsen, "the staffing, management, and organizational placement of usability groups are important issues that must unfortunately be left unresolved

... since virtually no research is available to resolve them" (1994). This remains true in large part today, with the exception of a few works in the field of technical communication. These scholars help put into perspective the struggles I faced with my venture.

Thus, aligned with reflections on the history of usability and UX in technical communication (Redish & Barnum, 2011), this case study provides stakeholders with further perspective on a host of questions for commencing and sustaining a collaboration of this ilk: What types of collaborations does an academic UX space require and support? How can a space complement academic curricula and the institutional mission? Who does the space serve? Who oversees the space and this work? How is it funded? What sustains those efforts? Further, by reflecting on the trials and tribulations of this long-term collaboration, this narrative details both the academic and industry consequences of my failures and the lessons learned from those failures.

■ The Vision of a UX Research Center

From its inception, the center was designed as a site where faculty and students would engage in research to apply disciplinary principles to real-world usability and UX problems, to contribute to the scholarship and practice of user-centered research, and to promote the application of user-centered principles by:

- Connecting curriculum and real-world client projects,
- Developing applied research opportunities,
- Responding to community and business needs, and
- Leveraging the center as a recruiting and retention tool.

Accordingly, the moment I stepped on campus, I began work with a newly formed faculty steering committee to author a proposal for a system-approved UX research center, which included my appointment as the center's director.[1] As director, I was solely responsible for cultivating and sustaining external client relationships while positioning the center as both a campus and regionally recognized resource, a UX research and teaching-and-learning space. I was also charged with the following responsibilities:

- Oversee the day-to-day operations of the center.
- Manage and coordinate usability projects in consultation with program faculty.
- Work with university program directors to infuse center programming into the curricula.

---

1. Based on the less-than-successful history of related efforts at our institution with no dedicated paid time, the center director received .25 reassigned time (the equivalent of one course per semester) for the work associated with developing, sustaining, and growing the center.

- Meet with the center's steering committee to help guide the center's short- and long-term goals.
- Ensure proper institutional procedures for engaging clients, including those related to contracts, budgets, and deliverables.
- Hire, train, and manage graduate assistants and undergraduate practicum students.
- Recruit external clients to generate revenue to support the center and director position.
- Assess the center based on its goals and provide yearly assessment reports to the dean, program faculty, and our professional advisory board members.
- Manage the center budget, maintaining budget authority jointly with the college budget manager.

Setting the Collaboration Stage

In order to do this type of UX work—that which straddles the lines of not only academy-industry partnerships, but also the push-and-pull between the inherent academic and administrative constraints and a free-market approach to building what is ostensibly a small business—I engaged myriad collaborators from three categories: UX clients, interdisciplinary colleagues, and administrators.

Granted a funded probationary status to move toward fiscal sustainability (to fund the director position and any associated center costs), the center was built on a revenue-generation model. As such, I was charged with determining services offered by the center, developing rates the center would charge for those services, and gaining institutional approval for those rates. The collaborative effort required to put the pieces in place to lead a revenue-generating center cannot be understated. I leaned on the expertise and experience of former professors, disciplinary colleagues, and my graduate school network to determine services and pricing in a higher-education setting. I connected with regional UX practitioners to inform the center's scope. I met with administrators and financial experts across my institution to develop systems and protocols. I consulted with various administrative units to navigate bureaucratic policies for contracts, payments, and vendor statuses with clients. I coordinated with facilities and IT authorities to plan and institute a physical center space for doing usability and UX research. I conferred with deans, department heads, and the center steering committee to determine short- and long-term goals for the center. I worked with a graduate student and graphic designer to develop a center identity—supported by a web and mobile presence, marketing collateral, signage, advertising, and documentation templates. These collaborative efforts culminated in an official three-day center grand opening event that aligned with World Usability Day, a hosted UX-themed Great Plains Alliance for Computers and Writing Conference in the fall of 2016, and the grand opening of the renovated building in which the center was housed. This was a monumental initiative, to be sure.

■ Revenue-Generating Collaboration Effort

Thus, after a year or more of planning, I began in earnest efforts to engage clients and generate income for the center. One of the major components of this UX collaboration, especially in a revenue-dependent model, was lead generation. Obviously, tapping an assortment of networks is essential for finding, contacting, and creating business relationships. Because my institution was a dedicated polytechnic that required practicum and/or internship experiences for all students—coupled with requisite professional advisory boards for all programs—I had a built-in set of industry connections on which to draw. Thus, I was able to immediately begin the process of reaching out to, setting up meetings with, and "selling" the services of the center to potential clients in our region. Contacts included an international communication company dedicated to online legal material, an industry-leading maintenance equipment company, a prominent plumbing-manufacturing corporation, and an American multinational conglomerate corporation operating in the fields of industry, worker safety, U.S. health care, and consumer goods.

One example of the collaborative effort required to generate revenue can be best understood through my relationship with the communication company. Over the course of three years, eight times I traveled the 140-mile roundtrip to the company headquarters on my own dime. I met with varied units, developed and pitched five proposals, and worked with administrative bodies from my university and the company for contracted and paid services. These efforts yielded a contract for a two-phased UX research study, generating nearly $16,000. Of the contracted payment, roughly 50 percent landed in the center's coffers (after university and unit overhead, administrative costs, user payments, study costs, etc.) to help support the center and director position. None of my other, similarly thorough efforts lead to any revenue. Sustaining a UX center solely from this inefficient and labor-intensive client revenue model proved to be more difficult than anticipated.

In order to complement my institutional networking efforts and optimize lead-generation time, I simultaneously began to tap my personal network of people working in industries that might need and benefit from the type of UX services offered by the center. In connecting with, for example, a SaaS company and a national outpatient diagnostic imaging company, I was able to produce two contracts totaling approximately $5,000. I also facilitated the landing of a supported summer internship by one of my excellent undergraduate students, for which I served as director and project consultant. While I was certainly able to be more efficient in these networking efforts, limiting the number of preliminary and fact-finding meetings, false starts, and negotiated proposals for scope of services, the effort did not equal the output; the amount of revenue did not support the time invested as the center director.

Pedagogical Collaboration Consequences

While the work-to-revenue balance from my lead generation was suboptimal, there was a silver lining: This networking provided my students with a host of opportunities to work with real-world clients in a UX context. Some of these opportunities came in the form of directed, paid internships for graduate and undergraduate students. For example, while my center's proposal to the university web development team to do iterative UX research on the design of our new university website was turned down—because, based on our university-approved center rate sheet, the desired services would comprise over a quarter of the project budget—I was able to negotiate, advise, and direct a single graduate student in doing over $15,000 (used for wages, overhead, and benefits) in UX work on the project that helped support their graduate education. This experience proved fundamental in their education and resulting post-graduation employment as a UX researcher.

Further, each semester I taught my undergraduate usability course during the center's operation, I was able to develop high stakes, authentic opportunities for students to engage, communicate with, conduct research for, and present findings to stakeholders in our region. While some of these collaborations were with industry and small business clients external to the institution, many were born from internal, interdisciplinary UX and usability needs. We developed assorted relationships and conducted projects with programs and units across campus. For example, we worked with the game design and development, interactive design, packaging, industrial design, and MFA in design programs. We took on as clients the university library, career services, learning information technologies, and enterprise information systems.

The Center's Demise

Throughout my tenure as the center's director, I had to turn down countless university units and UX needs due to budgetary constraints: Because of our approved rates and the revenue-generation imperative, unless units were able to pay the center for services or they were willing to have undergraduate students take the lead on the needed UX work, the center was forced to deny services to these campus entities. Consequently, I worked for over a year to pivot the center to a new model that exclusively served the UX needs of campus units, one where the center and its director would complete a specified number of projects per semester based on established selection criteria (e.g., priority, interface type, users served by the interface, alignment with institutional mission, etc.). Despite various attempted collaborations, which included a host of meetings with offices across campus, interviews with stakeholders, formal proposals to administration, and much interdisciplinary collaboration across academic units, the center was decommissioned and forced to shut its doors. I returned to teaching a full complement of courses in the fall of the 2019–2020 academic year.

■ Lessons Learned from Failure

While I learned much about UX collaboration throughout my time as director—with industry partners, institutional stakeholders, students, faculty, and colleagues across the country—for the purposes of this volume, several salient takeaways exist. I experienced first-hand how time-intensive and cost-prohibitive lead generation can be in an academy-industry collaboration that relies on revenue. This was not only problematic for the center's model, but also for involved faculty navigating tenure and/or promotion. Simply put, industry doesn't move at the same pace as academia. Industry partners' cadences, needs, urgency, projects, administrative processes, and budget-cycles don't necessarily align with semester calendars, tenure and promotion clocks, and center or university budgets. Illustrated through the communication company collaboration detailed above, this misalignment can be an impediment to producing enough income to support a center space and its staff. Accordingly, identifying institutional allies and an administrative collaborator for the work the UX space and its team engages is paramount. Creating partners who will express the importance of UX (to faculty, administration, industry contacts, and students) and collaborate on cross-disciplinary projects is invaluable in helping enhance campus understanding of UX and the role that a UX center might play.

Additionally (and unsurprisingly), a fundamental component of a successful UX space is an established, consistent institutional funding source that not only supports a dedicated position, but also funds research technologies, equipment, supplies, and various study needs as they arise. The potential for securing that source is directly related to collaborating with an individual or institutional unit that understands and values UX from an intellectual, academic, and industry perspective—someone who recognizes how collaborating on UX projects is beneficial for a variety of stakeholders across and beyond the university, including the students the institution serves.

■ Lessons Learned from Collaboration

Although the bulk of what I came to understand throughout my five-year venture smacks of "should have" and "could have" type lessons, there were some positive outcomes that made the center and related struggles worthwhile. This UX collaboration, even if it didn't lead to much contracted revenue, provided me, my academic program, and the university valuable connections not otherwise possible. One of the most satisfying professional consequences of my UX center involvement was the depth of relationships I developed across campus. Being a truly interdisciplinary field, UX provided me opportunities to get out of my academic "silo," and collaborate with faculty, staff, and administrators across campus. Not only did this provide me with a better personal and professional experience, but it also contributed to my expanding conception of UX as a field. Further, the networking born from industry lead-generation efforts produced numerous student internships with industry partners, several of which led to subsequent employment opportunities for our graduates. Relatedly, the established UX center connections produced several advisory board members who provided valuable industry insights, dialog, and direction to help guide our academic programming and kept us on the leading edge of professional and technical communication education. These two related groups—interdisciplinary colleagues and industry professionals—also contributed to my UX-related research efforts, many serving as interview participants, points of contact, or informal sounding boards on research projects. Thus, my time as center director, while ultimately suboptimal from a revenue perspective, contributed to my professional objective in earning tenure and promotion to associate professor and, I would argue, my current position in industry; without the opportunities I had during and after my time as center director, I wouldn't have had the requisite skills, qualities, and experiences to land a job as a UX researcher. The variety of projects, interfaces, stakeholders, and methods I engaged during my time as an academic proved paramount to my future success.

■ Takeaways and Conclusion

So, was attempting to build and sustain a dedicated UX space worth it? Yes. Could the effort have been more efficient, effective, and successful. Absolutely. Did I learn anything I might pass along to others considering such an endeavor? Unequivocally. While the existential lessons learned are certainly worth consideration, more pragmatically, those in a position to begin planning an institutional UX research center might attend to the following:

- Avoid the allure of a revenue-creation model when pitching to administration. While it will more likely yield support, the constraints to success far outweigh the financial proceeds.
- Highlight the professional, disciplinary, institutional, and student benefits that a supported UX research center affords.
- Align the center, its objectives, and its outputs with cross-institutional curricula by making connections with the varied (and there are many) departments, programs, and majors with UX interests—direct or peripheral.
- Seek to identify UX research needs and opportunities across campus to support the immediate value of the proposed center's creation.
- Develop a clear, measurable, and marketable model for supporting UX research needs within (primary) and without (secondary) the university, one including intake criteria, a typical schedule, and the scope of services that includes an associated fee schedule for different client types.

For those in industry hoping to learn more about UX research and what might be in your communities, consider the following next steps:

- Inquire about academic research at your local universities, as it is relatively less expensive than for-contract work provided by industry UX practitioners.
- Think about an academic research center as a personnel pipeline in industry environments without in-house UX—for internships and UX-minded technical communicators.
- Engage with academic UX researchers to help clarify how UX can provide value that impacts a company's financial bottom line.
- Solicit consultation to help those in industry (e.g., digital marketing or communication departments) who engage with third-party vendors to better understand the differences among UX, UXD, UCD, UI, ID, LxD, IxD, CX, usability, and various other initialisms surrounding our field.

According to our editors' CFP, "user experience work demands better collaboration." I would argue that *better* collaboration is *strategic* collaboration. Because of the complex nature of UX partnerships, they command acute rhetorical acumen. This case represents an evolution of that acumen, and were I less self-assured and more diligent in my formative, pre-launch research, I might have made some different choices. When I first conceived of and designed the center, I did so with an assumption akin to "if you build it, they will come." I naïvely anticipated that, during the prevailing industry UX culture at the time, developing a center to serve the varied UX needs of disparate stakeholders at bargain-basement rates (and superior quality) would obviously find success; surely, everyone needs UX, and the center would be a cost-effective solution for those in the region. The money would rain from the UX heavens, and the center would be able to find sustainability and even contribute to programmatic, departmental, and college budgets. Alas, the situation was far more complex in contemporary higher education culture, something I learned first-hand over my time as director. There were countless components that made the center fiscally untenable, and those factors align with this volume's emphasis. Collaboration—before and throughout the endeavor—is the key to success, and that success is more than likely not tied to revenue. It can be something so much more profound for academics wanting to do, teach, and grow UX, providing opportunities and experiences for myriad stakeholders within and without the academy. While I came to understand much about collaborating in UX contexts, one of the most striking lessons was that while people—both in academia and industry—think they value UX, most don't completely know what it is, where it lives, and what it can or should mean. Since the uninitiated don't fully understand it, it takes much to get would-be collaborators to support UX or purchase UX services from those who do. Working with stakeholders in a variety of environments requires time, dedication, and forethought. These collaborations are challenging and minimally lucrative when academically constrained, even if they are valuable for many across the university. While I still wear the center's failure as an academic "black eye," what it afforded so many (including me) who rubbed up against our hub of UX activity made it fruitful and fulfilling—a story worth telling.

References

Ismirle, J. (2018). *User experience research methods and contexts of use: A systematic literature review.* (Publication No. 10932371.)[Doctoral dissertation, Michigan State University]. ProQuest Dissertations & Theses Global.

Nielsen, J. (1994). *Usability Laboratories: A 1994 survey.* Nielsen/Norman Group. https://www.nngroup.com/articles/usability-labs/.

Redish, G. & Barnum, C. (2011). Overlap, influence, intertwining: The interplay of UX and technical communication. *Journal of Usability Studies, 6*(3), 90–101. https://tinyurl.com/yc7633bb.

Sauro, J. (2018). How to build a dedicated usability lab. *MeasuringU.* https://measuringu.com/build-usability-lab/

Part Two: Collaborations in Communities

5. Voice of a Community Partner: Challenges and Benefits of Novice Students Conducting Onsite Usability Tests

Billy Kangas
POPE FRANCIS CENTER

Chalice Randazzo
UTAH TECH UNIVERSITY

Abstract. Coauthored by a community partner and a UX educator, this chapter prioritizes the community partner's voice to explore challenges and benefits of having a class of novice students run onsite usability testing at a community site. Challenges included issues of time, space, and people (ethics, expertise, and participant availability). Benefits included buy-in from both students and the organization. Based on these experiences, the chapter provides a list of seven lessons for UX teachers and six lessons for community partners who want to undertake such a project.

A few years ago, Amy Kimme Hea and Rachel Shah (2016) observed that voices of community partners are notably missing from community engagement scholarship; and Shah (2020) recently expanded upon that observation. This dearth, they argued, can lead to reductively thinking about community partners "as 'others'—outsiders to our classrooms, our goals, and our scholarship" (Kimme Hea & Shah, 2016, p. 49). They called for more perspectives from community partners so that we can create and evaluate courses that truly engage communities. More recently, Carrie Grant (2022) noted that few studies "have measured community outcomes and examined the collaborative tactics that effectively lead to impactful partnerships" (p. 152). Her work added community partners' voices through excerpts of interviews she conducted with them. Importantly for this chapter, Grant (2022) emphasized the need to conceptualize communities and community members as engaged partners more than research participants.

This chapter builds upon that work by featuring a dialogue between Billy Kangas, a community partner, and Chalice Randazzo, a university professor. At the time of our partnership, Billy was director of community engagement at the Community Clinic, a nonprofit organization that provides medical and dental services, a food pantry, and other resources to underserved groups in our community. Part of his job was community outreach and visibility, which included partnering with several service-learning courses from different universities. Chalice was an assistant professor teaching a course in usability testing and user experience (UX) at a regional university in the Midwest. She had run project-based and service-learning courses for nearly a decade and had taught usability for several years, incorporated into larger technical communication courses or as standalone courses in UX and usability. This project, however, added something neither of us had done before: requiring students to run usability tests at a community partner's location.

Our below dialog focuses on the challenges and benefits of having novice students run onsite usability tests at a nonprofit community organization. This particular situation has not been well addressed in either UX or community engagement scholarship. The challenges of onsite testing (also called "in-situ" or "field" testing) have been observed in human computer interaction (HCI) scholarship (a great review is in Kjeldskov & Skov, 2014). Challenges include added time, trouble accessing space, and access to representative test participants (e.g., Holl et al., 2016; Kantner et al., 2003; Schell, 1986), all of which can cost more money (Fiotakis et al., 2009; Kjeldskov & Graham, 2003; Kjeldskov et al., 2004) and patience from stakeholders who are potentially already apathetic toward UX (Lopez Gil et al., 2016; Wale-Kolade & Nielsen, 2016). But this HCI body of scholarship does not consider the community nonprofit context, which differs in significant ways that Emma Rose and colleagues (2017) observed: nonprofits "fill gaps in infrastructure and services" (12), have limited resources, must comply with regulations, have "a fluid and dynamic workforce" (12), and—more than their corporate counterparts—"have existing and intimate relationships with their users" (30). These hallmarks require added commitment and resources from UX researchers, which Douglas Walls (2016) contends "goes against the ethos of more marketplace-driven development cycles where rapid prototyping and Agile development is emphasized" (4). In response to these unique needs, several community engagement UX scholars have embraced goals and methodologies from participatory design and contextual inquiry, which we briefly outline in the next section. Even those studies, however, have a limited set of examples where students ran onsite usability tests at a community nonprofit's site, and we use those as a launching point for our dialog about our collaborative project.

■ UX and Community Nonprofit Partnerships

In scholarship that discusses usability testing in community engagement partnerships, testing usually falls under larger umbrellas such as contextual inquiry, user-centered design, participatory design, HCI, and service learning. Much of this work had UX experts running onsite tests in community nonprofit contexts (Acharya, 2018; Camara et al., 2010; Durá et al., 2019; Hennes et al., 2016; Mara et al., 2013; Mara & Mara, 2015; Rose et al., 2017; Shivers-McNair & San Diego, 2017). In a few cases, students ran tests, which scholars have argued helps students become better user advocates (Cleary & Flammia, 2012) and helps students and instructors be more accountable to audiences (Shivers-McNair et al., 2018).

The context under which students run tests for community projects varies, with examples of actual onsite testing rarely discussed. Jeffrey Grabill's (2003) students ran lab tests, since onsite tests were not necessary for his project. Similarly, Kathryn Swacha and Kirk St. Amant (2021) had students test a website, but onsite testing was not required. J. Blake Scott (2008) provides advice based on partnering his courses with the Orlando Eligible Metropolitan Area HIV Services Planning Council, although it is unclear whether his students ran tests onsite or in a lab. Kathryn Swacha's (2018) students ran onsite tests on cookbooks with seniors from a local care center, and she uses that experience to explore embodied literacy as a key skill for technical communication. From HCI, Jonathan Lazar (2001, 2011) has published several works based on years of conducting service learning UX projects with community partners, using both onsite and lab testing with undergraduates.

Although the specific context varies, these UX scholars typically adopt goals and values from community engagement: reciprocity, empowerment, sustainability, and capacity building. Reciprocity of the project means that it must benefit the community as much as the researcher (Agboka & Matveeva, 2018; Grant, 2022; Walton et al., 2019). Empowerment of end users requires having community partners participate in defining the needs and objectives of a project (e.g., Acharya, 2018; Agboka, 2013; Grabill, 2000; Salvo, 2001; Shivers-McNair et al., 2019; Spinuzzi, 2005a; Sun, 2006; Walls, 2016). Importantly, reciprocity and empowerment require coalitional approaches; Cana Uluak Itchuaqiyaq (2021) reminds us to be advocates with oppressed groups—not speaking for them but building coalitions with them in order to do advocacy work. A third goal is sustainability, including sustainable relationships with community partners but more importantly as the sustainability of a community resource after a project finishes (Grabill, 2003). Grabill (2003) argues that a crucial component for sustainability is capacity building, where community participants become both willing and able to continue the project after the partnership ends: "Community networks, through both their development and their use, must leverage activities that increase a community's capacity for being productive—to write and create—with information technologies" (p. 144).

These goals require UX researchers to adapt methodologies based on the culture and needs of their community partner, especially with organizations that serve underrepresented populations (Hennes et al., 2016; Mara et al., 2013; Mara & Mara, 2015; Rose et al., 2017; Salvo, 2004; Walls, 2016). Adaptation is rooted in empathy: in tying UX to social justice, Sumana Harihareswara (2015) urges developers to use *disciplined empathy* to uncover bottlenecks that can lead to exclusion. Ann Shivers-McNair and colleagues (2018) directly link empathy with usability testing: "we ultimately approached usability testing as an empathetic, flexible, ongoing engagement with our audiences and users" (p. 39). Walls (2016) explains how this process affects UX methodologies and designers:

UX design professionals working with under resourced user populations must make moves to engage in robust ethnographic research [13], understand differences in culturally located explanatory metaphors [14], understand and adjust elements of participatory design [15], and persona development [16]. (p. 2)

Rose and colleagues (2016) detailed an example of methodological flexibility in their work with a community organization that helped people enroll in the Affordable Care Act (ACA). They modified the frequency of usability tests so they would not disrupt the organization's work, and they adapted their methods when space, staff, and linguistic limitations prevented ACA staff from participating in the usability tests.

The ethics of not interrupting a community partner's work, which Rose and colleagues (2016) followed in their ACA project, is in tension with the imperative to engage community participants. Participatory design requires researchers to find partners who are willing to help define project goals and understand community needs (Grabill, 2000, 2003; Hennes et al., 2016; Johnson, 1998; Shivers-McNair et al., 2019; Shivers-McNair & San Diego, 2017), and finding community end-users to participate in the design process is crucial (Mara & Mara, 2015; Salvo, 2001; Spinuzzi, 2005; Walls, 2016). Several scholars observe that social justice UX projects require more time to develop relationships, identify reciprocal projects, and conduct respectful contextual inquiry (e.g., Agboka, 2013; Chong, 2018; Rose & Walton, 2015; Salvo, 2004; Shivers-McNair & San Diego, 2017). This extra time can be seen in Grabill's (2003) phases of a community engaged UX project:

- Relationship building and (old-fashioned) community networking,
- Needs assessments through focus groups and interviews and information technology profiles (done in part with a technical writing class),
- Early versions of the web site (with technical writing class), and
- Usability testing and redesign (with technical writing class). (p. 136)

Extra time requires additional resources, paradoxically conflicting with the resource limitations of community nonprofit work. Many scholars, therefore, have published their experiences in navigating this paradox, although only a handful of those specify usability testing. And even fewer have discussed students running onsite usability tests in nonprofit contexts.

Our below dialog adds to these conversations by focusing on the challenges and benefits we encountered when students ran onsite usability tests at our community nonprofit's site. More significantly, we foreground the community partner's perspectives, answering Kimme Hea and Shah's (2016) call for including community partners' voices. In what follows, we discuss the project's context and timeline before moving into its challenges and benefits. The results are lessons for both instructors and community partners who want to embark on a collaboration where novice students run onsite usability tests.

■ Project and Context

The project was a partnership between Chalice's service-learning UX course and the Community Clinic. As we detail in this section, the UX course devotes a full semester to almost the entire life cycle of a project: identifying UX issues, creating a responsive deliverable, selecting UX methods for testing, and refining the deliverable. The course runs once per year with a new project almost each time it is offered; for example, one project was software documentation for a database system, while another was tutorials for first-year writing students. For the semester with the Community Clinic, the course had three graduate students and seven upper-division undergraduates.

Chalice met Billy, the Clinic representative, through the university's service-learning office, and they spent the next eight months identifying potential projects that would fit the needs of the Clinic and the course. Chalice shared her syllabus and old course projects with Billy as examples of what the course could do. Billy showed Chalice around the Clinic so that she could understand all the services that the Clinic provided, meet some Clinic staff, and see the physical context of the space. Billy also shared old documentation with Chalice as examples of what other classes had created for the Clinic.

By the time the UX course began in January, we had loosely identified several potential projects: kitchen instructions, medical and dental orientation materials, food pantry orientation materials, and database documentation. The audiences for each project differed: some documentation would be geared toward volunteers who were new to the Clinic, and other projects would be directed at volunteers or staff who had been with the Clinic for some time. With these preliminary plans in place, Chalice spent the first class session of the semester preparing her students to interview Billy; she purposely gave the students few details about the projects because she wanted them to understand the Clinic and the projects from Billy's point of view. Billy attended the second class session for a "client interview" where he provided students with the Clinic's mission, vision, stakeholders, services, and needs. This is also when Chalice started discussing ethical considerations with the class, which we detail more deeply later in this chapter.

Based on the initial client interview, the UX class spent the next few weeks narrowing project ideas and connecting them to timelines, workloads, and audiences. This included a site visit where Billy showed the entire class around the Clinic so that students could see the space, meet some of the staff, and take notes about the physical context of where documents would be used. This process resulted in two projects for the class:

- Half the class (five students) chose to create documentation for the Clinic's database system. The Clinic was transitioning between an old and new database system, and these processes were tied to important Clinic functions such as maintaining donor relationships. The Clinic had previous

documentation for some of these processes, but that previous documentation was predominately from the former database system. The new documentation would help standardize the way donors and volunteers were entered into the system. It would also help staff who were unfamiliar with the database processes or needed refreshers about the database.
- The other half (five students) chose to create orientation materials for running the Clinic's food pantry and farm stand. Each space had different processes, and multiple volunteers held different roles in each space: e.g., someone would check in customers while another person would help customers shop. The Clinic had existing documentation for each space, but there was debate about how accurate that documentation was. These orientation materials would be directed at new volunteers unfamiliar with the Clinic or food pantry.

Per the course requirements, both projects yielded two modalities of documentation: written documents that the Clinic could print and video tutorials that the Clinic could post to a YouTube site or internal server. While both of these projects had their challenges, this chapter focuses on the orientation materials because those had to be tested at the Clinic.

Site visits revealed several logistical factors that are pertinent to this chapter. First, the food pantry spaces had different hours than the rest of the Clinic, and those hours did not overlap with the UX class time. Second, other Clinic activities happened near the food pantry, and some of those overlapped with the first 15 minutes of class. Third, while the food pantry was connected to the main Clinic building, the farm stand was in a separate building next door. These locations affected access to the spaces, which was the fourth logistical factor. The reception area to the Clinic served as one entry to the food pantry, but there was a second entry to the food pantry that remained locked when the pantry was not open; the farm stand also had a large bay door that remained closed during our project, but it also had a side door that was locked during closed hours. And finally, some of the spaces were small enough that they created a tight fit with all the students in them; and there was limited parking space for the Clinic, meaning that a class of 11 people (Chalice included) made an impact on parking access for Clinic clientele. All of these factors affected the onsite testing situation.

Onsite usability testing happened in sixth week of class, and this chapter focuses on the challenges and benefits surrounding that test. However, some of the steps leading up to the onsite test will provide context:

1. **Obtaining the previous written documentation:** The Clinic provided previously written orientation materials to test. Students printed and reviewed them for design elements, but they had no way of knowing whether the content was accurate.
2. **Delineating tasks and documents:** The food pantry and farm stand typically had multiple volunteers working at a time, each with different tasks.

They were often separated: e.g., the person signing in customers worked in a different part of the pantry than the person helping customers shop. The previous documentation ran the tasks together in a single document. The UX class separated them in order to create documents that volunteers could take with them to different areas. The class settled on five tasks, each of which would need to be tested at a different station during onsite testing.

3. **Participant recruitment:** At the same time the class received documentation and identified tasks, we recruited representative participants. Billy was able to recruit some experienced Clinic volunteers and staff, while the students and Chalice found people who had never been at the Clinic. In total, we were able to recruit five participants for onsite testing.

4. **Securing space:** Chalice emailed the Clinic staff to check the testing schedule with them. As we explain later, the staff's response led us to constrain onsite testing to one day, which meant all onsite tests had to take place during the duration of one class session. This, combined with the number of tasks and participants, meant that participants would need to rotate between tasks. The class decided on three rotations, meaning that 1) each station would see three participants and 2) each participant would need to move three times.

5. **Practice testing:** Students practiced think-aloud protocols and post-test interviews, the two methods chosen for this project. Obviously, one purpose of these practice sessions was to train students how to moderate and observe. But it also had logistical purposes. Because the food pantry and farm stand were in separate buildings, the practice usability tests used two rooms at the university. We established how many pens, writing pads, and printed copies of the orientation materials we would need; who would greet test participants; who would track time on tasks; and who would escort test participants from one testing station to another.

All these steps affected the onsite testing. We will not detail testing results or how they applied to the final orientation materials, but some details about testing day are pertinent to the later discussion between Billy and Chalice. Onsite testing lasted 75 minutes and consisted of think-aloud protocols and short post-test interviews. The UX class split into five task stations that tested orientation materials for that task. Three of these stations were in the Clinic's food pantry, and the other two were in the farm stand next door, which Billy had to unlock when the UX class arrived. Chalice supervised the three food pantry stations, and Billy supervised the two farm stand stations. Each station had a student moderator, student observer, and participant, meaning that the UX class had a total of 16 people (including Chalice) onsite at the Clinic. The five participants rotated between three tasks; to coordinate their movements, all participants were given instructions on which stations they would visit, and students received instructions on where to escort their participant next.

The rest of this chapter is a conversation between us (Billy and Chalice) about the challenges and benefits surrounding this onsite test. In the next section, we discuss the challenges we faced from different sides of the partnership. We then move into the benefits of this process, some of which stemmed from logistical constraints.

■ Challenges: Time, Space, People, Expertise, and Attitude

Reciprocal, participatory community engagement partnerships necessitate involving end-users throughout the design process, being flexible with methodological approaches, and spending time observing users' activities even before a product is designed for those users. These goals require time, space, and people resources, all of which have been framed as challenges for in-situ researchers (e.g., Holl et al., 2016; Kantner et al., 2003; Kjeldskov et al., 2004). In community engagement partnerships, these challenges are also a burden on community partners, but community partners' direct voices have been largely absent from our scholarship (Kimme Hea & Shah, 2016). So, this section jumps between the community partner (Billy) and the UX instructor (Chalice) to understand challenges of time, space, and people from each partner's perspective. Based on our experience in this project, this section adds some additional challenges: expertise and attitude.

Time, Space, and People

Lazar (2011) noted that HCI projects run by undergraduate students have unique time challenges, and we also found those in our project. First, there is the timing of the class sessions themselves, which can fall into awkward times for community partners or participants. Second, there is the time constraint of the semester or quarter system in which the project takes place. These constraints, Billy points out, meant that the Clinic team had to invest additional time, space, and people resources. Chalice, too, felt that time constraints interacted with the challenges of finding space and people resources.

Billy

One of the most significant challenges of the work was the limited availability of the students. Although it was relatively simple to work with students on an individual level if the need arose, by in large most of the work for the project required most of the class participants to be available. This meant that time to collaborate often needed to fit the scheduled class time.

This limitation created some challenges. The times when the class was on site were precious. Documentation and testing needed to be done in multiple locations simultaneously, and without interfering with the operations of any of the programs.

In order to accomplish this, a lot of the work was spent preparing for these limited windows. We had to ensure there were the right volunteers available to help answer questions and test the documents the students were drafting. We had to coordinate with program managers to ensure the needed spaces could be made available, and we needed to ensure everyone was well informed about the goals of the day and their role in accomplishing those goals before anyone showed up.

When the groups arrived, we needed to be prepared enough to point everyone in the right direction and to let them go. As the staff point person attempting to manage multiple goals throughout the campus of our facility, I was really grateful that the students were well prepared and could lead their own work. The challenge of preparing the students really paid off when the students were on site. Instead of being pulled in multiple directions, I was able to invest my time in the areas where I could offer the greatest return for the students.

Chalice

I agree with all of Billy's points. Collaborative time on site was precious, so the class spent extra time preparing for our onsite visits. Before our tour of the Clinic, we reviewed the Clinic's website and any previous documentation they could provide us at that point. We also created a list of students' questions and a list of goals for observing the space (e.g., where do people use these documents, what type of audiences do these documents reach, etc.). Our onsite testing required perfected think-aloud protocols, practice sessions, and multiple written instructions for participants and students.

When it came to timing, I was most concerned about whether the Clinic's activities overlapped with class time. I did not want to disrupt their clients, and some Clinic activities were happening near the food pantry at the start of our class. So, we delayed the start of testing slightly, and I told students that they were to be polite, friendly, and quiet if other people were in the area. By coincidence, the food pantry and farm stand were both closed during our class sessions. This enabled us to test without disrupting those activities, but it also meant that we could not conduct contextual inquiry of the food pantry or farm stand volunteers while they were doing their work. Honestly, that was a small price to pay for not disrupting Clinic activities.

As Billy pointed out, time constraints overlapped with space and people resources. Since the onsite locations were in two different spaces, I could not be at both simultaneously to answer students' questions, give them pointers, or ensure they were being respectful. I would have liked to conduct two days of usability testing so that I could have supervised both locations, but that turned out to be logistically impractical. I emailed a potential schedule to one of the program managers that Billy mentioned, and her reply let me know that I was asking too much: "Those involved on this end of things need to have more discussion." The response let me know that I should have involved the program managers more directly while my class was deciding on whether we would create something that required onsite testing. Apologetically, I reported back to my students that we might have to scrap the onsite project. We were asking a lot of our partners, bringing 16 people onto their site who would fill their spaces and take up their parking. In the end, the program managers were okay with one day of testing, for which I am grateful. Condensing to one day meant that someone I trusted—Billy—would need to supervise one of our testing locations. It seemed natural for him to supervise the farm stand because he had to unlock it, anyway, since it was closed during our onsite testing time.

In retrospect, one day of testing was smarter because we would not have been able to obtain participants for two days. We had difficulty finding even five participants for one day. Class time was during regular working hours, so most people were at work or school. As Billy pointed out, some of the Clinic staff became our testing participants. This challenge led to some unexpected benefits because those staff had more expertise on our tasks than students did.

Expertise and Attitude

When UX, participatory design, or community engagement scholars talk about expertise, it is often to remind experienced UX scholars, researchers, and designers that community members are legitimate experts on a topic. In the case of this project, however, the students running the research were not experienced, much like the students in Lazar's (2011), Scott's (2008), and Swacha's (2018) work. The students in our project were novices on several fronts: with the Clinic's processes, with running UX research, and with documentation design. Working with novices, especially students in a course, creates extra challenges for community partners. Billy points out that a community partner is forced to enter into the pedagogical process, and not every nonprofit administrator will want to do that. He explains that this process requires open attitudes about mentorship, relationship building, and trust between community partners, students, and instructors.

Billy

Another challenge that I experienced was the need to be fully engaged in the learning goals of the class. Taking on a project like this required a high degree of trust between the instructor and myself. This project took the pedagogical process out of the controlled environment of the university classroom and placed it in the context of a living organization. If I hadn't taken time to help to mitigate the risks to the students and assist in transforming our space into a learning environment, the students could easily have felt lost.

I found that my own passion for seeing that students learned was a necessary skill. On multiple occasions I was able to sit down with students and talk about their own professional goals. This helped me to develop ideal projects that would connect students to relevant skills and expose them to environments where their educational development had professional applications.

Students can sometimes be really difficult to work with. They are still trying to figure out how to apply what they have been learning, and many of them have not developed basic professional skills. These deficiencies can result in more work, difficulties in accomplishing goals, and occasionally projects that simply don't meet the standards you would like. Without a heartfelt desire to see the students develop, this process could result in an overall frustrating experience for everyone involved.

Chalice

I can see Billy's point about expertise in the process and the product. Billy is adept at video production himself, so the video tutorials were less polished than he would have created. The database documentation was all right because those were just screen captures with voiceovers. But for the orientation materials, people had to act out the tasks in the food pantry and farm stand. Students were still learning how to create storyboards, shoot their videos, and edit those videos, and it didn't always go well: e.g., two students shot their videos in portrait instead of landscape, so they had to go back to the site and reshoot their entire videos. I could see another nonprofit administrator being disappointed with the quality of these products, especially for all the time and effort that Billy and his team put into the project.

Billy's points about cultivating mentorship attitudes and trusting relationships is key. Finding a community partner who has some experience working with students, as Billy did from previous partnerships with other instructors, is challenging but worthwhile. A trusting relationship also comes from time spent planning the project and then staying atop the project's progress—a challenge that becomes more manageable with practice.

In terms of expertise, I was also concerned about the students' lack of experience with the testing process. Several of them had never run a think-aloud protocol, and none of them had run a usability test with this many logistical considerations. They had to move participants between buildings and stations, keep time synchronized between physically separated stations, and ensure they all had the physical materials they needed; for example, we could not print more consent forms or orientation materials at the Clinic.

While quality and experience were definitely issues that arose from working with novice researchers, the greatest challenge for me was ensuring that students met ethical standards. During the onsite tour, I reminded students not to speak loudly or stare; they had to conduct their observations as discreetly and respectfully as a group of 10 people could. Before we went to onsite testing, we discussed participants' privacy and created consent waivers that went beyond our institution's IRB requirements. Also, before onsite testing, I reminded students that their testing wasn't as important as the people or activities already happening at the Clinic; for example, they could not ask the Clinic's staff for help or the clientele to move out of the way of a testing session. I was especially concerned about this on the testing day because I could not be with two of the groups; I am grateful that Billy was willing to be with them in the farm stand to ensure that things ran smoothly there.

Finally, during onsite testing, we unexpectedly had participants who had run the food pantry and farm stand. They spent the entire "test" correcting our materials, turning the test into an artifact analysis and interview session. When students worried because the test had gone astray, I encouraged them to let the participant write on the materials. This deviation allowed the class to discuss two things that would not have otherwise been possible. First, while user testing is not inherently participatory, a tenet of participatory design is to listen to end users' expertise. Second, these situations are common in testing, so we have to be flexible in our methodology based on our context. Those interactions stemmed from our inability to find enough participants, which resulted in several unexpected benefits that we discuss in the next section.

■ Benefits

Onsite testing required more effort from everyone involved: Billy and Chalice, certainly, but also the students and the Clinic team. It created challenges, but those challenges sometimes led to unexpected benefits. This section lumps all of those benefits under the umbrella of "buy-in": an attitude that encouraged people's commitment to the project, empowerment from the project, and belief in the project's merit. Billy observed that buy-in from students made them more engaged with the Clinic and led to better quality deliverables. Both Billy and Chalice also noticed how buy-in from the Clinic team led to a change in the organization's attitude toward documentation.

Buy-In from Students: Relationships and Deliverables

Time, space, expertise, and attitude were all challenges of onsite testing. But those challenges seemed to lead to deeper relationships between the class and the Clinic. Time constraints meant the class needed more preparation time before we went onsite, including students' online research about the Clinic's mission and vision as well as analysis of previous Clinic documents. This preparatory time also included the classroom interview with Billy and the onsite Clinic tour. Billy noticed that this process led students to be more connected with the Clinic's overarching mission and everyday processes, which he saw in the quality of their deliverables. Chalice also noticed how the onsite tour and testing, especially, allowed Clinic staff to see students' novice status and, in response, adopt a more mentorship attitude toward students. The combination of these factors deepened the relationship between partners in this project.

Billy

Students are very busy. Their mental and emotional energy is a limited resource. I wanted to ensure we got the very best of both from the students; this isn't something you can require. It's something that needs to be earned.

In my experience, student projects are notorious for being "phoned in." Students only give the effort they need to give in order to fulfil the course requirements and rarely give their whole heart to the needs of the organization they are serving with their work. This was not what we experienced with this project and I believe it was rooted in two choices that were made early on.

The first choice was for Chalice to take the time to understand and believe in the mission of the organization. We had met at the campus originally but she took time to come by, take a tour and learn about what we do. Surprisingly, there are few professors who invest their time in coming onsite. When this step fails to happen, there isn't mental or emotional energy invested from the faculty members, and the students pick up on this. They seem to intuit that a professor doesn't seem to care all that much about the organization and that they shouldn't either.

The second choice was the decision to bring the class onsite. This also gave them an opportunity to see the site for themselves and ask questions. This encounter created a fertile ground for the students to take an authentic interest in the work themselves. Giving them a "why" made them care a whole lot more about the "how."

Once students cared about the mission, the project became about more than the grade. It became an expression of the students' own values and goals. It allowed the hearts of the students to be won and this factor really showed through in the enthusiasm of the students and in the quality of their final results.

Chalice

Billy's comments reveal purposeful choices I made with this project, but I was also surprised by unplanned benefits. This was my first onsite testing experience, but my previous classes have done contextual observations, which opened opportunities for them to feel more connected to the community partner. So, I included contextual observation in order to foster closer relationships. What surprised me, though, was how onsite testing reinforced those relationships, both from students and Clinic staff. For example, a couple weeks after testing, I learned that some of my students had exchanged email addresses with one of the Clinic staff who participated in testing. Once students had a new draft of written instructions, they sent it to her for feedback, something I did not require them to do. I saw this as a mentoring relationship where students respected the staff's expertise and the staff recognized students' need for an expert. Onsite testing seemed to changed people's attitudes toward each other.

Like Billy, I noticed that this made a difference in students' commitment to getting the deliverables "right." The ones who sent drafts to the Clinic staff member were willing to go through extra drafting phases. In addition, two students filmed their initial video tutorials in portrait instead of landscape, and they were willing to go back into the site with me to re-film their entire tutorial. Certainly, this led to better portfolio pieces for them, but it also stemmed from their stated desire to produce something of quality that the Clinic could use without changes.

Buy-In from the Organization: Empowerment and Organizational Change

Time, space, people, and expertise challenges led to unexpected benefits of empowerment and organizational change. Time and space constraints meant that Billy had to be present for all the onsite activities, and he had to unlock the spaces and help run testing. The difficulty of finding testing participants led us to recruit Clinic staff who were not representative of our end users: we were aiming for inexperienced volunteers rather than experienced staff. But this ostensible failure had some unexpected benefits. Billy explains that it enabled Clinic staff to take ownership of the documents, give feedback on processes, and foster organizational change toward documentation and usability.

Billy

The whole process for us wound up being a pivotal moment in the culture of the organization. Before this project, I had struggled seriously with developing a value for documenting processes with some of the program leaders. One of the hang-ups in all of this was a fear of the unknown. People felt overwhelmed by the idea of documenting something and didn't have a good handle on what a success looked like.

The process of working with Chalice and her students exposed a critical number of our staff and volunteers to the field and helped us to develop a process, vocabulary and standard for what good process documentation looked like. In the months since then this initial boost has developed a much stronger value around process documentation in our programs. In many ways the students' projects were like a yeast which eventually helped the whole organization to rise.

One of the earliest benefits was buy-in. Staff and volunteers felt ownership of the final products since a significant number of staff and volunteers were invited into the process of developing the documentation and gave opportunities for feedback along the way. If we hadn't given so many opportunities for people to see themselves as co-creators, I believe the response to the documentation would have been critical. Instead, we experienced people who were passionate cheerleaders and avid users.

An unexpected additional benefit of this has recently emerged in light of the COVID-19 pandemic. Having a secure base of documentation helped protect our programs when many essential staff had to begin working from home as a result of the virus. Our familiarity with process documentation also allowed us to change programs as needed and provide quick and effective documentation of the changes for the many new volunteers who were stepping up to fill gaps.

Chalice

The Clinic staff's transformed approach to documentation was the benefit I least expected. It stemmed from the empowerment that Billy discussed above, and that empowerment was a direct result of not having enough people to run or take the usability tests. Because Billy had to unlock the spaces and help supervise the students during testing, he directly observed the testing process and recognized the goal of the test: to make documentation that people could use in context. The same is true of several Clinic staff and volunteers. Once they noticed that they had more expertise than students did, they stepped in with advice and realized they could shape something that would make their lives easier.

Several interactions since testing have demonstrated that this experience had some lasting impact on the Clinic's long-term documentation practices. For me, the biggest surprise came from the same program manager who had emailed me about the schedule. Roughly a month after our onsite tests, she asked whether I would give a workshop with the staff about usability testing. Seeing the test also affected Billy, who later told me that he now defined "good" documentation as something people could use, not just something that was accurate about a process. He bought the UX book that my students used for class. And as his above discussion points out, the change is still present over a year later, even having unintended benefits for adapting to the COVID-19 response.

▪ Lessons for Teachers and Community Partners

We (Billy and Chalice) were lucky that several of the challenges we faced led to unexpected benefits, although hopefully our discussion echoes other scholars' observations that this sort of project takes significant effort from community partners and instructors (Lazar, 2011; Scott, 2008). We both learned lessons about undertaking a project that involves onsite testing and novice researchers. As many scholars who do community engagement work have asserted (e.g., Cabrero et al., 2016; Camara et al., 2010; Grabill, 2003; Mara et al., 2013; Rose et al., 2017; Scott, 2008; Shivers-McNair & San Diego, 2017; Spinuzzi, 2005a, 2005b), each collaborative experience is unique and requires flexibility, so the lessons we provide in this section will obviously not apply to every situation. Still, they might prove helpful to some instructors and community members who are thinking of conducting onsite testing with novice student researchers.

Comparing his previous partnerships to this project, Billy outlines several pieces of advice to faculty who want to conduct any community engagement project:

1. **Review and adapt learning objectives in conversation with the partner organization.** Too often learning objectives do not reflect the context that a project needs to fit into. Understanding the needs and the capacity of the organization should be the first step as you are developing the course. Otherwise, you may find yourself working at cross-purposes with your community partners. This only builds antagonism.

2. **Build in flexibility to the process.** Expect the unexpected. Taking untested students into the real world will create unforeseen problems. Often students don't know how to navigate the kinds of problems that could arise. Give them permission to adapt and be proactive as you check-in to identify areas where change will be needed.
3. **Take a trip to your partner's site.** Faculty who take the time to see the location where their partners are working are more likely to understand both the opportunities and the challenges of the environment. This will only lead to better outcomes for students.
4. **Involve stakeholders in the organization as much as possible.** If a stakeholder is allowed to participate in the development of the project, they will be much more supportive of the work and will offer valuable perspectives along the way.
5. **Create opportunities for students to get to know the organization and pursue their own interests.** A student that is passionate about a project will put in a better effort. Creating space for students to find personal meaning in the project helps to motivate them, and it will show in the final deliverable.
6. **Uphold clear, professional standards.** At the end of the day, a partnership should be a benefit for both parties. An instructor must ensure that they do not allow poor-quality work to stand. Make sure the final product meets both your expectations and the expectations of the partner organization. Failing to accomplish the later goal will erode trust and will make future collaboration unlikely.
7. **Teach the organization as you teach the students.** Ideally your partners will emerge from this experience better educated and equipped to pursue further learning. Build in times for partners to learn about the process along with the students and be generous with resources that can help them develop their own capacity to work.

Billy's voice reinforces lessons that many scholars have emphasized for decades (e.g., Cleary & Flammia, 2012; Grabill, 2003; Lazar, 2001, 2011; Mara et al., 2013; Mara & Mara, 2015; Rose & Walton, 2015; Scott, 2008; Shivers-McNair et al., 2019; Walls, 2016). Teachers who are thinking about undertaking this sort of project should consider his and those scholars' advice. And just in case community partners read this chapter, he has a list of advice for them, too:

1. **Have motivations that go beyond the deliverable itself.** Community partners who place too much emphasis on the quality of the final deliverable could easily become disappointed. Therefore, we recommend other motivations that are guaranteed from a partnership, such as increased visibility with a college student population.

2. **Understand the learning goals of the course.** This advice has two benefits. First, it helps community partners understand what is realistic from the course: some courses do not have the timeframe, skill level, or learning outcomes that an organization needs. Second, it can help community partners feel like part of the teaching process by realizing how their expertise and their organization's goals fit into the course's learning outcomes.
3. **Be realistic about the resource commitments.** Communicate early, realistically, and frequently about what you can give in terms of time, people, and access (to physical resources as well as knowledge). Be conservative in your estimates. The teacher you partner with might (should) be able to provide options that you can scale to different levels of commitment.
4. **Take the time to get to know the strengths and weaknesses of the students.** Every student brings with them their own set of experiences. Take time to talk about the kinds of work that bring them joy, what they are proud of, and what kinds of work they find difficult and frustrating. You may not be able to connect each student with work that matches their skills and passions exactly, but having an awareness of areas of particular strength or areas in which students struggle will better equip a partner to provide additional supports in the areas that are most necessary and to plug students into the areas in projects where they are most likely to succeed.
5. **Try to help students connect the work with their personal goals.** Don't fall into the trap of thinking a student is only there to serve your needs. For the best collaborations, it is better to try to think of the ways that your projects can help students achieve their own goals. Take time to talk to students about what skills and experiences they are hoping to achieve. It's also beneficial to hear about their goals and dreams. Sometimes this can reveal opportunities to connect the work the student is doing to a larger ambition they have for their own lives. Making communication about student goals a part of the process helps position the experience as something or real value for the student's life.
6. **Set clear expectations, then repeat them.** Like any relationship, communication is critical when working with students. It is far better to *over communicate* expectations. Try to communicate expectations as clearly as possible and in as many ways as possible. You will not know the communication preferences for most students you work with and will not have prior experience to guide you. Expectations also need to be clear. Ideally, they are measurable and have concrete benchmarks with deadlines along the way. Check-in on progress and offer helpful feedback early in the process to ensure if something was misunderstood, it is corrected early on.

In response to scholars' advice as well as years of community engagement experience, Chalice has established a process she calls "prepared flexibility," which has requirements for both instructors and community partners (and looks like the "preparation and flexibility" concept that Scott's (2008) students developed during their projects). The next section weaves many of the above listed items into the prepared flexibility framework to demonstrate how that process looked specifically in the Clinic project. Our hope is that other faculty (and maybe even some community partners) can have an example of how those apply in UX community projects.

■ Prepared Flexibility in UX Community Projects

Billy's lists of lessons could be applied to any community project, which is not surprising considering the overlaps between UX and community engagement scholarship. Applying these lists to specifically UX projects echoes advice that Lazar (2011) gave to UX educators. Lazar (2011) forwards seven success factors for service-learning projects with undergraduate students, including having "community partners who believe deeply in the project and are willing to spend time with the students" (p. 586) and recognizing that "undergraduate students are not immediately experts in something that they just learned" (p. 587). In addition to these general tenets, we used the concept of prepared flexibility to make the UX course more successful.

Prepared flexibility starts with establishing, as much as possible, reciprocal goals and expectations early in the process. Above, Billy recommended that faculty adapt learning objectives in conversation with the community partner. Taken to an extreme, this process could result in hyperpragmatism, where academic goals are usurped by organizational ones. In addition, UX educators are often bound by the programmatic or course-learning outcomes agreed upon in curriculum proposals. But the academic goals of UX courses can be uniquely poised to adapt to almost any community project. For example, the program for Chalice's course used learning outcomes such as rhetorical awareness, process, multimodality, reflection, and genre conventions (adapted from the CWPA's "WPA Outcomes Statement for First-Year Composition"). Within that space, she was able to create UX-specific learning outcomes of user awareness, ethical UX research processes, and multimodal genre deliverables. All of those outcomes easily adapted to any community UX project without Chalice losing her academic autonomy; and, indeed, the course reached beyond the Clinic's needs, and Chalice was able to assess students' progress in those outcomes throughout the semester.

Prepared flexibility also requires flexibility on the part of the community partner, which is the crux of Billy's advice to community partners. Billy, for example, looked at projects from previous semesters as well as the upcoming syllabus and course schedule. He spent time understanding the UX-specific course learning goals, the timeline for the project, and the skillset of the students. For several months, we worked on loosely identifying several projects that would fit into the scope of both the class and the organization.

Despite the work that happens before the project starts, prepared flexibility does not mean solidifying full project details before a course begins; the UX course in our example did not have a project picked before we began the semester. Instead, prepared flexibility requires the reciprocity and collaboration valued in community engagement scholarship, which can be specifically applied to UX projects:

1. Identifying major milestones on a timeline, including contextual inquiry, (potentially) IRB approval, participant recruitment, testing, etc.;
2. communicating those milestones to community partners;
3. securing resources, including participants, spaces, and times to run onsite testing;
4. and, most importantly, being prepared to change when something falls through.

In our case, Chalice failed to tell all the program managers about the course's schedule, leading to the email that nearly stopped the onsite project. Although embarrassed and disappointed at the time, she and Billy had prepared backup projects that students could complete offsite. In addition, the UX class failed to secure enough participants who fit the traits of the end users. Our project showed us that unintended participants can provide unexpected benefits, so instructors might want to allow for some flexibility in recruitment (although, obviously, have as many participants as possible that exemplify the end users). Finally, Chalice failed to consider whether her class was scheduled at a day and time that worked for the Clinic's staff, so it was lucky that the UX course's days and times did not overlap with food pantry and farm stand activities. While building a schedule around a community partner is often impossible, we recommend it as much as possible, especially for a project that wants to do onsite testing. Being prepared but flexible allowed us to adjust to unexpected challenges.

Finally, although we did not discuss it in our list of advice, we want to mention that this sort of project is not ideal for inexperienced instructors or community partners. The logistical and ethical challenges we faced are not unique to our project—indeed, the issues we raised are well documented in the literature (Grabill, 2003; Hennes et al., 2016; Lazar, 2011; Mara & Mara, 2015; Rose et al., 2017; Rose & Walton, 2015; Scott, 2008; Shivers-McNair & San Diego, 2017; Swacha, 2018; Walls, 2016). Based on a study of students and instructors running usability testing in technical communication courses, Felicia Chong (2018) recommended that instructors take a usability course in order to be prepared to teach it. This advice is reasonable, as we found these challenges exacerbated in an onsite testing situation with novice researchers. It tried Billy's resolve as a community partner, and he drew from his experience working with previous classes in order to find motivation and patience. It tested Chalice's capacity for flexibility and planning, for which she drew from years of running project-based courses. We are not saying that new instructors or community partners cannot do these projects; but we recommend that one or both of the collaborators on such a project have some experience with the challenges of such a collaboration.

■ Conclusion

Scholars who employ usability testing in community nonprofit contexts point to community benefits such as empowerment and reciprocity. Still, these scholars acknowledge the intense resources needed to plan and run any community engagement UX project, even in situations with lab tests (e.g., Grabill, 2003) or UX experts (e.g., Mara & Mara, 2015; Rose et al., 2016; Shivers-McNair & San Diego, 2017). This chapter adds complexity to this discussion by exploring the challenges and benefits of an onsite test run by novice researchers.

Foregrounding the community partner's voice enables scholars to hear benefits and challenges of onsite testing from different perspectives. For example, community engagement scholars have talked for decades about the importance of building sustainable relationships between academics and community partners (Grabill, 2003; Hennes et al., 2016; Mara & Mara, 2015; Rose & Walton, 2015; Scott, 2008; Shivers-McNair et al., 2019; Shivers-McNair & San Diego, 2017). Billy points out that an individual class is only one contribution to a larger, sustained relationship between organizations:

> Another longer-term benefit of this was a strengthened relationship between the clinic and the university. Having a successful student project helped us to better define what parameters we would want to have in place when participating in future projects with the university. As a result, we have had greater comfort in working with faculty. Having a good relationship with the university offers a lot of great benefits. We have found an increase in financial support from alumni, new student volunteers and opportunities to collaborate with faculty on a wide range of issues. Not all of these are a direct result of the project, but I believe our collaboration with Chalice and her class played a significant role in deepening the overall relationship between our organizations.

Scholars who discuss community engagement or service-learning collaborations rightly stress the importance of individual instructors building sustainable and reciprocal relationships, and Billy's advice to instructors in this chapter reinforce those scholars' assertions. But individual instructors and scholars need to understand that the sustained relationship must be, from a community partner's perspective, larger than any single class or faculty member. This is true whether the partnership is UX or not.

Even more important is the sustainability of community resources after a project finishes. Grabill (2003) argues that this level of sustainability cannot be achieved unless the community organization builds capacity for the skills needed to sustain those resources. Billy's voice in this chapter demonstrates that, at least in some situations, onsite usability testing can have durable effects on end-users' empowerment and their capacity for creating, testing, and maintaining documentation. Interestingly, this capacity building was an unintended result of the unique challenges of this project: 1) novice students running tests (expertise challenges), 2) Clinic staff participating on testing day (people and space challenges), and 3) community partners' willingness to mentor students (attitude challenges). Sharing our community partners' voices, as Kimme Hea and Shah (2016) encourage, can help UX scholars understand different perspectives on the challenges and benefits of onsite usability testing.

Implications for Readers

By foregrounding the voice of a community partner, we have tried to provide insights about challenges and benefits of having a class of novice students run onsite usability testing at a community site. Challenges included issues of time, space, and people (ethics, expertise, and participant availability). Benefits included buy-in from both students and the organization.

Based on these experiences, the section titled "Lessons for Teachers and Community Partners" includes a list of lessons for UX teachers who want to undertake such a project, with another list of lessons for any community partners who might happen to read this chapter. The section on "prepared flexibility" clarifies how we implemented these lessons in our own UX project, with the goal of helping other educators and community partners who might want to undertake a similar partnership.

References

Acharya, K. R. (2018, August 3). Usability for user empowerment: Promoting social justice and human rights through localized UX design. SIGDOC '18: *Proceedings of the 36th ACM International Conference on the Design of Communication, 6*, 1–7. https://doi.org/10.1145/3233756.3233960.

Agboka, G. Y. (2013). Participatory localization: A social justice approach to navigating unenfranchised/disenfranchised cultural sites. *Technical Communication Quarterly, 22*(1), 28–49. https://doi.org/10.1080/10572252.2013.730966.

Agboka, G. Y. & Matveeva, N. (2018). *Citizenship and Advocacy in Technical Communication: Scholarly and Pedagogical Perspectives*. Routledge.

Cabrero, D. G., Kapuire, G. K., Winschiers-Theophilus, H., Stanley, C. & Abdelnour-Nocera, J. (2016, April 13). A UX and Usability expression of Pastoral OvaHimba: Personas in the Making and Doing. *Proceedings of the 2nd International Conference in HCI and UX Indonesia 2016*, 89–92. https://doi.org/10.1145/2898459.2898473.

Camara, S. B., Oyugi, C., Abdelnour-Nocera, J. & Smith, A. (2010). Augmenting usability: Cultural elicitation in HCI. In D. Katre, R. Orngreen, P. Yammiyavar & T. Clemmensen (Eds.), *Human work interaction design: Usability in social, cultural and organizational contexts* (pp. 46–56). Springer. https://doi.org/10.1007/978-3-642-11762-6_4.

Chong, F. (2018). Implementing usability testing in introductory technical communication service courses: Results and lessons from a local study. *IEEE Transactions on Professional Communication, 61*(2), 196–205. https://doi.org/10.1109/TPC.2017.2771698.

Cleary, Y. & Flammia, M. (2012). Preparing technical communication students to function as user advocates in a self-service society. *Journal of Technical Writing and Communication, 42*(3), 305–322. https://doi.org/10.2190/TW.42.3.g.

Council of Writing Program Administrators. (2019, July 18). *WPA Outcomes Statement for First-Year Composition (3.0), Approved July 17, 2014*. https://wpacouncil.org/aws/CWPA/pt/sd/news_article/243055/_PARENT/layout_details/false.

Dura, L., Gonzáles, L. & Solis, G. (2019, October 4). Creating a bilingual, localized glossary for end-of-life-decision-making in borderland communities. SIGDOC '19: *Proceedings of the 37th ACM International Conference on the Design of Communication, 30*, 1–5. https://doi.org/10.1145/3328020.3353940.

Fiotakis, G., Raptis, D. & Avouris, N. (2009). Considering cost in usability evaluation of mobile applications: Who, where and when. In T. Gross, J. Gulliksen, P. Kotzé, L. Oestreicher, P. Palanque, R. O. Prates & M. Winckler (Eds.), *Human-Computer Interaction—INTERACT 2009* (pp. 231–234). Springer. https://doi.org/10.1007/978-3-642-03655-2_27.

Grabill, J. T. (2000). Shaping local HIV/AIDS services policy through activist research: The problem of client involvement. *Technical Communication Quarterly, 9*(1), 29–50. https://doi.org/10.1080/10572250009364684.

Grabill, J. T. (2003). Community computing and citizen productivity. *Computers and Composition, 20*(2), 131–150. https://doi.org/10.1016/S8755-4615(03)00015-X.

Grant, C. (2022). Collaborative tactics for equitable community partnerships toward social justice impact. *IEEE Transactions on Professional Communication, 65*(1), 151–163. https://doi.org/10.1109/TPC.2022.3141227.

Harihareswara, S. (2015). User experience is a social justice issue. *The Code4Lib Journal, 28*. https://journal.code4lib.org/articles/10482.

Hea, A. C. K. & Shah, R. W. (2016). Silent partners: Developing a critical understanding of community partners in technical communication service-learning pedagogies. *Technical Communication Quarterly, 25*(1), 48–66. https://doi.org/10.1080/10572252.2016.1113727.

Hennes, J., Wiley, K. & Anderson, J. B. (2016, September 23). The Trail Reporter mobile application: Methods for UX research and communication design as civic agency. SIGDOC '16: *Proceedings of the 34th ACM International Conference on the Design of Communication, 24*, 1–5. https://doi.org/10.1145/2987592.2987620.

Holl, K., Nass, C., Villela, K. & Vieira, V. (2016). Towards a lightweight approach for on-site interaction evaluation of safety-critical mobile systems. *Procedia Computer Science, 94*, 41–48. https://doi.org/10.1016/j.procs.2016.08.010.

Itchuaqiyaq, C. U. (2021). Iñupiat Iḷitqusiat: An indigenist ethics approach for working with marginalized knowledges in technical communication. In R. Walton & G. Y. Agboka (Eds.), *Equipping technical communicators for social justice work: Theories, meth-*

odologies, and pedagogies (n.p.). University Press of Colorado; Utah State University Press.

Johnson, R. R. (1998). *User-centered technology: A rhetorical theory for computers and other mundane artifacts*. State University of New York Press.

Kantner, L., Sova, D. H. & Rosenbaum, S. (2003, October 12). Alternative methods for field usability research. SIGDOC '03: *Proceedings of the 21st Annual International Conference on Documentation*, 68–72. https://doi.org/10.1145/944868.944883.

Kjeldskov, J. & Graham, C. (2003). A review of mobile HCI research methods. In L. Chittaro (Ed.), *Human-computer interaction with mobile devices and services* (pp. 317–335). Springer. https://doi.org/10.1007/978-3-540-45233-1_23.

Kjeldskov, J. & Skov, M. B. (2014, September 23). Was it worth the hassle? Ten years of mobile HCI research discussions on lab and field evaluations. MobileHCI '14: *Proceedings of the 16th International Conference on Human-Computer Interaction with Mobile Devices & Services*, 43–52. https://doi.org/10.1145/2628363.2628398.

Kjeldskov, J., Skov, M. B., Als, B. S. & Høegh, R. T. (2004). Is it worth the hassle? Exploring the added value of evaluating the usability of context-aware mobile systems in the field. In S. Brewster & M. Dunlop (Eds.), *Mobile Human-Computer Interaction—MobileHCI 2004* (pp. 61–73). Springer. https://doi.org/10.1007/978-3-540-28637-0_6.

Lazar, J. K. (2011). Using community-based service projects to enhance undergraduate HCI education: 10 years of experience. *CHI '11 Extended Abstracts on Human Factors in Computing Systems*, 581–588. https://doi.org/10.1145/1979742.1979653.

Lazar, J. K. & Lidtke, D. (2001). Service-learning partnerships in the information systems curriculum. In J. Lazar (Ed.), *Managing IT/Community Partnerships in the 21st Century* (pp. 1–16). IGI Global. https://doi.org/10.4018/978-1-930708-33-4.ch001.

Lopez Gil, J. M., Urretavizcaya Loinaz, M., Losada, B. & Fernandez Castro, I. (2016). Field vs. laboratory usability evaluations: A study on a context dependent mobile application developed with an agile methodology. *IEEE Latin America Transactions, 14*(1), 339–348. https://doi.org/10.1109/TLA.2016.7430099.

Mara, A. & Mara, M. (2015, July 16). Capturing social value in UX projects. SIGDOC '15: *Proceedings of the 33rd Annual International Conference on the Design of Communication, 23*, 1–6. https://doi.org/10.1145/2775441.2775479.

Mara, A. F., Potts, L. & Bartocci, G. (2013, September 30). The ethics of agile ethnography. SIGDOC '13: *Proceedings of the 31st ACM International Conference on Design of Communication*, 101–106. https://doi.org/10.1145/2507065.2507080.

Rose, E. J., Racadio, R., Wong, K., Nguyen, S., Kim, J. & Zahler, A. (2017). Community-based user experience: Evaluating the usability of health insurance information with immigrant patients. *IEEE Transactions on Professional Communication, 60*(2), 214–231. https://doi.org/10.1109/TPC.2017.2656698.

Rose, E. J. & Walton, R. (2015, July 16). Factors to actors: Implications of posthumanism for social justice work. SIGDOC '15: *Proceedings of the 33rd Annual International Conference on the Design of Communication, 33*, 1–10. https://doi.org/10.1145/2775441.2775464.

Salvo, M. J. (2001). Ethics of engagement: User-centered design and rhetorical methodology. *Technical Communication Quarterly, 10*(3), 273–290. https://doi.org/10.1207/s15427625tcq1003_3.

Salvo, M. J. (2004). Rhetorical action in professional space: Information architecture as critical practice. *Journal of Business and Technical Communication, 18*(1), 39–66. https://doi.org/10.1177/1050651903258129.

Schell, D. A. (1986). Testing online and print user documentation. *IEEE Transactions on Professional Communication, PC–29*(4), 87–92. https://doi.org/10.1109/TPC.1986.6448996.

Scott, J. B. (2008). The practice of usability: Teaching user engagement through service-learning. *Technical Communication Quarterly, 17*(4), 381–412. https://doi.org/10.1080/10572250802324929.

Shah, R. W. (2020). *Rewriting partnerships: Community perspectives on community-based learning*. University Press of Colorado; Utah State University Press.

Shivers-McNair, A., Gonzáles, L. & Zhyvotovska, T. (2019). An intersectional technofeminist framework for community-driven technology innovation. *Computers and Composition, 51*, 43–54. https://doi.org/10.1016/j.compcom.2018.11.005.

Shivers-McNair, A., Phillips, J., Campbell, A., Mai, H. H., Yan, A., Macy, J. F., Wenlock, J., Fry, S. & Guan, Y. (2018). User-centered design in and beyond the classroom: Toward an accountable practice. *Computers and Composition, 49*, 36–47. https://doi.org/10.1016/j.compcom.2018.05.003.

Shivers-McNair, A. & San Diego, C. (2017). Localizing communities, goals, communication, and inclusion: A collaborative approach. *Technical Communication, 64*(2), 97–112.

Spinuzzi, C. (2005a). Lost in the translation: Shifting claims in the migration of a research technique. *Technical Communication Quarterly, 14*(4), 411–446. https://doi.org/10.1207/s15427625tcq1404_3.

Spinuzzi, C. (2005b). The methodology of participatory design. *Technical Communication, 52*(2), 163–174.

Sun, H. (2006). The triumph of users: Achieving cultural usability goals with user localization. *Technical Communication Quarterly, 15*(4), 457–481. https://doi.org/10.1207/s15427625tcq1504_3.

Swacha, K. Y. (2018). "Bridging the gap between food pantries and the kitchen table": Teaching embodied literacy in the technical communication classroom. *Technical Communication Quarterly, 27*(3), 261–282. https://doi.org/10.1080/10572252.2018.1476589.

Swacha, K. Y. & St.Amant, K. (2021). Lego™ learning: A scalable approach to pedagogy in the rhetoric of health and medicine. *Rhetoric of Health & Medicine, 4*(4), 446–474. https://doi.org/10.5744/rhm.4003.

Wale-Kolade, A. & Nielsen, P. A. (2016). Apathy towards the integration of usability work: A case of system justification. *Interacting with Computers, 28*(4), 437–450. https://doi.org/10.1093/iwc/iwv016.

Walls, D. M. (2016, September 23). User experience in social justice contexts. *SIGDOC '16: Proceedings of the 34th ACM International Conference on the Design of Communication, 9*, 1–6. https://doi.org/10.1145/2987592.2987604.

Walton, R., Moore, K. & Jones, N. (2019). *Technical communication after the social justice turn: Building coalitions for action* (1st ed.). Routledge.

6. Designing Virtual Reality User Experiences for a Nonprofit Organization: Perspectives from Engineering Graduate Students and Community Partners

Missie Smith
AUBURN UNIVERSITY

Felicia Chong
UNAFFILIATED

Abstract. In this exploratory qualitative study, a new graduate-level engineering course focusing on the intersection of virtual reality and augmented reality (VR/AR), user experience (UX), and social justice partnered with a local nonprofit organization to design a VR experience for middle school students. The purpose of our study was to better understand how the community partner and graduate students define and perceive success, what obstacles they think they experience, and what characteristics of the community partner they think would be ideal for such a VR/AR course, which is a highly technical domain for UX application. By analyzing students' reflections and interviews, coupled with the community partner interview, we found that even though most of the participants considered the project to be successful, their definitions and perceptions of success in collaboration varied and were closely associated with mutual positive engagement instead of the deliverable. Both the students' and community partner's personalities and attitudes, and even the instructor's, impacted their collaborative experience, which include qualities such as flexibility, open communication, maturity, and easygoingness. Although students described obstacles such as the lack of technical expertise, infrequent communication, and insufficient feedback, they also recognized the flexibility, creativity, and leadership that were necessary to successfully complete the project. We recommend clearly defining the expectations of the collaborative process by discussing the technical needs, assisting students in identifying potential approaches, and emphasizing the importance of establishing a relationship and communication channel with the community partner early on and throughout the project.

Recently, virtual reality and augmented reality (VR/AR) technology and user experience (UX) have been increasingly explored in writing and technical communication studies (Jones & Gouge, 2017; Tham, 2017; Tham et al., 2018). For example, VR/AR has been used for purposes such as audience analysis, multimodality, and peer review (Duin et al., 2016). In engineering, 3D VR/AR laboratories are frequently used to help students conduct complex analyses that may otherwise be cost-prohibitive (Vergara et al., 2017). Likewise, in the last decade, there has been a strong emphasis on promoting social justice in both technical communication (Agboka, 2014; Colton & Holmes, 2018; Jones, 2016, 2017; Walton et al., 2019) and engineering (Baillie et al., 2014; Leydens & Lucena, 2018; Lucena, 2013; Queiruga-Dios et al., 2021).

While promising, VR/AR presents unique challenges due to the advanced technical nature of the technology and its relative novelty. In addition, applying VR/AR technology when collaborating with external organizations, particularly nonprofit organizations involved with social justice issues, can present unforeseen challenges. Therefore, we must delve further into collaborator interactions to develop a better understanding of the impact of highly technical UX collaborations on both students and community partners, particularly at the graduate level.

In this case study, we analyze the collaboration between a graduate-level UX engineering course on VR/AR at a regional Midwestern university and a local nonprofit organization that serves underprivileged middle school students. Since this edited collection is centered on the idea that "for collaborations to work, all partners must buy in and experience benefits" (Introduction, p. 20), we focused our study on the perspectives of those engaged in collaboration, which in our case, included the graduate students and the community partner. The following questions guided our inquiry:

- How do students and the community partner perceive successful or unsuccessful collaborations? How do their perceptions impact their experience?
- What community partner characteristics affect the perceived impact of collaborations with graduate students in VR/AR courses?
- What obstacles stand in the way of productive UX on VR/AR partnerships? How can we work to overcome these obstacles?

Literature Review

For the last two decades, service-learning pedagogy has been widely advocated by educators in both technical communication (Bowdon & Scott, 2003; Cargile Cook, 2014; Sapp & Crabtree, 2002) and engineering (Bielefeldt et al., 2010; Litchfield et al., 2016) for improving students' professional skills. There are various models for incorporating service learning: for example, students can collaborate with a nonprofit community partner individually for an internship or a capstone project, or they can collaborate collectively with other students on a class-based or client-based project. In this section, we provide an overview of existing scholarship on measurement of project impact, characteristics of community partner, and obstacles and solutions in collaborations.

Measurement of Project Impact

There are three main ways to measure the effectiveness or impact of a service-learning project in the classroom: through examining student experience, quality of the deliverable, or community partner experience.

Focus on Students

Although there is a plethora of research addressing benefits and challenges of collaborating with nonprofit community partners for class-based projects, little scholarship in technical communication or engineering addresses both students' and community partner's perceptions on project impact. For example, in technical communication research, methods such as interviews, reflections, response papers, and quantitative and/or qualitative surveys (Bourelle, 2014; Matthews & Zimmerman, 1999; Sapp & Crabtree, 2002; Scott, 2008; Soria & Weiner, 2013; Walsh, 2010) are commonly used to assess student collaborative experience. Similarly, in engineering case studies that focus on a class-based service-learning project, researchers mostly measure student learning outcomes using surveys (Brown & Chao, 2010; Queiruga-Dios et al., 2021, Riley & Bloomgarden, 2006; Tiryakioğlu et al, 2009) and minimally address the community partner's perspective on the collaboration. Furthermore, most service-learning case studies tend to focus on undergraduate student experiences. As Richard Reddick and colleagues (2018) aptly pointed out, there is a lack of scholarship on the impact and effect of civic engagement on engineering graduate students. In fact, their study findings reveal that "engineering graduate students are not only motivated to serve in different community engagement capacities, but, moreover, find meaning in their service" (2018, p. 147).

Focus on the Deliverable

While success in collaboration can be measured using the quality of the deliverable that students produced for the community partner (e.g., Brown & Chao, 2010), Amy Kimme Hea and Rachel Wendler Shah (2016) warned that the deliverable is often used by "teachers and academics [to argue] for the value of and need for service-learning projects in technical communication" (p. 50). This is also in line with Juliette Butcher and Paul Jeffrey's (2007) argument that measuring success in collaboration using a tangible product "can generate an incomplete picture of achievement and fail to capture many (experiential) outcomes which may influence future collaboration intents or behaviour" (p. 1240).

Focus on Community Partners

Kimme Hea and Wendler Shah (2016) argued that in addition to having the instructor and student perspectives, it is crucial to hear from those "silent partners" who collaborated with students in our projects; therefore, they interviewed community partners who were involved in various sections of a professional writing course. While Lynda Walsh's (2010) research collected data from both the community partners and students who collaborated on the same projects, her end-of-semester community partner survey focused on the deliverable that students produced, and the community partners' experience on the collaboration process was largely based on her own observations.

Characteristics of Community Partner

Based on his experience as a technical communication instructor and service-learning program coordinator, Robert McEachern (2001) listed common characteristics of nonprofit organizations for instructors to consider, which include "passion for mission" (p. 216), "atmosphere of scarcity," and "individuals [having] mixed skill levels" (p. 218). Kimme Hea and Wendler Shah (2016) were concerned that some of the field's existing views on community partners (such as the ones laid out by McEachern above) can be "hyperpragmatic" in that "we run the risk of constructing partners reductively as 'others;'" (p. 50) by (over)focusing on the efficiency of collaboration logistics and the quality of the deliverables. To create successful service-learning collaborations, they listed four productive tensions that they argued need to be negotiated:

> These tensions include four main paradoxes: receiving resources requires giving resources, community partners are both teachers and clients, partnerships must involve clear plans but flexibility, and meeting community partner interests requires meeting student interests. (2016, p. 54)

There are also other technical communication studies that focus on the logistics and expectations of the community partners. For example, J. Blake Scott (2008) recommended that instructors establish long-term partnerships with organizations that can then serve as community partners, while others recommend letting students identify and locate service opportunities that align with their interests/values (Henson & Sutliff, 1998; Huckin, 1997; Matthews & Zimmerman, 1999; Nielsen, 2016). In Rebecca Walton's (2007) interview study of executive directors and volunteers from nonprofit organizations as potential service-learning partners for technical communication courses, she called for instructors to clearly establish each stakeholder's role and expectations, as well as discussing and articulating the criteria and definition of a successful project with both the students and with the nonprofit organization. With the advent of online technical communication classes, instructors are encouraged to collaborate with community partners who are responsive, especially where students want more interactions with the client (Bourelle, 2014).

Obstacles and Solutions in Collaborations

Not surprisingly, the bulk of technical communication and engineering literature on service learning has focused on positive student outcomes or success stories. For example, in technical communication, only a few studies explicitly mention obstacles found in collaborations, such as the community partner's lack of communication or guidance on the project (Bourelle, 2014; McEachern, 2001; Walsh, 2010), locating appropriate service opportunities (Nielsen, 2016), or students seeing service learning as charity, struggling with their roles in an unclear non-academic setting, and experiencing conflict as a team (Matthews & Zimmerman, 1999). Similarly, in engineering courses that integrated service learning, students can struggle with being inclusive in an interdisciplinary team (Brown & Chao, 2010) or being proactive in connecting with the community partner (Tiryakioğlu et al., 2009).

In one of the few engineering case studies that describe obstacles in detail, Donna Riley and Alan Bloomgarden (2006) listed multiple challenges that students in an undergraduate engineering and global development course faced when collaborating with a local bakery to identify pollution issues. First, students were asked to explore engineering technical pieces as needed instead of given a structured problem to solve, so students needed more context for understanding this framework and leading the project. Second, communication broke down between students and the community partner because students were not actively consulting with them. Third, students were seen as experts, which the researchers felt "implicitly devalues the knowledge and expertise held by community members" (Riley & Bloomgarden, 2006, p. 57). Fourth, due to the time constraints of an academic semester, where students had to acquire engineering knowledge and principles on the subject matter before solving the problem for the community partner, they were unable to quickly provide solutions.

Certainly, there is already a large body of literature that identifies best practices in university-industry research collaborations that can be applied to service learning projects, such as mutual trust and good relationship; good project management; mutual understanding and appreciation of motivation, interests and needs; clearly specified objectives and expectations; frequent, clear and open communication and feedback; commitment and continuity of both partners; close alignment of expertise and interests of collaborating parties; and, agreements on project roles and responsibilities (as cited by Butcher & Jeffrey, 2007, p. 1242).

However, Butcher and Jeffrey's (2007) examination of doctoral students' perceptions of success in collaborations with external organizations found that "perceived success is correlated not with factors which describe the formal structure of collaboration, but with factors that portray the experience of working together" (p. 1248). Similarly, H. J. Littlecott and colleagues (2017) surveyed and interviewed academics and practitioners who collaborated on the same project to determine their perceptions of success, and the researchers found that even though both stakeholders considered their project to be successful, where they based their positive views of success differed (e.g., deliverable/product versus process).

Below, we describe a case study in which we explore the complex dynamics when graduate students collaborate with external community partners. We start by describing the course design in detail, followed by the data collection methods and summary of findings. Finally, we discuss the case study in the context of relevant literature.

Course Design

Oakland University's (OU) ISE 5900/SYS 5900 Virtual and Augmented Reality course was designed by Smith in 2019 to help students develop technical VR/AR skills and learn UX methods, which they would apply when collaborating with organizations working on social justice initiatives in the Detroit metropolitan area. However, students could not choose the course based on the service-learning component, which was not listed in the course title or description and was first discussed in the introductory class. The instructor (Smith) had complete academic freedom and no constraints for content or partnerships. In addition to having lectures introducing theory, students participated in practicums where they could apply different UX methods found in *Universal Methods of Design*. For the purposes of the course, UX encompasses all aspects of the user interaction with the VR/AR system, and was addressed throughout the project lifecycle through discussions and feedback. Finally, students completed two projects in which they developed virtual or augmented reality applications, with the first being individually developed and the second being a collaboration with fellow classmates and a community partner. The 15-week course was developed with fully face-to-face (F2F) interaction in mind; however, due to the impact of COVID-19, we transitioned the course to fully online between weeks 9 and 10.

Reflection Assignments

Throughout the semester, students completed written reflection assignments. Reflections 1, 4, 5, and 6 focused on students' experiences in the class, with VR/AR technology, and with the community partner. Reflections 2, 3, and 7 connected students' projects back to course content including a subset of UX methods (specifically, design charettes and formal/informal interviewing) and VR/AR theory (presence, immersion, and fidelity) and encouraged deeper thinking about the material in the context of their work.

Projects

Students' course assignments included two hands-on projects (individual project and collaborative project, described below) where they developed a program in VR or AR. For each project, students developed an outline or storyboard to articulate the planned user experience, content, and interactions when using the VR/AR system. In addition to technical course requirements (deploy projects in Unity), students were required to write in reflection assignments and project summary documents about how each project addressed social justice issues described in the United Nations (UN) list of sustainable development goals (United Nations, 2024). Using Unity Software, students developed a virtual environment and placed digital objects in the environment that users could manipulate using student-defined interactions. Each project had to include a minimum of five different virtual objects and interactions. The individual project included only technical development within Unity, while the group project also included working with an external stakeholder to design a VR or AR system based on the needs of that partner. Thus, the students incorporated theory and practically applied UX methods from class to the group project. The course projects were based on similar assignments from the VR for the Social Good Initiative at the University of Florida (http://www.vrforthesocialgood.com/) and La Trobe University's CSE4AT3 Advanced Topics in Computer Science (Virtual Reality) taught by Dr. Richard Skarbez (https://www.richardskarbez.com/).

Individual Project

For the individual project, students were required to identify a social justice issue that could be, at least in part, solved by the use of VR/AR. They then designed and developed a short VR/AR activity that would address this issue by leveraging the inherent capabilities of VR/AR to make the user experience engaging. This project focused on building students' individual technical skills needed to develop applications in VR/AR with a compressed timeline (three weeks). For example, one student developed a VR game to encourage recycling by teaching users how to sort trash and recycling. When users sorted materials by placing them in the correct bins, they received visual feedback that they did the task correctly (i.e., their hands stayed "human"). When they did it incorrectly, for example, by throwing away a recyclable item, users' hands would incrementally turn into zombie arms.

Collaborative Project

After completing the individual project, students formed groups for their longer (10-week) collaborative project. The purpose of this project was to continue applying technical skills developed in the individual project while also incorporating collaborations with team members and the community partner. Because this graduate course was small (five students), the students chose to work as a single group. In line with recommendations from researchers such as Danielle Nielsen (2016), students were encouraged to identify potential community partners for the project who aligned with their interests and values. To ensure that at least one potential partnership was identified, the course instructor also sought out partners in the local area. The criteria for these partnerships were that they were nonprofit organizations focusing on social justice issues and were willing to partner with students on a project using VR/AR technology. To ensure the community partner's flexibility, the course instructor clearly explained that this was a pilot course that may not result in a viable VR/AR product. While students were given about three weeks to identify partners, none of the students brought recommendations, and therefore only the two potential partners identified by the course instructor were discussed by the class. The students then met as a team and selected the community partner that they felt would be the best fit for their group and this course.

After that, students worked together, along with feedback from the community partner, to design and develop a VR/AR project that could help the partner in some way. To ensure accountability and feedback, every few weeks, students had in-class discussions and completed a "Sprint Review" (in Weeks 6, 10, and 13) by showcasing completed work to gather feedback from the course instructor and, when possible, the community partner. The initial course plan included 10 weeks in which students could meet with the community partner to collect data, refine ideas, and implement changes using skills and methods learned in the class. However, due to COVID-19, students were only able to meet in person for the first five weeks of the project timeline (Weeks 4–9).

Community Partner

Based on the criteria and timeline above, the students selected the Michigan Youth Project (MYP) as their partner for the course project because of the focus on the UN's Sustainable Development Goal #4: *Quality Education*. They were given contact information and encouraged to reach out to MYP to better understand how they could apply their technical skills for the benefit of MYP. Based in Pontiac, Michigan, MYP was founded by Maggie Razdar in 2019 (Michigan Youth Project, 2019). Pontiac is located near Detroit, which is often known for its high unemployment and crime rates (Stebbins & Guneson, 2019). Similar to Detroit's history, Pontiac was once a thriving community due to the automotive industry, but it has recently been struggling with declining population, infrastructure, and educational resources, along with high violent crime rates (Mack, 2019; Wingblad, 2018). After volunteering in school systems in and around Pontiac, Maggie saw the lack of resources available to students and wanted to ensure a better education. Her goal is building students into independent learners by helping them improve reading, writing, and communicating skills through research. During MYP's first year, Maggie worked with 5th grade students in the Pontiac school system, across several elementary schools. The following year, she continued working with eight of those same students, now 6th grade Pontiac middle school students. Throughout the academic school year, students who participate in MYP complete a project examining the past, present, and future of their home city, and in this case, Pontiac, Michigan. The MYP participants' project would ultimately be presented to an audience of interested parties including their parents and community members. At the beginning of the partnership, MYP participants had just completed their projects about the past of Pontiac and were beginning to research the present and future.

The main social justice goal of the partnership was for OU students to introduce K–12 students in the local community to cutting edge technology like VR/AR, and to increase MYP participants' exposure to higher education. Through the process of co-developing a VR/AR project with OU students, the MYP participants would also see their ideas taken seriously and implemented into a project that could be shared with family or friends outside of MYP.

Project Outcomes

For this collaborative project, students were encouraged to own their learning by approaching or designing the project and applying their skills and new UX knowledge as they see fit. Students focused their design and development efforts highlighting research about the past of Pontiac from each MYP participant. Students developed a VR application for their project, also referred to as the VR "environment" or "world." The final project outcome was a VR environment with an interactive map of Pontiac including scenes highlighting six different MYP participant projects. OU students initially met with the MYP participants to learn about their projects and co-develop ideas. After initial meetings, students developed scenes based on MYP participant work, which focused on different elements of Pontiac history including music and arts, the General Motors plant, Woodward Avenue, Dr. Death (Jack Kevorkian), the asylum, and Chief Pontiac. Each scene included objects that could be selected to learn more details. After developing early project prototypes, OU students conducted informal interviews and usability assessments with MYP participants to determine how to improve the VR interactions in future iterations. Students completed as many changes as they could but COVID-19 interrupted course plans and limited access to lab computers. Therefore, to ensure that the MYP participants got some closure for the semester, the final project also included a video that could be shared with MYP participants showing the VR environment and available interactions, along with a description of the reasoning behind design choices and, finally, statements from each of the Oakland students about the overall experience and what they hoped the MYP participants could gain from it.

Technical Resources

As can be expected, a course aimed at developing VR/AR experiences requires a variety of technical resources. Each project required using free Unity software to develop a three-dimensional VR/AR project by using Unity's graphical user interface along with C# programming. While the software could be downloaded and used on students' personal computers, rendering graphics in 3D can be computationally expensive and may exceed system capabilities of some personal computers. Therefore, the course also included unlimited access to computers in the Human-Centered Engineering Lab on the OU campus to ensure student success. After developing a project in Unity, students could deploy or implement their projects on a variety of VR/AR hardware available as a part of the course including the Microsoft HoloLens (AR), Epson Moverio BT-350 (AR), and Oculus Rift (VR). Projects could be deployed directly onto the HoloLens, which essentially has its own internal computer, and graphics could be played on the Moverio through YouTube videos. On the other hand, the Oculus requires a relatively powerful computer and a high-quality graphics card (NVIDIA GT 960 4GB/AMD Radeon R9 290 or better) to process the graphics in real-time. None of the students in this class owned a personal computer capable of processing Oculus programs and therefore any Oculus programs had to be displayed in the lab.

■ Methods

After receiving Institutional Review Board approval (Oakland University #1544716), the instructor informed all students in this course about the option to participate in a research study. Early in the semester, Chong, who served as the external researcher and co-principal investigator for this project, visited class to explain the consent and research process and to collect consent forms. Throughout the semester, Chong kept track of students who participated in this study, and Smith did not know which students participated until after final grades for the semester were posted. Likewise, Chong interviewed students one-on-one after the semester, which enabled students to openly describe their experience without the presence of their instructor, who only listened to the interview recordings after the semester ended.

Table 6.1. Participant Overview

Student Name (Pseudonym)	Degree Seeking	Background	Gender	Employment	Previous Unity Experience
Anna	M.S.	Computer Science	Female	Full-time	Yes
Milo	M.S.	Engineering	Male	Full-time	No
Charles	M.S.	Design	Male	Full-time	No
Joe	PhD	Engineering	Male	Full-time	No
Thomas	PhD	Engineering	Male	Full-time	No

In order to participate, students needed to sign an informed consent document, but all analyzable materials were part of the course content, and no additional work was required. The purpose of this design was to minimize the impact to students and to maximize participation in the study. All five students enrolled in the course elected to participate in the research study, and their demographics can be seen in Table 6.1.

▪ Data Collection

The student materials that were analyzed include written reflections, completed projects, and an end-of-the-semester one-on-one online interview with Chong. The semi-structured interview allowed us to probe deeper into and seek clarifications on student responses and experiences without instructor presence. In addition to having student feedback, both of us solicited feedback from our community partner, MYP, by asking Maggie about her experience working with the graduate students, challenges faced, and recommendations for future collaboration, through an online interview at the end of the semester. All interviews were audio recorded and transcribed verbatim.

Data Analysis

Since this graduate course was offered by the instructor for the first time as an experiential pilot study, one of our goals was to gain insights into students' and community partner's experiences in terms of their collaborations that could improve future course offerings. Therefore, we used a qualitative research framework based on the grounded approach (Glaser & Strauss, 1967). This method allowed us to inductively analyze our data and identify themes that emerged.

Drawing from Meghan Barnes and Kathryn Caprino's (2016) method of analyzing service-learning reflections, we "searched for themes across the stories participants shared through written reflections and identified major themes and categories" (p. 564). Both of us acted as the analysts, where we individually read participants' reflections and listened to interview recordings to identify potential themes. Then, we discussed the themes we found based on our research questions and triangulated the data by corroborating our findings from multiple data sources (reflections collected throughout the semester and interviews) to ensure the quality and validity of our analysis.

Limitations

It is important to note that our study was based on entirely self-reported data and therefore limited to what the participants perceived. However, this perception is exceedingly important and merits further study. In addition, due to the disruptions caused by COVID-19, we were neither able to conduct user testing that was necessary with the MYP participants nor interview them directly on their collaboration experience. We believe that their opinion should be considered in future work; however, this would require parental consent, which may be a challenge working with minors in UX work.

Findings

Community Partner Perspective

We were interested in examining specific needs from the community partner when collaborating with graduate students in particular. Therefore, we asked Maggie about her experience, expectations, view on success in collaboration, and recommendations.

Previous Experience and Expectations

In terms of previous collaborations with other partners through MYP, Maggie found that the main challenge with some partners is that "they get their ego involved ... want to have their name tag on everything." Therefore, she recommended collaborating with organizations who share the same vision or goal. She believed that "educators are easier to collaborate with because they share similar goals."

While Maggie considered educators to be good collaborators, she also pointed out that even within university collaborations there can be significant differences in the partnership. She has now worked with undergraduate students and graduate students at OU in various capacities. Some students do not work directly with the MYP participants and instead work only with Maggie on the organization's websites and social media. Students from another class visit weekly to help MYP participants with their research, documentation, and communication, and Maggie found this to be helpful for the MYP participants because "seeing someone from university coming and helping them, they felt important because a lot of people don't give them credit and they feel like they have a voice."

While Maggie described positive aspects about all three types of service-learning approaches mentioned above, she made clear distinctions between collaborating with the graduate versus undergraduate students. Maggie does not have technical expertise in the VR/AR area; therefore, at first, she "had no idea" what the graduate students were doing for the project. Since the MYP participants who served as primary users had never experienced VR/AR technology prior to this project either, she had hesitations about the age difference between MYP participants and graduate students.

But after the project, Maggie was impressed that the graduate students "went to [the MYP participants'] level to collaborate with the kids." In her experience, undergraduate students were often "very timid with these kids," potentially because they are "afraid of Pontiac kids." She believed that when undergraduate students behave this way, it makes the MYP participants "even more uncomfortable" because "they just want to be kids." Conversely, she considered the graduate students' interactions with the MYP participants to be "perfect" and "comfortable" possibly due to the graduate students being "more educated" or "older." Therefore, she speculated that that was why MYP participants were actively asking questions and being more engaged, and she considered this project to go above her expectation because "it is something that the kids are asking for again. With other programs, they never asked for them again. So that just tells me that . . . something impacted [these kids]."

Maggie thought the partnership had "been a great experience" for the MYP participants because it exposed them to new technology. Maggie believed that MYP participants realized that technology they may have previously viewed just as "fun" could also be used to learn and could even potentially turn into a career path: "They were talking about 'Wow, you could actually create games. You could actually go to college to do that instead of just playing.' So, their vision became broader. It helped them to see it differently now."

Success in Collaboration

When defining successful collaborations, Maggie listed four reasons why she considered this collaboration to be successful:

1. Having a common goal and honest communication to achieve that goal. She defined a successful collaboration as:
    > Collaboration is [being] able to work together and going back and forth and communicating openly, coming up with conclusions or coming up with ideas [that are] going to work, and analyzing and really being open about it . . . with collaboration you have a purpose of working on one thing and you want to see how are we benefiting from it.
2. The instructor's open-mindedness, open communication, and flexibility. She thought that the instructor was "easygoing," "communicated well," and she appreciated the fact that the instructor was willing to "take a chance on this project."
3. Engagement and interest from the MYP participants. Maggie saw how MYP participants benefited from an engineering project that was "interactive" and "practical" because they typically do not like to just "sit and research." This is why "the kids [are] asking for it again."
4. Engagement and interest from the graduate students. She described them as "easygoing" and "respected the kids." The MYP participants felt "included" and that they were "part of the group."

Recommendations

When asked what we could do to improve this collaboration in the future, Maggie said that she "can't think of anything." However, she did wish they "had more time to even see more [of the VR projects]," and recommended introducing more collaborations and expanding the content to other domains.

Student Perspective

We were interested in examining graduate students' perspectives when collaborating with the community partner. Therefore, we asked students about what their expectations were, how they viewed their interactions with the community partner, what went well, and what they needed (but perhaps did not receive) in their interactions with stakeholders.

Previous Experience and Expectations for the Course

At the beginning of the semester, students were asked what expectations they have for the course (Reflection 1, Week 1). Out of the five students, only one (Anna) had prior experience using the Unity software; the other four students took the class primarily because they were interested in acquiring and enhancing skills and knowledge on VR/AR, with some expecting that the project would benefit their jobs (e.g., by collaborating with software developers more effectively or creating VR/AR projects that are resume-worthy).

Technical Expertise of Community Partner (Challenges and Benefits)

Students addressed the importance of understanding community partners' level of technical expertise for VR/AR in establishing expectations for the partnership. In their interviews, three students pointed out that the community partner's lack of knowledge about VR/AR resulted in minimal structure or stakeholder needs, which made the project challenging in different ways, for example:

- Charles had never worked with a nonprofit organization before and felt that he needed more information (e.g., scope and expectations) to move forward.
- Anna added that the lack of input required her team to "make a quick on-the-spot decision regarding scope and plan" and "just had to create it."
- Milo found it challenging to accommodate unrealistic expectations, for example, MYP participants wanted to have games incorporated into the scenes without realizing the amount of time and effort it would take.

Although Maggie and the MYP participants did not provide any technical requirements for the project, students also described the benefits of being able to lead the project:

- Milo, who is used to being "drilled" with technical questions at his engineering job, found that this collaboration was "not even stressful."

Instead, he was able to share in the excitement of "exposing kids to new technologies and trying to inspire them and . . . giving them new experiences and provoking their curiosity."
- Anna felt that the VR experience they designed "isn't being overshadowed by expectations an experienced user may have."
- Thomas added that "most of [the] times, you don't get all the information in [the] real world. You don't get exactly what you want. But here in this case, we got everything that we needed from them."

Communication with Community Partner (Quality and Frequency)

Students repeatedly mentioned the significance of working face-to-face with Maggie and the MYP participants by explicitly stating that they would have preferred increased interaction with the MYP participants to get more feedback or more substantial feedback. At the beginning of the project, students were able to meet with the MYP participants to watch them use the Oculus with an early project prototype. Even then, several students noted the difficulty of getting useful input from the MYP participants:

- Milo stated that the MYP participants "were unsure of how to give feedback," probably because "we were asking a lot from them for just being exposed to the technology."
- Joe found that watching students wearing the Oculus and reacting to the scenes, for example, saying, "no, that is not what I was expecting" was more helpful feedback than saying "you have done a really good job."
- Anna said the MYP participants "didn't really have a lot of input to give us on what they wanted this to be so we just had to create it . . . No input is kind of the same as giving us input in this case." She also found that the meetings were "chaotic" and "all a bit hectic" because they lacked structure.

As graduate engineering students, they were intentionally given the freedom to communicate with the community partner to gather the user feedback that they needed. Without specific directions on establishing a communication structure provided by the instructor, students had to be proactive in applying the data-gathering methods they learned in class. Watching the MYP participants interact in the environment in real-time allowed students to identify problems or challenges with the technical design, even though the client or users could not always articulate specific needs or requests. Therefore, Thomas wished that as a team, they could collect data via "questionnaires or feedback sessions." Likewise, Milo felt that more data collection using a survey was needed to measure the effectiveness of the VR environment they created, and that they "missed out on valuable data."

Students agreed that more frequent meetings with MYP participants would be helpful to gather useful information; however, they offered different suggestions about how much interaction would be sufficient for this project. Students recommended daily (Charles), biweekly (Anna), weekly (Milo, Thomas), or monthly (Joe) meetings with the community partner. Students were originally scheduled to meet with MYP five times throughout the semester, but two meetings were canceled due to COVID-19. In fact, COVID-19 was considered by the students as the primary reason for not getting enough feedback due to both canceled in-person meetings and closed buildings.

Although students acknowledged the importance of frequent meetings, none of them requested or pursued additional meetings besides those set up by the instructor (before COVID-19) even when they were given the contact information and were encouraged to do so. Milo was the only student who acknowledged that the team could have been more "proactive" to reach out to the community partner through email, but he realized that "it really wasn't Miss Maggie we were trying to talk to; we wanted to talk to the students."

Time Commitment

All students in this graduate-level class were working full time and taking full-time classes, not to mention that some have families. Although all students wanted more feedback and more interactions with the MYP participants, two also recognized that they had limited time. Anna said, "there was rarely a time when we were all available," while Charles pointed out that "everyone is learning [Unity by] themselves and everyone has their full-time job while having this class."

Even with their busy schedules, Joe thought that while it was "difficult" to work on the weekdays, they were able to find hours to work the project during weekends before COVID-19, and that he actually enjoyed the process because "we used to drink, eat, and do our work" together in the lab and "it was real entertainment for us." Additionally, students' commitment to the project and community partner was evident. For example, Milo stated that his team would still be "willing to meet up with the students even after the end of the course to talk to them and present our project."

Definition of Success in Collaboration

At the beginning of the semester (Reflection 1, Week 2), students were asked "How would you define success in collaborations?" Four students mentioned goals or tasks being accomplished, three students mentioned satisfaction, and only one student mentioned effective communication as elements of a successful collaboration. Similarly, in Reflection 6 and during the one-on-one interviews, students were asked, "How did your collaboration work out? Would you consider it to be successful? Why or why not?" Four out of five students considered the collaboration to be a success. The common themes were goals were met with a deliverable for and satisfaction from the community partner, as seen in their responses in Table 6.2.

Table 6.2. Students' Definitions of "Success in Collaboration" Pre-collaborative and Post-collaborative Project

Student	Pre-collaborative project	Post-collaborative project
Anna	Any success in collaborations would be defined as completing the task at hand so that all parties are satisfied and, ideally, would seek this type of collaboration again.	Our collaboration with MYP worked out wonderfully... We took their goal of education, used the resource of the research they have done, added the VR element, and came up with something I'm proud of. Definitely a success. Lots of "oohs and ahs" from the kids. I think everyone is happy with the results as far as I know.
Milo	Success, to me, in collaborations is when everyone has something to bring to the table and work toward a common goal.	It would be considered a success because by the end of the project we will have achieved the goals we began with: communicating our message and having a deliverable for the students to see.
Charles	The success in collaborations is that every collaborator achieves one or a few of the objectives with an investment lower than doing it alone.	A successful project is result-oriented. The collaboration worked out partially and got interrupted by the coronavirus outbreak. Although the students got so excited about our work, I would not consider it to be successful because [of] the lack of opportunities for them to experience the experience we created.
Joe	Team collaboration is very important when the goal to achieve is [the] same. People having knowledge and experience in the same domain can have effective communication to achieve excellent results.	Our team collaboration with Michigan Youth project worked really well, we collected data and feedback from the students and worked on different scenes. So, when the, like as a developer, we know what our end customer needs, then it's really easy to work on and produce something, right? What they can use.
Thomas	I think I am successful... [when collaborations are conducted in a] successful manner without any dissatisfaction from any group of people.	[The] project was shaped up very decently based on their feedback toward the experience. So, it's kind of a good collaboration. I felt and they were very supportive in the process of this project.

Multiple Project Impact

Although we did not explicitly ask students to describe their relationships with Maggie and/or the MYP participants, they all conveyed the positive impact they perceived the project had on both the community partner and on themselves, as evidenced by the statements that follow:

- Anna: "I feel that the partner we are working with for this project is, perhaps, much more rewarding and less challenging than most other partners we could have worked with . . . Even an 'I want to be an engineer.' was heard. New experiences were definitely given."
- Milo: "Ultimately, working with the students and Mrs. Maggie was a fun and rewarding experience. I like to think we made a positive impact on their lives and have encouraged them to want to dream big."
- Charles: "Our relationship with the community partner was a fun and joyful relationship in my opinion . . . It was admirable to me to know that there are people that truly want to make a difference in people's lives. Working with the students was also an awesome experience. I enjoyed seeing the students and hanging out with them."
- Joe: "I think we are really lucky to work with those kids . . . This project will definitely impact the students in a positive way to imagine their ideas and work with more innovative thoughts . . . But, overall experience of working with the community partner and my dedication to the project was really good. I have learnt so many new technical things in this project."
- Thomas: "It was a great experience for me when I met those kids at the Pontiac schools . . . and the stories that I heard from them and the approach they [had] towards their community. That felt like a great connection between the groups we have and those kids and the response we got from them and what they wanted to do."

Discussion

In the previous sections, we have described the course design, data collection methods, and study findings based on a graduate-level engineering course focusing on the intersection of VR/AR, user experience, and social justice. In the course, students partnered with a local nonprofit organization to design a historically based VR experience. The purpose of our study was to better understand how the community partner and the graduate students perceive success, what obstacles they think they face, and what characteristics of the community partner they think would be ideal for a VR/AR course, which is a highly technical domain for UX application. In this section, we will discuss our findings by addressing our research questions and connecting these findings with previous research.

How Do Students and Community Partners Perceive Successful or Unsuccessful Collaborations? How Do Their Perceptions Impact Their Experience?

Since this was an exploratory qualitative pilot study on a newly developed graduate-level VR/AR course, our goal was not to measure "success in collaboration" using objective metrics. Instead, we wanted to explore students' and the community partner's perceptions of success and how that might have impacted their collaborative experience.

Varied Definitions of "Success."

Our findings show that the definition of "success in collaboration" varied across students (as seen in Table 6.2) and the community partner. Since students in this class came from a variety of backgrounds, including interaction design, computer science, and engineering, their differing perspectives on success of a project like this could certainly be influenced by differences in educational background (as seen in Table 6.1). For one student, success is "result-oriented" and meant a technical output, while for some, success was determined by a combination of goals or tasks being accomplished, a deliverable, and satisfaction or support from the community partner. Likewise, Maggie's definitions of success in collaboration included both goals (working toward a common one) and specific personalities from individual collaborators (e.g., open, honest, respectful, easygoing). This resonates with Littlecott and colleagues' (2017) research on how perceptions of success can differ depending on the stakeholder.

"Unsuccessful" Does Not Equal a Negative Experience (and Vice Versa)

While we may traditionally align "unsuccessful collaboration" with a negative experience, that was not necessarily the case here. Even for the student who did not consider the collaborative project to be "successful," he still considered it to be an "awesome" experience because he admired Maggie's passion and enjoyed collaborating with the MYP participants. Similarly, although the community partner did not necessarily receive the deliverable that they were promised (to showcase at the MYP participants' presentation), Maggie still considered the collaboration a success because her definitions highlighted the importance of positive engagement from the stakeholders involved in this collaborative process: the instructor, the graduate students, and the MYP participants. Conversely, students who did consider the collaborative project to be successful still offered strong recommendations for improving the experience (e.g., more technical expertise from the community partner and more time with/feedback from users), which at first glance, may appear to indicate a highly unsuccessful collaboration. This is similar to Butcher and Jeffrey's (2007) findings, which correlated student perceptions of success with the social process of collaboration. In fact, they argued that:

> Much of the voluminous contemporary debate regarding the design and management of collaboration implicitly views the process as something to be engineered, manipulated, and somehow optimized. As a social process . . . the personal experience of research collaboration is necessarily imperfect, noisy, messy, and ultimately one of mixed emotions and outcomes, thereby constraining the impact of interventions based on a 'best model' prescription. (2007, p. 1248)

Mutual Positive Engagement/Relationship

There is a strong impact of mutual trust and good relationships on collaborations (as cited by Butcher & Jeffrey, 2007). When the instructor approached MYP as a potential community partner for her class, she did not foresee the strong effect of a mutual positive relationship between the graduate students and the MYP participants. It was not the explicit goal of the collaborative project to make both parties (graduate students and Maggie/MYP participants) enjoy working with each other. This is especially the case because the graduate students did not enroll to take a "UX in social justice" or a service-learning class, but were primarily interested in learning technical skills to develop VR/AR. Therefore, while Reddick and colleagues (2018) argued that some graduate students' motivation for service is likely based on their previous service engagement and therefore lead to a positive experience, our results suggest that these positive outcomes can be achieved even without the initial motivation to participate in such a course.

From the perspective of the community partner (Maggie's), simply giving the underprivileged MYP participants the opportunity to interact with university graduate students was a success in and of itself. For her, the additional exposure to both people and resources at the university could help MYP participants be more open and excited about future possibilities. Likewise, all graduate students mentioned the intrinsic benefit of interacting with the MYP participants, which resulted in positive outcomes for them (even for the one who did not consider the project a success). To take it even a step further, students might have helped broaden MYP participants' perspective by presenting future career paths and higher education options, and further contributed to their self-worth by taking them seriously and valuing their input.

This "byproduct" compelled us to consider how collaborations can be strengthened by identifying organizations that will have mutual benefit simply from interacting with university students. Further, despite the sudden change in instructional style and course requirements due to COVID-19, both collaborators felt that they had received positive benefit already from the few initial meetings.

What Community Partner Characteristics Affect the Perceived Impact of Collaborations with Graduate Students in VR/AR Courses?

Personalities and Attitudes

Both the students' and community partner's personalities and attitudes can impact collaboration. Based on her previous experience collaborating with undergraduate students on various projects, Maggie found graduate students to be good collaborators because of their maturity, inclusiveness, respect for, and comfortable interactions with the MYP participants. This resonates with Kimme

Hea and Wendler Shah's (2016) findings, where community partners "reiterated a primary motivation for their participation is the enthusiasm and energy that students bring to consultant projects" (p. 62). Similarly, Maggie described the instructor as being open-minded, easy going, flexible, and able to communicate well. These characteristics are important, as open communication was "most often discussed when . . . community partners . . . describe an 'unsuccessful' service-learning collaboration," and this applies to both instructor/student communication in discussing flexibility "when the situation does not proceed according to plan" (Kimme Hea & Wendler Shah, 2016, p. 61). Likewise, graduate students enjoyed working with Maggie and found this collaboration rewarding because of Maggie's easy-going nature and passion for the organization (McEachern, 2001), along with their ability to provide new, exciting, and inspiring experiences for the MYP participants.

Goals and Location

The community partner's location and goals/mission can impact collaboration. As an educational nonprofit organization, Maggie considered educators to be good collaborators because both share similar goals. Having "mutual understanding and appreciation of motivation, interests and needs" (as cited by Butcher & Jeffrey, 2007, p. 1242) is often considered to be an important characteristic of a successful collaboration. Our findings correlate with Kimme Hea and Wendler Shah's (2016), where they found that community partners do not necessarily want students to achieve the "exact same goals" as them—rather, "students who were able to set their own learning objectives were also more likely to foster a satisfying partner-student rapport and in turn create a better product" (p. 62). Furthermore, it is clear from Maggie's responses that she felt MYP participants were more engaged because of their positive VR/AR learning experiences and interactions with the graduate students during those face-to-face meetings. This was enhanced by the close proximity of the university and the MYP.

(Lack of) Technical Expertise

The community partner's technical expertise (or lack thereof) can impact collaboration. Since Maggie and the MYP participants did not possess the technical knowledge and skills that the students thought were crucial for the project, the community partner relied more heavily on the graduate students for their expertise. The project outcome, as evidenced in Maggie's comment, exceeded MYP's expectations and made it a positive experience for them. Similarly, these engineering students are familiar with the problem-solving process, so they recognized the benefits of being able to design the project by defining their own objectives and developing solutions. This additional ownership can be an asset, as it more clearly mimics real-world scenarios in which they, with their graduate degrees in engineering, may be looked to as "experts" on the topic at hand, as pointed out by Riley and Bloomgarden (2006). In those scenarios, they would need to be flexible in making high-level decisions based on constraints and (sometimes) moving goals. Therefore, a project like this gave them the chance to learn in a safe environment. For example, students initially over-planned and had to recognize their own resource limitations. In doing so, they realized that they needed to scope back the project to complete it on time. Unlike the undergraduate students in Riley and Bloomgarden's (2006) case study, graduate students in this course were able to act flexibly and creatively during their problem-solving process, which could be due to the "maturity" that Maggie described when comparing graduate students and undergraduate students.

What Obstacles Stand in the Way of Productive UX on VR/AR Partnerships? How Can We Work to Overcome These Obstacles?

(Lack-of) Technical Expertise

While the collaboration with MYP was a success by most accounts, it highlighted several obstacles to collaboration. Having "close alignment of expertise and interests of collaborating parties" (as cited by Butcher & Jeffrey, 2007, p. 1242) is considered to be another important characteristic of a successful collaboration. In this case, students found that even though both parties agreed on the deliverable, the technical expertise and experience were not mutually aligned, which is similar to the condition of "mixed skill levels" that McEachern (2001) used to describe nonprofit staff. More specifically, the lack of shared understanding of VR/AR technology made it difficult for students to understand the needs and desires of the MYP participants when they attempted to collect data. To overcome this challenge, students readily adapted their methods, such as by slowing down to have more intentional conversations or switching to observational data collection instead of relying on verbal feedback. Further, the chance to make decisions resulted in more freedom and more accurately reflected real-world scenarios, which may have contributed to a sense of ownership of the final deliverable. In addition, because the community partner had minimal expectations regarding the technical specifications of the deliverable, this meant that the students were more likely to be successful in meeting their expectations.

A potential solution to this challenge is to identify community partners who are not located in close proximity, but who share technical expertise in the topic area. However, a key benefit of this kind of community-based service-learning project is to engage students with the area around their university. While some researchers encourage students to find community partners that align with their own interests (e.g., Nielsen, 2016), finding technical expertise that aligns with the course content and/or student interest may limit the geographical location of community partners. It is unlikely, especially for highly technical VR/AR UX-based courses, to find a community partner that possesses the same technical expertise of the course in the same geographical area. Even in a large geographical area such as the Detroit metropolitan area, the instructor was unable to locate a nonprofit organization that focuses on social justice issues with VR/AR expertise.

Communication

Another challenge is the lack of structure in the communication and feedback process between students and the community partner (including both Maggie and the MYP participants). Similar to findings from previous researchers (e.g., Butcher & Jeffrey, 2007; Riley & Bloomgarden, 2006; Walsh, 2010), establishing useful communication channels is important but difficult for students. Even when students are encouraged to initiate and create that channel, they may not be prepared or motivated to create their own structure. Perhaps, this type of project stretches students in ways that they are not used to (two students explicitly mentioned in the interviews that this was their first service-learning project experience), and it requires building "soft" or interpersonal skills (e.g., communication, planning, project management) in addition to technical skills. As engineering students, they quickly and easily identified technical expertise as an area that they needed to develop, but may have overlooked these soft or interpersonal skills. Addressing the importance of these additional tasks can reinforce to students that communication and interpersonal skills are critical to the success of collaborations and therefore must be a key part of the plan. Thus, a potential solution is to clearly establish stakeholder roles and expectations for both the students and the community partner early in the semester (Walton, 2007). Instructors can also clearly define expectations for the process to encourage students to adopt best UX practices. By focusing on process expectations, rather than outcomes, students can be encouraged to, for example, communicate more frequently with the community partner. Therefore, framing the process is vital to ensuring the success of the process, which in turn should ensure a satisfactory deliverable at the end of the course.

Time Commitment

Finally, collaborations like this require a significant time commitment from the instructor, students, and community partners. One consistent theme across responses from both students and MYP is that more feedback and interaction is advantageous. One solution would be to connect students to community partners earlier in the semester, as recommended by Murat Tiryakioğlu and colleagues (2009). Even if the students do not yet have the technical knowledge to begin the process, requiring students to establish communication early can help them become more invested and can build the communication channels that are so vital later in the project timeline.

Students in this course were simultaneously full-time employees and students, which likely impacted their ability to devote significant time to the project. For example, much of their work had to be completed over the weekends. Yet, as

COVID-19 drastically changed the interactions toward the end of the semester, all students commented in class that they would like to maintain the connection with MYP, with one student writing in the reflection that he hoped to have the chance to present their final project to the MYP participants after the semester at a later date. Even though this was the students' first time collaborating with a community partner that does not have a long-term sustainable relationship with the department, instructor, or class itself, the perceived impact can be seen.

As Riley and Bloomgarden (2006) pointed out, the reality is that students have to leave at the end of the semester because the engineering curriculum does not typically allow for long-term commitments with students. Graduate students especially are often expected to focus primarily on research/scholarship and professional development (Reddick et al., 2018), which may hinder them from devoting a lot of time to community engagement or service-learning projects. Therefore, a possible solution may be to develop shorter collaborations and smaller partnerships where positive outcomes can be achieved with less time commitments.

■ Conclusion and Implications

The goal of our study was to explore graduate students' and community partner's perspectives to develop a better understanding of how a graduate-level UX engineering course on VR/AR can impact both stakeholders. Our findings show that there is clearly value for a highly technical course in partnering with organizations with varied levels of expertise as evidenced by the positive experiences of both students and the community partner. Yet ensuring the project is successful requires careful course design (described in more detail in Chapter 7), along with recognition that students and community partners will likely derive different meaning from the experience. We found that the varied definitions of success across students and the community partner resulted in a largely positive experience even when the project did not go as planned. Community partners may derive value from unanticipated sources which are independent of *project* "success," such as the positive value that our community partner felt resulted from interactions between MYP participants and university students. Successful collaborations may extend beyond scope of the planned project, and allowing space for adaptation can foster these benefits to create a more positive experience. Identifying community partners that are not only open to collaboration, but also are open to adapting as the project evolves will support the success of similar projects. Additionally, sharing common goals and close physical proximity further support collaborations. Yet regardless of these factors, when it comes to collaborating within highly technical graduate courses, obstacles such as technical constraints and required time commitment are likely to impact project success. Instructors can mitigate some of these obstacles by providing supporting infrastructure, particularly by clearly communicating both with students and community partners. Still, it's unlikely that all obstacles will be mitigated because of the complex interactions with multiple stakeholders. While there are many tradeoffs in this type of collaboration, in this case, the benefit gained across all stakeholders seemed to exceed the effort required to build it.

While this is an exploratory qualitative study on a pilot course that is limited to a small sample of participants in a very specific location, our findings contribute to scholarly conversations on productive partnerships in UX in that we offered both the perspectives of graduate students and the community partner. This is our way of answering the call of Kimme Hea & Wendler Shah (2016), who concluded their article by arguing that "we must conduct more technical communication service-learning research to include community partner perspectives" (p. 64).

As Butcher and Jeffrey (2007) aptly put it, "formality provides ambition, focus, efficiency, audit, whilst the informal engenders flexibility and independence. It is perhaps unsurprising that, irrespective of the measure used, some collaborative projects perform poorly" (p. 1248). While engineering projects are often based on formal project management structures, we found that informal elements such as mutual trust and good relationship, personalities or attitudes, technical expertise, goals and location, communication, and time commitment interweave and impact collaboration, sometimes in unexpectedly positive ways.

■ References

Agboka, G. Y. (2014). Decolonial methodologies: Social justice perspectives in intercultural technical communication research. *Journal of Technical Writing and Communication, 44*(3), 297–327. https://doi.org/10.2190/TW.44.3.e.

Baillie, C., Pawley, A. & Riley, D. (2014). *Engineering and social justice in the university and beyond.* Purdue University Press. https://doi.org/10.2307/j.ctt6wq5pf.

Barnes, M. & Caprino, K. (2016). Analyzing service-learning reflections through Fink's taxonomy. *Teaching in Higher Education, 21*(5), 557–575. https://doi.org/10.1080/13562517.2016.1160221.

Bielefeldt, A. R., Paterson, K. G. & Swan, C. W. (2010). Measuring the value added from service learning in project-based engineering education. *International Journal of Engineering Education, 26*(3), 535–546.

Bourelle, T. (2014). Adapting service-learning into the online technical communication classroom: A framework and model. *Technical Communication Quarterly, 23*(4), 247–264. https://doi.org/10.1080/10572252.2014.941782.

Bowdon, M. A. & Scott, J. B. (2003). *Service-learning in technical and professional communication.* Longman.

Brown, J. & Chao, J. T. (2010). Collaboration of two service-learning courses: Software development and technical communication. *Issues in Informing Science and Information Technology, 7,* 403–412. https://doi.org/10.28945/1216.

Butcher, J. & Jeffrey, P. (2007). A view from the coal face: UK research student perceptions of successful and unsuccessful collaborative projects. *Research Policy, 36*(8), 1239–1250. https://doi.org/10.1016/j.respol.2007.04.009.

Cargile Cook, K. (2014). Service learning and undergraduate research in technical communication programs. *Programmatic Perspectives, 6*(1), 27–51.

Colton, J. S. & Holmes, S. (2018). A social justice theory of active equality for technical communication. *Journal of Technical Writing and Communication, 48*(1), 4–30. https://doi.org/10.1177/0047281616647803.

Duin, A., McGrath, M., Moses, J. & Tham, J. (2016). Wearable computing, wearable composing: New dimensions in composition pedagogy. *Computers and Composition Online.* http://cconlinejournal.org/wearable/.

Glaser, B. & Strauss, A. (1967). *The discovery of grounded theory: Strategies for qualitative research.* Sociology Press.

Henson, L. & Sutliff, K. (1998). A service-learning approach to business and technical writing instruction. *Journal of Technical Writing and Communication, 28*(2), 189–205. https://doi.org/10.2190/0BT3-FVCX-3T9N-FVMR.

Huckin, T. (1997). Technical writing and community service. *Journal of Business and Technical Communication, 11*(1), 49–59.

Jones, J. & Gouge, C. C. (Eds.) (2017). Wearable technologies and communication design [Special issue]. *Communication Design Quarterly, 5*(4).

Jones, N. (2016). The technical communicator as advocate: Integrating a social justice approach in technical communication. *Journal of Technical Writing and Communication, 46*(3), 342–361. https://doi.org/10.1177/0047281616639472.

Jones. N. (2017). Modified immersive situated service learning: A social justice approach to professional communication pedagogy. *Business and Professional Communication Quarterly, 80*(1), 6–28. https://doi.org/10.1177/2329490616680360.

Kimme Hea, A. C. & Wendler Shah, R. (2016). Silent partners: Developing a critical understanding of community partners in technical communication service-learning pedagogies. *Technical Communication Quarterly, 25*(1), 48–66. https://doi.org/10.1080/10572252.2016.1113727.

Leydens, J. & Lucena, J. (2018). *Engineering justice: Transforming engineering education and practice.* Wiley-IEEE Press: IEEE PCS Professional Engineering Communication Series. https://doi.org/10.1002/9781118757369.

Litchfield, K., Javernick-Will, A. & Maul, A. (2016). Technical and professional skills of engineers involved and not involved in engineering service. *Journal of Engineering Education, 105*(1), 70–92. https://doi.org/10.1002/jee.20109.

Littlecott, H. J., Fox, K. R., Stathi, A. & Thompson, J. L. (2017). Perceptions of success of a local UK public health collaborative. *Health Promotion International, 32,* 102–112. https://doi.org/10.1093/heapro/dav088.

Lucena, J. (2013). *Engineering education for social justice critical explorations and opportunities* (1st ed.). https://doi.org/10.1007/978-94-007-6350-0.

Mack, J. (2019, October 3). *Which Michigan communities had the highest violent-crime rate in 2018? Mlive.* https://www.mlive.com/news/g66l-2019/10/2c291700cd8326/which-michigan-communities-had-the-highest-violentcrime-rate-in-2018.html.

Matthews, C. & Zimmerman, B. B. (1999). Integrating service learning and technical communication: Benefits and challenges. *Technical Communication Quarterly, 8*(4), 383–404. https://doi.org/10.1080/10572259909364676.

McEachern, R. W. (2001). Problems in service learning and technical/professional writing: Incorporating the perspective of nonprofit management. *Technical Communication Quarterly, 10*(2), 211–224. https://doi.org/10.1207/s15427625tcq1002_6.

Michigan Youth Project. (2018). Kids Standard. https://kidsstandard.org/michigan-youth-project.

Michigan Youth Project. (2019). The Michigan Youth Project, is one of Kids Standard's Newest Programs. Facebook. https://www.facebook.com/share/p/15J1cxTazF/.

Nielsen, D. (2016). Facilitating service learning in the online technical communication classroom. *Journal of Technical Writing and Communication, 46*(2), 236–256. https://doi.org/10.1177/0047281616633600.

Queiruga-Dios, M., Santos Sánchez, M. J., Queiruga-Dios, M. Á., Acosta Castellanos, P. M. & Queiruga-Dios, A. (2021). Assessment methods for service-learning projects in engineering in higher education: A systematic review. *Frontiers in Psychology, 12*, 629231–629231. https://doi.org/10.3389/fpsyg.2021.629231.

Reddick, R., Struve, L., Mayo, J., Miller, R. & Wang, J. (2018). "We don't leave engineering on the page": Civic engagement experiences of engineering graduate students. *Journal of Higher Education Outreach and Engagement, 22*(2), 127–156.

Riley, D. & Bloomgarden, A. (2006). Learning and service in engineering and global development. *International Journal for Service Learning in Engineering, 2*(1), 48–59. https://doi.org/10.24908/ijsle.v1i2.2084.

Sapp, D. A. & Crabtree, R. D. (2002). A laboratory in citizenship: Service learning in the technical communication classroom. *Technical Communication Quarterly, 11*(4), 411–432. https://doi.org/10.1207/s15427625tcq1104_3.

Scott, J. B. (2008). The practice of usability: Teaching user engagement through service-learning. *Technical Communication Quarterly, 17*(4), 381–412. https://doi.org/10.1080/10572250802324929.

Soria, K. M. & Weiner, B. (2013). A "virtual fieldtrip": Service learning in distance education technical writing courses. *Journal of Technical Writing and Communication, 43*(2), 181–200.

Stebbins, S. & Guneson, G. (2019, February 7). *These are the worst cities to live in America. Is yours one of them? USA Today*. https://www.usatoday.com/story/money/2019/02/07/worst-cities-america-50-places-named-least-desirable-call-home/39006457/.

Tham, J. (2017). Wearable writing: Enriching student peer review with point-of-view video feedback using Google Glass. *Journal of Technical Writing and Communication, 47*(1), 22–55. https://doi.org/10.1177/0047281616641923.

Tham, J., Duin, A., Gee, L., Ernst, N., Abdelqader, B. & McGrath, M. (2018). Understanding virtual reality: Presence, embodiment, and professional practice. *IEEE Transactions on Professional Communication, 61*(2), 178–195. https://doi.org/10.1109/TPC.2018.2804238.

Tiryakioğlu, M., Maxwell, T. E., Bird, C. P., Dempsey, B. W., Harbodin II, J. A., Laughner, J. R., Skelton, T. A., Wood, M., Şirinterlikçi, A. & Acharya, S. (2009). Integration of service learning into a manufacturing engineering course: A case study. *International Journal for Service Learning in Engineering, 4*(1), 44–52.

United Nations. (2024). The 17 goals. United Nations Sustainable Development Goals. https://www.un.org/sustainabledevelopment/sustainable-development-goals/.

Vergara, D., Rubio, M. P. & Lorenzo, M. (2017). On the design of virtual reality learning environments in engineering. *Multimodal Technologies and Interact, 1*(11). https://doi.org/10.3390/mti1020011.

Walsh, L. (2010). Constructive interference: Wikis and service learning in the technical communication classroom. *Technical Communication Quarterly, 19*(2), 184–211. https://doi.org/10.1080/10572250903559381.

Walton, R. (2007). Technical communication and the needs of small nonprofit organizations. *IEEE Professional Communication Conference (IPCC)*. 1–24. https://doi.org/10.1109/IPCC.2007.4464065.

Walton, R., Moore, K. & Jones, N. (2019). *Technical communication after the social justice turn*. Routledge.

Wingblad, A. (2018, October 8). *FBI's 2017 data shows fewer violent and property crimes across the county, but Pontiac still leads in many categories*. Oakland Press. https://tinyurl.com/42zdzn58.

7. Reflections on a Graduate-Level Engineering Service-Learning Project in a Virtual Reality and User Experience Course

Missie Smith
AUBURN UNIVERSITY

Felicia Chong
UNAFFILIATED

Abstract. This chapter summarizes the lessons learned in designing and implementing a graduate-level service-learning project in a virtual reality and user experience course. This type of cross-functional course and real-world collaboration provided a rich experience for graduate students (described in Chapter 6), although there were logistical issues that potentially hindered the collaboration and the learning process. This chapter provides practical recommendations to support the logistics of the course and to better align student learning with the intended outcomes.

University professors have the resources and flexibility to collaborate with community partners, and service-learning projects can be one way to broadly impact the surrounding community. While these collaborations can be rewarding, it is important to continually identify ways to improve these partnerships for the future. In this chapter, we discuss lessons learned from the service-learning collaboration described in Chapter 6, between graduate engineering students at a regional Midwestern university (Oakland University) and a local nonprofit organization (Michigan Youth Project) that serves middle school students from an under-funded school district in Pontiac, Michigan. Five graduate students were introduced to user experience (UX) methods and theoretical background of effective virtual reality (VR) and augmented reality (AR) experiences. To apply this knowledge, students learned Unity (3D development software), collected ideas from the community partner (CP), and collaborated as a team to develop a VR experience for the community partner. The community partner did not have a clear outcome in mind but requested a VR experience showcasing the history of Pontiac. Halfway through this collaborative project, the Oakland University campus closed due to COVID-19, resulting in a rapid transition to online learning and collaboration, and adjustments to the course objectives to account for these changes. Table 7.1 compares the original course objectives to the altered objectives as a result of COVID-19. Bold text indicates a substantial change from the original objective.

DOI: https://doi.org/10.37514/TPC-B.2025.2517.2.07

Table 7.1. Course Objectives for Students

	Original	Accepted
1	Identify potential project and partner	**Selected from** faculty-provided options
2	Develop initial project prototype	Developed initial project prototype
3	Apply feedback from CP (three times)	Applied feedback from CP (**one time**)
	Collect data using UX methods	Collected **unstructured verbal feedback**
	Analyze data and synthesize into meaningful insights	**Discussed feedback and highlighted pain points**
	Refined AR/VR experience	Refined AR/VR experience
4	Present final AR/VR experience to CP	**Produced video** showcasing work

In addition to the project, graduate students completed several written reflections throughout the semester where they discussed their collaboration experience and further connected the course content to their project; at the end of the semester, they were interviewed to gather additional insights about the course structure and recommendations for future curriculum. As explained in Chapter 6, students faced the typical logistical challenges associated with project-based learning such as needing more time, interactions or communication, and resources. This chapter, based on graduate student feedback and the instructor's experience, focuses on specific recommendations for building a successful collaboration and effectively teaching UX methods to graduate students in the context of a highly technical application.

Lessons Learned

Understand the Strengths and Limitations of Your Community Partner

Community partners have a variety of skill levels, technology experience, and goals. When selecting community partners, *consider their specific needs and abilities*. In this case, the community partner was comprised of novices to VR technology without a specific use case. Therefore, there was a lot of flexibility in the project outcome, which students appreciated. However, because of the community partner's lack of technical expertise in VR and low expectations for the project outcome, students were less motivated in applying the formal UX process, which would involve actively and iteratively seeking feedback and information from the users. Instead, students used general guidance from the community partners to develop the VR experience and waited until they felt they had accomplished the objectives to show the product to the community partner. As the course format switched to fully online due to COVID-19, students were unable to hold more face-to-face meetings with the community partner to showcase their project design, which they felt was integral to making the project successful. Therefore, they suggested that if the community partner was more experienced with VR technology, they could have more successfully collaborated remotely because of similar remote setups and more targeted feedback and questions. Depending on instructor course goals, there are circumstances where both novice and expert community partners are ideal. Prior to selecting a community partner, consider how their qualities will change project outcomes and the students' learning, application, and collaborative processes.

Define the Purpose of the Course/Project Clearly and Early

This course was designed to build a holistic course experience in which students both learn and apply VR/AR development skills and UX methods in the context of a social justice project. Since the formal course title and description did not include any reference to either UX methods or social justice, students indicated that their primary reason for taking the course was to build technical VR/AR development skills. However, through collaborating with the community partner, and especially interacting with the middle school students who are novice users, graduate students began to see the value in educating the community partner about VR/AR and that the positive impact was mutual. Designing a course that was mutually beneficial was a key part of the instructor's goals for teaching the class, and even though it was not part of the formal course title or description, students were receptive to participating in a project that had a positive impact on the surrounding community. For courses with a service-learning focus, sharing the reasoning for incorporating service learning in the class can help get students more excited about participating. That being said, having multiple course foci can also mean that unequal priority is given to different elements of the course. In this case, students did not prioritize finding a community partner, although this was part of the objectives. Instructors can help students better balance across multiple objectives by showing how each objective (in this case, VR/AR technical knowledge, application of UX methods, and social justice collaboration) directly corresponds to the course objectives. Therefore, by clearly articulating the course objectives at the beginning of the semester, instructors can help students establish their expectations and goals.

Connect Course Learning to the UX Process

In the interviews, students admitted that they never or rarely intentionally connected UX methods or theory such as personas to their project or data collection process. One student explained that applying methods was not useful because the community partner did not have a clear outcome in mind. Other students discussed the benefits of reflections, which required students to engage deeply with theoretical knowledge in the context of their applied work. As graduate engineering students, they were intentionally given the freedom to direct the project and work with the community partner to determine the ideal outcome. However, this lack of structure may have contributed to students' informal approach. To more effectively integrate course content with real-world application and facilitate communication and collaboration, *grade artifacts of the process* in addition to reflections and project outcomes, for example:

- Identification of potential community partners (name, contact information, and rationale)
- Meeting notes from group meetings (weekly or twice a week)
- Meeting notes from community partner meetings (biweekly)
- Outcomes from application of at least two UX methods with the community partner (e.g., interview notes, design charette drawings, and contextual inquiry notes)

Provide Infrastructure to Help Students Develop Technical Knowledge

All students reported that the need to rapidly develop technical programming skills was a barrier to the project, so they offered several unique recommendations on how to overcome this challenge. For example, students requested a *dedicated graduate assistant* to teach technical skills, *co-requisite classes* in which one focused on technical skill-building while the other focused on the collaborative project, and further integration of external asynchronous resources like *YouTube videos*. In this project, individual programming abilities clearly limited students' progress. While these recommendations may be helpful, they may not be practical in every course due to cost, time, and curricular constraints. The important takeaway is that for a course like this, instructors should expect students to struggle with the technical component and attempt to *put infrastructure in place to help students* develop technical knowledge at the pace that works for them.

Start the Project Early in the Semester

Because projects like these are limited to a semester schedule, timing is an important factor. Even though students stated that they needed even more skills development, they also wished that the collaborative project started earlier in the semester. Even if students do not yet have the technical skills, they indicated that *early meetings could focus on relationship building*. For courses blending technical skill building and application, there will rarely be enough time for both. Therefore, instructors should facilitate introductions early in the semester even if students are not yet ready to begin applying their skills. In doing this, students can begin to develop relationships with community partners so they can simultaneously start planning while still building technical skills.

Teach with a Variety of Styles

In this course, the instructor used a combination of classroom discussion, supplemental videos, reflection assignments, and interviews to help students better connect theory and application in a new topic area for them. Students mentioned that this varied approach to conveying knowledge helped them become more interested in the course. In-class *discussions* helped students develop better understanding topics and each other's perspectives. *YouTube videos* helped tie the concepts back to the project. Written *reflection assignments* integrated theory and application through targeted reflection assignments. The semester ended with a formal *interview* (conducted by the second author), which students believed was important to evaluate a student's understanding of the course. When designing a course teaching both highly technical skills and in-depth application, instructors should still provide space and opportunities for students to engage with the content in a variety of ways.

Use Accessible Software and Hardware

Technology access was a bottleneck for this work. While Unity is a free software, it requires minimum computer specifications to work properly. Similarly, VR/AR hardware is not yet widely accessible, so it is improbable that students would have access at home. After campus was closed due to COVID-19, some students were unable to access the VR/AR technology. Students felt that having *more access to the lab* would have helped them do more and better work because the lack of lab access severely impacted their progress. When possible, instructors should use accessible hardware and software or prepare a backup plan with the knowledge that not having adequate access will make teaching this type of specialized systems extremely difficult.

Implications

As a highly technical domain for UX application, VR/AR class projects can bring additional challenges to a service-learning collaboration. This chapter provides several recommendations based on practical experience for a course where graduate engineering students partnered with a local nonprofit organization to design a VR experience for novice users. First, the instructor should understand the community partner's specific needs and abilities. Second, ensure that the students have a clear path forward by explaining the purpose of the course and connecting course grades to UX methods. Third, support student success by providing infrastructure, connecting them with the partner early, teaching with a variety of styles, and using software and hardware that are accessible. Our recommendations resonate with findings in previous service-learning research. For example, David Blouin and Evelyn Perry (2009) suggested that instructors should partner with the community partner to develop the service component of their courses, share course objectives and learning methods with their community partner, and clarifies expectations and goals in writing.

■ Reference

Blouin, D. & Perry, E. M. (2009). Whom does service learning really serve? Community-based organizations' perspectives on service learning. *Teaching Sociology, 37*(2), 120–135. https://doi.org/10.1177/0092055X0903700201.

8. Critical Success Factors for Teaching an Accessible User Experience Project Across National Borders and Disciplinary Boundaries

Sushil K. Oswal
UNIVERSITY OF WASHINGTON

Zsuzsanna B. Palmer
GRAND VALLEY STATE UNIVERSITY

Rita Koris
BUDAPEST UNIVERSITY OF ECONOMICS AND BUSINESS

Abstract. Drawing on the data from the third year of a longitudinal study based on an international collaboration among three university faculty—one from Hungary and two from the United States—this reflective chapter narrates the lessons learned in engaging undergraduate students in a simulated client-provider relationship project that incorporated accessible user experience principles in entrepreneurial business planning and web design. While the participating instructors characterize this collaboration as a simulation, from the students' perspective, the pull of the project dwelled in the real life relationships developing out of the client-provider roles assumed by the collaborating groups from each university, the shared understanding of disability and accessibility acquired from the disability and design theory read and discussed during the academic term, and the heavy emphasis on the need for integrating disabled users in defining the overall user experience in each of the three classes.

We compose this piece based on our experiences of an online interdisciplinary and international collaboration project where students from two different universities in the US and a third from a university in Hungary work together to design accessible websites and business plans to attract customers with a variety of cultural and user needs and offer them meaningful and equitable user experiences. This project connects to a rich tradition of intercultural collaborations in the technical and professional communication (TPC) field that focus on developing intercultural communication competence, translation, report writing, technical communication skills (Cardon et al., 2022; Maylath et al., 2013; Starke-Meyerring & Andrews, 2006). Our practice has been to reflect on our teaching philosophy during and after every iteration of this collaboration for the purpose of identifying possibilities for improvements in how we deliver our curriculum through this project (Alvesson & Sköldberg, 2017). The purpose of this chapter is thus to share the notable lessons learned in delivering a curriculum that centers on user experiences (UX) for all. ISO 9241–210:2019 defines user experience as a "person's perceptions and responses resulting from the use and/or anticipated use of a product, system or service" (2019. 3.15). According to Nielson Norman Group, "user experience encompasses all aspects of the end-user's interaction with the company, its services, and its products" (Norman & Nielsen, 1998, "Summary"). A more comprehensive definition of user experience includes these elements: "a consequence of a user's internal state (predispositions, expectations, needs, motivation, mood, etc.), the characteristics of the designed system (e.g., complexity, purpose, usability, functionality, etc.) and the context (or the environment) within which the interaction occurs (e.g., organizational/social setting, meaningfulness of the activity, voluntariness of use, etc.)" (Hassenzahl & Tractinsky, 2006).

Whereas the concept of UX has moved TPC and human computer interaction (HCI) fields beyond the narrow concept of usability which centered on user cognition and user performance in human-technology interactions, the definitions of UX both by HCI and TPC experts leave out the accessibility aspect in the definition of user experience (Chong, 2012; Redish, 2010; Redish & Barnum, 2011). We extend earlier disability-centered UX definitions by Oswal (2019) and Sauer and colleagues (2020) from an inclusive design perspective as a holistic ecosystem within which a user experiences a human computer interaction, a technological or informational product or process, and any other conditions that shape the user's context of use. These conditions include an accessible interface for the technology on the user's end, ease-of-use in navigation, psychological and physical comfort in interactions, and an equitable reach to the affordances of the resource also for those users who might depend on common adaptive technologies, including keyboard-only input, screen readers, and voice input systems. Paying attention to the different conditions of user's context of use builds upon the awareness of accessibility in the TPC field that has been developed by the first book-length collection edited by Lisa Melonçon (2014) as well as more recent research published in the two *Business and Professional Communication Quarterly* Special Issues on accessibility edited by Oswal (2018) and Melinda Knight and Oswal (2018), and several scholarly works on different aspects of accessibility by others such as Sherrie Drye and colleagues (2023), Sherena Huntsman (2021), Brian Le Lay and Dan Card (2022), Oswal and Palmer (2022), and Palmer and Palmer (2018).

In the project described in this chapter, students in Washington work as accessibility advisors to students in Michigan who create websites for the business ventures proposed by Hungarian students. The Washington accessibility advisors also serve as user experience (UX) testers for the Hungarian business plans to make the proposed ventures more inclusive and to make the Michigan groups' website designs and content more usable and accessible for customers and consumers representing diverse cultures and abilities.

The breadth and depth of content areas for user experience pedagogy depends on the availability of resources—testing labs, access to participants, and the existing knowledge of students. Our web design and accessibility courses engaged students in select activities essential to the practice of UX design—conducting user research, training in content strategy, and making content design and development choices. In addition, students worked on visual design, interaction design, particularly in the context of accessibility for users with disabilities, and focused on the need for usability testing with disabled users while employing participatory design methods. The class in charge of the building of websites, as well as, the one serving as accessibility consultants, participated in persona design, journey mapping, and wireframe creation, as a part of designing meaningful and inclusive user experiences for all visitors to their websites. We decided to center accessible design issues in this project because we understand that people with disabilities form a significant portion of world-wide user population (WHO, 2019). We also know that no UX design can be adequate unless it can meet the needs of users with a variety of abilities (Urrutia et al., 2017; Yesilada et al., 2012). Last, we believe that UX design courses must help students inculcate the values of disability-inclusive design so that they do not perpetuate the regime of exclusionary UX designs still so common in web environments in their own professional practice as they enter the job market. Under the inclusive orientation of this international collaboration project, we view UX as a design proposition that embraces the needs, preferences, and desired experiences of users irrespective of the body/mind difference. We question and critique workplace practices that re-enforce disableist and ableist viewpoints (Bell & de Gama, 2019; Dale & Burrell, 2014). We further assert that all nondisabled users also do not sit in the middle of the Galton's bell curve and designers regularly take into consideration these differences (For critiques of Galton's bell curve, see Cowan, 1972, and Fendler & Muzaffar, 2008). A commonplace example of these considerations is that clothing, shoes, and most accessories—such as belts—come in different sizes and even further dimensions within these sizes—wide, narrow, tall, short, etc.; if these products are customized based on the needs of different types of users, technology products should also meet the needs of all users. We also posit that all technology—irrespective of what sort of body/mind its users possess—is assistive (Hendren, 2014).

In terms of content, this chapter specifically draws from our third annual iteration of our longitudinal study collected by the three collaborating faculty specializing in three interrelated but diverse fields—human-centered design, technical communication, and business English. Two of us are located in the United States in an interdisciplinary school and a writing studies program respectively, and the third was situated in an international relations program at the beginning of this collaboration and is presently teaching at a business university in Hungary. While our specialties remain relatively stationary, our students swap places as they move on to other coursework, complete their degree requirements, and graduate from college. Thus, it is a collaborative relationship which remains reasonably stable on the faculty side but shifts on the student side every autumn. Dependent on the vagaries of departmental course schedules and enrollment numbers for each class, our participating courses can change from one year to another requiring major and minor adjustments in the design of our collaboration. We also adjust student group sizes each year to reflect the class enrollment. What anchors our work to a reliable spot is our collaboration's focus on integrating disability and accessibility. We do this in all the three parts—business plans, websites, advisory documents—of the projects that each of our classes collaborate on with one another in a client-provider relationship, while remaining flexible and relatively low-tech about the choice of collaboration technologies from year to year.

On the student side, these three autumn terms, we have formed approximately six project groups. Each project group is made up of three teams, one at each location. In each class, the teams have three to five members. The three teams—one from each location—then make up a project group and function in a client-provider relationship with one another representing three business entities engaged in entrepreneurial venture planning, web design, and accessibility consulting respectively.

The reflective commentary presented here outlines what we have learned in engaging undergraduate students in this simulated client-provider relationship. The project incorporated the inclusion of accessible user experience principles into the process of our Hungarian students building up entrepreneurial business plans in small groups. The project for the Michigan students focused on designing and developing business websites for these Hungarian entrepreneurial ventures. At the same time, groups from the Washington campus supplied foundational disability and accessibility knowhow in short informational documents, providing usability and accessibility testing services both for business ventures and web development, and serving as UX experts in the overall scheme of things to the other two linked groups. Each Hungarian group was responsible for delivering a well-developed, inclusive entrepreneurial business plan by the end of the term whereas the Michigan teams built accessible websites to serve the proposed businesses by their linked Hungarian teams. The advisory information from the Washington groups took the form of a report on conceptualizing inclusive businesses, a manual for designing accessible websites, and multiple feedback reports on rough drafts of the business venture plan and the related website. Thus, each Washington team generated advisory documents for their linked Hungarian and Michigan teams within their project group toward the beginning of the project term, produced usability and accessibility test reports on the drafts of Hungarian business plans and Michigan websites during the term, and provided advice on an as-needed basis throughout the term. Since the design process in Hungarian and Michigan teams was iterative, they were in touch with one another, and with their linked Washington advisory teams throughout the drafting process. These interactions could happen via email, through Moodle Forums, or via prescheduled video meetings, and the drafts of the deliverables could also be exchanged using agreed upon technologies. In more recent iterations of this collaboration, our student cohorts have used Google Groups and Google Docs to carry on their collaboration work since these tools have gained a certain purchase on our campuses. To manage overall teaching schedules and to keep students on task, the instructors drew a commonly shared timeline with several synchronized deadlines for the three classes.

Our overall purpose in designing this collaboration was to create a learning environment where students might themselves create user experiences that might go beyond providing for those nondisabled users who are already well-accommodated and reach the users who have been excluded from meaningful net experiences for these full three decades of the World Wide Web (Aizpurua et al., 2016). While the participating instructors characterize this international and interdisciplinary collaboration among the teams within each project group from their three classes as a simulated learning environment, from the students' perspective, the pull of the project dwelt in the real-life relationships developing out of the client-provider roles assumed by the collaborating teams from each school. In addition, working relationships among groups were strengthened by the shared understanding of disability and accessibility acquired from the disability and design literature read and discussed during the academic term, and the heavy emphasis on the need for integrating disabled users in defining the overall user experience in each of the three classes. In comparison with most of the wide-ranging collaborations among distributed teams both in university and workplace contexts, our project continues to have an inclusive edge unmatched by other collaborations although we hope that other faculty will follow the success of our long-lasting collaboration.

Over these years, we have, by design, moved toward drawing the readings for our students from the formal and informal trade literature about and on accessibility—studies by technical communication and web design practitioners, blog entries discussing industry resistance to inclusive website development, and short how-to articles and book chapters describing accessible design—so that students could wet their feet with industry discourse in this area. (For examples of these readings, see Biddle, 2013; Henry, 2007; Horton & Quesenbery, 2014; Nielsen, 2001; Oswal, 2014; Sandnes, 2017; WebAIM, 2016). We believe our students can, and will, change the design market with their upbeat attitudes toward disability and help their employers capture some of this 15 percent market of disabled users often overlooked by business and industry (Biddle, 2013).

As we track the success factors in the design of this project—both from the perspective of learner and instructor satisfaction—we have discovered that our success has been dependent on the avoidance of certain traps relating to technology, overly limited focus on the multilingual aspect of projects, and emphasizing intercultural communication and learning without a context. For example, our project is not structured around the use of a particular technology which often limits other aspects of international learning. Such projects are technologically interesting (see the internet-mediated, audio-graphic conferencing project from Carnegie Mellon University by Hauck, 2007), but these projects do not intercept with other curricular goals as effectively such as teaching web design principles for intercultural audiences or entrepreneurial business development in international settings. We recognize that the question of technology acceptance and use goes beyond simple consumer or pedagogical choices as researchers in allied fields have given close attention to these matters (Alvesson & Kärreman, 2007; Venkatesh et al., 2012). We also realize that transnational and intercultural contexts similar to ours require dedicated TPC research on technology acceptance and use in distributed students teams. Likewise, bi-lingual collaborations solely reliant on telecollaborative exchanges for the purpose of language learning (O'Dowd, 2003; Ware, 2005) restrict the scope of such collaborations for faculty working in other knowledge domains such as access computing, web design, inclusive design, and business planning. Similarly, a large number of collaborations are centered on intercultural learning as a purpose in itself without a context for long-term learning (Muller-Hartmann, 2000). Such intercultural learning usually has limited applications for the workplace setting because these collaborations do not embed workplace contexts to show students how intercultural knowledge is essential for functioning adequately in today's globally networked work environments. We have, instead, let the intercultural and international learning happen through the processes embedded in the relationship building and maintenance activities for getting to the essential tasks for accomplishing the goals of the client-provider projects. As it might have been true in any local project, the technical communication practitioner learners and business planners in this collaboration from three locations across regional and national boundaries carry out their professional responsibilities in a simulated workplace context while connecting, interacting, and learning about one another's culture, language, and work orientations.

We provide a synopsis of two group projects executed by our tri-campus teams. One of the projects was centered on a proposed company that sells their organic beauty products online. The Hungarian team focused their business plan on emphasizing the unique characteristics of these products that are not only natural but also edible. The Washington team provided feedback on this business plan and made the Hungarian team aware of a wide array of demographics that need to be considered as customers. They also advised the Michigan team on creating a website structure and incorporating accessibility features—such as skip links and alt text—early on. The final website featured a wide array of products and was easily navigable and accessible. Another enterprise that was proposed by a Hungarian team was a yoga studio. As this enterprise was to be located in a brick-and-mortar building, the Washington team made the Hungarian team aware of the physical features that would make the location of this studio also accessible to people with disabilities. In addition, the Washington team tested the proposed website using the WAVE tool, and pointed out specific issues on the website that needed to be corrected in order to achieve better accessibility. This type of three-way interaction and collective iteration to produce deliverables is complex from the students' side, and this complexity becomes even more pronounced on the instructors' side. In the ensuing three sections, each of us instructors involved in the project share our thoughts on this collaboration.

Thoughts of The Human-Centered Design and Engineering Faculty on this Joint Pedagogical Venture

If I were to write about what I have learned from our collaboration, I would start with probably not that rash a claim that an international teaching collaboration first of all "is work" in the very rudimentary sense of the term—"to act, do, function, operate" and it is also associated with "tilling or ploughing the earth" for new growth (Oxford University Press, n.d.). Then, as a project, it is an ongoing attempt at developing a structure, or organization that could support a multi-year collaboration. This organization has to happen at several levels and in many areas—keeping all the pieces of the project together while keeping the colleagues apprised of one's movements; collecting the appropriate information for and about student project groups' work at the right time; constantly adding to and building on what already exists; and giving it the semblance of an order through a home-grown schema to keep it accessible for all the participants' use. And last, such a collaboration is a constant study of technologies involved, particularly when the so-called technologies of collaboration circulate so freely and are ubiquitous in faculty and student environments on almost every platform and in so many forms. We could say that a collaboration in the technical communication or human-centered design course is a combination of work, organization, and technology and this effort is as much about cooperation as it is a collaboration among the participants which also makes endless demands on the instructors' skills to coordinate all its pieces. Kjeld Schmidt (1991) describes the process in more measured terms when he writes, "cooperative work arrangements should be conceived of as emerging formations that change dynamically and involve distributed decision making" (p. 1).

On the social side of such international collaborations is the excruciating awareness of one's partners' desire to retain their autonomy and freedom to think their own ways—something that we in the United States—howsoever unknowingly—tend to overlook and assume that everything we do in this country is universal. One such practical learning happened at the end of the first year of our collaboration when our Hungarian partner had to correct one of my statements in a co-authored manuscript that characterized Hungary as an eastern European country. For them, the post-Soviet Hungary had nothing to do with its eastern past and it was very much a central European country. Not too different was the need to remember that outside the United States, faculty—like most other working people—go away from their university research, teaching, and academic chores on Friday and the weekend belongs to them, and to them only. The workaholic tendencies exhibited by most tenure-track U.S. research faculty, to them probably appears verging on the perverse. Another learning we keep on experiencing—like thousands of other faculty around the world—is about the extent of technology savviness our internet generation students actually possess which goes against our own presumptions about their digital native status (Ryberg et al., 2011). Beyond the exchange of information, drafts, and coordination of meetings via email, we always had some students who got lost in the Moodle pages, or should we say, got hung out in Google Hangouts. The takeaway for us is to introduce every technology for collaboration from square one and make sure that all our student cohorts are on board with every course activity in progress.

In closing, if we were to dig out the conceptual foundation of our collaboration, I would say that it rests on three posts: 1) a philosophy of work where meeting your collaborators' needs sits right next to your own; 2) a sociology of groups that remains fluid to avail the affordances of every moment of contact from student groups to student groups, from faculty to faculty, from faculty to student groups, and from student groups to faculty; and 3) an approach to technology based on necessity and meaningful use rather than on the compulsion to embrace the most recent fad on the market.

Thoughts of the Technical Communication Faculty on this Multi-year Project

Reflecting back on this collaboration project, I would highly emphasize how teaching as an ever-evolving and reflective practice becomes even more important in a collaboration project between classrooms than it is in a singular classroom (Ward, 2009). In our reflection process, we build on established observations about intercultural virtual collaboration within the TPC field such as the transatlantic project (Maylath et al., 2013) or the peer-review project involving technical communication students in two countries (Anderson et al., 2010) as well as more recent collaboration projects where students from several countries are included in report writing using Slack (Cardon, et al., 2022). To reflect, we also review the results of our multiyear research projects focusing on this specific collaboration (Koris et al., 2021; Palmer et al., 2021, Oswal et al., 2021). This reflection results in our understanding that while as an individual instructor one is only responsible for the learning outcomes within one's class, in a collaboration project such as ours, the learning outcomes can only be met effectively in one class when they are also met in the other two classes. In this sense, our collaboration project very much replicates the connections observed in contemporary conditions of distributed work (Treviranus, 2009) and is aimed at teaching students skills required in this environment (Paretti et al., 2007). As we continued to work on each iteration of the project, we take time to reflect on the successes and shortcomings of our previous method and design shared approaches that allow us to reach our individual classroom's goals. These reflections among us happen both on an individual basis as well as collaboratively. We take notes on our teaching regularly and share them with one another via email and phone calls as frequently as time permits. The observations recorded in these emails and notes from the phone conversations assist us in tracking how the nuts and bolts of our collaboration are working in our classes and also start our brainstorming as a team to seek out likely solutions for the hurdles confronted. In addition, as we gear up for a new round of this project, we hold planned meetings using conference call technologies like Zoom to sort out the details—specifically the details about the schedules of our classes since our academic terms begin at different times and the pacing of various assignments in each of the classes requires some serious juggling—to design the new elements we want to introduce to that year's project, and to foresee the problems we might face in the coming term due to the introduction of new elements. When possible, we also try to connect at academic conferences where we assess our recent successes and debacles while chartering our next moves. These in-person meetings have been easier for Sushil Oswal and me (Zsuzsanna Palmer) since we attend roughly the same conferences in the United States every year but Rita Koris also has been able to travel to one of the 4Cs Conferences in these years. Of course, these academic conferences were moved to the virtual sphere due to the COVID-19 pandemic. I might also note that some of our conversations spill out into our conference papers and provide us with further opportunities to reflect on this collaboration. To give our readers a sense of the kind of problems we address in our meetings from time to time, I share this example from one of our earliest reflection meetings: we noticed that during the first year of our collaboration our students were not interacting with other groups to the extent we had expected them to do. We also knew that the key to a successful project would be effective communication between groups, so we had to take a critical approach to deciding about different technologies to coordinate these communication encounters (Turnley, 2007). We had to openly discuss what sort of technological savviness we could expect from our students in each of the classes and what would be the appropriate technological median to serve all of them equitably and adequately.

Beyond deciding about communication technologies in tandem with the other instructors, I also had to determine which content management systems my students will use for building their websites. The use of a content management system was a necessity as only some of the students enrolled in my course possess sufficient coding skills to build a website from the ground up. One of the specific decisions that students needed to make in the first iteration of the project was choosing a content management system or a free website-building tool (Everett, 2014). The idea behind this decision was based on not having students go through a steep learning curve by letting them use a tool that they are already comfortable with. While this freedom certainly resulted in a quick start-up phase, students soon learned that the amount of changes they were able to make to their websites in order to make them more accessible varied greatly across platforms. For this reason, in the later iterations of the project we have expected all student groups to use the free version of the WordPress CMS and scaffolded their learning of this CMS before the start of the collaboration project. While this version of WordPress is still somewhat limited in the ways that accessibility can be customized, it has several templates that are developed to be accessible and also options for accessing and making changes in the actual code. In addition, this platform also allows students to get familiar with a content management system that improves their skills in component content management environments (Batova & Andersen, 2017).

Another reason why my pedagogy has evolved through the different iterations of the project was that I had to reframe this task three times for my different classes I was assigned to teach during our multi-year collaboration project. The first time around, I was teaching a business communication class for mostly IT majors, and thus I included business communication assignments such as proposals and progress reports into the project. In the second year, the project became part of a professional writing class where I had to foreground technical specifications and descriptions. In the third year, a web writing class was connected to the project, where I have replaced a formal proposal with creating personas, journey maps, and wireframes. All the while, I continued to improve the accessibility aspect of our project while incorporating readings about website accessibility (WebAIM, 2016) and including videos about how screen readers work. As we continue to work on this longitudinal collaboration among three instructors, I remind myself that with each new approach we take to this project, it is important to stay focused on our main shared objective, accessibility and accessible user experience, and to communicate this objective to our students in our classes, assignments, and shared online discussions in as many ways as possible.

The main takeaways for me from this project are principles that are connected to effective pedagogical practice in any classroom. First, the choice of technology in any course should be carefully weighed in order for it to facilitate collaboration without influencing its content. Second, while assignments might be similar from year to year, making these assignments relevant to students at all three institutions always involves improvisation and creativity. A slight change to the same project assignment can communicate so many different things across places and cultures. At the same time, when students are exposed to concepts across disciplinary boundaries, as our project's focus on accessibility does, they can be better prepared for their work life and civic involvement after college. Relying on these principles is something I myself learned from our engagement with disability and accessibility work that a social focus is essential for me to maintain the significance of longitudinal collaboration projects.

Thoughts of the Business English Faculty on this International Project

Online international collaboration projects are still a rare opportunity for many university students in Hungary. Being able to participate in the project provides students with a unique international experience that they would not gain in any other way. Internationalization and international collaborations are also becoming a high priority in European higher education to develop students' English language communication competence and increase their preparedness for employment (European Political Strategy Centre, 2017). Students lacking any form of global experience are often at a disadvantage when they step out to the European job market (Eurofound, 2019). It is our role to equip fresh graduates not only with marketable knowledge, but also with skills to facilitate their school-to-work transition. It is an unstated requirement of the business English curriculum to cover and teach these new sets of skills to boost students' English business communication competence with digital and transversal skills. Having gone through the implementation of our project for several years, we can see that students highly appreciate the achievements and personal skills development they undergo and the competitive advantage they gain as a result of their participation in the project. Students often report that their online collaboration and communication skills as well as their digital competence developed due to their involvement in the project.

The international collaboration project on my side was entirely embedded into the business English course curriculum combining theory with practice. Hungarian students had the opportunity to instantly apply the theories by collaborating with their international peers on the project tasks and deliverables. Also, they were able to demonstrate their business English language competence in meaningful and real-life exchanges with native speakers of English. Hence the project gave them a lot of instances for learning, practice, development, and confidence-building.

Accessibility and disability inclusion were originally not part of the business English university curriculum for the Hungarian students, but interdisciplinarity and awareness-raising on disability that became key elements of our project are highly valued by university leaders as these broaden the perspectives of our graduates. During the years, I could witness how the participating students became more and more accustomed to the concepts of disability and accessibility. They also became more open to the theoretical and practical applications of these concepts to their discipline. In the very first year, the participating student groups took disability less into consideration when working on their business ventures, while students in the third iteration of the project actively took up the challenge of accommodating disabled users, customers, and business partners. After having consulted with their peers in Washington advising on accessibility, the Hungarian students discussed and considered possible areas for inclusion in their business plans and proactively suggested solutions—such as adding a wheelchair ramp—for making their businesses accessible for users with various disabilities, thus adapting the concepts of accessibility learned from their peers. Thinking beyond their project assignments, one of the student groups also questioned the problems with elevators in one of the academic buildings on our campus as well as the overall accessibility of in-campus services. Another spontaneously reflected on the Hungarian public's attitudes toward disabled people that she had observed during her daily train commute to campus.

As for improvement for future implementations of the project, I constantly try to increase the work efficiency of the student groups. All three of us now incorporate more icebreaker activities—personal introductions, synchronous team meetings—for participants before the actual start of the collaboration. By experience, the teams where team members developed a good working relationship early on performed much better, were more effective in assigning and completing tasks, managed their time and resources more efficiently, and communicated with their partner teams more effectively while solving problems and creating streamlined business documents that incorporate accessibility and account for the needs of all users.

Based on my conversations with students, they felt that they gained three important benefits from this international project. First, they developed a new set of skills related to teamwork, online collaboration, and work efficiency that they considered highly marketable in finding a job after graduation. Second, they became highly confident in using new technologies and applications for collaboration that most of them had never used before, yet they thought that it would be essential to use in their future workplace. Third, they believed the project experience broadened their own disciplinary horizons and got an insight into disability and accessibility concepts, which would not have been possible otherwise. Therefore, the main takeaway of this project for me is that the project has proved to provide an outstanding opportunity for the students to acquire international experience without stepping out of their classrooms, try themselves out in a real work situation, and engage in interdisciplinary conversation with their peers.

▪ Conclusion

As our discussion shows, there are many considerations that need to be taken into account when planning and executing such complex projects. First, faculty interested in taking on such a project need to be able to see the benefits of such a collaboration and see how the inter-university teams in these projects can help students reach the learning objectives in their classes. Next, they need to find collaboration partners at other institutions who see the same benefits and are willing to do the extra work of coordinating these complex projects. Connecting with like-minded faculty can happen at conferences, through partner institutions or even through just cold calling to previously known colleagues across universities.

For example, the popularly known *IVEC* Conference, an international conference on the topic of virtual exchanges brings together dozens of university faculty from around the world and is a promising venue for finding partners for teaching collaborations. Study abroad offices on many campuses also offer advice on setting up such faculty collaborations, and more and more, universities are offering small grants to faculty for establishing such projects. Through planning of the timeline, collaboration method, and discussions around shared objectives, the project will slowly take shape and can be piloted with students from a single class from each campus. Every time the project runs, additional quantitative and qualitative data can be gathered about the effectiveness of the project through term end surveys and student reflections. Through iteration of such collaborations among faculty, new ideas are born that shape future iterations of the project. This evaluative aspect of such virtual projects also assists participating faculty in collecting data to support their case for funding for the additional time spent on preparation for this complex pedagogy while stressing the data provided by students about the novel instruction offered and skills quired by this internationally-minded pedagogy. We also want to add that this faculty collaboration continued during the two peak years of COVID-19 pandemic although classes from each campus endured the hardships imposed by the unusual circumstances arising out of this emergency.

As a teaching team that has gone through this iteration process several times at the time of publication of this collection, we have three additional takeaways for our colleagues to realize the overall success of such a multi-year pedagogical collaboration. Our first recommendation: always give a full hearing to your colleagues' ideas howsoever raw or unrealistic they might appear to your ear, and commit to working with them to develop and refine them further as you would do to your own. Our second recommendation: once you have settled on a theme or focus for your UX practice and teaching philosophy—disability and accessibility has been our chosen area of pedagogical development for ourselves, our curricula, and our students' learning—make a concerted effort together to integrate it in as many aspects of your participating course as you can while drawing on the group members' expertise and learning from one another as teachers, practitioners, and scholars. Finally, our third recommendation: maintain strong communication channels—formal and informal—among your team and your student groups, even during the busiest time of your teaching semester, to keep your finger on the pulse of each other's participating classes, to support one another, and to learn from your partners' location-specific circumstances and cultural differences. Through the different iterations of this collaboration project, each of us had developed our pedagogies significantly to ensure that the complex tasks of collaboration led to meaningful learning experiences in all three classes. Most importantly though, all three of us have arrived at the understanding that focusing our instruction efforts in all three classes on accessible user experience naturally led to a shared set of values and priorities. Acting on this shared set of values created a sense of urgency in our classrooms where students not only completed assignments but also participated in the valuable work of changing society, one business idea at a time.

Acknowledgments

We thank the editors of this collection and the anonymous reviewers for their useful feedback on the multiple drafts of this chapter.

We also invite our colleagues to undertake such collaboration projects involving distributed student teams to expand the sphere of interaction in their courses. Interacting with students from unfamiliar places and cultures can assist our students in mitigating the hegemonic effects of social media of our times.

References

Anderson, P., Bergman, B., Bradley, B., Bradley, L., Gustafsson, M. & Matzke, A. (2010). Peer reviewing across the Atlantic: Patterns and trends in L1 and L2 comments made in an asynchronous online collaborative learning exchange between technical communication students in Sweden and in the United States. *Journal of Business and Technical Communication, 24*(3), 296–332. https://doi.org/10.1177/1050651910363270.

Aizpurua, A., Harper, S. & Vigo, M. (2016). Exploring the relationship between web accessibility and user experience. *International Journal of Human-Computer Studies, 91*, 13–23. https://doi.org/10.1016/j.ijhcs.2016.03.008.

Alvesson, M. & Kärreman, D. (2007). Constructing mystery: Empirical matters in theory development. *Academy of management review, 32*(4), 1265–1281.

Alvesson, M. & Sköldberg, K. (2017). Reflexive methodology: New vistas for qualitative research. Sage.

Batova, T. & Andersen, R. (2017). A systematic literature review of changes in roles/skills in component content management environments and implications for education. *Technical Communication Quarterly, 26*(2), 173–200. https://doi.org/10.1080/10572252.2017.1287958.

Bell, E. & de Gama, N. (2019). Taking a stand: The embodied, enacted and emplaced work of relational critique. *Organization, 26*(6), 936–947. https://doi.org/10.1177/1350508418815424.

Biddle, T. (2013, April 3). User Testing for Web Accessibility. http://rss2.com/feeds/Six-revisions/72.

Cardon, P. W., Fleischmann, C., Aritz, J., Ma, H., Springer, A. & Springer, S. (2022-01-04). The influence of psychological safety and personality on technology acceptance of team-based technology in global virtual teams. *Proceedings of the 55th Hawaii International Conference on System Sciences.* https://doi.org/10.24251/HICSS.2020.045.

Chong, F. (2018). Implementing usability testing in introductory technical communication service courses: Results and lessons from a local study. *IEEE: Transactions on Professional Communication, 61*(2), 196–205. https://doi.org/10.1109/TPC.2017.2771698.

Cowan, R. S. (1972). Francis Galton's statistical ideas: The influence of eugenics. *Isis, 63(4),* 509–528. https://doi.org/10.1086/351000.

Eurofound (2019). *Living and working in Europe 2015–2018*. Publications Office of the European Union.

European Political Strategy Centre (2017). *10 trends transforming education as we know it*. Publications Office of the European Union.

Dale, K. & Burrell, G. (2014). Being occupied: An embodied re-reading of organizational "wellness." *Organization*, 21(2), 159–177. https://doi.org/10.1177/1350508412473865.

Everett, H. L. (2014). Consistency & contrast: A content analysis of web design instruction. *Technical Communication*, 61(4), 245–256.

Drye, S. L., Kelly, S. & Woodard, T. (2023). Professionals' understanding of accessibility regarding business communication materials. Business and Professional *Communication Quarterly*, 86(3), 235–256. https://doi.org/10.1177/23294906221133068.

Fendler, L. & Muzaffar, I. (2008). The history of the bell curve: Sorting and the idea of normal. *Educational Theory*, 8(1), 63–82. https://doi.org/10.1111/j.1741-5446.2007.0276.x.

Hassenzahl, M. & Tractinsky, N. (2006). User experience-a research agenda. *Behaviour & Information Technology*, 25(2), 91–97. https://doi.org/10.1080/01449290500330331.

Hauck, M. (2007). Critical success factors in a TRIDEM exchange. *ReCALL*, 19(2), 202–223. https://doi.org/10.1017/S0958344007000729.

Hendren, S. (2014, October 16). All technology is assistive: Six design rules on disability. *Wired*. https://www.wired.com/2014/10/all-technology-is-assistive/.

Henry, S. L. (2007). *Just ask: Integrating accessibility throughout design*. Lulu.com.

Horton, S. & Quesenbery, W. (2014). *A web for everyone: Designing accessible user experiences*. Rosenfeld Media.

Huntsman, S. (2021). Addressing workplace accessibility practices through technical communication research methods: One size does not fit all. *IEEE Transactions on Professional Communication*, 64(3), 221–234. https://doi.org/10.1109/TPC.2021.3094036.

International Organization for Standardization. (2019, July). *Ergonomics of human system interaction—Part 210: Human-centred design for interactive systems*. (ISO DIS 9241-210:2019). https://www.iso.org/standard/77520.html.

Knight, M. & Oswal, S. K. (2018). Disability and accessibility in the workplace: Some exemplars and a research agenda for business and professional communication. Business and *Professional Communication Quarterly*, 81(4). 395–398. https://doi.org/10.1177/2329490618811188.

Koris, R., Palmer, Z. & Oswal, S. (2021). Empowering cross-disciplinary learning through Online collaboration among students and faculty from business English, website building, and accessible design fields. *Journal of University Teaching & Learning Practice*, 18(7), 112–134. https://ro.uow.edu.au/jutlp/vol18/iss7/08/.

Le Lay, B. & Card, D. (2022, October 6). Toward an access-oriented field: Reciprocity as a guiding principle for capacity-building in technical communication. SIGDOC '22: *Proceedings of the 40th ACM International Conference on Design of Communication*, 24–31. https://doi.org/10.1145/3513130.3558974.

Maylath, B., Vandepitte, S., Minacori, P., Isohella, S., Mousten, B. & Humbley, J. (2013). Managing complexity: A technical communication translation case study in multilateral international collaboration. *Technical Communication Quarterly*, 22(1), 67–84. https://doi.org/10.1080/10572252.2013.730967.

Melonçon, L. (Ed.). (2014). *Rhetorical accessibility: At the intersection of technical communication and disability studies*. Routledge.

Muller-Hartmann, A. (2000) The role of tasks in promoting intercultural learning in electronic learning networks. Language Learning & Technology, 4(2), 118–144. http://doi.org/10125/25103.

Nielsen, J. (2001, November 11). *Beyond accessibility: Treating users with disabilities as people*. Nielsen Norman Group. https://www.nngroup.com/articles/beyond-accessibility-treating-users-with-disabilities-as-people/.

Norman, D. & Nielsen, J. (1998). *The definition of user experience (UX)*. Nielsen Norman Group. https://www.nngroup.com/articles/definition-user-experience/.

O'Dowd, R. (2003) Understanding "the other side": Intercultural learning in a Spanish-English email exchange. *Language Learning & Technology*, 7(2), 118–144. http://doi.org/10125/25202.

Oswal, S. K. (2014). Participatory design: Barriers and possibilities. *Communication Design Quarterly Review*, 2(3), 14–19. https://doi.org/10.1145/2644448.2644452.

Oswal, S. K. (2018). Can workplaces, classrooms, and pedagogies be disabling? *Business and Professional Communication Quarterly*, 81(1), 3–19. https://doi.org/10.1177/2329490618765434.

Oswal, S. K. (2019, October 4). Breaking the exclusionary boundary between user experience and access: Steps toward making UX inclusive of users with disabilities. SIGDOC '19: *Proceedings of the 37th ACM International Conference on the Design of Communication, 12*, 1–8. https://doi.org/10.1145/3328020.3353957.

Oswal, S. K., Palmer, Z. B. & Koris, R. (2021). Designing virtual team projects with accessibility in mind: An illustrative example of cross-cultural student collaboration. *Journal of Virtual Exchange*, 4, 1–27. https://doi.org/10.21827/jve.4.37192.

Oswal, S. K. & Palmer, Z. B. (2022). A critique of disability and accessibility research in technical communication through the models of emancipatory disability research paradigm and participatory scholarship. In L. Melonçon & J. Schreiber (Eds.), *Assembling Critical Components: A Framework for Sustaining Technical and Professional Communication*. The WAC Clearinghouse; University Press of Colorado. https://doi.org/10.37514/TPC-B.2022.1381.

Oxford University Press. (n.d.). Work. In *OED Online*. Retrieved June 9, 2020 from http://www.oed.com/view/entry/230217 *and* http:www.oed.com/view/Entry/201997.

Palmer, Z. B., Oswal, S. K. & Koris, R. (2021). Reimagining business planning, accessibility, and web design instruction: A stacked interdisciplinary collaboration across national boundaries. *Journal of Technical Writing and Communication*, 51(4), 429–467. https://doi.org/10.1177/0047281620966990.

Palmer, Z. B. & Palmer, R. H. (2018). Legal and ethical implications of website accessibility. *Business and Professional Communication Quarterly*, 81(4), 399–420. https://doi.org/10.1177/2329490618800241.

Paretti, M. C., McNair, L. D. & Holloway-Attaway, L. (2007). Teaching technical communication in an era of distributed work: A case study of collaboration between U.S. and Swedish students. *Technical Communication Quarterly*, 16(3), 327–352. https://doi.org/10.1080/10572250701291087.

Redish, J. (2010). Technical communication and usability: Intertwined strands and mutual influences. *IEEE: Transactions in Professional Communication*, 53(3), 191–201. https://doi.org/10.1109/TPC.2010.2052861.

Redish, J. & Barnum, C. (2011). Overlap, influence, intertwining: The interplay of UX and technical communication. *Journal of Usability Studies*, 6(3), 90–101.

Ryberg, T., Dirckinck-Holmfeld, L. & Jones, C. (2011). Catering to the needs of the "digital natives" or educating the "net generation"? In M. J. W. Lee & C. McLoughlin (Eds.), *Web 2.0–based e-learning: Applying social informatics for tertiary teaching* (pp. 301–318). IGI global.

Sandnes, F. E. (2017). On-screen colour contrast for visually impaired readers. In A. Black, P. Luna, O. Lund & S. Walker (Eds.), *Information design: research and practice.* (pp. 405–416). Taylor & Francis.

Sauer, J., Sonderegger, A. & Schmutz, S. (2020). Usability, user experience and accessibility: towards an integrative model. *Ergonomics, 63*(10), 1207–1220. https://doi.org/10.1080/00140139.2020.1774080.

Schmidt, K. (1991). Riding a tiger, or computer supported cooperative work. In L. Bannon, M. Robinson & K. Schmidt (Eds.), *Proceedings of the second European conference on computer-supported cooperative work ECSCW '91* (pp. 1–16). Springer. https://link.springer.com/book/10.1007/978-94-011-3506-1.

Starke-Meyerring, D. & Andrews, D. (2006). Building a shared virtual learning culture: An international classroom partnership. *Business Communication Quarterly, 69*(1), 25–49. https://doi.org/10.1177/1080569905285543.

Treviranus, J. (2009). You say tomato, I say tomato, let's not call the whole thing off: The challenge of user experience design in distributed learning environments. *On the Horizon, 17*(3), 208–217. https://doi.org/10.1108/10748120910993231.

Turnley, M. (2007). Integrating critical approaches to technology and service-learning projects. *Technical Communication Quarterly, 16*(1), 103–123. https://doi.org/10.1080/10572250709336579.

Urrutia, J. I. G., Brangier, E., Senderowicz, V. & Cessat, L. (2017, July). Beyond "usability and user experience", towards an integrative heuristic inspection: From accessibility to persuasiveness in the UX evaluation a case study on an insurance prospecting tablet application. In *International Conference on Applied Human Factors and Ergonomics* (pp. 460–470). Springer, Cham. https://doi.org/10.48550/arXiv.1806.11291.

Venkatesh, V., Thong, J. Y. & Xu, X. (2012). Consumer acceptance and use of information technology: Extending the unified theory of acceptance and use of technology. *MIS Quarterly, 36*(1), 157–178.

Ward, M. (2009). Squaring the learning circle: Cross-classroom collaborations and the impact of audience on student outcomes in professional writing. *Journal of Business and Technical Communication, 23*(1), 61–82. https://doi.org/10.1177/1050651908324381.

Ware, P. (2005) "Missed" communication in online communication: Tensions in a German-American telecollaboration. *Language Learning & Technology, 9*(2), 64–89. http://doi.org/10125/44020.

WebAIM (2016). Introduction to web accessibility. https://webaim.org/intro/.

WHO (2019). Disability and health. https://www.who.int/news-room/fact-sheets/detail/disability-and-health.

Yesilada, Y., Brajnik, G., Vigo, M. & Harper, S. (2012, April 16). Understanding web accessibility and its drivers. *W4A '12: Proceedings of the International Cross-Disciplinary Conference on Web Accessibility, 19*, 1–9. https://doi.org/10.1145/2207016.2207027.

9. Sustainability-Driven User Experience: A Strategic Approach to Interdisciplinary Collaboration

Tatiana Batova
UNIVERSITY OF VIRGINIA

Abstract. This chapter explores the integration of sustainability within user experience (UX) education, emphasizing the role of interdisciplinary collaborations. Drawing on author's experiences with Project Cities and EPIC (Educational Partnerships for Innovation in Communities), the chapter illustrates how these initiatives facilitate practical, community-engaged learning experiences. By detailing specific classroom practices, it underscores the necessity of adaptability in course structures and the profound impacts on student engagement. Educators are offered valuable strategies for embedding sustainability in UX curricula, fostering a learning environment that is meaningful, impactful, and relevant to current societal challenges.

In exploring ways to enrich user experience (UX) education, scholars have a unique opportunity to initiate collaborative projects with diverse disciplines and community organizations.[1] Such partnerships contribute to the development of comprehensive UX courses, fostering a deep understanding of UX principles among students and preparing them for collaborative endeavors in their future careers. User experience, as defined by Norman & Nielsen, encompasses all facets of the end-user's interaction with a company, its services, and its products, highlighting the multidimensional nature of UX. This case study underscores sustainability as a particularly fruitful area for multidisciplinary collaborations, demonstrating the potential for positive impact and innovation.

First, sustainability is inherently interdisciplinary because its problems are "too new, complex, wicked, hybrid, or too risky" to be resolved by an individual discipline (Schmidt, 2008, p. 58) and because human societies and ecological systems are very interconnected and co-adaptive (Dale & Newman, 2005). Second, sustainability has gained prominence in both Human-Computer Interaction (HCI) and UX, areas that are closely linked: HCI, often considered a precursor to UX in academic research, shares common ground with UX, particularly in terms of research focus and methodologies. This intersection has given rise to Sustainable Interaction Design (Blevis, 2007), emphasizing the need to integrate sustainability goals into user-centered design processes (DiSalvo et al., 2010; Goodman,

---

1. We extend special thanks to the Project Cities Program Manager and Partner Liaison Paul Prosser, and Program Director Anne Reichman for guiding us all through the program.

2009; Mankoff et al., 2007; Raghavan & Pargman, 2017; Silberman et al., 2014), and highlighted the value of learning from other design-focused fields like architecture (Shamonsky, 2018). Furthermore, it has led to the development of specific strategies for incorporating sustainability into design practices (Frick, 2016; Kramer, 2012; Meier et al., 2011). Third, sustainability has become an important learning outcome in higher education. The United Nations Education, Scientific, and Cultural Organization (UNESCO) has been advancing Education for Sustainable Development since 1992 (UNESCO, 2017). More and more universities, recognizing the need to promote sustainability education, include sustainability into their mission statements and learning outcomes (Zhan et al., 2015). For some degree programs, like engineering, accreditation criteria now include sustainability-related elements. For example, the criteria of the Accreditation Board for Engineering and Technology (ABET) state that student outcomes already at the baccalaureate level need to include "an ability to design a system, component, or process to meet desired needs within realistic constraints such as economic, environmental, social, political, ethical, health and safety, manufacturability, and sustainability" (ABET, 2015, p. 3).

While sustainability clearly provides opportunities to serve as an organic site for UX collaborations in educational contexts, how can instructors incorporate it as a focus in UX classes? In what follows I describe a case study that provides one answer to this question.

■ Context of the Collaboration and Collaborators Involved

In the fall semester of 2017, two of my classes conducted a project that focused on redesigning a community website with an eye toward sustainability. The two classes, named User Experience and aiming at guiding students through a typical UX project, enrolled 15 graduate and 22 undergraduate students with majors ranging from technical communication to engineering (e.g., graphic information technology and human systems engineering) to design. The learning objectives of the classes were to introduce students to the principles, techniques, and tools of UX design and teach them how to approach a UX design problem holistically. Combining theoretical analysis and hands-on learning, the assignments in the two classes included researching potential and current users, with their contexts, goals, and tasks and analyzing the results of this research; planning user-focused redesigns of the website and creating such redesigns as click-through prototypes; and evaluating the effectiveness of the redesigns. The deliverables included research reports (personas, tasks, and scenarios; findings; redesign recommendations) and prototypes with evaluation plans and ROI arguments.

The project was part of the *Educational Partnerships for Innovation in Communities (EPIC) Network*, a coalition of 30+ universities that partner with local communities to catalyze improvements in places we live in (Educational Partnerships for Innovation in Communities Network, 2017). EPIC argues that most sustainability issues happen at the community level. Yet, communities often lack time, resources, and political space to do things in new ways, so EPIC helps communities to put knowledge to practice by tapping into a local university's expertise: EPIC aims at matching local communities and universities in ways that advance the needs and benefits of both, all the while engaging with existing administrative structures. The EPIC program at ASU, Project Cities, carries out the mission of improving environmental, economic, and social balance in local communities and each year connects several classes with one or several local communities.

During the 2017–2018 academic year, Project Cities worked with the community of a town located 30 miles from ASU and surrounded by beautiful nature and historical sites; the community had experienced economic hardships in previous years but was rebuilding itself to improve its perceptions, vitality, and environmental approaches. Several classes took part in Project Cities at that time: User Experience, Landscape Design, Tourism Planning, Sustainable Solid Waste Management, Public Affairs Capstone, Socio-Economic Planning, History of the Wild, Projects/Community Based Theatre, and Planning for Sustainable Communities. The nine classes worked on four structured sustainability goals identified by the community stakeholders: improving the perceptions of the community and its sustainability, finding and promoting better ways of solid waste disposal, understanding homelessness, and planning and designing a space for an off-leash dog park. My UX classes specifically focused on community perceptions and sustainability as represented in the website for visitors and addressed the following goals determined through discussions with the community: identifying key audiences and stakeholders and better understanding their perceptions about the community; determining the strengths, weaknesses, and assets of the community; and exploring alternative and additional opportunities for existing programs.

EPIC through the Project Cities program had a tremendous impact on the success of the UX classes. Two dedicated Project Cities coordinators created liaisons between the community and the classes. These coordinators fulfilled multiple project management roles, from soliciting a proposal from the community and leading the negotiations about the goals and outcomes for all involved to drafting the memorandum of understanding between community, faculty, and students and organizing milestone events (e.g., introductions and visit to the community, final presentations, etc.). Once the projects were complete, the coordinators engaged a graduate assistant to create the final report based on community goals that combined the work of all classes.

■ Challenges of the Project

Although almost all products and services typically have touchpoints with sustainability, including it as a focus of the UX classes faced two major challenges. First, defining the term "sustainability" is fraught with disagreements. The foundational and most cited definition of sustainability appeared in the Brundtland

Report and included three dimensions: environmental, social, and economic; these dimensions aim at development that meets the needs of the present without compromising the ability of future generations to meet their own needs (UN, 1987). Over the years, this definition, however, received substantial criticism due to its unclear distinction between the three original dimensions and to excluding such possible dimensions as, for example, diversity, cultural vitality, and education. As a result, in 2015, the UN adopted a sustainable development agenda that included 17 large-scale interlinked goals (UN, 2015).[2]

Second, although the fields of UX and HCI agree on the importance of making sustainability a goal for research and practice, there are contradictions in what that means. Most agree that considering sustainability includes two main directions: decreasing the environmental impacts of interactions with technology and improving sustainability in other areas through design, e.g., by influencing eco-friendly lifestyles (Mankoff et al., 2007; Raghavan & Pargman, 2017). Yet, for example, whether decreasing energy consumption of developing digital information products and the resulting user interactions is an impactful endeavor is open for discussion. On the one hand, information technologies produce about 14 percent of total emissions if indirect energy is included in the calculations (*Belkhir & Elmeligi, 2018*). On the other hand, the footprint of computing constitutes only two percent of global energy use and efficiency gains can disappear due to rebound effects, e.g., Jevons's paradox (Hakansson & Finnveden, 2015; Jevons, 1906; Raghavan & Pargman, 2017; van Heddeghem et al., 2014). In addition, while some argue that "in the case of sustainable UX, people-friendly is also more planet-friendly" (Frick, 2016), others see the potential of sustainability goals being at odds with user-centeredness: "If we think of observing users and using this as the 'rightness' to infuse into design processes, we need to fully understand if and when what we observe are in fact sustainable actions" (Kramer, 2012). In such a way, users might actually need to be persuaded to act sustainably (DiSalvo et al., 2010).

■ Results of the Collaboration

To address the challenge of defining sustainability and determining its implications for UX, I introduced sustainability as a design challenge: How can we add sustainability goals when engaging in UX-focused website redesign?

Following Ann Dale and Lenore Newman (2005), who considered meaningful all-encompassing definitions neither possible nor useful in dealing with complex systems such as sustainability, I did not provide students with a single

---

2. No poverty; zero hunger; good health and well-being; quality education; gender equality; clean water and sanitation; affordable and clean energy; decent work and economic growth; industry, innovation, and infrastructure; reduced inequality; sustainable cities and communities; responsible consumption and production; climate action; life below water; life on land; peace, justice, and strong institutions; partnerships to achieve the goals.

definition of sustainability. Instead, I challenged them to compare the definitions from the Brundtland Report with the UN's large-scale goals, while also analyzing several short readings discussing the controversies of sustainability in HCI. As a result, students learned to see the purposeful ambiguity in defining sustainability as a productive arena for discussing the often-overwhelming sustainability goals in a specific context of a specific community with tangible, unique challenges: to tailor their own definition to "achieve concrete goals in their unique situation given the constraints of institutional history, existing frameworks, and structural and financial limitations" (Dale & Newman, 2005, p. 354). For example, using the UN goals to examine community needs and challenges, students combined the goals of creating resilient communities with economic growth and goals related to decreasing energy consumption and preventing pollution. As a result, they focused on conservation of resources (energy, finances, time) and user behaviors (recycling, free time activities).

Working on this design challenge, in addition to user and context research (content audit, comparative analysis, interview, survey, card sort, and usability testing), students communicated with community partners, with students of different majors in the UX classes, with students from other classes, and with Project Cities coordinators. They recruited and worked with users that reflected personas developed based on descriptions provided by the community (users for in-person testing were recruited from students' personal circles; users for remote testing were recruited through the educational partnership with TryMyUI). As a result, they worked on the following intersections of sustainability and UX throughout both their research and redesign projects:

- *Including sustainability into research.* Students argued that an effective approach to encouraging sustainable behavior is focusing parts of user research on sustainability, for example, including sustainability-related questions into surveys or interviews.
- *Developing personas, tasks, and scenarios.* Based on the results of their research, students included sustainability-related needs and goals into their personas, tasks, and scenarios (e.g., an environmentally conscious day hiker).
- *Including sustainability into content strategy.* Students started their projects with content audits and comparative analyses. For comparison, they selected the websites of communities that actively promote sustainable lifestyles during comparative analyses. Getting to know the content and information architecture of the website during content audits, students then suggested additional content about green tourism, garbage disposal, and recycling (which they could later adjust based on information from the tourism planning and waste management classes).
- *Uncovering inefficient design elements.* Students specifically tested the importance and usability of such website elements as an introductory video and a downloadable high-resolution information brochure because

both require more battery power for viewing. While the short video proved "fun" while only somewhat helpful, users typically tried to avoid downloading the PDF booklets, particularly on mobile devices.
- *Uncovering ineffective content.* Attracting visitors to the city through its website became an important part of both economic and social sustainability focus. It involved making the website attractive and easy-to-use. Based on content audits and user and stakeholder (e.g., current residents, business owners) research and thanks to feedback from other classes (e.g., tourism planning), students identified content that had little relevance for visitors or was ineffective.
- *Improving navigation and findability.* Students argued that navigation and findability are important factors for economic sustainability that also have the potential to preserve energy. Students focused on first testing navigation labels and then performing card sorts to determine the most intuitive navigational structures. Based on the results of the content audit and other user-research methods (e.g., interviews, observations), they also included content that was not on the website originally but was mentioned by most research participants (e.g., lodging). Including such content allowed users to find information quickly without having to leave the city's website. Based on the results of card sorts, user interviews, and conversations with community partners, students also suggested including quick filtering options for common searches, for example, family-friendly restaurants, dog-friendly hotels, outdoor activities for seniors, etc. Yet another element to improve findability was a filterable calendar of events.
- *Recommending a web Content Management System (CMS).* Because community partners wanted to make website design and upkeep more streamlined to save time and resources (and energy), students suggested switching from outsourcing website design to using in-house resources and talent and a web CMS. As a result, students included recommendations about web CMSs in their research findings.

While not each student engaged with every intersection of sustainability and UX described above due to the unique directions their projects pursued, they became familiar with these intersections through peer-review. As a result, they considered sustainable development as "a constantly moving target whose boundary domains evolve" (Dale & Newman, 2005)—just as the connection of UX and sustainability does.

Practical Implications

This project illustrated that sustainability can be a productive site for interdisciplinary UX collaborations, especially when students are encouraged to freely explore its meaning and relevance.

In the case study I describe, students got experience of working with a variety of stakeholders and disciplines, thus learning how to present the value of UX work. Including sustainability as a UX focus helped establish UX as a key stakeholder of the overall project, showing students that sustainability in UX is an exciting niche and an opportunity to showcase UX as a decision driver.

What is more, students learned how to engage with the definitions of sustainability productively and see possible connections of the pillars of sustainability (e.g., including green tourism and deleting a PDF brochure having both environmental and economic impacts). Understanding sustainability broadly is particularly beneficial in interdisciplinary contexts, where more space for various stakeholders to work toward a unique and constructive dialogue is necessary (Dale, 2001). In addition, students practiced how to address UX- and HCI-specific contradictions in sustainability work (e.g., focusing on green tourism as a means of persuasion). The project also helped them see traditional UX questions from the sustainability perspective (e.g., the value of good navigation in making a website intuitive, attractive, empowering—and energy efficient).

Focusing on sustainability in a UX class project helped crystallize two important practical implications for educators:

- *Search for existing collaborative infrastructures on your campus and nationally.* Sustainability is a topic for which one can often find existing *programs*. Its comprehensiveness can allow educators to leverage teaching partners on campus with already existing community connections and tap into the extensive infrastructure sponsored by EPIC. As a result, students in my courses benefited from a clear structure in communicating with the community, support network of Project Cities, connections to students in courses from a variety of disciplines, and opportunities to showcase their work within the university. Community partners benefited from the continuous nature of the project, with several new courses picking up the baton in the following semesters. I as a faculty member benefitted from establishing connections within the cross-disciplinary academic team and gaining visibility for the UX program. In addition, receiving the infrastructural support frees up faculty time and can allow the faculty member to be more experimental with class formats. Both classes I described were conducted in an intensive online format, which can make any faculty member shy away from collaborative, community-engaged projects due to time commitments, yet it proved to be a viable option in this case (Batova, 2021).
- *Be flexible with the elements of the course structure.* To ensure the success of your course, it is crucial to maintain flexibility in the course structure. Encourage open discussions with your students about the dynamic nature of the project and be prepared to adapt various elements of the course, such as communication channels and deliverables. You might consider

incorporating methodologies like lean UX, which allows for iterative testing and pivoting throughout the project. For example, based on the lean UX methodology, I decided on weekly units that focused on testing specific hypotheses that provided student teams multiple opportunities to adjust their work (Batova, 2021). When faced with challenges such as online communication with community partners or time constraints, promoting a structured team approach can enhance project management and ensure smoother collaboration. Even if certain outcomes, like clickable prototypes, are not required in the final deliverables, guide your students to compile and present their work in a manner that is accessible and useful to the recipients. The positive feedback from the community partners justified the flexibility-focused approach: research-driven recommendations and prototypes allowed them to allocate resources to the website redesign.

It is important to note that students' engagement in the two UX classes was very high; many of them commented on feeling that they can impact real change in a project that addresses one of the key issues our society faces today. Although graduate students were somewhat better equipped for the amount of work in the classes, the project appealed to all students, confirming that current cohorts of students are highly concerned about and willing to engage in sustainable behaviors (Fullerton et al., 2019; Petro, 2020).

■ References

ABET. (2015). Criteria for Accrediting Engineering Programs, 2018–2019. https://tinyurl.com/4a83rswd.

Batova, T. (2021). An approach for incorporating community-engaged learning in intensive online classes: Sustainability and lean user experience. *Technical Communication Quarterly, 30*(4), 410–422. https://doi.org/10.1080/10572252.2020.1860257.

Belkhir, L. & Ahmed, Elmeligi. A. (2018). Assessing ICT global emissions footprint: Trends to 2040 & recommendations. *Journal of Cleaner Production, 177*(10), 448–463. https://doi.org/10.1016/j.jclepro.2017.12.239.

Blevis, E. (2007). Sustainable interaction design: Invention & disposal, renewal & reuse. *Proceedings of the SIGCHI Conference on Human Factors in Computing Systems—CHI '07*, 503. https://doi.org/10.1145/1240624.1240705.

Dale, A. (2001). *At the edge: Sustainable development in the 21st century.* University of British Columbia Press.

Dale, A. & Newman, L. (2005). Sustainable development, education and literacy. *International Journal of Sustainability in Higher Education, 6*(4), 351–362. https://doi.org/10.1108/14676370510623847.

DiSalvo, C., Senger, P. & Brynjarsdottir, H. (2010). Mapping the landscape of sustainable HCI. *Proceedings of the SIGCHI Conference on Human Factors in Computing Systems*, 1975–1984.

Educational Partnerships for Innovation in Communities Network. (2017). About. https://www.epicn.org/about/.

Frick, T. (2016). *Designing for sustainability: A guide to building greener digital products and services*. O'Reilly Media.

Fullerton, S., McCullough, T. & Moore, D. (2019). Consumer actions and attitudes regarding initiatives directed towards sustainability: Assessing gender and generational gaps. *Association of Marketing Theory and Practice Proceedings*, 6. https://digitalcommons.georgiasouthern.edu/amtp-proceedings_2019/6.

Goodman, E. (2009). Three environmental discourses in human-computer interaction. *CHI '09 extended abstracts on human factors in computing systems*, 2535–2544. ACM.

Hakansson, C. & Finnveden, G. (2015). Indirect rebound and reverse rebound effects in the ICT-sector and emissions of CO_2. *Joint Conference on 29th International Conference on Informatics for Environmental Protection/3rd International Conference on ICT for Sustainability (EnviroInfo and ICT4S)*, 66–73. https://doi.org/10.2991/ict4s-env-15.2015.8.

Jevons, W. (1906). *The coal question: An inquiry concerning the progress of the nation, and the probable exhaustion of our coal-mines*. Macmillan.

Kramer, K.-L. (2012). *User experience in the age of sustainability: A practitioner's blueprint*. Morgan Kaufmann.

Mankoff, J., Blevis, E., Borning, A., Friedman, B., Fussell, S., Hasbrouck, J., Sengers, P. (2007, April). Environmental sustainability and interaction. CHI EA '07: *CHI '07 Extended Abstracts on Human Factors in Computing Systems*, 2121–2124. ACM. https://doi.org/10.1145/1240866.1240963.

Meier, A., Aragon, C., Peffer, T., Perry, D. & Pritoni, M. (2011). Making energy savings easier: Usability metrics for thermostats. *Journal of Usability Studies*, 6(4), 226–244.

Petro, G. (2020, January 31). Sustainable retail: How gen Z is leading the pack. *Forbes*. https://tinyurl.com/4zdjytvf.

Raghavan, B. & Pargman, D. (2017, May 2). Means and ends in human-computer interaction: Sustainability through disintermediation. *CHI '17: Proceedings of the 2017 CHI Conference on Human Factors in Computing Systems*, 786–796. https://doi.org/10.1145/3025453.3025542.

Schmidt, J. (2008). Towards a philosophy of interdisciplinarity. *Poiesis Praxis*, 5, 53–69.

Shamonsky, D. (2018). Developing a code of ethics for UX design: What we can learn from the field of architecture. *UXPA Magazine*. https://uxpamagazine.org/developing-a-code-of-ethics/.

Silberman, M., Nathan, L., Knowles, B., Bendor, R., Clear, A., Hakansson, M., Mankoff, J. (2014). Next steps for sustainable HCI. *Interactions*, 21(5), 66–69. https://doi.org/10.1145/2651820.

UN (1987). Our common future. http://www.un-documents.net/ocf-02.htm.

UN (September 25, 2015). Transforming our world: The 2030 agenda for sustainable development. https://sdgs.un.org/2030agenda.

UNESCO. (2017). *Education for sustainable development goals: Learning objectives*. UNESCO. https://tinyurl.com/39zhsy6fvan

Heddeghem, W., Lambert, S., Lannoo, B., Colle, D., Pickavet, M. & Demeester, P. (2014). Trends in worldwide ICT electricity consumption from 2007 to 2012. *Computer Communications*, 50, 64–76. https://doi.org/10.1016/j.comcom.2014.02.008.

Zhan, Z., Fong, P. S. W., Mei, H., Chang, X., Liang, T. & Ma, Z. (2015). Sustainability education in massive open online courses: A content analysis approach. *Sustainability*, 7(3), 2274–2300. https://doi.org/10.3390/su7032274.

10. How Long Have We Been Doing This Again? Establishing a Long-Term Interdepartmental UX Collaboration on Campus

Ashley Patriarca
WEST CHESTER UNIVERSITY OF PENNSYLVANIA

Kristin Williams
AVALIGN TECHNOLOGIES

Abstract. This chapter offers a picture of a multidisciplinary UX collaboration on a university campus that benefits students in an upper-level professional and technical writing course, as well as departments across the university. We also offer recommendations for colleagues beginning their own interdepartmental collaborations on campus and share sample materials for reuse or adaptation in similar courses at other universities.

Since Fall 2015, we've worked on a client-based collaborative project housed in a professional and technical writing minor course that tests the usability of our university's department websites. Although this type of client-based project often involves clients who are external to the university, we have found that this internal, interdepartmental collaboration can offer at minimum equal benefits for the students and clients involved. In our collaboration, we respond to a call from Therese M. Judge (2006), who urged faculty teaching upper-level writing courses to find opportunities for students to partner with departments across campus. We also build on the work of other teacher-scholars in technical communication, who have urged us to find ways to incorporate hands-on usability experiences for our students to prepare them for the changing workplace (Lauer & Brumberger, 2016) and to be rhetorically engaged citizens (Scott, 2008; Bartolotta et al., 2018). Our project also involves multidisciplinary collaboration at multiple levels: not only do we (the facilitators) come from different university departments and areas of expertise, the students in the course also come from a wide range of majors and possess a variety of strengths that contribute to the success of the collaboration.

In the sections that follow, we'll share information about our project and offer recommendations for colleagues beginning their own interdepartmental collaborations on campus. We also share sample assignments and course structures for adaptation or reuse in similar courses.

DOI: https://doi.org/10.37514/TPC-B.2025.2517.2.10

But First, Who Are We?

Ashley teaches the upper-level technical writing and usability class in which this project is housed. She coaches students through the day-to-day elements of the project, including issues with collaboration, project management, working with clients and users, usability research methods, and analyzing the data. She grounds students in the theory and practice of user experience and usability, ensuring that they understand the importance of what they are doing in this project.

Until her departure from West Chester in late 2021, Kristin worked as part of the university's web team, which develops, maintains, and supports all of the university's websites. She served as the class' point of contact for the web team and department clients. In this role, she represented department website goals to the students in the class and communicated the website's user needs to the web team and its department clients.

Why This Partnership Matters

This partnership has high stakes for our campus. University websites are a primary method by which current and potential students learn information about their programs, as well as critical information about campus resources and deadlines. First-generation college students are even more likely than their peers to seek information from university websites (Grim, et al., 2021), and approximately 30 percent of our university's students are first-generation students. This combination of factors makes the quality of our websites an equity issue on campus. More, our university is a regional comprehensive public university that primarily serves residents of our state: approximately 85 percent of our undergraduate students are in-state residents (West Chester University of Pennsylvania Institutional Research, 2021), with most of the remaining student population attending from an hour or less away. Through improving the university's communication and outreach to residents who wish to attend the university, our collaboration has directly helped our institution achieve its mission of serving our state.

Keeping the usability testing on campus has an immediate impact on students, as well. The course's students, who mostly come from the campus' professional and technical writing (PTW) minor or various computer science programs, gain valuable projects for their portfolios. Even more importantly, they are deeply invested in the projects as ones that will have an immediate impact on their own lives and on the lives of their friends and classmates. The students in the class also know that the university is responding to their concerns about key department websites through this collaboration. Even when students have a steep learning curve regarding usability, those connections to their peers and to their clients encourage them to remain active in the project. In this way, too, our collaboration contributes towards our university's mission to educate citizens who are deeply engaged with their communities.

■ Project Structure

In this section, we describe the specific contexts of the collaborative usability project and, when appropriate, connect to a Creative Commons-licensed version of the course documents. It's also important to note that this project has not always been structured in the way we describe below. It's grown significantly—expanding from a single, four-week unit in the course into a semester-long project that has completely reshaped the course itself—as we've learned more about our own collective strengths, our students' varied needs and background knowledges, and our department clients' needs. As we've gotten more skilled and more comfortable in working together, we have been able to respond to our contexts in a way that simply wouldn't have been possible back in 2015.

Introducing Key Concepts for the Course

Each iteration of the course begins with an individual website analysis assignment designed to familiarize students with usability concepts. This project provides critical scaffolding, given that few students enter the class with any exposure to usability (and sometimes even without prior exposure to professional writing classes). It also allows Ashley to identify and support any students who are struggling with usability, before those individual difficulties are hidden in the collaborative work.

To prepare for their website analysis, students read introductory works from the now-archived Usability.gov, professional and technical writing scholars focused on usability, industry professionals, and accessibility experts; more specific information about the readings throughout the course can be found in our sample calendar. Students also analyze and discuss case studies, including ongoing analyses of Instagram and recent website accessibility lawsuits, to understand *why* these details are so important. To assess their knowledge of these introductory concepts, students review the usability and accessibility principles of a website of their choice (or a nonprofit or research partner website when available, such as the local National Writing Project site). This project helps students learn concepts like the five elements of usability, as well as how to focus on website issues that are actionable. More, the project helps them understand the importance of usability and UX and become more critical, informed users of the websites they encounter on a regular basis.

Shifting into the Collaborative Project

At the end of the website analysis assignment, students begin to learn more about the practice of collaboration: how to handle difficult conversations and situations, what it feels like to research and write together, and how to manage a larger project such as the one they're about to begin. Ashley then divides students into groups based on a combination of individual schedules and strengths; the goal here is to eliminate one of the biggest challenges for collaboration among students, many of whom work at least one part-time job, commute over half an hour, and/or are caring for family members. Though students have significant time in class to work together on the project, they still need at least one common hour a week outside of class to meet, conduct tests, or complete other tasks during the project. Students then formalize their expectations and guidelines through a team plan.

Then, Kristin or another member of the Web Team meets with the whole class to discuss how the Web Team works with department clients to develop their websites, balancing the importance of usability and accessibility with the department's own goals for the website. She also introduces the department websites that the student groups will be testing that semester, and these websites usually represent a mix of academic departments (e.g., biology and music) and administrative departments that affect students across the university (e.g., financial aid and undergraduate admissions). These testing goals for these sites also vary: some clients' sites have been recently restructured and need feedback on a new iteration, while others are preparing for an upcoming site redesign. Each group gets to pick its websites out of a hat, with the opportunity to trade if the students wish to do so. If there are more client websites than groups, the remaining websites become in-class practice sites, so that those clients can also receive at least informal feedback on their websites to accomplish their goals.

Focusing on User Needs and Goals

As soon as each group has its assigned website, Ashley focuses on the different users their websites might have and what their needs are, using the contextual questions from St.Amant (2018) as a framework for the discussion. What tasks might users need to accomplish with that website? In what contexts do they encounter the websites? How might those user needs change over time? Then, students learn how to create effective tasks for study participants to complete, and they practice writing tasks for their assigned website. The user analysis and task development each become a smaller assignment that contributes to the larger usability report.

The class also discusses best practices for recruiting participants, and students learn about the challenges they might face in terms of that recruitment. Students then compose recruiting scripts for different audiences—including classmates, friends, faculty, and staff—and analyze the differences in each approach. Once the scripts are ready, groups can begin recruiting participants for their tests. Ideally, each group's participants represent a range of their assigned website's users. In some cases, this isn't possible, due to a lack of access to incoming students or perhaps a lack of participation from faculty or staff.

Usability Testing

Following J. Blake Scott's (2008) call for more hands-on student experience with usability methods in the classroom, Ashley creates space in several class meetings for students to practice different usability methods, such as card sorting, focus groups, system usability scales, and more. Students learn about the kinds of information each method can provide, the limitations of each method, and the need to balance both quantitative issues (such as "how long does it take to answer the question?") with qualitative details such as user satisfaction with the site. Ashley also models how to facilitate usability testing, with students taking turns being a participant or a facilitator. This practice helps the students troubleshoot their processes before any facilitation issues affect their testing data, and it helps them differentiate between their own status as facilitators and sometimes-users of the websites they are testing and that of the participants whose varied perspectives they need to learn. As Bartolotta and colleagues (2018) note, this differentiation can be challenging for students coming to usability testing for the first time, making this in-class facilitation practice crucial.

As the project continues, student groups design their own usability tests using a range of methods that address usability and accessibility. Then, they run those tests with their participants, focusing on content, organization, site architecture, and user satisfaction. Along the way, students contact Kristin or another member of the Web Team if they find items that require immediate correction (e.g., broken links or incorrect information). Communication is primarily via email at this stage, and that communication could be initiated by Ashley or by students in the class.

Once testing is complete, the students bring the data back to class and look for patterns as a group. As a class, students discuss how to report results and develop actionable recommendations. Then, the groups develop detailed usability reports for their assigned websites and present their findings and recommendations to department clients and representatives of the web team at the end of the semester. This presentation is key: it asks students to take the full project seriously, and it reminds them that the university is listening to their concerns through the enthusiastic attendance of the Web Team and department representatives.

What We've Learned

Each of us considers this partnership both sustainable and successful. As we prepare to enter the eleventh year of the partnership during the 2025–2026 academic year, we'd like to share a few takeaways for colleagues who might be interested in developing a similar project at their own universities.

Give Your Collaboration Time

When our collaboration began, we were both still new to our roles on campus, and we didn't know each other well. As a result, early iterations of the project were a little awkward, with each of us trying to figure out what would work best without stepping on each other's toes. Now, when Kristin or another member of the Web Team comes to visit the class at the beginning of each semester, one of us invariably asks the other, "How long have we been doing this again?" More, the time we've both invested in the collaboration has given us the ability to communicate openly about what's working and what isn't each semester. It's a partnership that now works so well that we sometimes forget all that we've invested to make it work.

Part of why it works so well is that we have different skills and backgrounds. Kristin brought the technical knowledge of implementing the recommendations, as well as an understanding of navigating the department clients' needs, and Ashley brought an in-depth knowledge of structuring professional writing research projects and teaching client-based writing. Neither of us could do this project alone. In this way, our collaboration mirrors that of the students each semester. Students come to the class from a variety of majors and minors, including computer science, English, communication studies, and/or the professional and technical writing minor. Thus, the students bring varying knowledge about web development and writing in plain language to their own collaborative usability tests.

Our familiarity also benefits students. Because students come to the class with varying levels of UX and usability knowledge, having a well-maintained partnership between the instructor and client representative eliminates an additional possible source of friction. They are then free to focus on grappling with the concepts and developing effective tests, rather than worrying about potential miscommunication between new collaborators.

For faculty and staff collaborating on UX projects at their own campuses, we recommend being patient with each other and with the process. Though faculty might be used to preparing students for collaborative projects, a partnership like this one might be new to you. As with any collaboration, some early awkwardness is to be expected. Check in with each other regularly, especially during the first iteration of the partnership, to ensure that everyone's needs are being met.

Keep Personnel as Consistent as Possible in the Beginning of the Collaboration

Ashley initially taught the course every semester out of necessity: the few other faculty members who could teach it were needed to teach other courses. However, that necessity offered an unexpected benefit: consistency in our collaboration. We've now grown comfortable enough with the project to be able to rotate our roles out: other faculty members have taught the course when Ashley was needed in other roles, and other members of the web content team have taken on Kristin's original role in the project now that she has left the university. It's clear from recent iterations of the project that we established a sustainable structure and comfort level that other folks can adopt and/or update as needed. This simply would not have been possible if other faculty members rotated into the course regularly at the beginning.

If you're considering a project like this one, we recommend keeping the personnel as consistent as possible in early iterations of the course. If you switch out personnel while you're still navigating early awkwardness, you will likely struggle to develop the familiarity that a truly deep, sustainable partnership requires.

Set Up Project Parameters Early in the Semester

In the early years of this project, students focused heavily on certain findings that simply couldn't be changed without a wholesale revamp of the website—for example, the placement of a contact button or the website search bar. Once we realized this, we filed the feedback for the next significant website rebranding, and we began to discuss what would and wouldn't be actionable in this situation early on every semester. Now, students can note these details if they emerge during user testing, but they're not positioned as time-sensitive within their reports. We've also learned to encourage students to report time-sensitive details (such as broken links) *before* completing their reports; doing so gives the Web Team action items that can be completed during the same semester. Students can then see their changes implemented in real time, giving them even more of an investment in the project.

When planning a partnership like this one, we recommend setting aside time for the staff partner to visit the class early in the semester: this allows the staff partner to establish project parameters at the beginning of the project. We also recommend consistent communication of time-sensitive information so that those issues can be corrected during the semester.

Scaffold the Coursework Appropriately for Your Students

Despite many of our students coming to the class from the PTW minor or computer science programs, many of them have no prior experience with usability or user experience. Some students even come to us with no prior professional and technical writing courses: for these students, the course fills a general education writing requirement or is an elective option within their major or minor program. The variety in backgrounds can be a strength when students get to the collaborative project; however, it presents an initial challenge for all of the students, who may need to know more about usability, web writing, and/or working with clients. Thus, we each must do a *lot* of scaffolding with students to ensure that they're prepared to discuss their findings with clients in a confident and professional manner. This kind of preparation isn't unique to this project; as Lee-Ann Kastman Breuch (2001) and others have noted, it's essential to any client project our students prepare. We have certainly found this to be true: As we have devoted more time to scaffolding and expanded the scope of the project, students' website recommendations have become richer, more clearly rooted in solid research, and easier to justify and implement for department clients. More, students are more comfortable interacting with the faculty and staff as experts themselves, and they're better prepared for handling challenging clients in future workplace situations.

If you're considering a project like this one on your campus, factor in your local contexts. Which students would be most likely to take this course, and why? What previous exposure have they had to UX, usability, or technical writing? These responses will help you scaffold the work in a way that is appropriate for your students. For us, we needed to build significant scaffolding for students to ensure the work was appropriate and useful for our department clients; in fact, we needed the full semester to give students the space to do the project well. If you work primarily with students who have previous exposure to UX & usability concepts, you may be able to build this project into half of a semester—or you may wish to continue with a full semester schedule and allow students to further develop skills in a related area (e.g., client presentation skills).

Limit Department Client Involvement Early on, but Encourage Them to Visit Presentations

Students found it harder to develop recommendations when clients visited at the beginning of the project: they felt more obligated to be kind and understanding of the clients' needs in a way that wasn't always productive for website critique. More, the students may have felt a power imbalance, as most department clients were faculty or department chairs who could have some impact on the students' college careers. However, it's clear that the department clients shared the same goals as the students themselves: improving these critical websites for their users. They *wanted* to be involved. The challenge for our collaboration, then, was balancing our desire to include our clients while offering students the space they needed to learn about the departments and test the websites.

We have found that the best results and recommendations have emerged when students are positioned as user advocates from the beginning, with Kristin or another member of the Web Team serving as the point of contact for department clients. Direct student-client contact is thus limited; however, indirect communication occurs throughout the project via Ashley and the Web Team, and students recruit members of the department community as participants. By the time students meet the website clients for presentations at the end of the semester, they are fully confident in the research they have completed and can recommend even significant changes to the website. This structure has been beneficial for our already over-stretched clients, too: they get to see the students as experts in how users interact with the department's website, and it limits the amount of time our clients are required to contribute throughout the semester.

They appreciate our attempts to be mindful of their time: when department clients redesign their websites, they frequently ask to have the class retest their sites.

If you're developing a partnership like this one on your campus, we recommend limiting client involvement at the beginning of the project. This choice allows students to develop the abilities and confidence they need to persuade their department clients. It also respects the time of your department clients, a strategy that encourages those clients to have their sites tested in multiple iterations of the course.

▪ The Partnership Evolves

This partnership is one that has proven to be sustainable, despite changes in personnel and even through changes wrought by the COVID-19 pandemic. Since we began writing this chapter, Kristin has left the university for a position in industry, and one of her former Web Team colleagues has taken on her original role in the partnership. In addition, two other English department faculty with expertise in web writing and user experience now regularly rotate in to teach the course when Ashley is not available. Our early emphasis on collaboration and trust has proven critical during these personnel changes: they've allowed us to respond quickly to the awkwardness of changes to the course, to the personnel, and to the very foundations of higher education.

More importantly, that emphasis has allowed us to react quickly and effectively to the most dramatic shift in the course since our partnership began: the shift to remote learning that occurred in response to the ongoing COVID-19 pandemic. On March 10, 2020, West Chester University announced that instruction would be remote for the remainder of the Spring 2020 semester (Fiorentino, 2020), and we remained in this mode through the entirety of the 2020–2021 academic year, even after other universities returned to in-person learning. Despite changes in instruction modality, as well as the significant pressure of teaching and learning during a pandemic, the collaboration—and students' course experiences—remained strong. Though neither author was involved with these iterations of the class, the faculty and staff who were involved with the course during remote learning leaned on the field's existing strengths in online pedagogy and distributed collaboration to help the collaboration succeed: they relied on existing strategies to help students connect in online learning and incorporated technologies that offered robust features for online collaboration (e.g., Slack, Discord, and Zoom).

▪ What's Next?

Given the scope of recent changes to the collaboration—new personnel, new mode of learning, a global crisis that has affected both physical and mental health—it would be unsurprising if our now eleven-year partnership had failed along the way. Happily, that hasn't been the case. Instead, with each new person who joins the partnership, as well as each new challenge that occurs, we learn new strategies to improve the course and make our collaboration richer and more sustainable. Although teaching this class remotely during the pandemic was not an easy task, student response to the format was positive: they appreciated having dedicated time to work together remotely to complete the usability research, and they were equally excited to add more workplace technology to their skillsets. Given that response, Ashley is now working with colleagues in the professional and technical writing minor to develop a permanent, hybrid face-to-face/online iteration of the course.

We're also thrilled to say that the work of students in the course is having a significant impact on the overall university website. Higher-order structural concerns that student groups identified through their research were addressed in recent (Fall 2021) major updates to the university's website branding and template. We anticipate that as departments continue to update their sites to take advantage of the new template, students in the course will provide feedback at multiple stages of the revision process. The new branding also means new testing based on changing user needs and priorities. Given the dramatic shifts in both due to the ongoing pandemic, updated testing is particularly essential for every academic and administrative department.

If you're interested in learning more about the course that supports this partnership, we offer assignment instructions, a sample course calendar, and more in a Google Drive folder at https://tinyurl.com/4u29aunu. All of these documents are licensed under Creative Commons CC-BY-NC-SA, meaning that you are welcome to distribute, remix, adapt, and build upon the material in any medium or format for noncommercial purposes only, as long as you credit Ashley as the creator of those works. We also welcome conversations about similar partnerships and encourage you to reach out to us if you have questions.

■ References

Bartolotta, J., Newmark, J. & Bourelle, T. (2018). Engaging with online design: Undergraduate user-participants and the practice-level struggles of usability learning. *Communication Design Quarterly*, 5(3), 63–72. https://doi.org/10.1145/3188173.3188180.

Fiorentino, C. (2020, March 10). *Health update: March 10, 2020*. West Chester University of Pennsylvania. https://tinyurl.com/32vpdrdz.

Grim, J. K., Bausch, E., Hussain, A. & Lonn, S. (2021). Is it what you know or who you know?: An information typology of how first-generation college students access campus resources. *Journal of College Student Retention: Research, Theory & Practice*, 26(1), 194–215. https://doi.org/10.1177/15210251211068115.

Judge, T. M. (2006). Service learning on campus. *Business Communication Quarterly*, 69(2), 189–192. https://doi.org/10.1177/1080569906900208.

Kastman Breuch, L.-A. M. (2001). The overruled dust mite: Preparing technical communication students to interact with clients. *Technical Communication Quarterly*, 10(2), 193. https://doi.org/10.1207/s15427625tcq1002_5.

Lauer, C. & Brumberger, E. (2016). Technical communication as user experience in a broadening industry landscape. *Technical Communication, 63*(3), 248–264. https://engl334w.wordpress.com/wp-content/uploads/2018/08/lauer-and-brumberger.pdf.

Scott, J. B. (2008). The practice of usability: Teaching user engagement through service-learning. *Technical Communication Quarterly, 17*(4), 381–412. https://doi.org/10.1080/10572250802324929.

St.Amant, K. (2018). Editor's introduction: Reflecting on and re-thinking usability and user experience design. *Communication Design Quarterly, 5*(3), 4–9. https://doi.org/10.1145/3188173.3188174.

West Chester University of Pennsylvania Institutional Research. (2021). *University enrollment*. West Chester University of Pennsylvania. https://www.wcupa.edu/deputy-provost/institutionalResearch/universityEnrollment.aspx.

11. Forming and Sustaining One Collaborative Service-Learning Partnership Around UX

Joseph W. Robertshaw
UNIVERSITY OF ALABAMA IN HUNTSVILLE

Abstract. This chapter describes the processes for setting up, managing, and maintaining a relationship with a community partner/client that yields valuable experiences for students and clients as they engage with concepts and tools of user experience (UX). It also presents five key takeaways from the lessons we learned through this experience that confirm ground and extend previous research.

In Spring Semester 2021, the technical writing classes I taught, both online and on-site, began participating in a user experience (UX) project to test the usability of our university library's website. They approached the project from a student user's perspective using tools and methods common to UX. We treated the experience as a client-centered service-learning project with a group of librarians, The Library Website Board, as our client. The students work in teams through online communication platforms to conceive, plan, propose, coordinate, execute and deliver their own UX study for the client in both written form and via remote presentation. The approach to service learning through UX offers significant value pedagogically, experientially, and it has produced actionable insight and usable data for the client. This article is an account of the formation of the partnership and the lessons learned in the first two iterations of this mostly online arrangement. There are more lessons, of course, but here I discuss five of them:

- Get the insight and approval of the leadership on both sides of the collaboration.
- Properly serve and respect the needs of all stakeholders.
- Work out a schedule and expectations.
- Make the rewards for stakeholders tangible.
- Never not working; always plan ahead.

A Bit of Background

The project did not spring from my forehead fully formed and dressed for battle. It was *phronetic*—born of wisdom gained through experience—as I worked at it from both ends. I teach business writing, technical writing, technical editing, and new media & rhetoric classes as a full-time lecturer in a business and technical writing program housed in an English department. That department lives within the College of Arts, Humanities, and Social Sciences, at a very high research activity university (R–1) in the Southeastern United States. The class rosters are typically capped at 20-ish students. Enrollments are majority white with a significant presence of Black, Latinx, Asian, and international learners. I also have many first generation and rural students. The class formats are a mix of online, face-to-face, and hybrid courses in a full-time teaching load of 15 credit hours per 16-week semester: four 3-credit courses and 3-credit hours of service to the department and the college.

Table 11.1. Project Schedule: October/November 2021

Week	Date	Due
8	Oct 4–10	UX Client Zoom Meeting + Release UX Tools (6th)
9	Oct 11–17	UX Audience Analysis (11th)
		UX Proposal (17th)
10	Oct 18–24	UX Progress Report 1 (24th)
11	Oct 25–31	UX Draft (31st)
12	Nov 1–7	UX Progress Report 2 (7th)
13	Nov 8–14	UX Progress CRC (14th)
14	Nov 15–21	UX Presentation (21st)
16	Last Class	UX Debrief Report (24th)

■ What We Do

I usually have two or three sections of the *Intro to Tech Writing* course. I divide each section into four teams, and each team has four to five students. This team size promotes the visibility and participation of each member: remaining small enough to be agile but robust enough to execute the labor the UX project requires. The project occupies weeks 8–14 of a 16-week term. We have a warm-up team exercise (Unboxing the Rubric in Week 2) and another smaller team project (WordPress Startup Guide in Week 5–6) before the UX project begins.

This scaffolded approach allows students to get to know their team members, come to understand basic roles of teamwork, and familiarize themselves with the communication platform Discord. These are all problems of preparing the students to meet UX for the first time and in a service-learning setting. This is not slavish nor dreaded labor for, as Dewey writes, "The difficulties that present themselves within the development of an experience are, however, to be cherished by the educator, not minimized, for they are the natural stimuli to reflective inquiry" (Dewey, 1910). My preparation translates to student learning and often to my own teaching innovation.

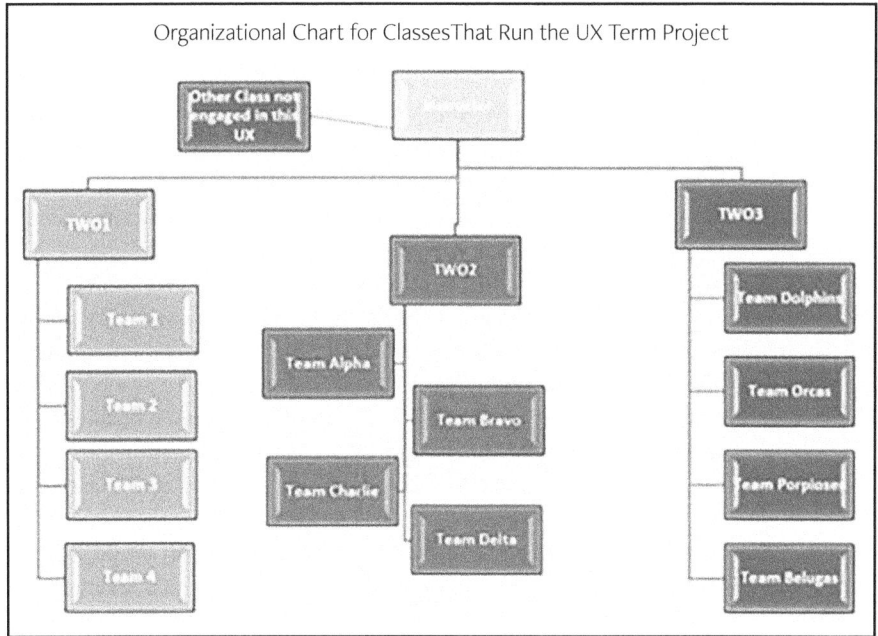

Figure 11.1: Organizational Chart.

When week 8 arrives, enough action and reflection has taken place in the front of the course that most team members are actively participating in their teams through a collective foundation of experience. At this point their familiarity with the tools of communication, the topics of the course, and some of the genres of writing permit them to start putting their skills to use in the UX Project.

Before the start of the term, I create a separate Discord *server* for each class section and invite the members to the platform in Week 2 during the *Unboxing the Rubric* activity. I chose Discord after formerly using Slack, Hangouts, Trello and Canvas because Discord seems to offer the most functionality in one place, presenting a simpler interface. Each server contains several *channels*:

- A general channel for text-based chat
- A Voice/Video channel for conferencing
- A Links & References channel for important reference information distribution from the instructor
- An Off-Topic channel for sharing interests and jokes to foster community

To make this scene more manageable for students, each team member profile is assigned a *role* as they enter the server with a role and the leaders get an additional *leader role* and a *specific team leader role*, which provides some extra permissions. The leader role affords all leaders access to the leaders' lounge: a place for leaders to share tips and tricks about leadership. The teams are also given private team space on a discord server that the instructor maintains. Each team receives a chat channel for asynchronous communication and a voice/video channel for conferencing. Only members of a given team can see their teams' private channels. Only leaders can see the Leader Lounge. Being very aware of the complications surveillance can create, and out of respect for their workspaces, the instructor does not enter these private workspaces unless summoned by the team that owns the space. Even then, it is to answer that summons and then return to the default posture of supervisor/consultant. All class members can send direct messages (DM's) to all other members as well.

The UX project kicks off when the client releases the Call for Proposals (CFP) and I place it into Canvas. The CFP summons teams to a Zoom meeting by asking for two representatives from each team to attend the meeting. At the zoom meeting the Library Website Board (two to five members, one of whom is a SME for library web design), present their need and the scope of their areas of study. I act as a facilitator as team representatives make inquiries and seek clarifications.

When the meeting is complete, I release a link to a wonderful database that a student at my university developed. That database helps students locate, explore, understand, and select the tools that can answer the CFP, while staying within the scope of the area of study. Many students have never encountered user research, outside of the opinion survey, and they may require suggestions of tools that fit the research questions they develop. I tend to allow exploration and then suggest a few if choosing becomes too difficult. The Library Website Board has also offered their own pro-teams' data from tools such as HotJar, and their search history database as supplemental data. The UX Lab on Campus also offers many tools like GazePoint eye-tracking software & hardware, and observation rooms. Most recently, our clients offered four sites of inquiry from which our teams may choose.

Sites of Study

- Organization of supplemental study guides–often referred to as LibGuides
- User navigation to LibGuides and
- User interaction with The LibGuides
- Usability of the library website landing pages

The student research teams then select one of the proffered sites of study and write a proposal explaining how they will create a test for observation, select appropriate UX tools, gather participants, make observations, process and interpret data, and construct communications to deliver their results in written form and in multimodal format. I hold that critical thinking students engage in during the decisions about their study's design as a key threshold experience that must be lived, and cannot be downloaded. Teams will often observe volunteer participants that vary widely in demographic groups, from peers in other courses, to other college students, and even outsiders, depending on the type of user the team is interested in most. As participants navigate the site of study, observations take place on Zoom, in a lab, or sometimes offsite in person, with researchers recording the participants' clicks and missteps, timing their successes, and noting their confusions. If the observations are conducted in person, then the teams designate on-campus students for that task and then process the data from the observations together. UX teams manage their own projects with Gantt charts, MS Teams, or Trello spaces as they work together on Google Docs and Office 365. They conference on Discord to compile their observations and make sense of what they witnessed. Teams are neither instructed to provide recommendations nor are they prohibited from doing so, as the data collection and interpretation alone is quite a robust learning experience. Even so, teams often construct wireframes to aid in presentation of suggested revisions for their site of study. Student groups have even made mock-ups using the snipping tool to rearrange visually and spatially the existing elements of their site of study to illustrate suggestions to improve user navigation.

In executing this project teams construct process documents including: a proposal, communication in formal emails, two progress reports, a draft, a final written report, a multimodal presentation, and a reflection/debrief report. The first progress report, the draft, and a debrief report are submitted only to the instructor, but the other deliverables are submitted to the clients. These submissions require responses. I offer critique on all of them.

As part of course prep, I also worked with the clients to construct form-letter response boilerplate that they could add a few lines to thereby minimizing the effort required on their part when receiving 12 copies of many of the deliverables over the course of the term. It must be noted that it can be very easy—because librarians are also teachers at heart—for them to expend too much time and effort in responding to the teams. This would tax them heavily and could easily spoil our partnership. Respect for the time of the client, and the students, does place an initial increased weight on the instructor until proper systems and materials have been developed to reinforce that value of respecting labor. We develop these systems and resources in meetings between clients and instructors as we attempt to maximize student-client contact but minimize client labor. Negotiating the proper amount of labor with the client—which approximates the involvement of a private client in the world who hires an outside UX analysis team to gather data on their user interactions—is imperative to the success of the project. It would be unethical to place too much labor on the client, while allowing too little would render the experience inauthentic for the students. The role of the instructor, before the project begins, involves consulting and planning with the client, just as well as acting as a consultant for the student researchers during the project.

This careful negotiation can help authenticate the experience for the student, but I do iterate frequently that every client has different needs and refer researchers frequently to their audience analysis from the beginning of the project as an important diagnostic tool. At the end of the project, the clients select and notify two to three finalists from the presentations and accompanying reports. All teams receive a letter from the client with the finalists garnering a higher degree of personalization. The clients then post their Finalist Selections and a short write-up thanking the teams on the library's publicly accessible newsletter. This functions as a resume line for the participants.

Benefits of this Collaboration

Who benefits from this collaboration? That is a great question that I am often asked when I talk about this project, and it is a question that I wrestled with before the partnership was formed. The work involved in launching such a project is significant and the chances of sustaining a partnership less than certain. I considered three main stakeholders when I decided to pursue this radical pedagogical shift and added one more after the partnership commenced. The short answer is, everyone benefits.

Table 11.2. Stakeholder Benefits

Stakeholder	Benefits
Students	Immersion in a work-like setting, doing actual research for a real client, with the possibility of authentic documented outcomes.
Client	This client gets to serve their customer base while collecting valuable feedback on their current procedures, products, and services.
Instructor	The classroom becomes a site of study for the instructor as well as the environment for their teaching praxis.
University	Many studies rank family and friend recommendations very highly, as important influences in college choice (U.S. Department of Education, 2018). Consistently, employers have ranked internships, volunteerism and work experience as top assets they seek (Thompson, 2014). This project can provide some exigence for creating these conditions. The cycle spirals upward when graduating students who came to the university based on the recommendations, or results, of friends find full employment, quickly and easily, and they in turn share that news with friends and family.

Lessons Learned

Both the problems and successes of this project have taught us about what makes a service-learning UX collaboration useful and what makes them full of "messy learning" (VanKooten & Berkley, 2016). It is hoped that these few considerations might save time, effort, and woe for a reader who is hoping to undertake a project such as ours.

Lesson 1: Get the Bosses Onboard

In our case, Michael Manasco and Doug Bolden, the lead clients, and I both sought the approval of our supervisors who were responsible for our academic units and even invited them to some of the preliminary organizing meetings on Zoom, which they attended. Once they were convinced of the validity of the aims of the partnership, and the potential rewards for the students and the client, we were given the go-ahead. To attempt something as arduous as this project without support would be folly. And so, the lead clients and I laid the groundwork for the structure of the project together and then, without making any assumptions, approached the supervisors with the plan and a dream, instead of just a dream. With the offer of support from both academic units we felt confident to proceed.

Lesson 2: Be Mindful of the Stakeholders' Needs

1. **Client Needs:** Time seemed to be in short supply as we approached the second iteration of the project—and the surprise second-act of the COVID-19 pandemic—which made the clients reluctant to enter into a second iteration of the project, so, as a matter of pedagogical *praxis*, I began seeking ways to make their labor load lighter. First, we created form letters from the correspondence they created in the first run of the project and reduced the number of documents they needed to produce as clients, without harming the students' needs in the process. The client cannot become the instructor but rather must fulfill their part of this arrangement: a client with problems who is seeking data toward solutions. Importantly, it is also up to the instructor to model, for the team leads, the importance of the need to protect the clients' time.
2. **Students' Needs:** Most students have other classes and, increasingly, families and jobs in addition to their full course loads. I have tried to remain vigilant about making sure that the workload is distributed, and also that students learn to distribute it. I make it clear in the beginning of the project that this will be less academic and more like a work experience. I ask them to plan two to three hours per week for the labor that it will take to serve the needs of the client. I provide links to scheduler websites and ask them to find and agree on a common meeting time to hold meetings, and meeting minutes, each week for about 30 minutes or so to support their asynchronous communication on Discord with live updates, reports, and task assignments. As many students do not have experience in leadership roles, these have to be coached even as the concepts and tools of UX are introduced.
Students may also need emotional support while learning to collaborate. The concept of labor-based organization is foreign to many and the idea of a class that asks for applied tacit and implicit knowledge can be bewildering when they have been largely engaged to this point with explicit knowledge through tests and quizzes. There is no value in hiding the differences in the kinds of tacit knowledge expected, the paths one can take to gain that knowledge, and the practices needed to perfect the

employment of the knowledge. The instructor must be transparent about what the students are supposed to learn and what they are supposed to do with what they learn. This transparency, and a little empathy, can help clear up the confusion inherent in exploring the hitherto unknown, liminal spaces that lay within the thresholds of new learning.

3. **Instructor's needs:** To be clear, in making this work I have violated some of my own needs and requirements. This course is normally the sort of course taught by a tenured or tenure-track professor and the experiences of a course like this one can drive research for them. For that sort of a situation, the overlap of research and teaching is productive and beneficial. A higher teaching load and no requirement—nor allotted time—for research forces a deficit of time upon the instructor. Since I very much enjoy teaching the courses however, I have borrowed time from other activities in my life. I have not shorted my family, but rather, have sacrificed much of my hobby and leisure time in exchange for the grading and commenting that always accompanies teaching writing-intensive classes. The group submissions on many of the deliverables do ease that stress somewhat later in the term but there are many extra hours invested in office hours, online in Discord, clarifying instructions, helping groups reach consensus, or providing extra genre models for some of the students.

Lesson 3: The Scheduling Thing is Critical

It is imperative to map out the deliverables, but equally essential to consider school calendars, client and instructor travel, and student workloads. Moving the final products for the UX project into week 14 and allowing weeks 15 and 16 for reflection, review, and portfolio construction shifts the most strenuous labor away from finals week and helps the students manage their time more easily. This shift also allows time for the clients to read and view all the submitted UX Reports before making selections from among them. The shift also provides the instructor with time to grade the products before final grades are due. The careful planning of deliverables also provides students with free time for semester breaks and with a schedule upon which to build their project management plan.

Lesson 4: The Reward for All Stakeholders Should Be Tangible

The rewards for the stakeholders are not merely byproducts of the process. By rewards here I mean tangible tokens. The sweat equity everyone invests in the project should yield a material benefit that the stakeholder can show to another person and say, "Hey! Look at this!" For the students in this case we have letters of thanks, and the teams that really excel have a publicly available document that praises their work. The clients get copies of the UX reports and the multimodal presentations that accompany them. The instructor receives the opportunity to do research and write. For a person with a PhD in rhetoric and writing, yes, this is a tangible reward.

Lesson 5: Always Keep Working and Thinking Ahead

Instructors should cultivate multiple partnerships to increase the project's flexibility. It is my plan to cultivate another partnership or two and then rotate them through. The hope in this move is to avoid undue stress on any one client-partner so that my welcome will not be worn out. One partner can only make fair and reasonable use of a certain amount of data and only at a certain frequency interval without the risk of becoming redundant and thereby unnecessary—a condition that devalues the data. Multiple client partners would present a greater selection of needs, and allow for a cooling period for each client-partner, in which, the repetition of data collection would become useful once more as a longitudinal interval and comparative analysis tool.

What's Next?

Like Troy Polamalu and Head & Shoulders, I am never not working. For the project: in the short term, the library client and I plan to re-sight our targeted sites of study and retire others recently completed. We can then move to a different site of study within the library website. I will also cultivate more partnership both across campus and off campus. I hope to continue this habit and run the UX Project with a client once per year in the Fall Term, changing sites of study after each iteration. This will in effect provide a longer cooling window for each site of study, even within the same client partnership. To supplement the Spring Semester, I would like to seek out smaller businesses who would like to have their digital footprint analyzed to see if it is making the impact they desire. Our UX project can offer this assistance even as the students explore the tools and methods of UX Studies. It is possible that these ties to the community could also prove to be beneficial to the university, and longstanding. In the way of campus partners, I have recently reached out to [our on-campus business incubator] to inquire if there is a place for us in their ongoing efforts.

In the classroom, I hope to narrow the selection of tools with a directed list based on the type of study the client needs each term. I am also of a mind to increase the reflections that the students do over the term, so that I can better monitor their foundational learning. It is clear that not all technical writing students will use their acquired skillsets in the same way, or for the same purposes, but it is conversely clear that the collaborative writing and the genres of writing that these students engage with in the UX project are transferable skills that are useful to them.

Since our university has a newly developed UX minor and a graduate certificate—logically these may develop further as time moves forward—I also see my UX project, in the third-year undergraduate technical writing course, as the toe-dip for students to check the UX studies water. This should present a river of opportunity at the confluence of the principles of lean technical communication (Johnson et al., 2018) and core of service-learning sustainability (Cushman, 2002). Even so, I am mindful of the fact that rivers must be fed by streams, and similarly, students need to see the usefulness that research and writing can create together before they will wade into the current. This project can become a sustainable part of the ecology of my technical writing class. As I see students I have taught landing jobs, in part, because of the experiences they had in the UX project, and other projects like it, I can see other ripples the experience makes as my little stream rolls away to the sea, to eventually make the rain.

■ References

Cushman, E. (2002). Sustainable service learning programs. *College Composition and Communication, 54*(1), 40–65.

Dewey, J. (1910). *How we think*. D. C. Heath.

Johnson, M. A., Simmons, W. M. & Sullivan, P. (2018). *Lean technical communication: Toward sustainable program innovation*. Routledge.

Thompson, D. (2014, August 19). *The thing employers look for when hiring recent graduates*. *The Atlantic*. https://www.theatlantic.com/business/archive/2014/08/the-thing-employers-look-for-when-hiring-recent-graduates/378693/.

U. S. Department of Education. (2018). *Factors that influence student college choice*. NCES. https://nces.ed.gov/pubs2019/2019119.pdf.

VanKooten, C. & Berkley, A. (2016) Messy problem-exploring through video in first-year writing: Assessing what counts. *Computers and Composition, 40*, 151–162.

Part Three: Collaborating with Users

12. Twitch and Livestreaming as User Experience Platforms

Amelia Chesley
EMBRY-RIDDLE AERONAUTICAL UNIVERSITY, PRESCOTT

Cody Reimer
UNIVERSITY OF WISCONSIN, STOUT

Abstract. This chapter examines Twitch.tv for its potential as a platform for user experience (UX) collaborations and research. Twitch has the potential to support many common UX methods, enable combinations of old and new methods, and open possibilities for serendipitous research discoveries via wide sampling of random participants. We analyze the features and affordances of Twitch from a theoretical standpoint, review existing UX and UX-adjacent work present on the platform, and explore how game companies specifically, and other companies more broadly, can leverage Twitch's features for productive UX work and adapt established UX methods for use with the unique affordances of the platform. We acknowledge the risks involved in using a public and sometimes toxic platform, but ultimately argue that mainstream tools such as Twitch can make UX research more visible and can help center previously marginalized voices and perspectives for more empathetic UX work.

Hiko is a streamer on the website Twitch.tv, broadcasting his real-time gameplay of a new hero shooter from Riot Games, *Valorant* (2020). It's the end of May, 2020. Thousands of people watch Hiko play, some dedicated members of the massive community he has cultivated, others simply interested in the much-hyped game, set to launch later in the year. As they watch, viewers set the chat panel scrolling with questions, emotes, banter, and comments, which Hiko's moderators filter, answer, relay, and highlight.

In addition to the screencast of his gameplay, Hiko uses two webcams: one showing his face as he concentrates on play and chats with his viewers, and one showing his mouse hand which glides and flicks to aim his hero's weapon in *Valorant*. As new viewers tune in, they are greeted with a popup indicating that Hiko uses an eye tracking extension called Tobii Ghost. Overlaid on the screen showing his gameplay, a blue circle flits and flows to indicate where on the screen Hiko is looking at any given moment: a glance at the scoreboard, a glimpse at the game's mini-map (as in Figure 12.1), a look hovering near his targeting reticule, or skimming his skill's cooldown indicators at the bottom of the game's interface.

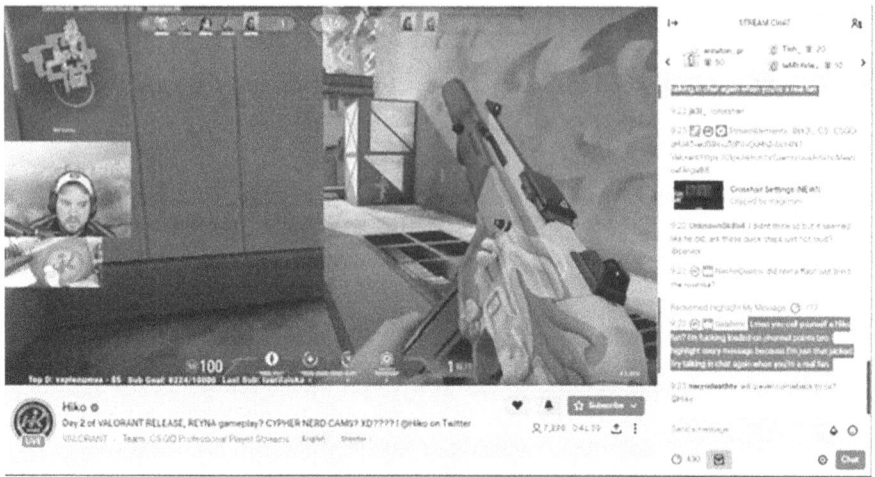

Figure 12.1. Screenshot of Twitch streamer Hiko broadcasting gameplay of a forthcoming game, with an eyetracking extension enabled, visible as the blue circle, top left.

Viewers in the chat ask how the game compares to another popular first-person shooter. Hiko muses aloud on the subject. Another viewer asks whether eyetracking is enabled. A moderator commands a chatbot to relay info which links to the Tobii Ghost website and clarifies the eyetracker's specifications: the tracking circle doesn't display on mobile or Firefox browsers. Hiko reiterates to viewers that the extension is, indeed, turned on. He verbally checks in with his in-game teammates to coordinate tactics and strategy. He reflects on his own gameplay and on the game itself.

Hiko plays and does well at both winning the game and entertaining his audience. The number of viewers watching the stream rises. Riot Games' decision to give him access to the closed-beta game appears to have been savvy. He's drawing attention to their new title by broadcasting his playthrough experience. One wonders to what extent Riot is leveraging the user-data Hiko's channel is generating—physiological data from Tobii Ghost, concurrent think-aloud (CTA) data on his observations about the game's UI and design and balance, a corpus of text and emotes from an ad hoc focus group, and so forth—to polish their game prior to its official public launch.

However the developers at Riot Games may be analyzing and learning from the wealth of data generated by Hiko's Twitch stream, it's clear that this nexus of critical gameplay, spectatorship, and technology can be considered a site of informal user experience research (UXR) for anyone interested in learning from and with users. Twitch makes it possible to watch users' screens, users' faces, users' eye movements, and much more, alongside their audiences' responses. In the case of Hiko and *Valorant*, both player and viewers are users experiencing the game;

Twitch, Riot Games, and the various tech developers involved with both companies are also stakeholders in this collaborative, mediated user experience.

Twitch's multimodal affordances and interactions, as described above, make it a worthwhile platform for robust, collaborative, multimethod user experience (UX) work. Livestreaming media in general, and Twitch in particular, offer possibilities for collecting and storing UX data, conducting UX research (and meta-UX research), or hosting UX collaborations; livestreaming platforms can be part of reconfiguring what public UX looks like in ways that are mutually beneficial to a wide range of parties. Given these platforms' growing popularity and relatively open, lower-cost tools, the variety of informal, agile, user-centered UXR studies that might be conducted on and with spaces like Twitch can help broaden and strengthen UX's reach and influence beyond game design. The potential methods and research questions we offer provide a starting point from which more organizations might move to follow the example set by Riot Games and its fairly public, open collaborations with university researchers (Hsu, 2015) and its players (Reimer, 2017), all in pursuit of more positive experiences for users.

Game companies in particular have the opportunity to leverage the dynamic environments and interactions afforded by Twitch in exploring and developing user-centered collaborations and research. In fact, Twitch already logs plenty of data about users—the devices and browsers they use, the games they play, when, and for how long—and shares it with game developers (Twitch, 2020). As streaming non-gaming activity becomes more common on Twitch, there is potential for other industries to be involved in this kind of user research as well. Through leveraging the popularity and customizability of the Twitch platform, UX researchers and designers can collaborate with each other and with users across distances and cultures even without expensive lab space or centralized equipment.

Of course, Twitch is not the only site for livestreaming. Over the last decade, livestreaming has grown in popularity and cultural relevance, giving rise to numerous other services (e.g., YouTube Live, Facebook Live, Instagram Live, Vimeo Enterprise, LinkedIn Live, TikTok Live, Restream.io) that offer similar capabilities. Of these platforms, Twitch is the oldest and most established among gaming industries and gamers, dating back to 2011. Because, as Katherine Payne and colleagues (2017) recognize, Twitch "was developed for and adopted by gamers rather than organizations" (p. 96), it has become widely available and accessible for viewers and developers such as those behind the Tobii Ghost eye tracking extension. This openness and potential for Twitch to host users with a wide range of experience levels makes the platform a valuable space for finding, attracting, recruiting, and participating with everyday users. The maturity and relevance of Twitch for gaming research prompt us to limit our discussion to Twitch, while acknowledging that other streaming platforms likely afford many of the same UX possibilities we discuss in this chapter. To be clear, we are not claiming that Twitch is the only, or even the best, platform for UX collaborations. It is, however, a useful starting point for thinking about possibilities.

In this theoretical exploration of UXR with and on livestreaming platforms, we hold up gaming as a lens for two reasons: historically, game development and UX have overlapped a great deal, and the popularity of games makes them a ubiquitous example of how UX design and research matter in popular culture and everyday life. This chapter reviews some history of the overlap between UX and videogame development, provides an overview of Twitch as an interactive platform (along with discussion of its benefits and risks), and explores how Twitch can be (and has been) leveraged for productive UXR. We discuss how core features of Twitch can be adapted for use with established UX methods, tools, and approaches and begin to envision potential collaborative research trajectories. We end with a call for more research and collaboration between UXR and livestreamers, noting the need for close attention to the risks and limitations of Twitch specifically.

■ Games Research & UX

Videogame industries have long embraced usability-adjacent concepts such as iterative design and playtesting, but until the last decade they have lacked an overarching definition, framework, and consensus for how user research principles could be applied throughout the various phases of game development. In her book on UX and game design, Celia Hodent (2018) notes that games-UX principles were still coalescing in the early 2000s, and that even in 2008 when she joined Ubisoft—one of the largest game studios in the world—games UX still wasn't "a thing." However, it's not as though the games industry was unaware of UX. Early games user research (GUR) distinguished itself from UX by nuancing differences between users and players (Lazarro, 2008; Lazzaro & Keeker, 2004). Nicole Lazarro (2008) defines UX as "the experience of use, how easily and well suited to the task, what the person expects to accomplish" and player experience (PX) as "the experience of play. How well the game supports and provides the type of fun players want to have" (p. 320). She contrasts the different purposes in UX (productivity) and PX (entertainment) by focusing on the rhetorical nature of games, and in so doing she illuminates the challenges that researchers face in applying general UX goals to the specialized medium of videogames. Nevertheless, players *are* users of a game, and games are experiences, so it would seem that UX principles should apply, in some cases and degrees, when researching players' experiences.

Some dissonance between UX and PX has driven many games industry members to conceive of UX as dealing primarily with technicalities of the game's user interface (UI), while PX principles should inform the design of the game as a challenging but rewarding player experience. As the differences between UX and PX, UI and design were explored, various efforts at GUR appeared, including: RITE, rapid iterative testing and evaluation (Medlock et al., 2002); SAGA-ML, semi-automated gameplay analysis by machine learning (Southey et al., 2005); and TRUE, tracking real-time user experience (Schuh et al., 2008). Graham

McAllister and Gareth White (2015) identify other contributions to early GUR, pointing to Chuck Clanton's assertion (1998) that good games are decided by good gameplay, which Larsen (as cited by McAllister & White, 2015) tried to investigate by examining how professional reviewers rated games. They also identify efforts to unify heuristic measures in a "GameFlow process" (Sweetster & Wyeth, 2005), and measure and define immersion (Jennet et al., 2008). Like UX, PX and its principles grew haphazardly within various competing companies and academic fields. There was "no overarching definition of what a game user experience entails or a defined UX framework" (Hodent, 2018, p. 98); industry practitioners and academics alike were all introducing concepts and strategies for improving player experience.

Scholarship on GUR identifies the industry's debt to the field of Human Computer Interaction (HCI) in guiding its approach to UI-UX—often branded as GRUX (games research on user experience). GRUX is not limited to UI or HCI, however, despite its debts to those fields. In her edited collection *Game User Experience Evaluation*, Regina Bernhaupt (2015) indicates game development's approach to UX is beholden to the field of HCI. McAllister and White (2015) also point to early HCI-UX work in games, citing Anker Helms Jørgensen (2004) and Steve Cornett (2004). Others, like Hodent, strongly value Don Norman's conceptualization of UX, and take issue with HCI because it "does not consider the whole experience people have with a product" (Hodent, 2018, p. 99). Along these lines, games researchers have been mindful of uncritically adopting HCI's methods and principles. Randy Pagulayan and Dennis Wixon (2008) warn about the dangers of "hot research topics" and of treating as novel what has already been established by other fields; they argue for interdisciplinarity so long as it is done with "due diligence in studying games and their unique challenge and culture" (p. ix). Their insistence on interdisciplinarity is not only out of respect for varied contexts, but also out of timeliness; in GUR, a classical approach slowed things down and was too sterile for iterative design efforts. Games researchers' efforts to contextualize usability methods for games often resulted in "discount" usability methods, owing to usability's origins in productivity applications and the resultant inconsistency for leisure applications (Amaya et al., 2008).

Games research eventually began to include non-traditional usability research aims and rely on increasingly multimethod approaches. Previously, research had concerned itself with player attitudes: how did players *feel* about the game, its play, its UI, its flow? Collecting this kind of attitudinal data was often the aim of playtesting, though it's worth noting that there is still no single shared definition or approach to such testing. In contrast, Pagulayan and Wixon (2008) advocate for the value of behavioral data: what players *do* in the game, rather than how they *feel* about it. This shift away from player attitudes to behaviors came about in part because of the growth of virtual gaming worlds and game development's need for user research after product launch. This evolution became behavioral game telemetry.

Game telemetry is "data logged from clients or servers about how players play games, or conversely about how the game client itself responds to player behavior" (Drachen, 2015, p. 137). Its low costs and high yield data make game telemetry especially attractive in comparison with more resource-intensive playtesting.[1] Games analytics and GUR overlap where they concern users (Drachen, 2015). Both contribute to multimethod approaches and allow researchers to triangulate behavioral (typically quantitative) data with GUR-supplied attitudinal (typically qualitative or semi-quantitative) data (Drachen, 2015, p. 140).

An example of this marriage between attitudinal and behavioral data is Microsoft Game Studios' early multimethod GRUX approach, TRUE—tracking real-time user experience. Facing a need to "understand what issues people encountered late in the game, why they were having those difficulties, and have a good idea of what we needed to do to fix those problems," the team initially considered think-aloud testing but felt they "couldn't afford the ~160 hours of observation time that testing would cost" (Schuh et al., 2008, p. 239). The team's solution, TRUE, uses three categories of in-game surveys (event-based, on-demand, and time-based), gathers necessary contextual data with game telemetry (e.g., build number, participant ID, timestamp, player position coordinates), and video captures on-screen play, and then maps player position with survey data. TRUE thus enables triangulation across behavioral data (e.g., heatmaps of player deaths on a particular level) and attitudinal data (e.g., that the level was particularly confusing for players, rather than an enjoyable challenge). Once researchers identified a problem, they could collaborate with the designers to diagnose and address the problem. Eric Schuh and colleagues (2008) write about one such instance in another case study, explaining "After watching these videos, the designers were able to immediately pick up on a subtle nuance in the game mechanic that only they were able to identify" (p. 249). Multimethod research yields UX data that empowers collaboration among designers, researchers, and players. With such multimethod approaches, researchers can understand both what players are doing in the game (their behavior) and how they feel about the game (their attitudes) and use this more complete understanding to guide design decisions.

Hodent's (2018) analysis of games and UX similarly supports multimethod approaches. She cites the challenges of single methods like think-aloud protocols and explains that "verbal protocol analysis seems to be much less suitable to address the level of enjoyability of the game, to investigate the potential engaging power of a game: Having to think aloud is 'killing' the experience, or at least changing it" (Hodent, 2018, p. 66–67). Jettie Hoonhout's (2008) treatment of think-aloud research offers some solutions about the costs and challenges.

---

1. Jakob Nielsen & Thomas Landauer's (1993) suggestion of five users per test to keep costs low cannot apply to experiences that take dozens of hours to complete, as is the case with some videogames.

She contrasts the strictness of think-aloud methods of K. Anders Ericsson and Herbert Simon (1984) with the opportunities McAllister and White might call "discount" usability, explaining that "in a usability evaluation context adopting a less strict approach to think-aloud studies than advocated by Ericsson and Simon does result in usable and useful data about important product aspects" (Hoonhout, 2008, p. 67) so long as the protocol's limitations are acknowledged. Those limitations, in part, require careful attention to participant selection, representativeness, and recruitment of "people who are relatively at ease with thinking aloud while performing a task" (Hoonhout, 2008, p. 68).

Even with careful consideration of think-aloud limitations, however, Ericsson (2006) reminds us that "verbal reports are only one indicator of the thought processes that occur during problem solving. Other indicators include reaction times (RTs), error rates, patterns of brain activation, and sequences of eye fixations" (p. 229). Tom Tullis and Bill Albert (2013) observe that retrospective think aloud (RTA) is gaining popularity among usability professionals as a way to benefit from user insight without disrupting their focus during testing. Hoonhout (2008) suggests an alternate, informal approach still useful for usability wherein the researcher analyzes comments, adding that it "should be adopted only in combination with other forms of data collection, for example logging of interactions, recording observable behavior, conducting a close interview, and perhaps administering questionnaires, to ensure a richer 'picture' of the issues" (p. 71). These indicators are precisely the sort of data streaming services gather as a matter of their function.

Many in the UX field acknowledge how rarely developers have the time and resources to create ideal situations for thoroughly testing and evaluating user experiences for their games (Hodent, 2018; McAllister & White, 2015). Even the most carefully designed UX tests are never perfect; developers must often prioritize what matters most, both for players (Hodent, 2018), and for collaboration with designers (Schuh et al., 2008). This is a good reminder that in industry, quick actionable data is de rigueur, and not necessarily the same as academic rigor. With game design's need for quick iteration and cheap, actionable data, it makes sense to forego some of the strictness of think-aloud protocols, to supplement them with a multimethod approach akin to TRUE, to triangulate attitudinal and behavioral data to bring to designers for informed discussion and decision-making. On Twitch, as players verbalize their decision-making processes and engaging with an ad hoc focus group of viewers, their stream is recorded and archived for posterity, their chat often moderated and full of viewer text and emote reactions; in this space we see readymade triangulation, ripe for further research in GRUX as well as UX. We must also recognize that imperfect or less-than-ideal situations necessitated by expedience for iteration must never come at the cost of participant and researcher safety. UX Researchers considering studies through livestreaming platforms, especially one such as Twitch, must safeguard against potential harassment and abuse, especially in racist, sexist, toxic public spaces (Gray, 2020).

▪ Twitch and Its Users

Twitch bills itself as a community for people involved in creating their own entertainment. As a platform, Twitch brings content creators, audiences, sponsors, and other stakeholders (product designers or developers, brands, and researchers) together. Collaboration can range from large team projects to one-on-one tutorials. On Twitch, almost anyone can access rich video streams or recordings of people around the world using a wide range of tools, often in the context of their regular lives, from almost anywhere.

The Twitch platform affords streaming support, video-on-demand (VOD) capture, chat moderation, graphic overlays, screen sharing, live chat, and more. It is free to broadcast and view, generating revenue from advertising and optional subscriptions. Common affordances used by most Twitch broadcasters include webcams, microphones, notifications regarding subscribers or donations, added music, and social media tie-ins (Sjöblom et al., 2019). Twitch streamers often customize their channel pages and videos by adding overlays and other thematic elements to accompany the base video stream. The Twitch platform also includes live audience chat where viewers can type messages to the streamer and to each other during each livestream. Interaction like this, among streamers and audience members who may be experts or novices or anywhere in between, creates opportunities for learning by watching and through discussion (Payne et al., 2017).

As a media platform, Twitch has technologically, culturally, and socially enabled streamers to find and build an audience, to promote both personal and corporate branding, and position themselves as both influencers and entertainers, entering into "media industry work" in a manner no platform previously afforded (Taylor, 2018, p. 35). For many popular streamers, their work on Twitch is a full-time career (Johnson & Woodcock, 2017). Streamers with the time and inclination to stream regularly can partner with Twitch for the privilege of earning ad revenue from their streams. Other streamers ask for donations and/or earn a portion of Twitch viewers' subscription fees (Hamilton et al., 2014). Streamers and the labor they perform are imbricated in a host of capitalist industries, the gaming and esports industries most prominently. Twitch becomes a workplace for many who rely on the platform for self-promotion, networking opportunities, and income from sponsors, donors, and subscribers. The streamer from our opening anecdote, Hiko, streams professionally; he generates income by subscriptions and by the promotions enabled by his broadcasts. Not all Twitch streamers participate in order to earn money, however. T. L. Taylor (2018) articulates six types of motivation for players to stream their gameplay, only two of which are financially motivated (Taylor, 2018). For others, Twitch remains primarily a site for entertainment and social interaction.

Although a majority of content streamed via Twitch is gaming-related, the roots of the platform go back to more general, everyday-life streaming. The 2007 livestreaming website Justin.tv hosted several categories, the most popular of which was for gaming; in 2011, the gaming category was split from the rest of the site and branded Twitch.tv. The original site where users around the world livestreamed anything at all is no longer online—Justin.tv simply redirects to Twitch, which is now a property of Amazon.

Streaming categories on Twitch today include hundreds of game-specific categories ranging from Chess to the latest Mortal Kombat to The Legend of Zelda. Taylor (2018) demonstrates just how dynamic streaming spaces have become since their origins in the early 2000s, noting that non-gaming streams were only officially allowed on Twitch as of 2016. Before that year, non-gaming content was "actively prohibited" (Taylor, 2018, p. 64). Today, non-gaming Twitch categories like Talk Shows & Podcasts, Food & Drink, ASMR,[2] and Makers & Crafting include streams from people cooking, playing tabletop games, doing yoga, and making things—using all kinds of implements from workout equipment and power tools to looms and spinning wheels.

These streams and the resulting videos can be instructional as well as entertaining. A convention among livestreamers is to think aloud about their decisions and actions, talking to and with their viewers about the game as an intentionally designed experience. In fact, streamers are strongly incentivized to talk through their activities and connect verbally with audiences; this is part of the performance they offer to viewers. Such thinking-aloud activity layered onto a stream's visual elements is a key part of the "exteriorization of an otherwise unspoken ludic process," as Taylor (2018, p. 81) characterizes streaming. For UX professionals, understanding such unspoken, tacit processes is a crucial part of understanding, empathizing with, and serving users in the context of their lived experiences with a given product or process.

Empathy has become a foundational concept for user-centered design and related research methodologies, often listed as the first step in any iterative design process. But the ideal of individual empathy isn't enough. As we consider Twitch as a platform for multimethod UXR, we must acknowledge its implications in ratifying systemic issues of injustice. However playful games and gamespaces may appear, they often harbor and perpetuate toxic cultures (Hsu, 2015; Paul, 2018), particularly with regard to existing power structures. Acknowledging UX as a historically, systemically white and male discipline, Vivianne Castillo (2018) calls out UX's "inability to discuss, acknowledge and absolve the effects of unchecked white privilege and male privilege within our leadership, organizations, conferences, and research" (para 3). Without addressing systemic problems of racial and gendered privilege, there is little chance of breaking down those systems in order to build more equitable user experiences. Thus, our considerations of Twitch as a platform for UXR must be tempered by an awareness of systemic bias and an explicit understanding that, currently, not every user's experience and participation is valued equally or compensated fairly. We must be especially wary of inviting at-risk populations into toxic spaces solely for the benefit of

---

2. Autonomous sensory meridian response

our research needs. If researchers choose to use these spaces, they should do so with an eye toward actively valuing the cultural knowledge work of marginalized populations (Chan & Gray, 2020; Gray, 2017). That is, UX researchers must move beyond empathy and consistently work to amplify marginalized voices, address the harmful effects of bias and privilege, and promote anti-racist and anti-sexist policies and practices within and beyond the gaming industry.

■ UX on Twitch

In this section we review and describe UX or UX-adjacent work already happening on Twitch. The examples we include were discovered through exploring Twitch organically, searching the site, and sharing our own experiences as Twitch users. These examples demonstrate how livestreaming on Twitch corresponds with UXR practices and interests, highlighting a convergence of opportunities for observational and telemetric data on attitudes and behaviors across several modes. Videos subtitled with "New Player Experience," often also tagged "blind [sic] playthrough" or "first playthrough," are common on Twitch. Part of the appeal of Twitch embraces the desire for collaborative, community-based gaming, even in single-player videogames; this is evident in the popularity of first experience playthroughs, where viewers get to see the streamer experience a game for the first time. Twitch users' interest in initial ludic experiences extends to UX researchers, too. We found various clips including mentions of UX and usability as topics that streamers are aware of and interested in (bornfreetwitch, 2019; krosmarc, 2019; wright4thejob, 2022) and some UX professionals and enthusiasts with a presence on Twitch (derScharni, 2020; GameUserX, 2018). Another major category included formal presentations on topics related to UX. These collections show that people interested in UX have already identified Twitch's value for hosting such research. We also saw various simple recordings of traditional in-lab usability and user testing scenarios on Twitch (alexgwin, 2013; FranstarMTG, 2013; GameCircus, 2012). Most of these tests contain either recorded video of users interacting with a mobile device or a screen-capture (with audio, sometimes with a webcam to capture users' faces) of activity on a website. The existence of UX videos like these affirms the practical value of Twitch for such work and supports our call in this chapter for more research and exploration into what it can offer.

As we saw with the streamer Hiko in our opening section, UX-adjacent data collection tools and technologies are prevalent on Twitch. Along with the video recording, webcams, and eyetracking already mentioned, some Twitch streamers also use technologies that track and display the interactions of their hands and game controllers. For example, Twitch user AccountingNightmareSA (2019) streams playthroughs of *Devil May Cry 5* that include an icon showing her controller inputs in the bottom right corner of the video (Figure 12.2). As she presses buttons, the corresponding icons light up in sync with the gameplay being streamed. This controller-input map allows viewers to watch and potentially learn the controller

Twitch and Livestreaming as User Experience Platforms 217

techniques she uses and could also provide valuable data about this user's interactions and experience with both the hardware and software of the game.

Figure 12.2. Screenshot of AccountingNightmareSA's DMC5 stream with controller map displayed bottom right.

A webcam view of TheMainManSWE's (2020) controller (Figure 12.3) is included in his stream of *Tekken 7*, which adds even more context than the dynamic controller map in the previous example. Here, viewers can see specific hand and finger positions in relation to the controller, so we see not only which buttons the player is pushing but also how he does so.

Figure 12.3. Screenshot of Tekken 7 stream. The webcam showing the streamer's hands is at bottom middle right, to the left of the streamer's face.

The eyetracking extension described earlier, Tobii Ghost (now "Tobii Eye Tracker 5"), is another example of a UX tool being used for livestreaming. This eyetracking system (Figure 12.4) has been developed and promoted by a global assistive technology company, Tobii. As part of a partnership with machine-learning startup Mobalytics, Tobii is applying eyetracking in esports training (Tobii, 2020; Ewalt, 2020). A post on the Tobii Blog pitches the technology to potential clients as a method for training professional gamers, specifically *League of Legends* players (Tobii, 2020). Mobalytics hopes to use the data gathered via Tobii to analyze and understand the strategies of professional gamers and thereby derive professional standards against which aspiring pro gamers can then measure their own gameplay: "For instance, Mobalytics' studies have found that top *League of Legends* players look at the mini-map almost twice as often as average players: By using the eye-tracking system, the software can tell a user whether they need to check it more or less often" (Ewalt, 2020, para. 5). The eyetracking system can provide this data not only to game companies, but also to players individually, allowing them to evaluate and reflect on their own player experience.

Increasingly convenient and affordable, eyetracking has many applications within and beyond UX studies as a source of physiological user data. This adaptation for professional esports is an example of UX-related collaboration opened up via Twitch. Professional gamers and their coaches study eyetracking data to hone their competitive edge, game companies leverage the data to understand their users and improve their products, and other streamers use it for added entertainment value, enabling their viewers to see where they look on screen and further shrinking the techno-mediated intimacy gap between streamer and viewer.

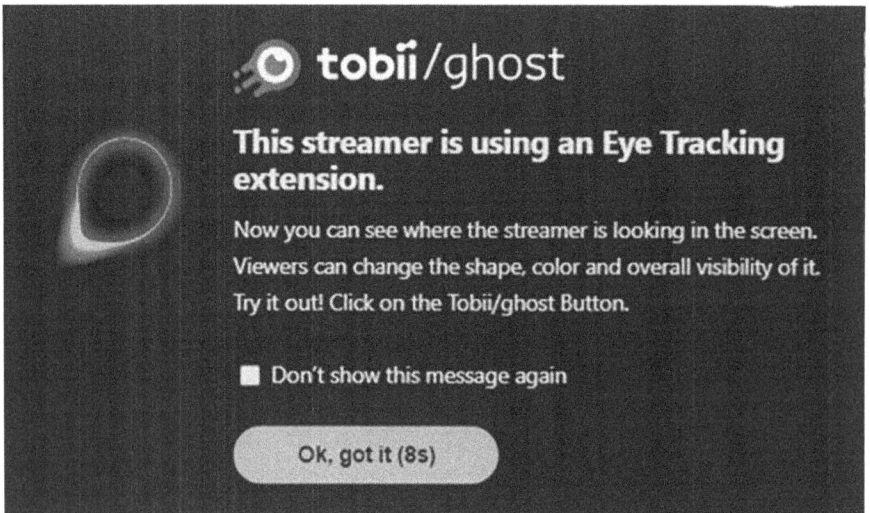

Figure 12.4. Screenshot showing the Tobii Ghost extension popup message.

We acknowledge that the examples covered here are centered in gaming and therefore won't necessarily illustrate the potential of Twitch to capture diverse user experiences in other areas. Because Twitch has long tailored itself to and prioritized gamers and their experiences, it may be that accessing the same kinds of data about user experiences in other arenas—crafting, fitness, etc.—may not be as simple or convenient, since the platform's affordances may be less meaningfully developed for non-gaming streamers and audiences. However, it is worthwhile to consider the platform's potential, particularly as non-game categories (e.g., IRL, Talk Shows & Podcasts, ASMR, Food & Drink, etc.) grow in popularity and as livestreaming becomes more mainstream across a variety of industries.

UXR Methods and Livestreaming

Many of the elements of everyday Twitch streams already incorporate classic UX tools and methods in some way, as we saw in the previous section. The following sections offer considerations for Institutional Review Board approval and ideas for research-based applications, trusting readers to consider how, where, and when livestreaming UX may be useful (see Rohrer, 2014). We also discuss prominent features of the Twitch platform and outline specific ways each can be integrated with existing UX tools and methods. The technical details of setting up and managing a Twitch stream are beyond the scope of this chapter, but we hope to provide points of inspiration for bold experimentation and innovation.

Navigating Institutional Review Board Processes

Obtaining IRB approval or exemption is valuable for any research involving human participants. Because UXR is not often concerned with producing generalizable knowledge, it commonly qualifies for exemption. Nevertheless, it is important to consider how participants will be informed of the study's parameters, whether and how any personal identifiable information will be gathered, and how that data will be protected and secured.

Because Twitch and most other livestreams are public broadcasts with VODs publicly available, we encourage researchers to consider using chat moderators or auto-moderators to make consent information available to participants, as appropriate. Chat functions can also convey details about the scope and aim of the research, its potential for publication, and relevant privacy considerations. Researchers should carefully consider where and how their participants will join the study: those invited to the platform are less likely to understand its public nature and the resultant privacy implications than those who arrive of their own volition. Researchers might consider enabling the subscriber-only chat feature and providing subscriptions (and thus chat capability) only to those who consent to participate in the study. This model could also serve to verify participants are not legally minors.

Livestreaming in general and Twitch in particular offer exciting new opportunities for collaboration in UXR, but researchers are well served when they respect their participants by engaging IRB processes or protocols to ensure participant safety.

▪ Affordances and Applications

A range of UX methods—think-aloud protocols, observations, usability testing, gathering psycho-physiological and other metrics—can all be applied within a livestreaming context (Figure 12.5). Below, we describe several potential opportunities for multimethod UX. To be clear, these observations are not meant to be an explicit guide to enacting UX on Twitch, but a theoretical overview of how existing Twitch features can be leveraged in conducting, teaching, or exploring UXR.

Figure 12.5 shows a screenshot of Hiko's stream (the same used in Figure 12.1), with specific features boxed and enumerated. Each element contributes to the interactive experience of the livestream: (1) the broadcast itself, the shared screen of the streamer; (2) the webcams overlaid on the stream, and the streamer's microphone; (3) the chat box, where viewers and moderators communicate through text and emotes; (4) the channel title and other relevant meta-data that accompanies the VOD capture of the broadcast; and (5) the eyetracking circle implemented with Tobii Ghost, here used to represent Twitch extensions in general.

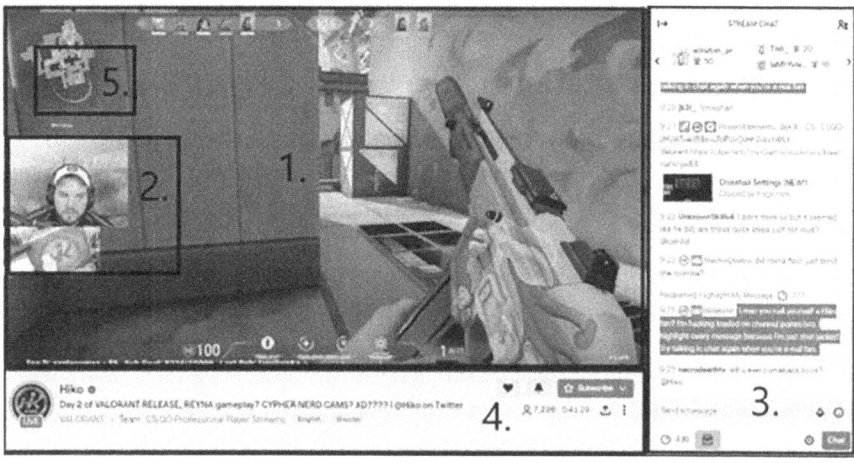

Figure 12.5. Screenshot of Hiko's stream (the same used in Figure 12.1), with specific features boxed and enumerated.

Screen Broadcasting

Observing a user interact with a tool or product is the most fundamental method of usability testing. Twitch and other livestreaming services were built to allow viewers to see and follow along with streamers' on-screen activity. Conducting the simplest observation or delving into a more expansive contextual inquiry or ethnography can "produce ecologically sound data and can generate profound insights regarding user activities and their meaning" (Kim et al., 2008, p. 444). Accessing video of users' experiences via livestreaming can be a relatively simple, low-cost way of collecting observational data if participants already have the equipment and know-how to broadcast. Streaming the activity of a user's desktop via screensharing allows for synchronous observations, as well as later analysis if the stream is archived (see the section on VOD, below).

Twitch observations may involve sampling a wide selection of Twitch streams for general insights about certain groups of users or a certain game, or a more controlled observation with intentional user recruitment. The question of who to recruit as the streamer for a UXR project mainly hinges on when during the development process the research is being conducted. During a "closed beta" phase, outside experts are invited to play and test the product. Closed beta typically occurs just prior to launch, and playthroughs at this stage are often used to help finetune mechanics and balance as well as stress-test servers. Streamers given a key to participate in a closed beta pose an opportunity not unlike expert heuristic evaluations—they are savvy with the genre and type of software, well-versed and professional in their critical consumption or use, and able to identify resonances and dissonances between this experience and others. Alternately, UXR may prefer an insider, an internal employee, to broadcast or record. Though perhaps less likely to be versed in the work of broadcasting and thinking aloud than a streamer, they may be more representative, easier to find, or better disposed to engage with the product at a valence useful for that development phase. In any case, setting up UX observations over Twitch should be relatively simple if participants are already familiar with the platform or willing to learn it.

One significant constraint to recognize when working with Twitch is the public-by-default nature of livestreaming. Twitch does not currently allow for most streamers to purposefully limit viewership to a certain group or to require a password or login to access live Twitch content, but in response to an increase in targeted harassment the platform has implemented new tools, such as requiring a verified phone number to participate in chat (Parrish, 2021). In any development phase where the company is uncomfortable with broadcasting the product to the public, they would need to account for exposure, liability, privacy, and the like. The platform does not permit private streaming, although there exist imperfect ways to remain hidden from general viewers (Luci, 2020). This means that any UX work performed on Twitch will technically be public and perhaps prone to disruption. Distractions from the streamers' physical space or irrelevant comments from chat participants could somewhat dilute the data. As is the case in many online spaces, there is potential for disruptive or uncooperative behavior, trolling, flaming, toxicity, racism, sexism, and other unwanted intrusions. If researchers are to use Twitch or other online streaming services, they must anticipate and plan to identify and mitigate abusive behavior using tools such as chat moderation.

Streaming on-screen activity is only part of how Twitch might be used for observations. By combining the affordances of microphones, webcams, and chat, UX researchers can gather additional user data for triangulation and participatory design work. The affordances of visual, audio, and interactive chat media are discussed in the sections below.

Webcams & Microphones

Webcams are one of the primary means streamers use to connect with their viewers. They are common, although not required, among streamers, with many streamers using multiple webcams, such as Hiko's webcam for his mouse; some streamers even use webcams to showcase their pets. Professional streamers invest in high quality recording hardware to elevate the quality of their broadcasts. Seeing streamers' reactions comprises a central part of the experience for many viewers, not unlike the common "reaction" video genre on platforms such as YouTube. The ability to see the streamer can also permit qualitative, observational research, enabling UX researchers to see reactions such as pain points (Fei, 2018).

As is the case with webcams, microphones function as a mainstay of the broadcast experience. They are the primary channel through which streamers communicate with viewers. In the case of Twitch specifically, the nature of the broadcast compels the streamer to articulate their reactions, thoughts, and opinions. Often streamers will reflect aloud on the game's design or interface, bringing to bear their prior gaming experiences and unique user perspectives. The widespread convention of talking aloud while livestreaming means that Twitch is host to many popular streamers who are adept at something akin to concurrent or retrospective think-aloud (CTA/RTA), who embrace the "Let's Play" genre: videos and walkthroughs where streamers demonstrate a videogame to viewers, either broadcast live or recorded, edited, and uploaded later (Let's Play Archive, 2007; PBS Digital Studios, 2013).

Recall the importance of "people who are relatively at ease with thinking aloud while performing a task" (Hoonhout, 2008, p. 68). Whether or not they're broadcasting Let's Plays or walkthroughs, streamers are incentivized to talk through their decision making, prompted both by viewer questions and remarks in chat, but also through the nature of streaming-as-performance. Recall, also, the value placed on multimethod approaches to complement the thought processes laid bare through think-alouds (Hoonhout, 2008; Tullis & Albert, 2013). Twitch specifically and streaming platforms generally are well-suited to mix and match such methods to suit context and improve validity, and accuracy.

If the test participant is a practiced streamer, they may need little guidance to provide useful data through CTA/RTA, whereas internal participants may need more. But the value of streamers' microphones reaches beyond think aloud practices. Audio broadcast means streams can include interviews, either prompted through moderators in chat or through co-hosts. Interviews conducted or designed by UX researchers can yield different data than CTA/RTA and fit within a product's development phases more soundly. The ability to broadcast and record screens with an audio-video complement broadens UX researchers' options for the methods they employ at various phases of development. The chat function makes the breadth of options more dynamic still.

Chat & Chat Moderation

The chat features on Twitch allow for real-time conversation and interaction between streamers and their viewers, as well as among viewers from around the world. Very popular channels often employ moderators to manage the chat portion of their streams, in order to discourage or prevent inappropriate messaging and/or maintain the boundaries of a particular viewership via gatekeeping practices. Streamers can also amplify viewer comments and bring their questions into the central stream itself by repeating or responding to that content verbally. The affordances of chat and moderation could allow UX researchers to coordinate Twitch-based UX testing or to collect user feedback via modified interviews, surveys, questionnaires, and focus groups. Setting up any given Twitch stream as a user testing scenario could be relatively straightforward, provided that participants are already familiar or have time to familiarize themselves with Twitch beforehand and provided that the prototype or product being tested is available to them. Streamers could be provided with a game or other product to use and then follow chat-based instructions for completing a series of specific tasks.

Along with observing users' behavior, asking users about their experiences is another classic method for learning about what they need or want from a game or product. When implemented carefully, user surveys and questionnaires can be invaluable for accessing users' perceptions and experiences. The Presence, Involvement, Flow Framework (PIFF) and Core Elements of Gaming Experience (CEGE) questionnaires from Bernhaupt (2015) are established tools for assessing the UX of videogames. Questions from these instruments or others could be relayed to the streamer and/or their viewers via the Twitch chat interface. Given the conventional dynamics of livestreaming, where viewers communicate with streamers in this multimodal way, this type of data collection wouldn't necessarily interrupt gameplay or distract users, especially if done with respect to Jun Kim and colleagues' (2008) provisions about survey types and/or done with the coordination of trained chat moderators. Third party surveys (such as the PIFF and CEGE) could also be linked via Twitch chat for users to complete offsite.

Another method for collecting user input involves focus groups. This method is especially useful for market research and early stages of UX development, since focus groups allow researchers to learn more about what users expect and need, as well as what they're collectively excited about. Holding focus groups via Twitch chat won't be the same as doing so in person but does come with the built-in benefits of easily stored text-based interaction as opposed to bulkier audio recordings. For a Twitch focus group, the streamer could lead a demonstration and ask for audience input, or a chat moderator could lead participants through questions about the ideas or activities being streamed. Focus groups may not work as well on very popular channels without heavy moderation. Scheduling specific "focus group" streams for specifically invited groups of users, or restricting chat to subscriber-only mode, could be ways to productively limit participation, although these tactics may not be available for all channels (Parrish, 2021).

When streamers choose to preserve the chat portion of their livestream, the saved chat transcripts can become the basis for other modes of deeper UX research, including corpus analysis and ethnography.

Video on Demand (VOD)

Twitch's built-in VOD gathers the chat exchanges in addition to the audio-visual broadcast. This allows researchers to return to the archive in perpetuity to analyze streamer facial and vocal reactions, viewer reactions, and questions/comments from chat. The value of archived broadcasts for multimethod UXR shines within the triangulation depicted in the case studies of the TRUE method described above. When the quantitative, behavioral data suggested there was an issue (i.e., too many players were dying on a particular level), researchers were able to use qualitative data from the video-recorded play to "drill down" and, in collaboration with designers, quickly identify the cause—in this case, that enemies on that level threw grenades "faster and with less of an arc," thus making them deadlier (Schuh et al., 2008).

Recorded footage can provide attitudinal data to contextualize the issue, framing researchers' understanding of the quantitative data (i.e., number of deaths) with the emotional reactions from the player (e.g., looks of concentration or confusion combined with shouts of joy or frustration). While visual reactions are an imperfect indicator of attitudinal data, they can be triangulated with think-aloud protocols from streamers' microphones, and returned to for consideration in the context of the shared screen in the archived VOD.

Extensions (for Eyetracking and More)

An impressive range of extensions is available to Twitch streamers—from static overlays to dynamic displays of data (e.g., live stats trackers) and more interactive elements to boost viewer engagement (e.g., suggestion boxes, stickers, polls). Twitch supports several extensions meant to integrate with specific games, scheduling and countdown extensions, loyalty and recognition extensions, streamer analytics extensions, music extensions, and extensions for polls and voting. Some of these work with openly available stats or other application programming interface (API) data on the web, while others are linked to specific hardware. Extensions can gather and display data overlaid on a stream or facilitate unique kinds of interaction among viewers. The eyetracking tools Hiko and others are using work through the Twitch extension Tobii Ghost (circled in Figure 13.1); controller input maps like the one used in AccountingNightmareSA's stream (see Figure 13.2) are javascript extensions. These and other analytics extensions are obvious points of interest for UXR. These tools may be useful for collecting other physiological data from users, as well as other telemetric data or user feedback for later triangulation.

The intersection between Twitch extensions and UX work suggests a wealth of future possibilities for collaboration. Documentation is available on Twitch for any would-be extension developers, and Twitch encourages users to add any extensions they want to see and use. Future research and experimentation could involve conceptualizing and building specific UX-focused Twitch extensions. Established Twitch developers, UX researchers in academia and industry, and even other tech companies (like Tobii) might collaborate to make UX work on Twitch even more agile and accessible.

Accessing UX data via these various features of the Twitch platform, rather than in a more formal UX lab setting, means accepting some amount of unpredictability in exchange for the benefits of convenient online access and timeliness. A loss in formal rigor is offset by the benefits of quicker data collection and more agile iterations of analysis and testing. The opportunities for triangulation afforded by Twitch can help mitigate the drawbacks of this trade-off. For many designers, production cycles move too quickly for the types of rigor sought by academics. Using Twitch to gather user data and feedback more quickly allows for UX research to be useful even during the demanding timelines upheld in the games industry. And perhaps because of the relative informality of such public UX, unexpected or serendipitous discoveries may be more likely to be considered seriously, rather than merely noted as interesting afterthoughts.

▪ Envisioning New Collaborations

Because Twitch remains significantly gaming-centric, the types of studies we envision begin within that realm and venture beyond it only slightly. Foundational UXR in Twitch gaming circles may build a basis from which non-gaming UX work can draw inspiration. As we think about making the most of Twitch as a hub of UX collaboration, there are several key questions and possible research trajectories we envision as necessary starting points. This section lays out what we perceive as important areas of inquiry, pointed research questions, potential for collaboration, and problems facing that work.

Game development and UX research are both collaborative yet often tightly controlled spaces. Josh Zimmerman (2014) explores how almost any collaboration between game developers and players/fans is often carefully and strictly managed by the developer—part of maintaining the power dynamics where developers control their intellectual property, tightly manage proprietary information, and shape games discourse to serve their profit-based interests. The prominence of non-disclosure agreements (NDAs) among game developers further evinces these power dynamics. The use of NDAs and the secrecy that rationalizes them complicates workplace studies that would seek to investigate the relationship between developers, fans, UX/PX, and technology such as Twitch. So, while a workplace study focusing on streamers and their collaborations with game developers might be an ideal starting place for any research focused on streaming's value for and impact on product development, the hurdles/barriers of NDAs commonplace in videogame development make such research difficult. In cases where NDAs complicate or stymie inquiry, we suggest an alternate approach—reaching out to the gamers who have been sponsored to stream by game developers, and those broadcasters' viewers.

Bernhaupt (2015) provides an overview of the applicability of UX methods during game design and development phases (see Bernhaupt's table 1.2, p. 6), indicating that some data able to be gathered from streamers may be less useful or even useless at the point during the development that streamers are typically asked to showcase the game. For instance, she indicates that focus groups and interviews are useful during conceptualization and prototyping, but not once the pre-production phase begins. However, several important applications stand out as both lining up with sponsored streaming (which usually occurs in late production) and the types of data Twitch streaming offers, namely observation, playtesting, physiological UX evaluation, experiments that include game controller evaluation, heuristic-based evaluations, video heuristics, and behavioral game telemetry.

We wonder, then, how well sponsored streams lend themselves to producing data useful for such methods. If streamers are being approached from a largely marketing perspective, to promote the game as it nears release or a big update, how are their streams and the constituent elements used to gather UX/PX data, if at all? Moreover, if NDAs prohibit or complicate the researchers' access to workplace studies on use of streamer data, what can we learn about this power dynamic from the streamer, stream, and viewers? We encourage further research here, including inquiry targeting the collaboration between Twitch streamers and developers/designers, but also involving UX practitioners and academics. Specifically, we pose some initial questions:

- How are game companies currently collaborating with streamers via Twitch (or other platforms)?
- What are the common processes/workflows practiced among streamers who partner with game companies?
- What variations are evident among streamers' think-aloud behaviors, and how do these behaviors align (or not) with similar protocols in UX fields?

- How do the contexts of Twitch and in particular the presence of an internet audience affect a participant's thinking aloud?
- How do streamers understand the role(s) of their viewers within their work and collaborations?
- How do Twitch viewers understand the work of the streamers they watch (in terms of performance, use/demonstration, competition, etc.)?
- What comparable partnerships happen via Twitch in non-gaming circles? Are there emerging opportunities for sponsorship non-gaming industries should be aware of?

We envision a potential research trajectory built on these questions would begin with interviewing a selection of sponsored Twitch streamers on their experiences with how they collaborate with game companies, with their audiences, and others. Researchers might begin by asking:

- What were the stated goals of the sponsorship? Was it explicitly intended to promote and market the game, or were there other goals?
- Who began the sponsorship process? Who approached whom? Did the streamer solicit the company, or the other way around?
- Who from the game company was involved in the sponsorship? Was it the developer? Marketer? Other?
- With which organization/company departments did they interact?
- Were there specific criteria the streamer was required to meet prior to the collaboration?
- What kinds of instruction were they given for accessing game content? for streaming? for communicating with viewers/fans?
- How does the streamer consider and engage their viewers when streaming sponsored content as opposed to non-sponsored content?
- Were there other stipulations or agreements in place as to the nature of character of the sponsored stream?

Following preliminary interviews, researchers might design surveys or focus groups around the most interesting findings. Additional findings from such surveys could form the basis for more in-depth research into specific Twitch-UX applications, such as think aloud protocols for streamers or analysis tools for developers. Using Twitch for UX-based collaborations offers a value-multiplier for sponsored streaming: if companies are paying streamers to market their game anyway, they might also get valuable data with which to improve their design or development, and streamers may find that an attention to or use of think aloud protocols maps onto and perhaps even improves viewer engagement. Even in cases with no sponsorship, if researchers can better understand how streaming practices produce useful user research data, independent game developers and small studios—the sort with limited resources for UX—can more affordably and efficiently conduct such research. Academics also stand to benefit from these findings when conducting user research from a distance.

■ Limitations and Ethical Responsibilities

There are limitations and risks to collaborating via Twitch, some of which we have touched on above. The distributed, public nature of Twitch means that UX work on such a platform can be easily interrupted or derailed. Confidentiality and privacy are difficult to manage on such an open platform, to the extent that if the product being tested is not ready for the public or if participants prefer anonymity, any benefits of using Twitch may be outweighed by these ethical concerns. Livestreaming tools other than Twitch may be more practical in certain contexts.

Perhaps more importantly, researchers and professionals should be mindful and equitably inclusive as they seek collaborations with Twitch users. As a gaming-centric space, Twitch undeniably harbors toxic racist and sexist cultures (see Gray, 2017, 2020; Paul, 2018; Taylor, 2018). Researchers considering Twitch-based UX hold an obligation to center marginalized voices and perspectives in their work and must allow and support radically inclusive representation (in gaming and in UX) to counterbalance the overrepresentation of white male participants in such spaces. Researchers might begin by recognizing the harms of racially color-blind approaches to UXR (Sano-Franchini, 2017), by adopting careful and considered chat moderation practices, and by listening to and acting on recommendations from marginalized steaming communities.

Addressing the effects of privilege and systemic inequalities will always be especially important for building products and systems that are user-centered for more than merely a subset or even a majority of users. The obligation to do so extends beyond the fields of UX and game design into product design, interface design, and communication design of all kinds (Acharya, 2018; Noble, 2018) as well as academia (Walton et al., 2019). Although our discussion of these issues here is inadequate, acknowledging these realities and our responsibilities for addressing such issues is undeniably important. By inviting and supporting (financially and socially) the participation of users from as many backgrounds and ability levels as possible, UX researchers have the potential to open conversations and build connections across historically divided groups, widening access to and awareness of UX along the way. Doing so will be an important part of working past the ingrained privilege still common in UX generally (Castillo, 2018).

■ Conclusion

This chapter has not covered all potential ways UX principles and methods can be taken up via Twitch and similar livestreaming spaces, but the examples described above and our speculative exploration of how to apply a variety of UX methods on Twitch show that livestreaming services offer productive multimethod platforms for collaborative UX research. Although games have been our focus in this chapter, leveraging Twitch and other livestreaming platforms for UX is likely possible beyond the gaming industry. The affordances of Twitch make it especially useful for multimethod research and collaboration for researchers in any sector of UX invested in collaborating to make positive change for users. The openness and the popularity of Twitch, a platform where hundreds of thousands of users are already showcasing their use of a variety of interfaces and tools, make it a noteworthy site for further research and investigation.

∎ References

AccountingNightmareSA. (2019). *Devil May Cry 5—Nero Bloody Palace (Stream 05/04/19)* [archived Twitch stream]. Twitch. https://tinyurl.com/nkvw9wht.

Acharya, K. R. (2018, August 3). Usability for user empowerment: Promoting social justice and human rights through localized UX design. SIGDOC '18: *Proceedings of the 36th ACM International Conference on the Design of Communication*, 6, 1–7. https://doi.org/10.1145/3233756.3233960.

alexgwin. (2013). *usability test 1* [archived Twitch stream]. Twitch. https://www.twitch.tv/alexgwin/video/49873772.

Amaya, G., Davis, J. P., Gunn, D. V., Harrison, C., Pagulayan, R. J., Philips, B. & Wixon, D. (2008). Games user research (GUR): Our experience with and evolution of four methods. In K. Isbister & N. Schaffer (Eds.), *Game usability: Advice from the experts for advancing the player experience* (pp. 35–64). Morgan Kaufmann Publishers.

Bernhaupt, R. (2015). User experience evaluation methods in the games development life cycle. In R. Bernhaupt (Ed.), *Game user experience evaluation* (pp. 1–10) Springer.

bornfreetwitch. (2019). *UX* [archived Twitch stream]. Twitch. https://www.twitch.tv/bornfreetwitch/video/425465268.

Castillo, V. (2018, June 24). *An overdue conversation: The UX research industry's Achilles heel*. UX Planet Blog. https://uxplanet.org/an-overdue-conversation-the-ux-research-industrys-achilles-heel-3524b1c6f908.

Chan, B. & Gray, K. (2020). Microstreaming, microcelebrity, and marginalized masculinity: Pathways to visibility and self-definition for Black men in gaming. *Women's Studies in Comm, 43*(4), 354–362. https://doi.org/10.1080/07491409.2020.1833634.

Clanton C. (1998, April). An interpreted demonstration of computer game design. In *CHI 98 Conference Summary on Human Factors in Computing Systems* (pp. 1–2). ACM.

Cornett, S. (2004, April 25). The usability of massively multiplayer online roleplaying games: Designing for new users. *CHI '04: Proceedings of the SIGCHI conference on Human factors in computing systems*, 703–710. https://doi.org/10.1145/985692.985781.

CouchTeamGaming. (2018, August 27). How much money do small Twitch streamers make [Video]. YouTube. https://www.youtube.com/watch?v=fkMnWJ6xl3Q.

derScharni. (2020). *The UX and Chill Show* [Twitch channel]. Twitch. https://www.twitch.tv/derscharni.

Drachen, A. (2015). Behavioral telemetry in games user research. In R. Bernhaupt (Ed.), *Game User Experience Evaluation* (pp. 135–168). Springer.

Ericsson, K. A. (2006). Protocol analysis and expert thought: Concurrent verbalizations of thinking during experts' performance on representative tasks. In K.A. Ericsson,

N. Charness, R. R. Hoffman & P. J. Feltovich (Eds.), *The Cambridge handbook of expertise and expert performance* (pp. 223–241). Cambridge University Press. https://psycnet.apa.org/record/2006-10094-000.

Ericsson, K. A. & Simon, H. A. (1984). *Protocol analysis: Verbal reports as data.* MIT Press.

Ewalt, D. (2020, January 3). The pro gamer's secret training tool? Eye tracking. *Forbes.* https://tinyurl.com/2s445n6s.

Fei, R. (2018, February 11). *Personas, jobs to be done, user needs = goals + pain points.* UX Collective. https://uxdesign.cc/personas-jtbd-user-needs-goals-pain-points-7eaa81976f0.

FranstarMTG. (2013). *Usability study* [archived Twitch stream]. Twitch. https://www.twitch.tv/franstarmtg/video/50823054.

GameCircus. (2012). *Phillip Paplinko usability* [archived Twitch stream]. Twitch. https://www.twitch.tv/videos/46223117.

GameUserX. (2018). *[ENG] The Witcher 3: Wild Hunt + all DLC + game UX evaluation [PART 1.1]* [archived Twitch stream]. Twitch. https://www.twitch.tv/videos/292359981.

Gray, K. L. (2017). They're just too "urban": Black gamers streaming on Twitch. In J. Daniels, K. Gregory & T. M. Cotton (Eds.), *Digital sociologies* (pp. 355–368). Policy Press.

Gray, K. L. (2020). *Intersectional tech: Black users in digital gaming.* Louisiana State University Press.

Hamilton, W. A., Garretson, O. & Kerne, A. (2014, April 26). Streaming on Twitch: Fostering participatory communities of play within live mixed media. *CHI '14: Proceedings of the SIGCHI Conference on Human Factors in Computing Systems* (pp. 1315–1324). http://doi.org/10.1145/2556288.2557048.

Hodent, C. (2017). *The gamer's brain: How neuroscience and UX can impact video game design.* CRC Press.

Hoonhout, H. (2008). Let the game tester do the talking: Think aloud and interviewing to learn about the game experience. In K. Isbister & N. Schaffer (Eds.), *Game usability: advice from the experts for advancing the player experience* (pp. 115–126). Morgan Kaufmann Publishers. https://tinyurl.com/yc3k2wr9.

Hsu, J. (2015, January 27). Inside the largest virtual psychology lab in the world. *Wired.* https://www.wired.com/2015/01/inside-the-largest-virtual-psychology-lab-in-the-world/.

Isbister, K. & Schaffer, N. (2008). *Game usability: Advice from the experts for advancing the player experience.* Morgan Kaufmann Publishers.

Jennett, C., Cox, A. L., Cairns, P., Dhoparee, S., Epps, A., Tijs, T. & Walton, A. (2008). Measuring and defining the experience of immersion in games. *International Journal of Human-Computer Studies, 66*(9), 641–661. https://doi.org/10.1016/j.ijhcs.2008.04.004.

Johnson, M. R. & Woodcock, J. (2017). "It's like the gold rush": The lives and careers of professional video game streamers on Twitch.tv. *Information, Communication & Society, 22*(3), 336–351 https://doi.org/10.1080/1369118X.2017.1386229.

Jørgensen, A. H. (2004, October 23). Marrying HCI/usability and computer games: A preliminary look. *NordiCHI '04: Proceedings of Third Nordic Conference on Human-Computer Interaction, 393*–396. https://doi.org/10.1145/1028014.1028078.

Kim, J. H., Gunn, D. V., Schuh, E., Phillips, B., Pagulayan, R. J. & Wixon, D. (2008, April 6). Tracking real-time user experience (TRUE): A comprehensive instrumentation solution for complex systems. *CHI '08: Proceedings of SIGCHI Conference on Human Factors in Computing Systems* (pp. 443–452). https://doi.org/10.1145/1357054.1357126.

krosmarc. (2019). *Woaaaaaah. Denkt doch mal an die usability!* [archived Twitch stream, unavailable as of publication]. Twitch.

Lazzaro, N. (2008). The four fun keys. In K. Isbister & N. Schaffer (Eds.), *Game usability: Advice from the experts for advancing the player experience* (pp. 317–343). Morgan Kaufmann Publishers.

Lazzaro, N. & Keeker, K. (2004, April). "What's my method?" A game show on games. *CHI EA '04: CHI '04 Extended Abstracts on Human Factors in Computing Systems* (pp. 1093–1094). https://dl.acm.org/doi/abs/10.1145/985921.985922.

Let's Play Archive. (n.d.). *The history of the Let's Play Archive*. Let's Play Archive. https://lparchive.org/history.

Luci. (2020, May 7). *How to private stream on Twitch*. Stream Scheme. https://www.streamscheme.com/how-to-private-stream-on-twitch/.

McAllister, G. & White, G. R. (2015). Video game development and user experience. In R. Bernhaupt (Ed.), *Game user experience evaluation* (pp. 11–36). Springer.

Medlock, M. C., Wixon, D., Terrano, M., Romero, R. & Fulton, B. (2002, July 8–12). Using the RITE method to improve products: A definition and a case study [Presentation]. 11th Annual Usability Professionals Association Conference: Humanizing Design, Orlando, FL, United States.

Nielsen, J. & Landauer, T. K. (1993, May 1). A mathematical model of the finding of usability problems. *INTERCHI '93: Proceedings of the INTERCHI '93 Conference on Human Factors in Computing Systems* (pp. 206–213). https://dl.acm.org/doi/10.5555/164632.164904.

Noble, S. U. (2019). *Algorithms of oppression: How search engines reinforce racism*. New York University Press.

Pagulayan, R. & Wixon, D. (2008). Games user research at the crossroads. In K. Isbister & N. Schaffer (Eds.), *Game usability: Advice from the experts for advancing the player experience* (pp. vii-x). Morgan Kaufmann Publishers.

Parrish, A. (2021, Sept. 29). Twitch announces new safety tools in the fight against hate raids. The Verge. https://tinyurl.com/mtyj5j84.

Paul, C. A. (2018). *The toxic meritocracy of video games: Why gaming culture is the worst*. University of Minnesota Press.

Payne, K., Keith, M. J., Schuetzler, R. M. & Giboney, J. S. (2017). Examining the learning effects of live streaming video game instruction over Twitch. *Computers in Human Behavior, 77*, 95–109. https://doi.org/10.1016/j.chb.2017.08.029.

PBS Digital Studios. (2013, September 3). Why Is LET'S PLAY So Huge? [Video]. Youtube. https://www.youtube.com/watch?v=pQ9bpcdMd_U.

Pires, K. & Simon, G. (2015). YouTube Live and Twitch: A tour of user-generated live streaming systems. *MMSys '15: Proceedings of the 6th ACM Multimedia Systems Conference* (pp. 225–230). https://dl.acm.org/doi/10.1145/2713168.2713195.

Reimer, C. (2017). Dialogic, data-driven design: UX and League of Legends. In L. Potts & M. J. Salvo (Eds.), *Rhetoric and experience architecture*. (241–257). Parlor Press.

Rohrer, C. (2014, October 12). *When to use which user-experience research methods*. Nielsen Norman Group. https://www.nngroup.com/articles/which-ux-research-methods/.

Sano-Franchini, J. (2017). What can Asian eyelids teach us about user experience design? A culturally reflexive framework for UX/I design. *Rhetoric, Professional Communication, and Globalization*, *10*(1), 27–53.

Schuh, E., Gunn, D. V., Phillips, B., Pagulayan, R. J., Kim, J. H. & Wixon, D. (2008). TRUE instrumentation: Tracking real-time user experience in games. In K. Isbister & N. Schaffer (Eds.), *Game usability: Advice from the experts for advancing the player experience* (pp. 237–265). Morgan Kaufmann Publishers.

Sjöblom, M., Törhönena, M., Hamaria, J. & Maceya, J. (2019). The ingredients of Twitch streaming: Affordances of game streams. *Computers in Human Behavior*, *92*, 20–28. https://doi.org/10.1016/j.chb.2018.10.012.

Southey, F., Xiao, G., Holte, R. C., Trommelen, M. & Buchanan, J. (2005). Semi-automated gameplay analysis by machine learning. *Proceedings of the AAAI Conference on Artificial Intelligence and Interactive Digital Entertainment*, *1*(1), 123–128. https://doi.org/10.1609/aiide.v1i1.18727.

Sweetster, P. & Wyeth, P. (2005). GameFlow: a model for evaluating player enjoyment in games. *ACM Computer Entertainment*, *3*(3), 1–24. https://doi.org/10.1145/1077246.1077253.

Tullis, T. & Albert, B. (2013). *Measuring the user experience: Collecting, analyzing, and presenting usability metrics* (2nd ed.). Morgan Kauffman.

Taylor, T. L. (2018). *Watch me play: Twitch and the rise of game live streaming*. Princeton University Press. http://watchmeplay.cc/.

TheMainManSWE. (2020). Highlight: Tekken 7 ranked [archived Twitch stream]. Twitch. https://www.twitch.tv/videos/576069073.

Tobii. (2020, Feb. 4). Tobii and Mobalytics kick off beta tests featuring eye tracking analytics for League of Legends players. Tobii Corporate. https://tinyurl.com/3n7fd6zw.

Twitch (2019, June 26). *Superfans welcome: Subscriber streams are coming to Twitch*. Twitch Blog. https://tinyurl.com/mryphrre.

Twitch. (2020). *Insights & analytics*. Twitch.tv. https://dev.twitch.tv/docs/insights.

Walton, R., Moore, K. R. & Jones, N. N. (2019). *Technical communication after the social justice turn: Building coalitions for action*. Routledge.

wright4thejob. (2022). User experience design for a bike tail bar! Switches and indicators mechanical and electrical design. [archived Twitch stream, unavailable as of publication]. Twitch.

Wodtke, C. (2018, August 16). The design of everyday games [Video]. YouTube. https://www.youtube.com/watch?v=bhxhL6ChYko.

Zimmerman, J. (2014). Psyche and eros: Rhetorics of secrecy and disclosure in game developer–fan relations. In J. deWinter & R. Moeller (Eds.), *Computer games and technical communication: Critical methods and applications at the intersection* (pp. 141–156). Ashgate.

13. Collaborating on the Interface: Rhetorical and Hermeneutic Theory for User Experience Design

Eric J. York
IOWA STATE UNIVERSITY

Abstract. In this chapter I take up a longstanding problem in design, the question of how meaning gets made, and consider the question in the context of graphical user interfaces. After developing satisfactory definitions for experiences and interfaces, and after tracing how semiotic theory, as conceived in interface studies, developed as a way to avoid the messiness of language, I argue it propagates a simplistic view of communication merely as a process of using sign systems to encode and decode meaning. Subsequently, I develop an alternative conception of meaning-making in interfaces that combines rhetorical and hermeneutic theories of invention and interpretation to articulate a theory of interfaces as sites of participatory collaboration. This view asks designers and researchers to reconsider how they see their relationships with users and advises a questioning and listening approach in UX studies.

> *Qui non intelligit res, non potest ex verbis sensum elicere./*Those who don't understand *things* can't elicit sense from *words*.
> – Martin Luther (as cited by Gadamer, 2004, p. 173, emphasis added)

> Users spend most of their time on other sites. This means that users prefer your site to work the same way as all the other sites they already know.
> – Jon Yablonski, Jakob's Law.

The polymorphous nature of graphical interfaces presents problems for both designers and users. Where text, color, typography, images, videos, animations, and icons come together, their various communicative systems bunch and overlap in complicated ways. Occasionally with great effort, an interface can recede almost entirely from view; more often, interfaces present users with interpretive problems stemming from their design—*What does this symbol mean? How does this process work? What does this button* actually *do?* For researchers, the problems are acute. Faced with the formidable task of describing, modeling, and making predictions, scholars over the past three decades have turned to a wide variety of theories to explain observational data and guide their research. It can be difficult to know which questions to pursue, given the abundance of theoretical models, and it can be difficult to resolve incommensurability between theories that subvert and contradict one another. In a recent collection, for example, Ehren Pflugfelder (2017) identifies "a few dozen methods" and describes "a maze of options" (p. 168). Evolving from its earliest days as a body of largely prescriptive aphorisms and a list of dos and don'ts (de Souza, 1993), UX research has branched out in almost as many directions as there are researchers. Some evaluate neural activity and biometrics using methods developed in the natural sciences, some conduct standardized assessments (using tools such as the SUQ and PSSUQ) and apply statistical methods, and some analyze emotional states using ethnographic and other more qualitative methods (Skorin-Kapov et al., 2014). Some are testing how many milliseconds it takes to locate and click a button, others are measuring what effect clicking it has on heart rate and brain activity, and still others are asking the users how clicking a button makes them *feel*. Like interfaces themselves, interface studies are polymorphous.

While there are certainly strengths to this polymorphism, one of the most important issues we face, consequentially, is the need for a coherent body of theory to better integrate these different methods and support more systematic inquiry. Certainly, there have been prior attempts to formulate such a unifying theory—one of which, semiotics, serves as my foil for this chapter—however, it turns out that adequately theorizing the design and evaluation of user interfaces is quite complicated. As an exercise, let's imagine what might comprise such a theory. Given the field's history, the theory would likely need to retain its interdisciplinary heritage and remain a patchwork but must somehow coherently represent the uniquely dense and varied nature of interfaces as well as account for both their creation and their interpretation—in other words, it must explain how such complicated, multimodal "texts" are created and used as well as the affective, cognitive processes involved in both their production *and* their interpretation. That's already a lot to do, considering how complicated subjects of cognition, memory, and behavior are. Additionally, and in keeping with a tradition we've found indispensable, this theory should be amenable to experimentation and, ideally, predictive of observable phenomena. It would need a clearly defined terminology coherent enough to retain explanatory power across disciplines, yet flexible enough to be relevant in domains such as business, marketing, and other industries. Finally, it would need to address the ethical dimensions of interface design: how interfaces relate people to one another socially and economically, for example. This is a big job and even sketching a general outline, admittedly incomplete as this, is daunting. Interface studies seems to impinge on every sphere of human endeavor.

Obviously, fully developing such a unifying theory is more than I can accomplish here, so I'll focus instead on a single, longstanding question that illustrates why previous attempts at formulating a unifying theory have failed and what such a theory must look like to succeed. By focusing on one significant issue (the interpretation question), and the field's primary response to it (semiotic theory),

I hope to show the relationship to rigor and science that any potential unifying theory must establish if it is to actually unify the various aspects of the field in tension. The question of interpretation has long preoccupied UX researchers and has been posed and addressed in various ways over the years. Fundamentally it's about how meaning gets made in interfaces. How do designers imbue a largely arbitrary collection of signs, images, colors, shapes, and microcopy with enough meaning for users to perform extremely complex tasks, such as creating virtual imagery, trading stock portfolios, or maintaining very large databases, using them? How do people elicit enough meaning from often ambiguous visual systems to still make reliable decisions? Where does the meaning of design elements such as lines, colors, icons, or emojis come from? How is it produced or assigned? Perhaps most importantly, why does it go wrong? These and others are all variations of the interpretation question which boils down to the need for a theory to describe the process of making meaning from signs.

Aside from being a longstanding issue, the interpretation question is pertinent for other reasons. It encompasses both halves of UX studies—design and research/testing, which are increasingly in tension—and comprises the place where they both overlap. Interpretation is a critical concept for both subdisciplines because it's instrumental to both. UX designers must know to some extent how their designs will be interpreted and UX researchers must know to some extent how the users interpreted and failed to interpret the interface. Interface interpretation is the central process that UX is concerned with, no matter the specialization. The act of interpretation is when designers, all different kinds of users, researchers, and even nonhumans, must come to agreement about what things mean, about how things are—at least, if the communication is to be successful.

This question is also pertinent because for decades the main response to the call for a unifying theory of UX, which was semiotics, was claimed by proponents to offer a science of interpretation. Members of more scientific disciplines can become frustrated with the messiness, the illogic, that is seemingly endemic to interface design. As Mihai Nadin (1988) tellingly asks, why can't interface design be "more like science" and why can't interface designers "be more like engineers?" (p. 272). If semiotics attempts to brings the rigor of science to the messiness of design, the prevailing theory of interpretation in UX likewise harkens to a mathematical theory of communication that seeks to reduce communicants to senders and receivers, and messages to signal and noise. In this model, the process of design and interpretation is a process in which designers encode meaning into interfaces using signs and later, users decode them, reassembling the message by associating the signs with their intended meanings. In providing the rhetorical-hermeneutic response to the question of interpretation, my argument not only refutes semiotics as the science of language, but it also likewise and by the same token discredits a mathematical model of communication that has proven inadequate for understanding how designers create and users engage with interfaces.

After dispensing with some definitional issues, this chapter examines the question of interpretation as it's been framed, illustrating its complications with examples of interface elements, and establishing a vocabulary for discussing interface artifacts. The main body of the chapter provides a substantial critique of the most significant candidate for a unifying theory, namely semiotics, and proposes an alternative one grounded in rhetorical hermeneutics, showing how it better explains the way designers create and users make sense of interfaces. Drawing on Gadamerian philology and tracing its roots to the rhetorical concept of *technē*, the chapter argues that the most productive view of interfaces is not one of systems of signs and symbols where meaning must be encoded by designers and decoded by users, but instead a view that sees interfaces as part of a living language whose terms are in constant flux and whose creation and interpretation requires authentic dialogue between parties, dialogue that is generative, rather than representative, of meaning. Furthermore, rather than being stubbornly illogical, merely flawed conduits of meaning, interfaces are instead sites of profound and extensive collaboration where humans and nonhumans, despite barriers, come together to communicate with one another, to act and to change. Ultimately, I envision this collaboration as a kind of hermeneutic friendship informed by rhetorical prudence, and I discuss the implications of this view for UX design, pedagogy, and research.

■ Defining User Experiences and User Interfaces

According to the International Organization for Standardization (ISO, 2019), user experience is defined as the "perceptions and responses that result from the use and/or anticipated use of a system, product or service" (3.15). The definition states, "this includes the users' emotions, beliefs, preferences, perceptions, comfort, behaviours, and accomplishments that occur before, during and after use" and goes on to explain:

> [user experience] is a consequence of brand image, presentation, functionality, system performance, interactive behaviour, and assistive capabilities of a system, product or service. It also results from the user's internal and physical state resulting from prior experiences, attitudes, skills, abilities and personality; and from the context of use. (3.15).

So, according to this, user experience is the sum of one's "perceptions and responses" broadly conceived, encompassing what happened before, during, and after use, and is the result of a varied set of concerns at least some of which (such as "internal and physical state") are entirely outside the control of designers and even users themselves. Given this definition, how could one ensure a good user experience? Designers would need divine knowledge of individuals and an omnipotent control over things well outside the scope of a given project. Rather than this laundry list of a definition which apparently excludes nothing, we could use some more practice-oriented language.

Marc Hassenzahl (2008), arguing against a prior version of the same standard, provides just such a definition, one that, he claims, "shifts attention from the product and materials . . . to humans and feelings" (p. 12). The shift to humans and feelings is productive for three main reasons: it emphasizes the dynamic and temporal dimensions of interactions (now incorporated into the current version of the standard, but not present then); it provides a primary object of analysis: the "stream of passing momentary feelings" (Hassenzahl, 2008, p. 12); finally, it includes a way to talk about and test a class of phenomena difficult to pin down. Hassenzahl calls this the question of "how UX is 'made'" (2008, p. 12). Building on the ideas that "experience itself is an ongoing reflection on events . . . a constant stream of self-talk" (Hassenzahl, 2008, p. 11) which always includes "a momentary feeling of pleasure and pain in various intensities" and which "regulates our behavior" (p. 12) and the fact that, in an ongoing experience, we always have access to a sense of whether we feel good or bad at any particular moment, Hassenzahl ultimately defines user experience as "a momentary, primarily evaluative feeling (good-bad) while interacting with a product or service" (p. 12). This definition, while much shorter and more direct than the ISO standard, also has the advantage of telling us what user experience actually is: an evaluative mode of thinking.

However, this definition is incomplete (as Hassenzahl himself acknowledges) because it doesn't address the "critical question of how UX is 'made'" (2008, p. 12). Hassenzahl proposes a corollary, that "Good UX is the consequence of fulfilling the human needs," which he categorizes into autonomy, competency, stimulation, relatedness, and popularity (2008, p. 12). While we may quibble over this taxonomy (and as we've seen, subsequent standards revisions have chosen a different one), we can't argue with the experimental results which support his hypothesis (Hassenzahl, 2008) and in any case, our interest is not with experiences in general but with one kind of experience specifically: the graphical interface. We can extrapolate enough from Hassenzahl that users are constantly making judgements about how interface elements make them feel, and that, in principle anyway, an interface succeeds at creating a positive user experience when it fulfills some set of human needs, however they are defined.

Similarly, the ISO defines a user interface as "all components of an interactive system (software or hardware) that provide information and controls for the user to accomplish specific tasks" (2019, p. 1) sweeping in "all components" providing "information and controls," and coupling them with the ability to "accomplish specific tasks" and doing little else. Like the previous standard, it's vague enough that nearly anything could fit. According to this definition, I could use a hammer to interface with a house, and therefore it misses the opportunity to identify the characteristic most salient to interfaces of all kinds: their primarily linguistic composition. All the various elements of an interface, the buttons and switches, the menus, even the colors and arrangements—the things that actually "provide the information and controls"—all share one common purpose: to enable communication, and they do this primarily by communicating their intent through their representation—in other words, their function is represented by their appearance. While not every component of an interface is linguistic in nature, the interface as a whole is a linguistic composition because it is comprised of various elements whose arrangement and combination allow it to be used for communication.

This linguistic composition is what distinguishes interfaces from common tools. I do not mean to restrict the term "linguistic" only to the alphabetic kind, the language used verbally and in writing, but instead to include all forms of language, including the visual and the gestural. As the father of modern hermeneutics, Hans Georg Gadamer (2004) writes, "Being which can be understood is language" (p. 470). In this view, because being can only make itself understood through language, being itself is language. So, the hammer doesn't interface with the house, but in the subtly beckoning curve of the handle we do find an interface because it is communicating with us. A person, the designer, communicates through a kind of gestural language to another person, the user, to seemingly say: "grasp me here and swing me so this other place strikes." The hammer can't interface with a house, but a human can interface with either a hammer or a house by way of the language of affordance. This language of affordance is still nevertheless language, even though it utters not a word, and in the same way shapes, colors, textures, space, sounds, and other media are also language, albeit nonverbal.

So, we must revise the standards definition to be more specific. We should define a user interface as consisting of the linguistic components of an interactive system that enable human and nonhuman communication. This definition more finely distinguishes not only the character of interfaces but also the specific uses to which they are put. It's not just any components, but the linguistic ones, and not just any tasks, but communicative ones. This allows us to discriminate between interfaces and common tools, for example. Even more usefully, this definition also makes available what we might call the "stuff" of interfaces, that is, what they are made of. However, some examples are needed before we can explore this more fully.

■ Multimedia and Intermedia Composition

Figure 13.1 shows interface elements one might find on a number of websites: a hyperlink, a pause button, a dropdown, and so on. By contrast, Figure 13.2 shows a children's music-making app ("Bandimals"). Aside from the first being a collection of generic elements and the second being a finished commercial app, or the first containing mainly website elements while the second contains mainly mobile ones, or that the audience for the first is primarily adults and the audience for the second is mainly children; or that the first is monochromatic and the second uses color, or any number of other surface differences we might mention, these contrasting examples nevertheless illustrate several characteristics inherent to and common among graphical user interfaces as a class.

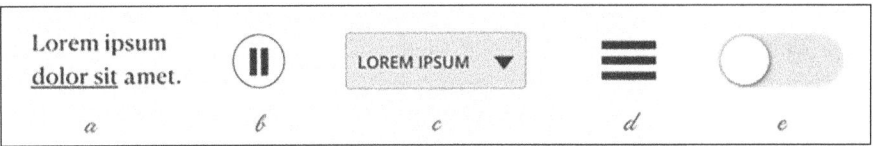

Figure 13.1. Generic interface elements a. hyperlink; b. pause button; c. dropdown; d. menu; e. switch.

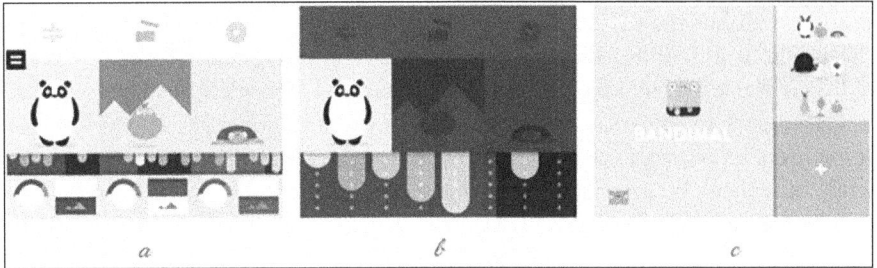

Figure 13.2. Screenshots from the "Bandimals" app a. Home; b. Play; c. Create New.

In Figure 13.1c, a textual element i.e., the lorem ipsum, (one medium), appears alongside graphical elements, a rectangle, and a triangle (another medium). In Figure 13.2, in the fully developed app, this is even more apparent as the images, colors, arrangements, icons, motions, and actions all exist together in juxtaposition on the screen. Not only do the elements that comprise interfaces exist as multimedia, which is to say they are made up of different media, but they are also intermedial, meaning part of them exists between different media, as more than the sum of the different parts. The interface of a mobile app will adapt when viewed on a larger display and so is intermedial in this way, and each element is also intermedial in its local context. For example, the icon representing the main menu in Figure 13.2a is also a button that, when pressed, slides down a portion of the screen to reveal additional options. The element is both an icon and part of an animation. To understand it only as an icon is distorting, to say nothing of the sounds that become music when icons are tapped in sequence. Even the relatively simplistic elements in Figure 13.1 are intermedial. Each figure is part of a composite whose elements work between and among different media. All interfaces consist of elements in multiple media and all interface elements exist at least partially between media, as well.

Because graphical user interfaces have this composition, we cannot read an interface as we would read a text, experience it like an animation, look at it like a photograph, or watch it like a video, even though an interface may include all these things. Instead, it is more. And this brings us to another point about these examples, one that has more direct bearing on our discussion: the question of representation. Readers may notice that the elements in Figure 13.1 are significantly more familiar, perhaps one might say more standard, than the equivalent elements in Figure 13.2. While there isn't a one-to-one correspondence between subfigures, 13.1a roughly corresponds with the word "INFO" in 13.2c, as both are hyperlinked text, and 13.1d corresponds roughly with the small black square in 13.2a, as both are menu icons, and comparing them highlights the originality of the latter. Also, there are additional nonstandard icons in Figure 13.2 such as the "play," "save," and "record" buttons in the top panel and the volume and image controls in the bottom panel of 13.2a, the dots and highlights panel in 13.2b, and all but the plus sign and grid arrangement in 13.2c. But—and I know this is wholly anecdotal—despite this nonstandard iconography, my eleven-year-old daughter used the app without issue whereas I struggled to make sense of it. Our theory must do something to address this additional curiosity. How can some users know what these seemingly arbitrary signs and arrangements mean, while others can be mystified? Why would an adult with expertise in interfaces be worse at reading one than a child?

■ Semiotic Theory in UX Research

Interface studies scholars have advanced several candidates for an overarching theory of UX, the most important of which is semiotics. However, it's important to note that semiotic theory in interface studies as described here is not the same kind of social semiotics Gunther Kress and Theo van Leeuwen (2021) memorably figure as a "semiotic landscape" (p. 9)—something at once both natural and shaped. Prior to that, Ben Barton and Marthalee Barton (1987) had presented a balanced analysis of the semiotic approach as part of their study of simplicity in design. Drawing on visual rhetoric, they noted problems "when a visual representation may be invested with multiple meanings," and called it "a semantic incompatibility" (1987, p. 19), but neither could they completely accept a definition of graphics purely as a "monosemic (unique-meaning) system" (p. 14), and with inimitable style conclude that it's never practical to insist on purity and that design is a process of making compromises (1987). In the decades since, technical communication scholars have tended toward a polysemic (multiple-meanings) view of language and visuals congruent with the core idea that "reality is actively constructed rather than passively reflected in signs" (Yu, 2023, p. 321). By contrast, the kind of semiotic theory I outline in this section belongs to the other tradition in which signs passively reflect reality, instead of constructing it, and where the ideal is that each sign should mean one and only one thing.

At first, there may be some points to recommend a monosemic view. Semiotic theory was already well established by the mid–1980s when user interfaces were first garnering scholarly attention in the engineering community. Arising out of the work of linguist Ferdinand de Saussure and logician Charles Sanders Peirce and later updated by, among many others, author and critic Umberto Eco, the theory of semiotics is systematically applied to interface studies by Nadin (1988), augmented by Clarisse de Souza (1993), and taken up by a welter of scholars in the 2000s. Semiotic approaches to interface design continue to the present day with Muhammad Islam and Harry Bouwman (2016), Daniela Fogli (2017), and Vito Roberto and Elio Toppano (2019). Semiotic theory may be appealing largely because it purports to be the science of language. Through extensive categorization, it seeks to make language as predictable as mathematics (see Nadin, 1988, de Souza 1993, and Islam & Bouwman, 2016 for examples). Perhaps most importantly, semiotic theory appears to answer two questions which the "computer community" found to be critical: as Nadin (1988) frames them: "(1) Why isn't the design of computer interfaces more like science? and (2) Why can't the people who design interfaces be more like engineers?" (p. 272). As a purported science of language, semiotics seems to offer the computer community a way out of problems posed by the messiness of design.

In the computer community, proponents of semiotic theory have made some extravagant claims that haven't exactly been borne out by the research. Nadin (1988) writes, "If there is a science of interface (computer interface or any other kind), then this science is semiotics, and the pan-logical semiotics established by Peirce seems appropriate to interfaces. Once they accept this affirmation, computer scientists and engineers should have no problem . . ." (p. 273). In a similar vein, de Souza (1993) writes "if designers are led to conceive of systems [*i.e.*, interfaces] as a distinctive type of message they are sending to users, an engineered metacommunication artifact, many of the misunderstandings and deadlocks possibly occurring in human-computer interaction can be avoided" (p. 754). However, empirical research since then has belied such hopes and shown semiotics are not panacea. In their analysis of induction-based research methods in which general rules are inferred from specific data, Paul van Schaik and colleagues (2012) find significant problems with a model in which designers are senders and users are receivers of information and in which, as Nadin (1988) puts it "once the user accepts a language, he will apply it according to the rules the designer embedded in the interface, and their communication, mediated by a certain machine, will take place" (p. 274). According to this view, once users decode the meaning that designers have encoded, everything works smoothly.

To the contrary, these authors cite "a wealth of empirical evidence" suggesting that, "rather than doing complex (weighted and summated) calculations to induce, people use relatively simple cognitive strategies" such as "simple rules" and "heuristics" (van Schaik et al, 2012, p. 11:2). The lengthy process of building up a mental model of the language of a given system of signs does not appear to be in operation. Instead, people form judgments much more quickly. Neglect of this fact, the authors argue, "can easily lead to false conclusions" and "spurious" effects. Instead, the authors explain, "'beauty' should be thought of as an affect-driven, evaluative response to the visual Gestalt of an interactive product," which, because of "its predominantly affective nature makes it very quick" (p. 11:4). Instead of calculating beauty, people feel it; instead of formulating logical rules, people intuit them. Ultimately, the authors contend, in absence of a sufficient understanding of how such inference works, "the theoretical justification of a model is almost impossible" (p. 11:3). Likewise, reporting on the results of empirical study, Islam and Bouwman (2016) conclude that "user interpretation . . . is nearly impossible to predict based on the meaning of the sign or . . . the sign itself" (p. 134). Aside from these decidedly unfavorable results, research based in semiotics has some benefits. For example, Islam and Bouwman (2016) give us the useful concept of the "interface sign" (p. 122), and de Souza (2005) begins to move the field beyond a theory of signs with her discussion of the ontological and epistemological dimensions (p. 337–338) of interfaces.

■ Interface Signs and Symbols

To move beyond a theory of signs, we must recognize that the inability of a linguistic theory to predict human behavior is not indicative of a limitation of the theoretical model, but instead reveals a characteristic inherent to all linguistic systems. I'm tempted to crack the old programmer's joke, "it's not a bug, it's a feature," because, as we've seen from our survey, linguistic systems are more unpredictable than they ought to be. Language, despite the imposition of scientific methods and taxonomy, remains stubbornly intractable, difficult to pin down, liable to slip away leaving the researcher holding vapor. This ungraspable quality to language has been noted by some of the most prominent thinkers in the Western tradition and it ultimately leads us to inquire into the nature of thinking itself. So, we begin on the ground de Souza approaches in her later work: the ground of ontology, specifically, the ontology of signs and symbols.

Gadamer is perhaps, alongside Paul Ricouer, Jurgen Habermas, Gianni Vattimo and a handful of others, the most significant figure of twentieth century hermeneutics. His encyclopedic *Truth and Method* was first translated into English in the late 1970s and only became widely available in 1989. As a result, it probably wouldn't have enjoyed as much currency as semiotic theory did for scholars like Nadin and de Souza; nevertheless, the hermeneutics developed by John Dewey, Wilhelm Dilthey and Friedrich Schliermacher and revolutionized by Gadamer were engaged in a similar project to semiotics to bring to the humanities the rigor enjoyed by mathematics and the sciences. Gadamer's differed radically, however, from other attempts to systematize human language. Whereas Peirce's semiotics, Gottfried Leibniz's *characteristica universalis*, John Wilkins' "Real Character," Cartesian rationality, etc. all seek to impose scientific methods onto human language, Gadamer's hermeneutics explicitly rejects such imposition. It identifies a fundamental feature of language, its speculative nature, that makes such scientific surety impossible. However, fully understanding this difficult-to-grasp characteristic of language requires us to first establish some key concepts such as the ontological differences among signs, symbols, and works of art, the structure of the hermeneutic circle, and centrality of language itself to being.

Gadamer (2004) describes signs and symbols as "the two extremes of representation" (p. 145). At one end of the spectrum is "pure indication which is the essence of the sign" and at the other, "pure substitution which is the essence of the symbol" (p. 145). Indication and substitution can be present in mixed amounts so that a particular composition consists of greater and lesser amounts of each. At one end, "a sign," Gadamer writes "is nothing but what its function requires; and that is to point away from itself. To fulfill this function, of course, it must first draw attention to itself. It must be striking: that is, it must clearly foreground itself and present itself as an indicator," however, Gadamer is careful to point out, it cannot be *too* striking or cause readers to linger over its beauty "for it is there only to make present something that is absent and to do so in such a way that the absent thing, and that alone, comes to mind" (2004, p. 145). The same is true of all signs, Gadamer tell us, "There is something schematic and abstract about them, because they point not to themselves but to what is not present" (2004, p. 146). The examples in Figure 13.1 exhibit this schematic or abstract character—they are like diagrams of art, proto-figures, skeletons, or scaffolds that have preserved the function of the visual but lack its full aesthetic.

a   *b*   *c*   *d*

Figure 13.3. Several common symbols of trust. a. McAfee; b. PayPal; c. TRUSTe; d. Better Business Bureau.

Symbols, however, are not merely signs, but also something more. Instead of merely pointing to something that is not present, a symbol also makes present the thing it points to by standing in for it, by representing it. Gadamer writes a "symbol not only points to something; it represents it by taking its place. But to take the place of something means to make something present that is not present" (2004, p. 147). Each of the examples in Figure 13.1, is mere sign pointing to what is not present: the underscore points to a hyperlinked resource; the downward caret points to a list that is not yet visible, and likewise for the menu icon. The pause button and toggle switches both point to and recall physical objects which perform analogous functions. However, the examples in Figure 13.3 are not only signs, but also symbols of various kinds of trust. These trust symbols, often appearing on webpages in the header or footer, on payment forms, and alongside payment buttons, serve a different purpose. Rather than signaling that something is not present, they instead symbolize something that is present, in this case trust, verification, accreditation, and so forth.

Normally, signs and symbols are given their meaning through an act Gadamer (2004) calls "institution." He writes: "Artificial signs and symbols alike do not . . . acquire their signifying function from their own content but must be taken as signs or as symbols. We call the origin of their signifying function their 'institution'" (2004, p. 148). The examples in Figure 13.3 have such an institution. When the Better Business Bureau unveils their trust badge, it becomes imbued with meaning: thereafter it represents the accreditation of the body. However, the same is not true of the examples in Figure 13.1. The venerable underscore has signified a hyperlink since the first days of the internet, however not all hyperlinks are indicated by underscores, so what of those that use different colors or typography? From where does that meaning stem? While a downward-pointing caret may carry meaning from other systems, where does the meaning of the menu icon come from? Whoever first used it didn't institute it in the sense that a Department of Transportation decrees what traffic signs means. Instead, as Gadamer writes of works of art (as opposed to signs and symbols): "The public act of consecration or unveiling that assigns its purpose does not give it its significance. Rather, it is already a structure with a signifying function of its own, as a pictorial or non-pictorial representation, before it is assigned a function" (2004, p. 147). Works of art are functionally and structurally different from both signs and symbols and this is what gives them additional dimensions of meaning.

The difference between signs and symbols on the one hand and works of art on the other stems from their relationship with things that are not present. While a sign or a symbol may be instituted with meaning, a work of art already carries its own system of meaning to which its parts are arranged in relation. Thus, Gadamer distinguishes between those signs and symbols which merely carry meaning and artistic elements "whose own content points beyond them to the whole of a context determined by them" (2004, p. 149). It is no coincidence that the example Gadamer chooses to illustrate is the art of architecture. Architecture, Gadamer explains, both responds to the space around it and structures the space within it, a process he calls a "twofold mediation . . . [which is] namely to draw the viewer's attention to itself, to satisfy his taste, and then to redirect it away from itself to the greater whole of the life context which it accompanies. As the art which creates space," Gadamer tells us, architecture "both shapes it and leaves it free" (2004, p. 150). Interfaces are a lot more than a collection of signs and symbols. Although made up of signs and symbols, interfaces also structure space and, through the structure of this space, provide structure for the content that resides within it. Interfaces are more akin to the art of architecture than they are to a system of signs and symbols, and so in this dimension alone, semiotic theory, which stops at signs and symbols, fails to account for what we observe.

■ The Speculative Structure of Language

However, the problem with a narrowly construed semiotic theory is not merely that it misclassifies interfaces as signs when they should actually be seen as a specific type of architecture; there is a more fundamental misapprehension yet that, once revealed, does away altogether with any ideas about a science or mathematics of language. Gadamer explicitly rejects the notion of "a pregiven system of possibilities of being for which the signifying subject selects corresponding signs;" he writes: "a word is not a sign that one selects, nor is it a sign that one makes or gives to another; it is not an existent thing that one picks up and gives an ideality of meaning in order to make another being visible through it" (2004, p. 417). Language cannot be reduced to a mere system of signs because it carries within itself generative power. There is a paradox in language that cannot be explained away or avoided, represented by what Gadamer calls "the speculative structure of language" which involves achieving a "speculative unity" (2004, p. 470). On the meaning of the word "speculative" Gadamer writes he uses it in its common sense as well as how it was used by eighteenth-century philosophers, having the nature of being reflected (from the Latin *speculum*, or mirror). This dual meaning is no coincidence. As Gadamer writes of moments like this: "one must always count on finding the technical and the freer use of a word juxtaposed" (2004, p. 415). The multiple meanings of "speculative" point precisely to the generative power of language Gadamer is trying to explicate and for which the word "speculative" stands as synecdoche.

In Dawn Opal and Jacqueline Rhodes's (2018) discussion of how user-centered design has become "intertwined" (p. 71) with rhetoric and composition studies, the authors draw on the idea of *speculative design*, that is, a design concept that calls for exploring "alternative, fictional scenarios [and] asking what-if questions" engaging in "a form of play" that "invites makers to make-believe" (p. 77). So, language is speculative in this sense, as way to pursue creativity through play, but it is the relationship between speculation and reflections or mirrors which we must examine more closely. The metaphor of a reflection in a mirror is useful in understanding what it means for words to have "speculative unity" (Gadamer, 2004, p. 470). Imagine a mirror with a candle in front of it. There two candles, the original, what we might call the real, and its reflection, which is like a copy. But, unlike a true copy or duplication, this reflected candle doesn't exist except as a reflection, whereas a real copy of the candle would exist on its own. But for our reflected candle, if the original is taken away, the reflection ceases to exist; by the same token the reflected candle is only lighted if the original candle is lighted, and so on for every trait. Unlike a copy or duplicate, the reflected candle is bound to the original in this way. Gadamer, following Hegel, assigns the original and the copy-as-reflected a sense of belonging-together. As Gadamerian scholar Kathleen Wright (1986) puts it: "what is at issue (*die Sache*) and its meaning as expressed and reflected in language seem to be two and distinct. Nonetheless insofar as the meaning of what is at issue appears only as expressed and reflected in language, they belong together" (p. 207). Like the candle reflected in the mirror, the meaning of a word only has its existence in relation to the word itself. The word and its meaning are bound together like a candle and its reflection.

This is what Gadamer means when he writes: "everything that is language has a speculative unity: it contains a distinction, that between its being and the way that it presents itself, but this is a distinction that is not really a distinction at all" (p. 470). The reflected candle is a separate candle in the sense that it is not the original, but it is not different enough that the original could be lighted and the reflected one not, or the original be broken and not the reflection. This speculative unity, this distinction without a distinction, has the quality Wright calls "double-directionality" (Wright, 1986 , p. 207). According to Wright, there are two directions: from the object into the mirror and from the reflected object in the mirror back out into the world. While the object in the mirror remains the same as a result of its being a reflection, the original object gains something beyond itself: it is now the original candle instead of just a candle, even though it only gains this additional meaning as a result of its appearing in the mirror. While this analogy is simplistic, it illustrates how representation in language is generative: more is made than what is provided; meanings multiply. Originals take on reflections and in so doing, gain identities.

Language is generative in another way as well and grasping this also means solving what Gadamer calls "the great dialectical puzzle of the one and the many which fascinated Plato as the negation of the *logos*" (2004, p. 453). As we've seen, an object and its reflection in language have a paradoxical kind of being, that of quasi-duality, and this gives rise to the generative aspect of language, to its multiplicity. Gadamer accuses Plato of turning away from the puzzle, of taking "only the first step." Gadamer writes:

> For there is another dialectic of the word which accords to every word an inner dimension of multiplication: every word breaks forth as if from a center and is related to a whole, through which alone it is a word. Every word causes the whole of the language to which it belongs to resonate and the whole world-view that underlies it to appear. Thus every word, as the event of a moment, carries with it the unsaid, to which it is related by responding and summoning. The occasionality of human speech is not a casual imperfection of its expressive power; it is, rather, the logical expression of the living virtuality of speech that brings a totality of meaning into play, without being able to express it totally. (2004, p. 453)

In this passage, Gadamer elegantly expresses a number of relationships: a new definition of dialectic (different from Plato's, Aristotle's, or Hegel's), the concept of language as a center and its momentary, occasional quality, the concept of the unsaid and the fundamentally revolutionary idea that it is the unsaid in language that makes it infinite. Gadamer reminds us that, while words may represent things, they may also fail to represent things, or represent them only partially or be used to represent other things because of a perceived similarity. They can be used metaphorically, ironically, sarcastically, iconoclastically. Language in use happens this way: roughly, playfully, with terms pressed to serve purposes for which they weren't intended.

Observing that "in verbal consciousness there is no explicit reflection on what is common to different things," and there is a "widening experience, which looks for similarities, whether in the appearance of things or in their significance for us," Gadamer ultimately argues that "The genius of verbal consciousness consists in being able to express these similarities. This is its fundamental metaphorical nature, and it is important to see that to regard the metaphorical use of a word as not its real sense is the prejudice of a theory of logic that is alien to language" (2004, p. 428). In other words, to condemn language for not being logical is to criticize it on the grounds of logic, not on language's own ground which affirmatively includes the ability to be used in a sense outside of or even contrary to its meaning. For this most important reason, an interface is not a collection nor a system of signs because it is part of a living language in which individual terms are not only representative of meaning but also themselves generative of meaning. Just as a word may resonate with the unsaid to produce heretofore unindicated meaning, so too might an interface sign resonate with the totality of other signs to produce additional meanings.

Because language has this property allowing "an infinity of meaning to be represented within it in a finite way" (2004, p. 461), it has significant implications for the act of understanding. A hermeneutic experience, Gadamer tells us, has "its own rigor." This is because a thing can only present itself to the hermeneutic experience with a special effort: that of "being negative toward itself" (2004, p. 461), so that an interpreter must constantly keep at arm's length countless incorrect interpretations, everything that is not the meaning suggested by the text itself. This constantly unfolding process of interpretation, Gadamer tells us, takes the form of a series of conjectures. He writes, "explicating the whole of meaning towards which understanding is directed forces us to make interpretive conjectures and to take them back again" and that this "self-cancellation of the interpretation makes it possible for the thing itself—the meaning of the text—to assert itself" (2004, p. 461). Thus, the infinity constantly suggested by language is accounted for in the interpretive act, winnowed away by a process of conjecture so that only what is common remains. In order for this commonality to become apparent, to enjoy a hermeneutic experience, the rigor that Gadamer writes is required is an "uninterrupted listening" (2004, p. 461). It is within this listening, which cannot be interrupted because it is an active kind of listening, that hermeneutic experiences exist. Active listening, or what rhetoricians have called "rhetorical listening" strongly implies collaboration.

■ Rhetorical Technē and Cunning Intelligence

Once we've given the hermeneutic response to a unified theory for interface design and evaluation, our burden remains incomplete. We've shown that a scientific, mathematical understanding of interface languages will always elude our grasp because interface signs are not merely signs but living nodes in a network of conversation that is always reflecting, always changing and being changed. But we've yet to explain what we ought to do as a result. Do we throw up our hands, saying "language is paradox" and just put pseudo-random signs into place as we go? Do we cease evaluating interfaces or putting consideration into our designs because we cannot say with mathematical certainty how they will be received? Of course not, and so we must turn away now from theories of interpretation and toward a theory of production: specifically, to the rhetorical concept of *technē*. Rhetorical *technai* (plural of *technē*), such as the core process of conjecture outlined below, provide us precisely the explicitly unscientific methods that should guide the production of interfaces. While hermeneutics gives us a way to understand the analysis of communication, rhetoric is more suited to describe the production of texts. The concept they have in common is conjecture. The act of conjecture is essential, as we've seen, to an authentic interpretive experience, but as a rhetorical *technē*, the concept of conjecture is also essential to the process of invention.

More than simply being one of the "states" Aristotle laid out in *Nichomachean Ethics* "by virtue of which the soul possesses knowledge" (Barnes, 1989, p. 1799), rhetorical *technē* has a rich history covering more than two millennia. One prominent scholar of this ancient tradition, Janet Atwill (1998), attempts to reach beyond Aristotle to recover what she argues is a "neglected tradition of rhetoric embodied . . . in Protagoras' political *technē* and Isocrates' *logon technē* and preserved, in somewhat modified form in Aristotle's *Rhetoric*" (p. 1). For Atwill:

> a *technē* is never a static normative body of knowledge. It may be described as a *dynamis* (or power), transferrable guides and strategies, a cunningly conceived plan—even trick or trap. This knowledge is stable enough to be taught and transferred but flexible enough to be adapted to particular situations and purposes. (1998, p. 48)

We see here how language in general and interface language in particular seems to operate like a *technē*. It is dynamic and resists normative imposition yet remains stable enough to be grasped. It can, and indeed must, be adapted to different purposes and in different circumstances. Like interpretation of the word, Atwill writes how "*technē* is never reducible to an instrument or a means to an end. Instead, art intervenes when a boundary or limitation is recognized, and it creates a path that both transgresses and redefines the boundary" (1998, p. 48). Thus, not only is it a mistake to think that the interpretation of interfaces could be subjected to science, but it is also a mistake by the same token to subject the creation of interfaces to science. The state of *technē* is by its nature transgressive of boundaries, its function to escape limitations, to defy easy categorization, and, most importantly, it "creates a path," or, alternatively, shows the way.

Atwill's *technē* is animated by the particular kind of thinking the ancients called *mêtis*, or cunning intelligence. *Mêtis* operates in domains where the weaker must overcome the stronger, where time and terrain are always shifting, where forms are hard to identify and fix, and where surface appearing stands opposed to true nature. In the deceptive world of *métis*, only a cunning mind has the tricks necessary to master the always-changing moment. Atwill writes, "the significance of *technē* often lies in the power of transformation *métis* provides" (1998, p. 56) and she goes on to chart several connections between the kind of intelligence denoted by *métis* and the kind that leads to the development of *technai*. In argumentation, one such process is known as conjecture, and it has its etymological roots in celestial navigation and the plotting of a journey by the stars. Like *technē*, it "creates a path." The ability to reason by conjecture plots its course by mapping like and unlike things. It's worth mentioning that one of the primary synonyms listed in most thesauri for "speculate" is "conjecture": the same reasoning by analogy we've seen in speculative thinking.

Aristotle recovers a form of this intelligence with the theory of prudence elucidated in *Nichomachean Ethics* and rehabilitates the kinds of knowledge that "are subject to contingency and directed towards beings affected by change" (Barnes, 1984, p. 316), calling this *phronesis*. These kinds of knowledge are employed by the prudent one, the one who possesses *phronesis*, as Aristotle writes "whose actions are oriented towards an end and who must always appreciate the importance of opportunity and understand that he is operating in a domain in which there is no stability" (Barnes, 1984, p. 316). Nevertheless, Aristotle is at pains to distinguish *phronesis* from mere cunning, writing: "[it] is more than mere intuition; it is a type of skill founded upon 'deliberation aimed at a good result' (*euboulia*), which is different from the ability 'to do things with a particular aim in view'" (Barnes, 1984, p. 317). For Aristotle, what distinguishes the two is their ends: *phronesis*, or prudence is cunning aimed a good result.

In either case, the person with *phronesis* operates by and through a process based on conjecture. The *phronimos* "can only reach his goal if he conjectures . . . his route with the aid of the signs that his flexible intelligence enables him to recognize, compare and use to the full" (Barnes, 1984, p. 313). Thus, cunning intelligence enables the prudent one to "recognize, compare and use" signs, and it enables the prudent one to do so very rapidly. As linguistic scholars Marcel Detienne and Jean-Pierre Vernant write, this "intelligence that is at work in action," this "indirect and groping knowledge," is also what allows the *phronimos* to excel in "in forming the best opinion thanks to the most rapid reflection" (1978, p. 313). This rapid process recalls the effect noted by van Schaik and colleagues (2012). Recalling their observation that inference is "affect driven" and so is "very quick" (p. 11:4), we see a clear relationship between the kinds of inferences users make regarding interfaces and the kinds driven by *phronesis*. It seems a parallel process is at work both in the rhetorical creation of the interface by designers and in the hermeneutic interpretation of the interface by users: a process that proceeds indirectly and crookedly, unscientifically, by mapping the similarities and differences between like and unlike things, by formulating conjectures which account for the speculative nature of language. This parallel process, the apparent fact that both designers and users proceed largely through conjecture, brings us at last to our final insight: that it is most productive to view the interface as a site of collaboration between users and designers.

■ Interface as Ongoing Collaboration

Collaboration between users and designers requires a particular kind of authentic relationship that is based on a shared moral and ethical framework. Like Aristotle, Gadamer also sees a moral, ethical dimension to the process of conjecture which comprises *phronesis*. It is within this ethical dimension that we find the proper way to conceive of this relationship, as a kind of friendship, and of the interface as a site of participatory meaning-making. This friendship requires the kind of prudence that Gadamer describes when he writes "*phronesis* allows us the self-knowledge of moral reflection" because it is not about knowledge in general, not about technical knowledge or the application of it, instead it is about knowledge of a "concrete moment" and that this kind of wisdom "has meaning only when the parties are in friendship. That is, no matter how wise you are, you can only give advice if you are in a relationship of belonging together, if you care what happens to the other. This is friendship" (Gadamer, 2004, p. 320). This hermeneutic friendship, this "belonging together" is the same word Gadamer uses to describe the relationship between an object and its reflection in a mirror and between a concept and its expression in language. Thus, we see that the essence of the hermeneutic friendship is the same kind of speculative unity employed in language. Words have speculative unity, but so too do speakers and listeners. They reflect each other and in that reflecting gain additional senses of being the being that is language. Now, perhaps, Gadamer's exhortation that, "[b]eing that can be understood is language" (2004, p. 470) is at last made plain. For us to be understood by one another means in a sense that we must become language. Not only is the interface a collaboration through language, but it shows how this collaboration functions: a hermeneutic friendship brought about through *phronesis*.

As we've seen, a proper understanding the hermeneutical event of language implies that we should turn away altogether from seeking a science or mathematics of interfaces and instead try to focus on the kinds of human relationships that allow for better understanding in the first place. If we cannot establish a science or mathematics of interfaces, and if our best tools are the processes of speculation, on the part of the interpreter and conjecture on the part of the designer, processes which are one and the same, then UX studies must embrace the messiness of language and rediscover the freedom of speculation, of alternative meanings, of ambiguity and play.

The concerns that van Schaik and colleagues express when they address the concept of beauty seem to be particularly productive in this regard. Both Gadamer's hermeneutics and rhetorical *technē* have potentially useful contributions to make here. In particular, as Gadamer observes, there is a close relationship between beauty and light. Noting how light also has a kind of speculative unity, namely because "[l]ight is not only the brightness of that on which it shines; by making something else visible, it is visible itself, and it is not visible in any other way than by making something else visible" (2004, p. 477), Gadamer argues near the end of *Truth and Method* that "This means that beauty has the most important ontological function: that of mediating between idea and appearance.... It finds its concrete form in the concept of participation ... and concerns both the relation of the appearance to the idea and the relation of the ideas to one another" (2004, p. 476). This suggests a fruitful line of inquiry may be studies of light and beauty, of the optics of the human eye and of the understandings of visual perception and cognition documented in design discourse, such as in the work of Rudolph Arnheim and Edward Tufte. Indeed, the entire field of visual rhetoric seems well poised to make contributions along these lines.

Likewise, UX designers could benefit from approaching the interface not as an always imperfect medium that ultimately fails to accurately convey meaning, but instead as a collaboration in which a multiplicity of meanings is possible. By understanding their complementary relationship to users, designers should come to view interfaces as places where people can play at communication, where prudence, discretion, and wisdom are watchwords, places where certainty is impossible, and appearances are always shifting. For design pedagogies, more attention could be paid to developing the productive capacities of Detienne and Vernant's cunning intelligence, the ability to adopt "an oblique course" and which makes "intelligence sufficiently wily and supple to bend in every conceivable way" with a "gait so askew" that it is "ready to go in any direction." The task of design, then becomes, through cunningly twisted methods, to chart "the straightest way to achieve" (1978, p. 6) the good end.

What does this good end look like? Gadamerian scholar Wright relates Heidegger's "two extremes of solicitude ... an inauthentic and an authentic way of everyday being with another" (1986, p. 197). The first is "a way that leaps in and dominates" and the second a way that "leaps forth and liberates." In the first way, it "takes the other into one's care such that care is taken away from the other and instead provided for the other," while in the second, it "takes the other into one's care in order for the other to develop the ability to take care of himself" (Wright, 1986, p. 196). These ways of being have their correspondence in Gadamer's inauthentic and authentic dialogue and help explain what the good end would actually entail.

Gadamer makes his point by crediting Plato and Aristotle with the unintuitive fact that "it is more difficult to ask questions than to answer them" (2004, p. 356). When we dispense with this notion, however, we can make "the critical distinction between authentic and inauthentic dialogue" (Gadamer, 2004, p. 356). Gadamer goes on to explain: "To someone who engages in dialogue only to prove himself right and not to gain insight, asking questions will indeed seem easier than answering them" (2004, p. 356) because there is no risk of failure. However, being able to ask the right question is in fact the authentic way to conduct a dialogue. Gadamer writes: "In order to be able to ask, one must want to know, and that means knowing that one does not know" (2004, p. 357). This latter way "leaps forth and liberates" (Wright, 1986, p. 197) because as the questioner moves into the unknown, the questioner is free from having to be right. This is an authentic way of belonging together because it allows the other partner in the dialogue the ability to answer the question, it accords the respect of not knowing the answer and thus making a collaborative answer possible. Here we find perhaps our best recommendation to guide the design of interfaces: not that they should seek to specify meanings, but that they should approach meaning as an open question, something to be negotiated between designers and users. Something to be asked, rather than answered.

This idea, that questions should come first, is already built into the structure of UX studies. The testing phase of development already explicitly acknowledges the priority of the question. Whenever a tester sets a task and asks about various missteps along the way, or about various perceptions, judgments, and feelings, he or she is explicitly concerned with breaking open the meaning of the event. A healthy UX process is always asking questions of users. What are the right questions to ask? For example, while we might ask a user to describe how they feel when interacting with an interface, more collaboratively we may also ask what they take the signs to mean or even what other signs they think might be more apt. This view of collaboration invites us to see users as fellow designers who can provide not only insight, but direction, and this practice should be more regularly incorporated into UX methods.

Finally, much of hermeneutic and rhetorical theory remains undiscovered by user experience studies. As a rhetorician, sometimes reading UX theory gives me *déjà vu*, as a patient scholar rediscovers an ancient concept and gives it a new name. Although Hassenzahl argues convincingly that "User Experience (UX) is not just 'old wine in new bottles'" (2008, p. 11), there is still a strong sense of the familiar. It's not that UX is reiterating old understandings, rather it's more like a feeling of returning home. So, part of the task of rhetorical UX is to better articulate the points of connection between theories of rhetoric, language, and philosophy with the empirical studies done in laboratories. According to what we've seen, there is no need to make this a one-to-one correspondence, or a strictly scientific endeavor, but merely to suggest similarities and differences, as I have done here. To speculate. To conjecture. And most importantly, by doing this to invite discussion, further questions, and an ongoing conversation. This is the larger work toward which I hope this theory contributes.

■ References

Atwill, J. (1998). *Rhetoric reclaimed: Aristotle and the liberal arts tradition.* Cornell University Press.

Barnes, J. (Ed.). (1984). *Complete works of Aristotle* (Vol. 2). Princeton University Press.
Barton, B. F. & Barton, M. S. (1987). Simplicity in visual representation: A semiotic approach. *Iowa State Journal of Business and Technical Communication, 1*(1), 9–26. https://doi.org/10.1177/105065198700100103.
de Souza, C. S. (1993). The semiotic engineering of user interface languages. *International Journal of Man-Machine Studies, 39*(5), 753–773. https://doi.org/10.1006/imms.1993.1082.
de Souza, C. S. (2005). Semiotic engineering: Bringing designers and users together at interaction time. *Special Theme—Papers from Members of the Editorial Boards, 17*(3), 317–341. https://doi.org/10.1016/j.intcom.2005.01.007.
Detienne, M. & Vernant, J. P. (1978). *Cunning intelligence in Greek culture and society.* Harvester Press.
Fogli, D. (2017). Weaving semiotic engineering in meta-design: A case study analysis. *Semiotics, Human-Computer Interaction and End-User Development, 40*, 113–127. https://doi.org/10.1016/j.jvlc.2017.04.002.
Gadamer, H. G. (2004). *Truth and method* (J. Weinsheimer & D. G. Marshall, Trans.). Bloomsbury Academic.
Hassenzahl, M. (2008, September 2). User experience (UX): Towards an experiential perspective on product quality. *IHM '08: Proceedings of the 20th Conference on l'Interaction Homme-Machine* (pp. 11–15). https://doi.org/10.1145/1512714.1512717.
Kress, G. R. & Van Leeuwen, T. (2020). *Reading images: The grammar of visual design* (3rd ed.). Routledge.
Islam, M. N. & Bouwman, H. (2016). Towards user-intuitive web interface sign design and evaluation: A semiotic framework. *International Journal of Human-Computer Studies, 86*, 121–137. https://doi.org/10.1016/j.ijhcs.2015.10.003.
ISO (2019). ISO 9241–210: 2019 Ergonomics of human system interaction—Part 210: Human-centred design for interactive systems. https://www.iso.org/obp/ui/en/#iso:std:iso:9241:-210:ed-2:v1:en.
Nadin, M. (1988). Interface design: A semiotic paradigm. *Semiotica, 69*(3–4), 269–302. https://doi.org/10.1515/semi.1988.69.3-4.269.
Opal, D. & Rhodes, J. (2018). Beyond student as user: Rhetoric, multimodality, and user-centered design. *Computers and Composition, 49*, 71–81. https://doi.org/10.1016/j.compcom.2018.05.008.
Pflugfelder, E. (2017). Methodologies: Design studies and techne. In L. Potts & M. J. Salvo (Eds.), *Rhetoric and experience architecture* (pp. 166–183). Parlor Press. https://files.elfsightcdn.com/1d8413c1-4044-4752-8a80-5eef266f8355/fe27149c-fe7b-4645-b642-7f93ffe3fad5.pdf.
Roberto, V. & Toppano, E. (2019). Multimedia analysis and design: A conceptual framework. *Multimedia Tools and Applications, 78*(10), 14029–14043. https://doi.org/10.1007/s11042-018-7136-5.
Skorin-Kapov, L., Dobrijevic, O. & Piplica, D. (2014). Towards evaluating the quality of experience of remote patient monitoring services: A study considering usability aspects. *International Journal of Mobile Human Computer Interaction, 6*(4), 59–89. https://doi.org/10.4018/ijmhci.2014100104.
van Schaik, P., Hassenzahl, M. & Ling, J. (2012). User-experience from an inference perspective. *ACM Transactions on Computer-Human Interaction, 19*(2), 1–25. https://doi.org/10.1145/2240156.2240159.

Wright, K. (1986). Gadamer: The speculative structure of language. In B. Wachterhauser (Ed.), *Hermeneutics and modern philosophy* (pp. 193–218). State University of New York Press.

Yu, H. (2023). Visual. In H. Yu & J. Buehl (Eds.), *Keywords in technical and professional communication* (pp. 319–326). The WAC Clearinghouse; University Press of Colorado. https://doi.org/10.37514/TPC-B.2023.1923.2.39.

14. Achieving Veteran-Centered Design: Case Study of the Human-Centered Design Process Used During the Vets.gov Project

Jeffrey M. Gerding
XAVIER UNIVERSITY

Abstract. This chapter examines how human-centered design emerged as a guiding philosophy for the U.S. Digital Service at the Department of Veterans Affairs (DSVA), focusing specifically on how user experience research was conducted for Vets.gov, a website that serves as a hub for all veteran digital services. Based on artifact analysis, a site study, and interviews with two UX researchers in the DSVA, this case study sought to examine the specific methods, design processes, and ethical challenges facing the Vets.gov team as they conducted UX research with veterans. In addition, this chapter provides an overview of core tenets from human-centered design scholarship and calls upon inclusive design as a critique of and complement to traditional UX processes. The chapter concludes by identifying three ethical dimensions of UX research with veterans—compassion, accessibility, and respect—and offers multiple takeaways and implications for technical communication and UX practitioners and scholars.

Over the past decade or so, human-centered design (HCD) has played an increasingly central role in the development of services and products within the Department of Veterans Affairs (VA), resulting in a period of cultural and institutional change for an agency whose primary mission is caring for veterans and their families. As of 2021, the VA was the second largest cabinet department in the Executive Branch of the United States government, with an annual discretionary operating budget of $104.6 billion, behind only the Department of Defense at $703.7 billion and the Department of Health and Human Services at $108.4 billion (Office of Management and Budget, 2022). Because it is one of the largest customer-service-oriented agencies in the federal government, the VA has a greater incentive to apply user-centered design approaches than most other departments. In his testimony to the U.S. Senate Committee on Veterans' Affairs in January 2016, former Secretary of the VA Robert McDonald noted the importance of adopting design thinking to better serve veterans. Among his priorities for transforming the VA were "improving the veteran experience" by "focusing on human-centered design . . . and working with leading design firms to learn and use the technology associated with improving every interaction with clients" and "improving the employee experience—so we can better serve Veterans" (McDonald, 2016).

By emphasizing human-centered design as a way to improve the experience of both veterans and those who work to serve them, Secretary McDonald made a deliberate attempt to move the VA toward a more holistic understanding of veterans not just as users of a service, but as people whose experiences, backgrounds, and perspectives shape how and why they interact with the VA. During his brief tenure as Secretary of the VA, McDonald also oversaw the creation of the Digital Service at the Department of Veterans Affairs (DSVA), one of several smaller agency teams within the larger U.S. Digital Service, a "tech startup" founded by former President Barack Obama in 2014. The stated mission of the U.S. Digital Service (USDS) is "to deliver better government services to the American people through technology and design" (Mission). Due to its unique position within the Executive Office of the President, the USDS and its agency teams like the DSVA created a wide range of services for a diverse cross-section of American citizens.

This chapter focuses on one such project: Vets.gov, which was later merged with the flagship Veterans Affairs website, VA.gov (https://www.va.gov/). Developed between 2015 and 2018, the Vets.gov project was a complete redesign of websites through which veterans access essential services like healthcare and educational benefits. Importantly, Vets.gov was also a massive effort to apply principles of human-centered design and the methods of user experience re search to improve the digital experience for millions of veterans.

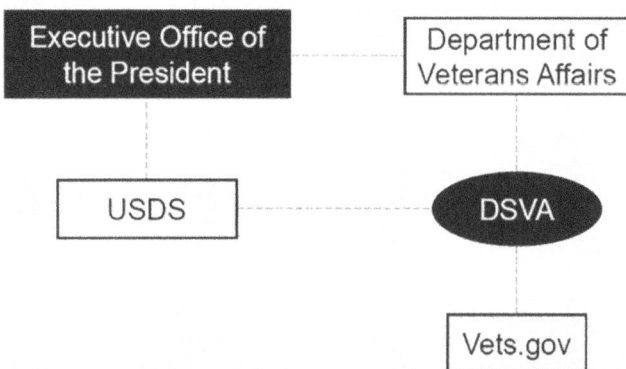

Figure 14.1. A visualization of the relationships between the U.S. Digital Service (USDS), Department of Veterans Affairs (VA), Digital Service at the Department of Veterans Affairs (DSVA), and the Vets.gov Design Team. The VA is a cabinet department within the Executive Office of the President; the USDS is a technology startup within the Executive Office of the President; the DSVA is an agency team within the USDS that was chartered by the VA from 2015 to 2018; Vets.gov was a project developed by the DSVA and later merged with VA.gov.

This case study emerged from interviews with two UX researchers in the DSVA, a site visit to both the DSVA office and USDS Headquarters in Washington, D.C., and analysis of a broad range of documentation, including press releases, reports, blog posts, GitHub repositories, and government websites. By triangulating all this data, I sought to examine the broader context for human-centered design in the Vets.gov project and provide specific accounts of the methods, principles, and practices that directly informed the work of the DSVA and has continued to influence veteran experience initiatives in the broader VA. This chapter ends with discussion of three ethical dimensions of veteran-centered research that emerged from my study—compassion, accessibility, and respect—and considers how this ethical framework for veteran-centered user research has remained resilient in an ever-changing Department of Veterans Affairs.

■ Case Study Background

Before describing how the case study was conducted, it is necessary to introduce the key institutions featured prominently in the remainder of this chapter. Founded in 2015, the U.S. Digital Service at Veterans Affairs (DSVA) was the oldest of seven "agency teams" operated by the USDS within the federal government (U.S. Digital Service, 2017). These Digital Service agency teams were supervised by the main U.S. Digital Service but operated independently within individual executive departments (see Figure 14.1), each of which maintains its own office space and signs a separate four-year charter with the USDS. As the government technology trade website *NextGov* explains, "The charters essentially act as franchise agreements between Digital Service headquarters and the agency teams. After agreeing to a charter, agencies can use a USDS-developed hiring process that accepts and reviews resumes and funnels potential applicants to agencies" (Moore, 2016). While the Digital Service agency teams are autonomous, they report back to the USDS and have regular "all-hands" meetings at USDS HQ where representatives from each agency team share updates on their work.

Each agency team worked with its respective department to identify projects that would have the most significant impact on users. An impact report marking the two-year anniversary of the USDS in 2016 describes a "digital application for health care built with Veterans, not for them" (White House, para. 4) as a primary example of the UX initiatives pursued by the DSVA. According to the report,

> Previously, less than 10 percent of applicants used the Veteran Online Application for a simple reason: the form would not open for most users. The application was a fillable PDF that required Veterans to use Adobe 8 or 9 via Internet Explorer. More than 70 percent of U.S. Government traffic comes from Chrome, Safari, or Firefox, meaning that more than 70 percent of visitors would have trouble accessing the healthcare application. (Office of the Press Secretary, 2016)

That a seemingly simple change like going from a PDF to a digital form can have such a significant impact on so many veterans highlights the immediate impact the DSVA had on modernizing UX within the VA.

In early 2019 the DSVA's charter with the VA expired and was not renewed, at which point it was "absorbed" by the VA Office of Information and Technology, which is part of the Office of the Chief Technology Officer (CTO) of the VA. In an interview with *FedScoop*, Charles Worthington, CTO of the VA, described the reorganization of the VA's IT initiatives into his office as an opportunity to "scale" and expand the work that had been done by the DSVA, including the continued development and research for new tools, forms, and apps within VA.gov (Chappellet-Lanier, 2020). And in March 2022, the White House proposed a $5.8 billion budget for the VA's Office of Information Technology "to support cybersecurity, financial management business transformation, claims automation and the infrastructure readiness program," as well as an additional $1.8 billion for "health records modernization" (Hewitt Jones, 2022). Though the VA's information technology and digital services mission continues to evolve to this day, this particular case study is an examination of a narrow moment in time—roughly 2014 to 2019—when the DSVA was a satellite agency team, Vets.gov had not yet been integrated into the larger VA website, and human-centered design was still emerging as a foundational set of principles for veteran digital service design. Documenting this era of innovation and experimentation reveals much about the kinds of partnerships, collaborative efforts, and user-centered research that led to the foundation on which future VA information technology initiatives would stand.

Vets.gov and VA.gov

Launched in November 2015, Vets.gov was one of the U.S. Digital Service's signature projects and is listed prominently on their online portfolio of work (U.S. Digital Service, n.d.). Described to me by former USDS Director Matt Cutts as a "unified front" for all veteran services, Vets.gov was intended as a cohesive and consistent "front door" for the veteran user experience. Prior to the development of Vets.gov, as many as 500 separate websites existed for the range of services provided by the VA (e.g., applying for insurance, tracking a disability claim, etc.), each with a unique design and interface and its own password and username. According to the U.S. Digital Service's (2017) Report to Congress, many of these services are also based on outdated technology. Vets.gov, in contrast, was designed to be a single access point through which veterans can "discover, apply for, track, and manage their benefits online." Designed according to modern web development practices, Vets.gov was mobile-first and cloud-based, supported multiple browsers, and used entirely open-source code.

The Vets.gov design team, which was comprised of both DSVA employees and government contractors, relied on contemporary technological best practices to solve problems both complex and mundane. In a *Medium* blog entry describing the technologies used in the project, Alex Yale-Loehr and Raquel Romano (2017), note that "the only remarkable part of [their approach] is that it's actually happening inside government, where software development has generally fallen far behind the pace of that in the tech sector." By aligning the values of human-centered design with the development practices used in both the technology industry and open-source community, the Vets.gov team was able to forge a path toward modernizing electronic systems in government without compromising values.

In 2018, more than a year after site visits for this chapter were completed, Vets.gov "was expanded and ultimately migrated to the VA's primary web domain," VA.gov, where it continues to be managed by a team of individuals from across the VA, including some who worked on the original Vets.gov project with the DSVA (Chappellet-Lanier, 2020). Since merging the DSVA with the VA's Office of Information and Technology's Office of the Chief Technology Officer and migrating Vets.gov to VA.gov, the VA's flagship site has experienced a notable rise in traffic. In a report published a year after the re-launch, *NextGov* noted that

> Veterans submitted nearly 600,000 education forms through the new site in 2019, a two percent increase since the site was overhauled . . . Disability compensation submissions filed digitally rose 27 percent to 291,000; pension submissions increased by 59 percent with 8,000 Veterans filing; and burial requests almost doubled, increasing 91 percent to 6,500 submissions. (Boyd, 2019)

And in January 2022, VA.gov set a single-month record of 1.5 million unique individual users, "a roughly 20 percent increase compared to" the year prior (DigitalVA, 2022). Although the Vets.gov project may have ended in 2018, the effort to establish an accessible, inclusive, and user-centered "digital front door" for veterans clearly endures.

■ Research Design and Methods

This chapter emerged from a much broader dissertation project that used a multi-case study research design to examine the user-experience methods applied to digital service design in the U.S. federal government. A case study research design was selected because, as Robert Yin (2003) notes, case studies are effective for research where contextual conditions are "highly pertinent to your phenomenon of study" but contain "many more variables of interest than data points" (p. 13). Because my goal was to examine cases where user experience research was applied within federal agencies, I had to first determine where this kind of work was being done and by whom. After researching the larger digital services movement and its various embodiments in the U.S. federal government, I began sending "cold" emails to several agencies of interest, to which I received few responses and only one interview.

Separately, a colleague put me in touch with a contact in the federal government who ended up playing the pivotal role of ethnographic "gatekeeper," allowing me to send my recruitment letter to people I would not have had access to otherwise. This process of recruiting participants through word of mouth and networking is described as snowball sampling, which begins "with a small sample of people who are readily available and easy to contact and then expands the sample by asking each participant to recommend other potential participants" (Koerber & McMichael, 2008). Although snowball sampling is a form of convenience sampling, it fit the exploratory nature of this project and allowed me to slowly build relationships as I conducted interviews and gained greater access to participants and sites. While this technique does not result in a randomized sampling that would allow for generalizable results, it does allow access to participants that I would not otherwise have known about, which in turn led to greater awareness of the scope and scale of the phenomena I sought to study. Three interviews formed the basis of this chapter: two UX researchers on the Vets.gov team, "Sarah" and "Maria" (both pseudonyms), and former U.S. Digital Service Administrator Matt Cutts, who met with me at the USDS headquarters and provided useful background information and historical context for this chapter.

Semi-Structured Interviews

Given the high degree of variability and uncertainty within my study, it was critical to proceed inductively and iteratively, with the scope and focus adjusting as new data was collected, initial impressions recorded, and further opportunities encountered. The case featured in this chapter was selected after conducting over a dozen initial semi-structured interviews with employees across different parts of the federal government. By conducting these interviews *before* identifying which cases I would feature in my study, I was able to cede a measure of control to participants, who were invited to respond to my interview protocol in whatever way they felt was important. Beginning research with interviews also allowed me to first develop an awareness of the work different agencies and offices perform and then later select cases from among those projects mentioned by participants. To better understand the values, practices, and methods used in the Vets.gov project, semi-structured interviews were selected to gather firsthand accounts from members of the DSVA in July 2017. Several interviews with technologists who worked at the DSVA were conducted but ultimately omitted from the final case study as the focus of the research narrowed to include only the Vets.gov project.

A semi-structured interview protocol allowed for significant flexibility in responses, both to accommodate a range of participants with different titles and responsibilities, and to allow for responses from both current and former government employees. The primary goal of the interviews was to get participants to reflect on one or more of the projects they worked on during their time in government and to interpret other aspects of the questions (e.g., technology, users, expertise, etc.) as they saw fit. This was particularly important because I did not want to lead participants to specific topics or influence how they responded; rather, I wanted participants' responses to guide me toward topics and ideas they felt were valuable or important which could be explored further through follow-up questions. Because this was one case study of several conducted as part of a much larger study, the questions were written to be deliberately broad so that the same protocol could be used for each case. Questions included on the IRB-reviewed interview protocol are listed below:

1. In your current position or role, what is one typical digital service or civic technology project you have worked on?
2. What recent projects illustrate how users are integrated into your projects? What methods or techniques are used to facilitate this interaction?
3. What is one example of how your organization/agency/office communicates about your work to the public? What tools are most often used? What responses did you receive from citizens?
4. When collaborating with those who do not specialize in your area of expertise, how do you explain the purpose of your organization/agency/office and the work that you do?

Interviews were conducted either by video conference or in-person and recorded to ensure accuracy and allow for transcription, which was done using a commercial transcription service and checked for accuracy. Interview data were analyzed using NVivo to code within and across interview transcripts, as needed to triangulate responses from multiple participants. Ethnographic memos were also written to develop further connections between key concepts that emerged in coding. For instance, while coding transcripts for this chapter, "trust" emerged as a critical concept with multiple meanings and was mentioned with regards to veterans' trust in the VA to meet their needs; VA employee's initial distrust of "outsiders" in the USDS; and DSVA's attempts to build trust within the veteran support network. Teasing out these various meanings of "trust" enabled connections to artifacts and observations from site visits. Together, each of these nodes led to a more nuanced and interconnected understanding of the relationships that exist in the digital service movement between designers, users, and stakeholders.

Artifact Analysis

While interviews were useful for gathering a participant's perspectives in their own words, it was necessary to triangulate this data with information found in various artifacts and documents online to create connections and more accurately describe concepts and terminology used in each case. In my project, this process allowed me to examine a range of artifacts to understand the role they play as a source of methods, procedures, and values. The artifacts selected for this project can be broken down into five general categories:

- Reports published by offices and agencies within the VA, such as the VACI.
- Blog posts on *Medium* published by technologists with the USDS and DSVA.
- GitHub repositories connected to specific web pages, like the Vets.gov Playbook.
- Congressional testimony and press releases issued by the VA, the White House, etc.
- Government websites and individual web pages such as Vets.gov, VA.gov, DigitalVA, etc.

Artifacts were discovered in three ways: through independent online research, by direct reference in participant interviews, and from secondary sources. Artifacts were read closely to determine their relevancy to the case and identify connections to other data points. Several dozen artifacts were read and annotated while only a dozen or so were included in the final text. Artifacts were excluded for a variety of reasons, most commonly due to lack of relevance as the scope and scale of the project naturally narrowed during research. As described in the interview section, Nvivo was used to develop connections between interview transcripts and artifact annotations. This proved particularly useful for this case study as several participants referenced documents that would not have been found independently, such as those created by older or less visible agencies like the VACI. After reading interviews notes and final transcripts I was able to locate copies of several documents that I would then read, annotate, and add as nodes on Nvivo to indicate the connection between data points. The more connections I observed the more likely a document was to be featured in the case study.

Site Visits

The final source of empirical data for this project was a series of site visits conducted during a trip to Washington, D.C., in July 2017. During my week-long trip I was able visit a number of offices, including two sites pertinent to this chapter: the headquarters of the U.S. Digital Service, where I was given a tour and conducted a brief interview with former Administrator of the U.S. Digital Service Matt Cutts; and the office of the U.S. Digital Service at the Department of Veterans Affairs (DSVA), where I received a tour, conducted two interviews, and observed a retrospective meeting of the Vets.gov design team. During these visits, I took notes, made observations, drew sketches, recorded audio, and took photographs where permitted. After each visit, I wrote an ethnographic memo that contained a description of the visit, sketches of the office space, relevant quotations, any questions that required further investigation, and connections between the site visits and interviews or artifacts previously examined. Despite the short duration of site visits, they provided ample opportunities for triangulation, which gave the study a level of contextual richness that would have been missing had only interviews and document analysis been conducted.

Limitations

The most significant limitation of this project is the lack of generalizability created by the decision to use a looser and more inductive sampling technique. Snowball sampling has several recognized limitations, including its reputation as "accidental" and "opportunistic," the risk of overgeneralization of results beyond a narrow population, and a general lack of acceptance in interdisciplinary scholarship (Koerber & McMichael, 2008). While this technique was justified by time constraints and the unique difficulty of gaining access and permission within the federal government, these limitations were a constant challenge with which I had to grapple. In addition, my own position as a researcher external to the federal government was another significant limitation. Though I tried as much as possible to allow interview participants to shape the direction and scope of the study, my understanding of the topic is still constrained by my status as someone outside of government. Finally, site visits were significantly limited in terms of the amount of time I was able to spend at each site, ranging from a few hours at the DSVA office to just 30-minutes at the USDS HQ. As one would expect, security also limited where I could go and what I could observe during my site visits to federal buildings.

Applying Human-Centered Design to Serve Veterans

As both a design philosophy and a research process, human-centered design prioritizes considerations of "the needs, perspectives, and input of users" (Walton, 2016, p. 406). In the introduction to their special issue on human-centered design and technical communication, Mark Zachry and Jan Spyridakis (2016) write,

> HCD is fundamentally about accounting for and reflecting shared human values in the creation of the technologies, artifacts, and systems that humanity shares in the collective pursuit of life. Recognizing that values vary from context to context, and that they are subject to change as people and technologies interact, we remain grounded in the assumption that human values are primary and should guide the world that people collectively create. (p. 394)

Placing collective human values at the foundation of design activity attempts to shift control of technology away from system-centered models. As Rebecca Walton (2016) writes, "a key issue of discussion is whose perspectives, expertise, and goals should direct decision making: In other words, which humans should be at the center of HCD" (p. 406).

Recognizing the need to design systems that are fundamentally humane, and not just efficient and easy to use, is one reason "human-centered design" has challenged "user-centered design" as the preferred term since the 1990s, Walton (2016) argues. While the latter "frames people solely as users," the former "emphasizes the importance of having users themselves provide input to shape design" (Walton, 2016, pp. 404–405). Similarly, Emma Rose (2016) argues that using the term human-centered design rather than the more common user-centered design "moves away from the idea that we are focusing on people solely in their relationship to and use of technology" (p. 428). It is not enough "to consider users and their needs alone"; instead, designers and UX researchers must adopt "a principled stance to understand the lives, needs, and values of vulnerable populations . . . to ask different questions and . . . bring about different, and more equitable, design solutions" (Rose, 2016, p. 443). Though there have been many different interpretations and definitions of human-centered design, they all share a common basis in applying empirical research conducted with actual users of a product "to drive the design solution" (Friess, 2010, p. 42). The four principles of human-centered design, according to Don Norman (2019, July 23), are "ensuring that we solve the core, root issues, not just the problem as presented to us;" "focusing on people;" "taking a systems point of view;" and "continually testing and refining our proposals, ensuring they truly meet the needs of the people for whom they are intended" (section 1). Norman further identifies three issues that must be addressed in the application of human-centered design to large, complex problems: "proceed slowly, with incremental, opportunistic steps;" design systems that "provide understandable explanations;" and involve "local communities . . . in determining the outcomes" (section 3) not just technologists and specialists.

Refocusing user experience research around these principles and best practices illustrates the need for user experience researchers to acknowledge their work as "a sustained dialogue between user and designer" (Salvo, 2001, p. 288). Michael Salvo (2001) examines user-centered design as a continuum based on the degree of interaction between users and designers. Specifically, he focuses on the far end of the spectrum, "user-centered design strategy with a high degree of dialogic interaction" (Salvo, 2001, p. 288), which can lead to blurring of boundaries that traditionally exist between users and designers. "In dialogic ethics," Salvo explains, "the self is constituted through its interactions with the other. Identity is created in the interplay between self and other, a making of one's self through communication. When one engages another person as an individual, as a person, one recognizes the humanity of the other" (2001, p. 276). In her analysis of Salvo's argument, Rose (2016) notes that dialogical ethics emphasize ethical responsibility of researchers to become advocates for the needs and interest of users *and* for more ethical application of user research within broader design processes. "Dialogical ethics are critical to researchers," she explains, "because they help us avoid the deployment of usability practices that are motivated solely by commercial interests and that focus on efficiency above all else. Dialogical ethics require us to be with the user in their discomfort and frustration" (2016, p. 429).

Toward More Inclusive UX Design Practices

Inclusive design has emerged as an important complement to human-centered design practices, one that centers the needs of marginalized users who are too often ignored in the creation of new digital tools and user interfaces. According to Alita Joyce of the Nielsen Norman Group, inclusive design is a set of methodologies that "enable people of all backgrounds and abilities," with the goal of "fulfilling as many *user needs* as possible, not just as many users as possible" (Joyce, 2022). One of the most frequently cited definitions of inclusive design comes from Microsoft: "Inclusive Design is a methodology, born out of digital environments, that enables and draws on the full range of human diversity. Most importantly, this means including and learning from people with a range of perspectives" (Microsoft, n.d.). In her introduction to the special issue about inclusive design published in *Intercomm*, the magazine of the Society for Technical Communication, Huatong Sun (2021) describes inclusive design as a process of empowering communities from within. "Being consciously aware of our systemic and personal biases," she notes, "is an important step leading towards" a design process that foregrounds humility, empathy, and reciprocity. "Through this process, we help users utter their own voices and plant seeds to nurture culturally sustainable changes mutually," rather than imposing external preferences, timelines, biases, and hierarchies on partner organizations and the communities they serve (Sun, 2021, p. 5).

Inclusive design is thus a necessary reminder that user-centered and human-centered design practices can easily be exclusionary to marginalized populations, despite the best intentions of designers. In her book *Design Justice*, Sasha Costanza-Chock (2020) presents a compelling critique of user-centered design. "Design always involves centering the desires and needs of some users over others," they write. "The choice of which users are at the center of any given UCD process is political, and it produces outcomes (designed interfaces, products, processes) that are better for some people than others (sometimes very much better, sometimes only marginally so)" (Costanza-Chock, 2020, p. 77). Because designers often "unconsciously default to imagined users whose experiences are similar to their own," Costanza-Chock argues, this "relatively small, but potentially highly profitable" set of users form the "unmarked" dominant group whose needs are prioritized. In the United States, this unmarked group is comprised of people who are "(cis) male, white, heterosexual, 'able-bodied,' literate, college educated, not a young child and not elderly, with broadband internet access, with a smartphone, and so on" (2020, p. 77). Catering to the needs of this unmarked group contributes to what Costanza-Chock terms "the spiral of exclusion," through which

> design industries center the most socially and economically powerful users, while other users are systematically excluded on multiple levels: their user stories, preferred platforms, aesthetics, language,

and so on are not taken into consideration. This in turn makes them less likely to use the designed product or service. Because they are not among the users, or are only marginally present, their needs, desires, and potential contributions will continue to be ignored, sidelined, or deprioritized. (2020, pp. 77–78)

Applying the methods of inclusive design begins with understanding the fundamental need to change the underlying causes of marginalization within designed systems. As Kat Holmes (2018), former Principal Director of Inclusive Design at Microsoft, writes in her book *Mismatch: How Inclusion Shapes Design*, exclusionary design results in difficult interactions between end-users and "access points" (e.g., tools, technologies, spaces, relationships, etc.). When a user attempts to participate in an interaction that is not easy for them to access, they can attempt to "adapt [them]selves to make the interaction work," but often "no degree of creativity will make it possible to use a solution that simply doesn't fit a person's body or mind" (Holmes, 2018, p. 2). Such "mismatched interactions" are "barriers to interacting with the world around us," "a byproduct of how our world is designed," and "the building blocks of exclusion" (Holmes, 2018, p. 2). Inclusive design, in contrast, begins with three basic principles: "recognize exclusion," "learn from human diversity," and "solve for one, extend to many" (Holmes, 2018, p. 13). "An inclusive designer," Holmes notes, "is someone, arguably anyone, who recognizes and remedies mismatched interactions between people and their world. They seek out the expertise of people who navigate exclusionary designs. The expertise of excluded communities gives insight into a diversity of ways to participate in an experience" (2018, pp. 56–57).

Inclusive design is particularly important for the application of user-centered and human-centered design practices in government digital services given the long history of mismatched interactions and exclusionary design prevalent in government access points. Historically marginalized and under-represented populations have a relationship with government service providers—like the VA—that is informed by generations of unequitable treatment and oppression within deeply-rooted systems of discrimination. Trying to build trust in and reliance on human-centered designs within such systems without first identifying and addressing the systemic problems that lead to the "spiral of exclusion" will only continue to perpetuate, reinforce, and strengthen the privileging of "unmarked" end-users. In a post to the U.S. Digital Services blog, Digital Services Expert Suzanne Chapman (2018) argues that inclusive design "isn't just about accessibility . . . or compliance, it's about the whole experience." While the VA has ostensibly always been "veteran-centered," many veterans have had mismatched interactions with VA services. Though the DSVA sought to do things differently, UX design can easily perpetuate exclusionary practices.

Chapman tells a story that effectively illustrates this problem: while conducting user-experience research with a veteran who had Parkinson's disease, the participant struggled to remember questions posed by the researchers, had difficulty using the provided computer mouse to access the interface being tested, and "said he probably wasn't the best person to get feedback from" (Chapman, 2018, para. 1). This veteran's experience, Chapman writes, made him "exactly who we want to make sure our site works for" and as a result the design team "collectively made it a priority to ensure we were deliberate in our research, design, and content practices" so as not to reinforce the spiral of exclusion that led to this participant's marginalization in the UX research and design process in the first place. This recognition, and the resulting commitment by the design team to address this mismatched interaction, is the first step toward slowing and eventually ending the spiral of exclusion experienced by this veteran and the countless others who rely on VA services.

When applied to the design of services for veterans, human-centered design and inclusive design must take into consideration the unique life experiences and backgrounds of those who have served in the armed forces. According to the National Center for Veterans Analysis and Statistics, as of January 2022 there were 19.1 million veterans in the United States, of which:

- 2.4 million were Black.
- 1.5 million were Hispanic.
- 0.9 million were American Indian/Alaskan Native/Other.
- 0.4 million were Asian/Pacific Islander.
- 2 million were women.
- 8.8 million were aged 65 years or older.
- 5.26 million received disability accommodations.
- 0.84 million received education benefits.

While this community is unified by both the unique experiences of servicemembers as well as common access to and reliance on government programs and services (e.g., pensions, life insurance, education benefits, health care, etc.), interactions with the VA system are not monolithic. According to the 2014 *Minority Veteran Report*, published in 2019 by the U.S. Department of Veterans Affairs, "In 2014, minorities comprised 22.6 percent of the total veteran population in the United States. By 2040, they are projected to make up 35.7 percent of all living veterans" (para. 3). Human-centered UX design initiatives like those described in the remainder of this chapter can perpetuate the marginalization of veterans if they do not actively acknowledge and intentionally work toward addressing inequities within their own practices and systems.

Human-Centered Design Initiatives in the VA

Frustration with government services is a familiar experience to many Americans. For veterans and their dependents and survivors, however, there can be few other options for accessing essential benefits. A 2014 report by Ruskin et al. (2014) titled "Toward a Veteran-Centered VA" describes the unique problem of services for veterans: "As a service-delivery government agency, unlike comparable service providers in the private sector," authors Mollie Ruskin and colleagues write, "the VA does not compete for business of our customers. As a result, we may take for granted the loyalty of our customers and miss the opportunity to understand their core needs and motivations" (Ruskin, et al., 2016, p. 7). Because many veterans rely on the VA for benefits that they often cannot get elsewhere, such as health insurance or funding for college, the risks associated with what Robert Johnson (1998) terms a "systems-centered" approach to design are much higher. In a systems-centered design, Johnson writes, "the technology, the humans, and the context within which they reside are perceived as constituting one system that operates in a rational manner toward the achievement of a predetermined goal" (1998, p. 25). Avoiding a systems-centered orientation requires acknowledging the inherently limited perspectives of researchers and designers. As Ruskin et al. explain,

> From within our organization, we cannot fully understand what it feels like to approach our services. We are acquainted with the acronyms, we know the business lines and service offerings. We may think a sign is clear or that a form makes sense. Yet we, the dedicated people who deliver vital services to Veterans, cannot fully grasp what it feels like to access these services—unless we ask. (2016, p. 7)

The solution detailed in the report is to embrace "the research tools of a Human-Centered Design process" by speaking directly with veterans and their families "about their experiences with the VA and how our services fit into the fabric of their lives" (Ruskin, et al., 2016, pp. 7–8)

Over the last fifteen years, concerted efforts have been made within the VA to modernize the department's approach to technology, design, and user experience. One of the first such initiatives, the VA Center for Innovation (VACI), was founded in 2010 "to identify, test, and evaluate new approaches to the agency's most pressing challenges" (VA Center For Innovation, 2017). Until it was merged with the Veterans Experience Office in 2019, the VACI was at the forefront of promoting human-centered design in the VA, including publishing two documents that together outline how the HCD process can improve the development of services for veterans. The first, Toward a Veteran-Centered VA, was released in 2014 and provides an overview of human-centered design methodology, including definitions, methods, and misconceptions. The report also presents the results of a pilot study with the dual-purpose of "test[ing] the usefulness and application of a human-centered design methodology within the context of the VA" and collecting data "to understand veterans' experiences interacting with the VA, identify pain points in the present-day service delivery model, and explore opportunities to transform these interactions into a more veteran-centered experience" (Ruskin, et al., 2014, p. 1).

The second document, known as the HCD Toolkit and published in 2015, offers project leaders within the VA an introduction to "the HCD process, goals, and activities you can use with your teams to design and deliver new programs, services, and products for Veterans" (Veterans Affairs Center for Innovation, 2015, p. 6). The toolkit is organized into four stages of human-centered design—frame, discover, design, and deliver—and offers a breakdown of several possible steps within each stage. For example, the discovery stage includes a detailed explanation of both contextual and ethnographic research as well as an explanation of several different approaches for analyzing collected data to identify insights. The toolkit also presents case studies for each stage based on work completed by UX researchers and design teams in the VA Center for Innovation. One case study described in the "discovery" section of the toolkit summarizes a pilot study of HCD research methodology conducted in 2014, which "surfaced themes about the needs, perceptions, and expectations of Veterans" and "helped guide the development of more veteran-centric efforts, including the work of the new Veterans Experience Office at VA and of VA offices across the country" (Veterans Affairs Center for Innovation, 2015, p. 30). Together these two documents preserve an important history of human-centered design methodology within the VA, highlight the extensive work that was done to scale HCD methods for expansion to other parts of the department, and establish a solid foundation for future initiatives, including the Vets.gov project.

While much of this work continues, the institutional structures that support it are in a continuous state of flux. In 2019, for instance, the VA Center for Innovation became the similarly named VA Innovation Center, but its mission shifted significantly, from exploring research and design practices to creating new service models for the Veterans Health Administration. Much of the VACI's HCD efforts are now continued by the Veterans Experience Office (VEO), which was created by former Secretary McDonald in 2016 "to enable VA to be the leading customer service organization in government so that veterans, their families, caregivers and survivors Choose VA" (Veterans Experience Office, 2019). What follows, then, is a description of the human-centered design research that occurred during the five-year period during which the DSVA developed Vets.gov but before it merged with VA.gov.

▪ Veteran-Centered User Experience Research

The design process used by the Vets.gov and later VA.gov design teams resembled in many ways the process identified in the VA Center for Innovation's "HCD Toolkit," but reflects the specific approach to HCD used for such a large and complex project. This process is best described in the Vets.gov Playbook

(Veterans Affairs, n.d.), a set of design principles that provided the foundation for the work of the Vets.gov team and that has since been migrated to VA.gov. The Vets.gov Playbook contains seven sections detailing the team's process and best practices, including a design guide, an editorial and content guide, a migration strategy, and a description of the team's HCD process. As the introduction to this page notes, "We've asked our customers what they want and need and we've designed in response to that. We've tested and made adjustments based on their feedback and will continue to do so as we add new features and information to the site" (Veterans Affairs, n.d.). The VA.gov HCD process is subdivided into three stages—discover, design, and measure and refine—and the full list of steps within each stage has been provided in the Table 14.1.

Table 14.1. A Description of the Three Stages of the VA.gov Human-Centered Design Process as Described in the Vets.gov Playbook (Veterans Affairs, n.d.)

Discover	Design	Measure and Refine
"Conduct user research."	"Generate potential solutions."	"Build new services or products in agile increments."
"Synthesize findings to define user needs."	"Translate ideas into prototypes."	"Release new offerings with feedback loops included."
"Formulate statement of the problem to solve."	"Conduct tests with users."	"Continuously monitor and refine to increase user satisfaction."
	"Refine based on feedback."	
	"Prepare for implementation."	

Four Types of User Research in the DSVA

Because the Vets.gov design team worked on multiple components of the website at various stages of development and for a range of stakeholders and users, the human-centered design process just described is critical for keeping teams organized and ensuring the same basic process is replicated consistently on every part of the project. This also means that user research is potentially conducted at every single step, from initial discovery phases at the very start of the process, all the way through identifying and resolving user-reported bugs after delivery. Through interviews with Maria and Sarah, two UX researchers on the Vets.gov team, I was able to get an even more complete sense of how the team handles the massive amount of user research conducted for every component of the Vets.gov project. As Sarah explained, user research plays a pivotal role in how the team approaches its work: "everything we do is very much . . . user-centered. That is a core principle for everything we do. It is not questioned by anyone on the team . . . It's just a fully baked-in part of the process."

Achieving Veteran-Centered Design 271

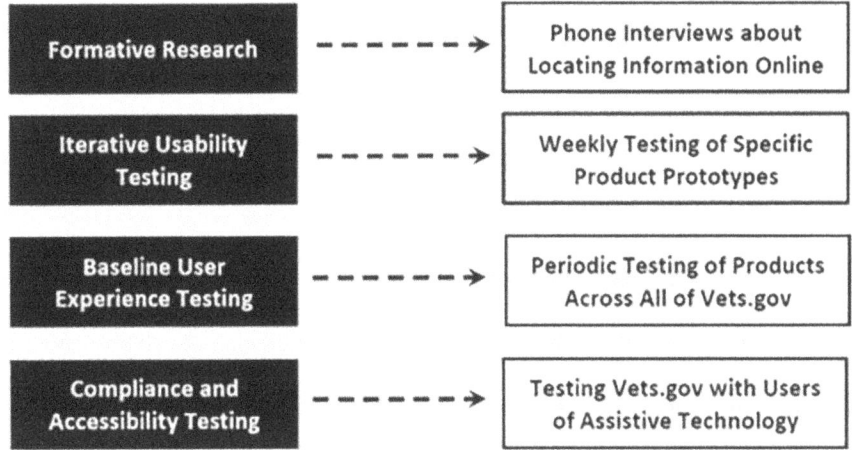

Figure 14.2. A visualization showing the four types of user research conducted by the Vets.gov design team.

The research process used by the Vets.gov team includes four broad types of user research: formative research, iterative usability testing, baseline user experience testing, and compliance and accessibility testing (see Figure 14.2). Though the order below roughly follows the progression of the product development cycle, each of the four types can be used at multiple points throughout the design process.

Formative Research

Formative research occurs at the very beginning of the process as the team determines what product they are working to improve. According to Sarah, the team does not usually begin a project knowing which existing tool or form they are going to modernize; rather, the product they will work on is determined through interviews with stakeholders and by gathering information about existing systems. Maria described this type of research as "exploratory" and noted that it was on the opposite end of the research continuum from usability testing. For example, during exploratory testing the team might conduct phone interviews asking broader questions about where veterans go online to find information. "[T]he VA has a very large amount of content about health on its many websites," Maria explained. "What of that is relevant for this particular website that is hosting benefits and services, and what kind of health information do veterans even come to the VA for versus other sources?" Formative research allows the team to better understand "the greater sphere of ways veterans want information" and their overall "relationship with the military and the VA." Results from formative research allows the team to identify elements of Vets.gov that have a high impact on the veteran experience and could be prime candidates for redesign or the development of new tools.

Iterative Usability Testing

Once the team has decided where their efforts are most needed, iterative usability testing is conducted on a particular product with a constantly changing group of veterans. This testing occurs at any stage of the process, whether this is gathering impressions of an early prototype; toward the middle of a development cycle to isolate a particularly complicated problem; or at the very end of the process after extensive testing has already been completed. As Maria told me, "I'm personally willing to test things at any stage whether it's just words, card sorting, talking through something—sketches, an online prototype, something that's not clickable . . . we'll look at whatever's available to get the team the answers to make decisions that they need to keep working." The ultimate goal of iterative testing, Sarah explained, is to get continuous feedback: "we interact with veterans every single week primarily through the usability testing that we're running . . . So, three to five [participants] would be our average number of interactions per week." Though this is a small number of participants, prototyping occurs frequently with the goal "to get every new feature on the site in front of veterans two-to-three times before launch." In addition to weekly iterative testing, the team also conducts longitudinal studies with as many as thirty veterans from across the country participating in remote moderated testing for several weeks. While most of the research conducted by the team is done through remote screen sharing, Maria noted they were able to conduct in-person usability testing with one veteran service organization (VSO). This allowed usability researchers to observe tasks being completed by "a few different people [using] their own custom set-ups with some different accessibility tools" that could not be observed otherwise.

Baseline User Experience Testing

Baseline experience testing, in contrast, is more holistic in nature, occurs less often, and is conducted longitudinally. As Sarah noted, baseline testing often begins with researchers observing "maybe ten kind of general tasks that span across the whole site and all the different tools. Obviously, we can't go deep in any of those, but can people find what they're looking for and do they understand what they've found?" Because it focuses on the broader experience of using the entire website, rather than one particular tool or form, baseline testing is not as deep as continuous testing. However, it can provide the team with data to make comparisons across multiple iterations of the site, which allows them to examine "how . . . those changes add up and improve the whole experience." Like formative research, baseline testing allows the team to make decisions about where to prioritize their time and resources based on direct input from and observation of veterans completing typical tasks on Vets.gov.

Compliance and Accessibility Testing

Finally, compliance and accessibility testing ensure websites are usable for veterans with cognitive impairments, motor skills impairments, and those who use assistive technology. As Sarah explained, compliance is "often referred to as a sort of coding challenge, that you want to make sure your sites are coded well . . . but there's also the parts not talked about as much, [such as] how do you design for accessibility so it's not just the downstream coding thing, but how do you make sure that what you're designing is accessible?" By combining "rigorous automated testing" of the code and design elements of the website with qualitative usability research, the team strives to account for the unique needs of veterans who use assistive technology when accessing services online.

Participant Recruitment and Community Outreach

Because of the sheer amount of user testing conducted on Vets.gov, participant recruitment poses a unique problem for the DSVA. As Maria explained, the demand for feedback from veterans is often greater than their ability to recruit participants: "We haven't had a ton of research capacity on [our] team compared to how fast the designers and developers are moving. It's awesome that we have a lot of demand for veteran feedback, but it's been a bit of a struggle to keep up sometimes." The primary method of recruitment is from other veterans and family members. According to Sarah, "veteran-to-veteran" recruitment has been effective, but they have to be careful about over-saturation and being respectful of veterans' right to privacy:

> We have a lot of different methods of trying to find people . . . There's a really strong veteran-to-veteran support network. We try to be careful about that because veterans get spammed a lot and, on the surface, people who've never experienced usability testing [laughs] might see it as weird. So, we've tried to be really careful about our language and use a VA email address connected to it and things like that.

Outreach takes a number of other forms, including printed materials, like fliers and palm cards; phone calls to friends and family of VA employees; direct recruitment through veteran service organizations (VSOs); and more unproven or experimental methods, such as posting to veteran Facebook groups and subreddits or placing ads on Craigslist. The team also makes a conscious effort to recruit beyond the D.C. area to ensure participants are more fully representative of the veteran population as a whole.

Recruitment is complicated by several factors. First and foremost, there is no single listserv or other form of mass communication that can reach every veteran, nor are there simple ways to send messages to specific niche groups of veterans. "With 22 million veterans, you would think [recruitment] would be relatively easy," Sarah said, "but it is one of our biggest challenges lately because we do it so often. And sometimes, we just need any veteran; sometimes, we need a veteran who has already engaged with the VA in some way.

So, [there are] 22 million veterans and I think the number of veterans who have interacted with the VA in some capacity is down to like 9 million . . . then it just keeps getting smaller and smaller depending on how niche of an audience we're looking for." A second, related problem is that depending on what tool or component of the website is being tested, researchers may need to recruit veterans who have recently used a particular service on Vets.gov. As Sarah explained further, "we have some . . . individual tools that we're testing where it's important that [participants] have been through that process or are currently going through whatever process it is . . . And somewhat recently so that the memory's fresh."

Finally, the VA is careful to avoid spamming veterans by overusing communication channels or specific recruiting methods that could potentially risk damaging integral partnerships with VSOs and other organizations that advocate on behalf of veterans. Such organizations are critical not just for participant recruitment, but also for establishing long-term collaborations between the DSVA and the broader veteran community. For instance, Maria described a project the team was working on when I visited the DSVA office in July 2017 that involved conducting usability demonstrations with representatives from VSOs. Because they are highly protective about their members, this project was as much about gaining the trust of VSOs and informing them of the process veterans go through when they participate, as it was about getting feedback on the process itself. As Maria described it, the project involved conducting "a sample session with [the VSO representative] where we're going to look at part of the website and I am going to run the conversation like we do when we get veteran feedback and [they] get to experience that as what it's like from the veteran's side. And then we . . . give [them] time to answer their questions about our work and . . . ask whether they're willing to send information about our work to some of their members." By taking time to model the research process for VSO representatives, the team seeks their trust and attempts to earn their support in encouraging VSO members to see the potential value of and impact from their participation in UX research.

This outreach initiative with community-based organizations like veterans service organizations ultimately reveals a significant difference between human-centered design within the Department of Veterans Affairs and user research conducted in other areas of government: direct collaboration with the community of support built around veterans. Because this community existed long before Vets.gov was established and will continue to exist long after the current services are outdated, the team must work to establish their reputation within this diverse and ever-changing community. Even if veterans rely on services from the VA and have few alternatives to access services, their advocates hold power and influence within the system. To gain the trust and support of these advocates, the Vets.gov team actively embedded ethical interactions with veterans into their ongoing research and design processes.

Three Ethical Dimensions of UX Research in the DSVA

Based on my analysis of interviews conducted with Maria and Sarah, I have identified three ethical dimensions of user-research in the VA Digital Service: compassion, accessibility, and respect. These dimensions are particularly important for the development process embraced by the VA to achieve the ideals of advocacy and human dignity indicative of a more ethical approach to service design. While these dimensions reflect only the DSVA's practices, and not necessarily those adopted by the Department of Veterans Affairs more broadly, they indicate a promising trajectory for using human-centered design methods in the design of services for veterans. Because Vets.gov was a stated priority of the main U.S. Digital Service and received considerable attention in the press and elsewhere outside of government, its potential impact on applications of user experience research within the VA and the entire federal government is considerable.

Compassion: "No, we actually care about your opinion."

A veteran-centered approach to design acknowledges that the services provided to veterans have a direct impact on user's lives, both in the sense of providing more effective access to necessary services (e.g., healthcare, insurance, etc.) and by reducing the barriers of access and "pain points" in the process. It also means considering how users' lives are impacted by a design and valuing their expertise even if it clashes or contrasts with views of designers, programmers, or administrators. A more compassionate approach to user research requires more than just acknowledging that users can contribute to the design process; it also requires researchers to demonstrate that participants' contributions will be valued, respected, and used in good faith throughout the design process. As Maria explained, because many veterans already have a complicated relationship with the VA, researchers have to acknowledge that participants' experiences will be complex and varied:

> It's been surprising how emotional the work has been . . . a lot of veterans have had pretty negative experiences with the VA over the years. It's a really big system and over the years, some parts have worked less well for veterans. And so, it has been pleasantly surprising how much just asking someone's opinion on something can make a difference in that and saying, "No, we actually care about your opinion, your feedback, and your experience in the moment."

Acknowledging this complicated history, rather than ignoring it in favor of a more positive spin, is critical for addressing inequitable and exclusionary practices. After talking with DSVA employees, it is clear that compassion for veterans and the desire to use their technical skills to make government services more effective and transparent drives many technologists to public service in the first place. But as Sarah noted, outside of the DSVA employees of the VA are similarly service-oriented but are new to the philosophy of human-centered design. "Even though they might be bureaucrats and lifelong employees of the organization," she said, "for the most part, they are deeply invested in making things better for the veterans. They just maybe don't have the full understanding or sort of modern way of figuring out how to solve those problems." Linking such commitment with the established practices of UX, human-centered design, and inclusive design thinking ensure compassion leads to actual change.

Accessibility: "Just because it passes compliance does not mean it's user friendly."

A key component of design for the Vets.gov team is achieving 508-compliance. Within the federal government, accessibility of electronic information is regulated by Section 508 of The Rehabilitation Act of 1973, which was revised in 1998 to set new precedents that apply "to all Federal agencies when they develop, procure, maintain, or use electronic and information technology" (U. S. General Services Administration, 2024, para. 1). Specifically, to comply with Section 508, "agencies must give disabled employees and members of the public access to information that is comparable to the access available to others" (U. S. General Services Administration, 2024, para. 2). Accessibility is particularly important for the VA, Sarah noted, because "we do have a lot of users who have full range of disabilities . . . that's why they're using the VA: because they need support and resources for injuries and health impairments and old age."

For the Vets.gov team, key components of accessible design include using plain language, simple design aesthetic, mobile-first design, and developing with assistive technology in mind. Plain language is critical, according to the "Editorial and Content Guide" in the "VA.gov Playbook" (Veterans Affairs, n.d.) because "language communicates our humanity. In the context of a website, it conjures up the people on the other side of that glowing screen. It engages, builds trust, and guides visitors through processes and information that can be stressful and confusing." For Maria, plain language is less a design principle and more a guiding philosophy that extends to all of her interactions with participants and stakeholders:

> User experience work has a lot of jargon, as does government work, and so you may notice I've been calling them "feedback sessions" rather than "user testing." . . . That's one of my personal missions, to use language that's more comfortable for our participants as well as our partners in and out of government that we're working with.

Checking off the requirements for compliance does not necessarily mean that a website is accessible, yet alone inclusive. Rather than viewing 508-compliance as a "big stamp of approval at the end of the process," Sarah explained, the Vets.gov team builds accessibility into the process from the beginning. Usability testing plays a key role in determining usefulness to a diverse range of veterans, particularly those who use assistive technology. Even after the code has gone through automatic testing and has been determined to be in compliance, the team continues to do usability testing because, as Sarah put it, "just because something passes compliance does not mean it's still user friendly. You can have something that passes all of the tests but it's still garbage . . . everything can pass but still be hard to use." The design aesthetic for Vets.gov, according to the Playbook, "aspires to be honest, transparent, respectful, and accessible to all visitors" (Veterans Affairs, n.d.). While compliance is important for achieving legal requirements, for the DSVA accessible design was a baseline internal expectation.

Respect: "They've been burned before by shiny people coming in wanting to change the world."

Placed within context of the institutional history of the VA, the digital services movement is only the most recent attempt at changing or "modernizing" established systems and processes. As Sarah explained, previous attempts at introducing new methods or practices have been attempted but failed often enough for career VA employees to be suspicious of any change perceived as being introduced from the outside. Sarah told a story from the early years of the DSVA where the team was more active with outreach and encountered resistance from others within the department:

> they tried to go around and talk about the things that they wanted to do and how they sort of aimed to operate and people just were like, "Okay. I don't care. Goodbye." Just like, "Yeah. I talked to some group two years ago that said the same thing and they didn't do anything and I talked to somebody three years before that and they never did anything." You know? They've been burned many times by these shiny new people coming in wanting to change the world and had not really worked or had worked in really small scale.

Implementing change respectfully acknowledges that the principles of human-centered design and inclusive design must extend to the process of design and not just the products. Any change must thus be done in a way that puts trust in people over the system and acknowledges both the successes and failures of those who advocated for change previously.

Respect is particularly important in a large and complex organization like the VA, where new initiatives, policies, and leaders come and go frequently while many career employees continue to work on the same projects and with the same tools for decades and across multiple administrations. Given that the DSVA's charter lasted for only four years, a longitudinal view is necessary for retaining institutional memory and for allowing philosophies like human-centered design and inclusive design the time and resources necessary to become effective on a larger scale. Treating veterans with respect and dignity is a primary stated goal of the VA and a point that has been repeatedly emphasized by the department's leadership, but it remains a constantly moving target.

Conclusion

In many ways, this chapter serves as a time capsule of sorts, documenting the practices, policies, and initiatives that existed during a particularly narrow timeframe. Over the six years that I conducted this research, much has changed about the offices, teams, and initiatives documented in this chapter. Despite large-scale institutional change, there has been some degree of continuity from one iteration to the next; remnants of prior efforts that preserve the institutional memory of projects that have come and gone. For instance, since the end of the Vets.gov project and the lapse of the DSVA's charter in 2018, most of its projects were absorbed into other parts of the Department of Veterans Affairs. The DSVA still exists but now operates within the VA's Office of Information Technology rather than as a chartered agency team of the U.S. Digital Service. The existing Veterans Experience Office emerged directly from the work on human-centered design completed by the VA Center for Innovation, which has since shifted its mission away from research. But the work completed by the VACI, like the two documents described earlier in this chapter, are still accessible from VA websites. Similarly, to some extent the DSVA I observed no longer exists. And yet its work can still readily be found online and, perhaps more importantly, its influence continues in the work of its successor team—the VA Digital Service team housed with the VA Office of the Chief Technology Officer—which is at once distinct from and inherently connected to an earlier era of veteran experience design.

Since I began this research in 2016 there have been three presidential administrations and four secretaries of the VA. With each administrative shift, I feared the day when the USDS or the DSVA would simply disappear overnight; though this has not (yet) happened, there have been many changes to how, where, and to what extent human-centered design is practiced. As an outside observer, I frequently questioned whether UX and HCD would still be a priority to each incoming administration. But if anything, I have been surprised by the *resiliency* of these principles and practices, which have lasted far beyond the initiatives and partnerships through which they were initially developed. As such, human-centered design shows signs of long-term integration into the institutional fabric of the Department of Veterans Affairs. Part of the unique identity of the VA is that its mission endures as long as there are veterans who still depend upon its services. While administrations change, institutional structures rise and fall, and initiatives come and go, the *demand* for continuous improvement to veteran services will exist as long as there are veterans, their families and dependents, their supporters and allies in various organizations, and a broader coalition of advocates working on their behalf. The alphabet soup of offices and initiatives created to improve the veteran experience over the last decade (VACI, DSVA,

VEO, etc.) illustrates the necessity of such initiatives in the VA, the complexity and scale of the problems they were meant to solve, and the realization that such impactful and challenging work cannot be the responsibility of any single project, team, or office.

Implications

The implications from this research for technical communication practitioners, researchers, scholars, and educators are numerous. First and foremost, this research stresses the importance of examining public sites of UX design, particularly within imposing and often opaque governmental institutions. Though getting access can be challenging, UX in government is an under-studied area of research that can complement work conducted in corporate, nonprofit, and academic sites. Methodologically, this study underscores the importance of ethnographic approaches to studying UX design. The slow, inductive, iterative approach taken in this project was imperative for studying such a complex and multifaceted phenomenon. In particular, triangulating data collected through artifact analysis, site visits, and interviews allowed for unexpected, serendipitous, and *kairotic* moments to surface that made for a stronger (if somewhat unwieldy) study. The results of this study offer many paths for further research, including expanding ethnographic methodologies in studies of UX design teams, identifying further cites of governmental and civic UX design, examining other nontraditional sites of UX design, and continuing to develop theories using human-centered and inclusive design as foundational concepts.

For practitioners of UX and TC, both the research and design practices of the DSVA and the broader ecology of materials created to establish human-centered design in the VA can be instructional for launching new projects or updating existing initiatives. The experiences described by Maria and Sarah offer a number of important insights for any UX team, and the many artifacts cited throughout this chapter provide concrete, actionable steps teams can take to replicate an HCD-influenced approach to user experience design. For example, artifacts like the HCD Toolkit, USDS Playbook, and DSVA GitHub repositories are public and open source, meaning they can be modified or expanded upon by those who may want to learn from, experiment with, or replicate best practices of the U.S. Digital Service. Further, the inclusive design literature surveyed here offers an important reminder that even the most well-intentioned applications of UX and HCD principles can very easily perpetuate exclusion and oppression of historically marginalized populations. Technologists, UX researchers, and technical communicators unfamiliar with inclusive design principles would benefit from surveying the many readings, trainings, and programs that have emerged around inclusive design and design justice.

Finally, this case study is a potential resource for teachers and students of technical communication who wish to deepen their understanding of UX practices, human centered design principles, and inclusive design. Integrating case studies into technical communication courses at all levels of higher education can make such work accessible to students for whom user experience can often seem abstract. Further, students at both the undergraduate and graduate level may benefit from reading this case study of government UX design, as it can inspire further research into governmental UX, promote curiosity about public and open-source design practices, and even foster a commitment to pursuing UX in various public sector contexts, including all levels of government, nonprofits, civic tech organizations, civic hackathons, and more. My sincere hope is that this case study, which emerged from my dissertation research, may also inspire other graduate students to aim high when identifying public sites of UX research to study.

Acknowledgments

This ethnographic case study could was only possible with support from employees of the Digital Service at the Department of Veterans Affairs. I am grateful to everyone who responded to emails, devoted time to interviews, and welcomed me into their office. Of course, I can't thank any of them by name, so pseudonyms will suffice: thank you, Maria, Sarah, David, and William, for making this research possible.

References

Boyd, A. (2019, November 8). More vets are taking advantage of digital services through new VA.gov. *NextGov*. https://tinyurl.com/52uzx5sp.

Chapman, S. (2018). A quick guide to inclusive design. The U.S. Digital Service. *Medium*. https://tinyurl.com/397pje7d.

Chappellet-Lanier, T. (2020). Looking for "balance," U.S. Digital Service team adapts to changes at VA. *FedScoop*. https://www.fedscoop.com/us-digital-service-veterans-affairs-transition.

Costanza-Chock, S. (2020). *Design justice: Community-led practices to build the worlds we need*. MIT Press.

DigitalVA. (2022). VA.gov hits 1.5 million-in-a-month milestone. https://www.oit.va.gov/news/article/?read=va-website-hits-milestone.

Friess, E. (2010). The sword of data: Does human-centered design fulfill its rhetorical responsibility? *Design Issues*, 26(3), 40–50. https://doi.org/10.1162/DESI_a_00028

Hewitt Jones, J. (2022). President's budget includes $1.8B for health records modernization at the VA. *FedScoop*. https://www.fedscoop.com/biden-budget-2023-va-health-records-modernization/.

Holmes, K. (2018). *Mismatch: How inclusion shapes design*. MIT Press.

Johnson, R. R. (1998). *User-centered technology: A rhetorical theory for computers and other mundane artifacts*. State University of New York Press.

Joyce, A. (2022). Inclusive design. *Nielsen Norman Group*. https://www.nngroup.com/articles/inclusive-design/.

Koerber, A. & McMichael, L. (2008). Qualitative sampling methods: A primer for technical communicators. *Journal of Business and Technical Communication, 22*(4), 454–473. https://doi.org/10.1177/1050651908320362.

McDonald, R. A. (2016, January 21). Testimony of Secretary of Veterans Affairs Robert A. McDonald before the United States Senate Committee on Veterans' Affairs. D1E4CDA5-AEB1-4DC1-B63C-8B680BA15365.

Microsoft. (n.d.). Inclusive design. Retrieved November 24, 2024 from https://www.microsoft.com/design/inclusive/.

Moore, J. (2016). Lack of funding means several agencies won't be getting digital service teams after all. *Nextgov.* https://tinyurl.com/4kdmh977.

National Center for Veterans Analysis and Statistics. (n.d.). VA benefits and health care utilization. Retrieved April 10, 2022 from https://www.va.gov/vetdata/docs/pocket cards/fy2022q2.pdf.

Norman, D. (2019). The four fundamental principles of human-centered design and application. JND.org. https://jnd.org/the-four-fundamental-principles-ofhuman-centered-design/.

Office of Management and Budget. (n.d.). Budget of the U.S. government: Fiscal Year 2022. Retrieved April 10, 2022 from https://www.whitehouse.gov/wp-content/uploads/2021/05/budget_fy22.pdf.

Office of the Press Secretary. (2016). Transforming government services through technology and innovation. The White House. https://tinyurl.com/9uncwccr.

Rose, E. J. (2016). Design as advocacy: Using a human-centered approach to investigate the needs of vulnerable populations. *Journal of Technical Writing and Communication, 46*(4), 427–445. https://doi.org/10.1177/0047281616653494.

Ruskin, M., Schleuning, A., Tavoulareas, E. & Chapman, M. (2014). Toward a veteran-centered VA: Piloting tools of human-centered design for America's vets. Department of Veterans Affairs Center for Innovation. https://library.alnap.org/system/files/content/resource/files/main/Toward_A_Veteran_Centered_VA.pdf.

Salvo, M. J. (2001). Ethics of engagement: User-centered design and rhetorical methodology. *Technical Communication Quarterly, 10*(3), 273–290. https://doi.org/10.1207/s15427625tcq1003_3.

Sun, H. (2021). Empowering from within: Uttering voices and planting seeds. *Intercom, 68*(3), 4–8.

U.S. Department of Veterans Affairs. (2019, June 4). Minority veteran report. https://tinyurl.com/3v28shua.

U.S. Digital Service. (n.d.). Mission. Retrieved October 13, 2024 from https://www.usds.gov/mission.

U.S. Digital Service. (n.d.). How we work. Retrieved April 10, 2022 from https://www.usds.gov/work.

U. S. Digital Service. (2017). The United States Digital Service report to Congress. https://www.usds.gov/report-to-congress/2017/07/.

U.S. General Services Administration. (2018). IT Accessibility Laws and Policies. November 24, 2024 from https://www.section508.gov/manage/laws-and-policies/.

Veterans Affairs. (n.d.). Vets.gov playbook. https://tinyurl.com/y3cyrk5s.

Veterans Affairs Center for Innovation. (n.d.). About VACI. Internet Archive. Retrieved November 24, 2024 from https://tinyurl.com/469hfnfv.

Veterans Affairs Center for Innovation. (2015). Designing for veterans: A toolkit for human-centered design. https://www.vets.gov/playbook/downloads/vaci-project-toolkit.pdf.

Veterans Affairs Innovation Center (2019). About the VA Innovation Center. https://web.archive.org/web/20200605005501/https://www.innovation.va.gov/about.

Veterans Experience Office. (2019, March 29.) Veterans, family, and community engagement. U. S. Department of Veterans Affairs. Internet Arhcive. https://tinyurl.com/nfk9pdde.

Walton, R. (2016). Supporting human dignity and human rights: A call to adopt the first principle of human-centered design. *Journal of Technical Writing and Communication, 46*(4), 402–426. https://doi.org/10.1177/0047281616653496.

The White House. (2016, August 09). Impact Report: Transforming Government Services through Technology and Innovation. https://tinyurl.com/9uncwccr.

Yale-Loehr, A. & Romano, R. (2017, June 15). Vets.gov: A modern software development environment in government. The U.S. Digital Service. *Medium.* https://tinyurl.com/yc5288dd.

Yin, R. K. (2003). *Case study research: Design and methods* (3rd ed.). Sage.

Zachry, M. & Spyridakis, J. H. (2016). Human-centered design and the field of technical communication. *Journal of Technical Writing and Communication, 46*(4), 392–401. https://doi.org/10.1177/0047281616653497.

15. Collaborating Through Usability in Health and Medical Contexts

Kirk St.Amant
LOUISIANA TECH UNIVERSITY AND UNIVERSITY OF LIMERICK

Abstract. New technological developments have resulted in patients performing an ever-increasing range of health-related activities. In these situations, the usability of the associated product is central to non-healthcare professionals performing different processes effectively. As a result, understanding the audience's expectations becomes key to both the usability of the product and the safety of the user. This chapter presents an approach for collaborating with patients to identify their usability expectations based on core cognitive factors that affect the use of items. By focusing on certain cognitive concepts, individuals can identify a patient's usability expectations for factors of access, comprehension, and acceptability. They can then use these findings to develop products the related audience more readily understand and can more easily use. These ideas and this approach, however, is not tied to medical situations. Rather, individuals can employ them to foster effective collaborations for identifying the usability expectations for different groups, situations, and settings.

The nature of many medical processes means collaboration is often central to healthcare (Morley & Cashell, 2017).[1] Hospital visits, for example, usually involve different individuals—from check-in personnel to nurses to physicians—collaborating to collect a patient's health information. In other cases, such collaborations are more direct as when nurses, anesthesiologist, and surgeons interact during an operation. Because such collaborations generally occur in dedicated healthcare settings, individuals often view these dynamics as involving healthcare professionals and happening in specific medical contexts. As a result, patients are often overlooked as central collaborators when developing medical products, procedures, or documentation. Changing healthcare practices, however, mean patients need to become core collaborators when developing healthcare activities or designing medical products—including documentation.

The last decade has seen rapid growth in technologies dedicated to personal health and wellness (Fortune Business Insights, 2020; Phaneuf, 2020). These products range from wearable health monitors to informational websites to DIY videos on healthcare processes. These situations, however, focus on non-medical professionals performing wellness activities outside of formal healthcare contexts (Heath, 2016; Resnick, 2019). In such cases, usability becomes central to effective

---

1. I wish to acknowledge the Eunice C. Williamson Endowment in Technical Communication for providing support used in the development of this chapter.

health and wellness, for failure to use a technology effectively or perform a process correctly could result in flawed care and/or injury (Clark & Israelski, 2012; Zhang et al., 2003).

Creating usable healthcare products for such situations involves understanding who is using these products as well as where, when, and how such usage occurs (Melonçon, 2016, 2017; St.Amant, 2020). Addressing this situation requires patients to collaborate in the development of

- New medical technologies to be used by patients and/or their families
- Emerging healthcare practices to be performed by non-healthcare professionals
- Informational/instructional materials associated with such technologies and practices

The challenge becomes fostering such collaborations in a way that makes patients central to these processes. The solution involves user experience (UX) approaches that focus on patients as central collaborators in such activities.

This entry offers a theory-based approach to engaging in such collaborative interactions when examining UX dynamics in medical contexts. Specifically, the entry presents an approach for collaborating with patients to develop usable healthcare *materials*, or the health-related products patients use and the related documentation they rely on when using such products. Known as localized patient experience design (L-PXC), the process involves working with patients to identify:

- Where they engage in healthcare activities
- What factors they associate with usability during such processes
- Which psychological factors guide patient usability expectations in these contexts

Identifying such factors, can help UX professionals create materials (i.e., healthcare product s and associated documentation) that more effectively address user expectations for contexts of care (Melonçon, 2017; St.Amant, 2017a).

▌ Cognition and Conceptualization

Products reflect the assumptions and expectations of their creators (Pacey, 1996; St.Amant, 2017a; Sun, 2012). This is because humans use mental models to guide how they conceptualize ideas and understand processes. For example, when most of us are told to "create a user guide," we hear the words "user guide," and our minds access a mental model of what this item is (Eyal, 2014; Lindstrom, 2010). This mental model is an "ideal" representing what we think our final product should be. We then try to create something that resembles that ideal—continually comparing our in-progress work to this ideal in order to replicate that mental model. This approach often guides how we produce everything from a wearable devices and apps to the documentation that accompanies these items.

When individuals use materials (i.e., products or associated documentation), they engage in a similar cognitive process. If told to perform an activity, such as "call your office from your mobile phone," individuals access a mental mode of what that process involves (Eyal, 2014; Lindstrom, 2010). This model includes what individuals need to do and what they need to use to perform the related task. Individuals then replicate the process that appears in this mental model and assume doing so will yield expected results.

The mental models that guide actions and influence usability are not innate. Humans learn them through repeated exposure over time. The more I encounter a "user guide" with certain features, the more I form a mental model noting something should have those features for me to recognize it as a user guide (Aitchison, 1994; Rosch, 1978). If I encounter different user guides, I will note the features common across them, and these common features form my idealized concept of "user guide." I then access this idealized version, called a *prototype*, when thinking about this item (Aitchison, 1994; Rosch, 1978). Over time, I become so accustomed to a user manual resembling a related prototype that I no longer consider what features a user manual should have; rather, I rely on the related mental model to reflexively direct my expectations and actions (Ratey, 2002).

The same situation applies to how I conceptualize the process for using an item. My experiences have taught me how I and others perform a process, and these experiences form a metal model for thinking about such activities. The resulting model includes:

- What I think objects used in that process should look like and do
- Who (if anyone) assists with these activities
- How to identify such person (e.g., by a uniform)
- Which actions I (or others) need to perform in order to achieve a particular objective

These mental models for activities are *scripts* consisting of the prototypes of items and persons I associate with the related process so I can identify and use them (for items) or interact with them (for individuals) during the activity. Such scripts also include mental models for how I expect actions to be done when I or others perform a task (Tomkins, 1978, 1987). Again, the more I perform or observe a process over time, the more the related script becomes embedded in my subconscious until I can perform an activity reflexively. Unfortunately, a lack of interaction and collaboration with others can result in mental models causing usability issues.

■ Problems with Products and Processes

Problems arise when the mental models of the product or document creators do not match those of the intended users of those products or content (Aitchison, 1994; St.Amant 2017b). I, for example, might think of checking blood pressure as something done at my physician's office where a nurse uses an analog sphygmomanometer and a stethoscope. You, however, might conceptualize this process as something you do yourself using an automatic blood pressure cuff while seated in your office at work. Both processes involve a common objective, but the different mental models that guide such activities will affect how we communicate about the related task.

Consider if I created blood pressure monitoring instructions for you. My instructions might include actions such as "Allow the nurse to apply the blood pressure cuff and position the stethoscope." Such content reflects my mental model, which identifies these actions as essential to this process. You, however, might read these instructors and become confused, for the process I describe is not the one you use when checking your blood pressure. As a result, you might guess at certain activities, perform processes ineffectively, or decide not to use my instructions at all.

This situation involves three usability-related problems based on my assumptions of:

1. Objects unfamiliar to you (e.g., analog sphygmomanometer) that you cannot identify or use.
2. Individuals who will perform the process (e.g., a trained nurse vs. an untrained patient).
3. Setting where the process occurs (e.g., physician's vs. personal office) and what activities can be done there.

In this example, the cognitive model I associate with a particular healthcare processes reflects my own experiences (St.Amant, 2017b). Yet this model could vary from yours due to our different experiences associated with that same activity. The resulting differences could affect how successfully you can use my instructions to perform the related healthcare process. Without awareness of such issues, this problem can occur every time the mental model of a product developer or content creator diverges from that of the intended user. Such situations can create health disparities that affect the equity of care whenever the experiences of different groups and communities are not considered or included when developing health-related products or content for those groups or communities (Braveman, 2014). Such problems can be particularly acute for marginalized groups that have been historically excluded from various healthcare processes and the development of related products or documentation (Baah et al., 2019; Sevelius et al., 2020).

Addressing such situations involves an inclusion-based approach focused on identifying the mental models an audience employs to perform processes and use items. Collaboration, in turn, becomes central to avoiding such issues. The more product developers and content creators collaborate with members of the intended audience during the design and drafting process, the better they can identify and address the mental models audiences associate with usable products and usable content. This requires product developers and content creators to realize they cannot assume how an audience will use an item. Rather, they need to interact with and collaborate with their audience (i.e., users) to understand the mental models influencing usability expectation. Such approaches mean viewing users as central collaborators in the overall design and creation processes. In healthcare situations, such collaborations require the involving patients—the intended users of products and content—throughout development processes to create effective products and documentation. Product developers, content creators, and UX professionals alike therefore need to view patients as central participants, or *patient collaborators*, who play an active role in design and development activities throughout the content creation/product development process.

▪ Expanding Understanding of Users

In healthcare contexts, a central usability problem involves how product developers and content creators conceptualize their users. When these developers and creators access the mental models that guide their activities, they often do so with a particular end user in mind—an idealized version of who the users are. These developers and creators then focus on producing texts, images, and products for that audience (Lindstrom, 2010; St.Amant, 2017b). These assumptions, however, often reflect the developer's or the creator's experiences and associated assumptions of who the end user is.

This approach might have worked when access to health-related products and content remained relatively restricted to formal healthcare venues where they were primarily used by trained healthcare professionals. Today, this situation has changed as a range of heal and wellness technologies now exist for use by individuals with no healthcare background (Heath, 2016; Resnick, 2019). Such factors radically shift:

- What users know about health and medical processes
- What users are able to do and can use when performing a process
- Where users will engage in a task

Addressing such factors is central to creating health-related products or content audiences can use.

The changing nature of healthcare further contributes to this situation. The length of hospital stays in the U.S. continues to decrease as does the time U.S. patients spend interacting with healthcare providers (Bryant, 2017; Frakt, 2016; Linzer et al., 2015;). As such, individuals are becoming increasingly responsible for performing their own healthcare activities or doing so for family members, friends, or neighbors (Gittel, 2009; Gouge, 2016; Woods, 2019). The rise of electronic health records and artificial intelligence in healthcare further complicates this situation by increasingly requiring individuals to enter health and medical data into different systems via various interfaces (Das, 2019; Dunn, 2017; Heath, 2016;). Finally, the market for products like wearable healthcare technologies continues to grow as does the number of wellness technologies targeted at non-healthcare professionals (Dunn, 2017; Fortune Business Insights, 2020; Phaneuf, 2020).

These situations mean product developers and content creators cannot assume who the audience for healthcare information or technologies will be (Melonçon, 2016, 2017). Nor can they assume who to collaborate with when creating healthcare products or medical content. Rather, the collaborators for this emerging context need to be the patients who will use such materials. The challenge becomes determining how to collaborate with patients to tap their expectations for activities in a context of care—or the locations where healthcare processes occur. Such collaborations require strategies that help product developers, content creators, and UX professionals interact with patients to identify associated usability expectations for such contexts of care. Additionally, these collaborations must make patients central participants in the research, development, and design of healthcare products and related documentation/content (e.g., visuals and texts).

■ Locations, Experiences, and Expectations

Location often influences usability expectations (St.Amant, 2017b, 2018). Humans learn to perform processes in a particular setting, and these experiences shape mental models for using products and contend (St.Amant, 2018). If you have only tested your blood sugar levels in a formal healthcare setting like a hospital, your mental model for this process reflects these experiences. If, however, most of your experiences involve testing your blood sugar levels yourself while at home, then you have a different mental model for what this process entails.

In both cases, the healthcare objective is the same, yet the approach for achieving it differs per what usability entails based on the individual's experiences (Duhigg, 2012; Lindstrom, 2010). In the hospital setting, the perspective of patients is often that of passive participant. Materials designed for them might therefore reflect what patients should allow to be done *to them* and *for them*. The individuals who perform the process, the phlebotomist who draws blood and the lab technician who analyzes it, are the actual users of products and content associated with this process. These individuals have a certain knowledge of the topic, training in the process, and expectations of tools used during an activity.

Conversely, patients who monitor their own blood sugar assume the role of one who performs the process and use associated materials (i.e., products and documentation). The materials these individuals use would thus differ from those created for trained healthcare workers based on the background, training, and tools available to the patient. These factors mean each group (i.e., trained healthcare provider and untrained patient) might have different mental models for a process, and such differences often reflect the location where each process occurs.

In both cases, usability in a location focuses on:

- Who in a location performs an activity.
- What those individuals use in that location to perform the activity.

Product developers and content creator need to address both contextual factors to meet the usability expectations of the intended audience (St.Amant, 2017a). The dynamics of such contexts of care, however, can vary depending on what is available in a setting (St.Amant, 2017a). The challenge becomes identifying the contexts of care individuals associate with using medical products and healthcare documents. The more patients perform healthcare activities, use medical technologies, or review wellness-related content themselves, the greater the prospective variations across contexts of care.

Addressing this situation requires product developers, content creators, and UX professionals to identify the "who" and "what" aspects for a context of care. Collaborations with the patients who will actually use products or documentation in these contexts thus becomes essential to achieving this objective. Fostering such collaborations requires the realization that not all parties have common context of care experiences. Rather, product developers, content creators, and UX professionals need to invite members of the intended audience to participate in the development of the healthcare products and content they will use. Maximizing interactions with and input from the related audience is central to these activities, and localized patient experience design (L-PXD) can facilitate such processes.

▌ Complexities of Contexts of Care

Context of care expectations reflect more than location. They bring with them assumptions of who performs a process, what they use, and what such processes entail (Tompkins, 1978, 1987). Earlier examinations of these ideas focused on localization (i.e., creating items for the setting where they are used) and examined usability expectations in different international healthcare situations (St. Amant, 2017a, 2017b). The shift to patient-centered care mirrors this need to understand the local contexts where individuals use health-related products and content. As such, a localization-focused approach seems well suited for collaborating with patient groups on healthcare-focused product development and content creation.

This approach to understanding how local contexts affect patient expectations is localized patient experience design (L-PXD). It is based upon of Lisa Melonçon's (2016, 2017) patient experience design (PXD) methodology that was later adapted by St.Amant (2017a) to address cross-cultural contexts via international patient experience design (I-PXD). I-PXD applies usability concepts to local healthcare contexts in order to localize (i.e., adapt) content for international settings. L-PXD applies the I-PXD approach to any location—international, domestic, regional, or local—to identify user expectations for contexts of care. In so doing, L-PXD makes patients central development and design collaborators by focusing on three factors:

1. *Access:* How patients access healthcare products and content in the context where a healthcare activity occurs.
2. *Comprehension:* How well individuals can use healthcare products and content in a context of care based on their understanding of
   - Biomedical processes and practices associated with a healthcare process.
   - Uses of tools, technologies, and documentation related to such processes.
3. *Acceptability:* How readily individuals accept product and content as credible and will use such products and content in a context of care (see St.Amant, 2017a).

This focus helps product developers, content creators, and UX researchers collaborate with patients to identify their expectations for different contexts of care (St. Amant, 2017a, 2017b).

Access

Access is central to usability, for how patients access materials in a setting affects their usability and design expectations. L-PXD (St.Amant, 2017a) examines access in terms of:

- *Mode of Access*: The mode individuals associate with accessing healthcare products and content in a setting establishes design expectations for using items (e.g., printed books lying flat or videos organized into easy-to-stop/rewind clips). Different modes also require certain environmental factors to use items in a location (e.g., ample light for reading printed texts or internet access for viewing online videos).
- *Time of Access:* When individuals access materials can affect the activities they can undertake (and how they can perform them) in a location. Performing healthcare processes in an empty, quiet location allows individuals to focus on a task. Doing so when that space is filled with other people can affect one's ability to focus on that activity.
- *Materials and Access:* The materials available in a location—be they tools, technologies, or documentation—affect what activities individuals can perform there. If the items associated with a caregiving process are not present in a location, alternative products, processes, or content needs to be developed to achieve the related healthcare objective in that setting.
- *Mechanisms for Access:* During a healthcare process, individuals might need to obtain information or tools from or share details with individuals outside of the context of care. Such factors could include requiring

information or sharing details about what occurred or accessing tools for performing follow-up processes. If and how individuals access such external factors affects what they can do in a context of care. Identifying how individuals access outside information and products or share information with others is crucial to such understanding healthcare activities.

These factors can affect how individuals perform processes in a context of care. Collaborations with patients can help identify such factors in order to develop products and content that meet related expectations for healthcare processes.

Comprehension

Access to materials does not ensure their use; individuals also need to *comprehend* content, designs, and products in order to:

- Recognize what items are
- Understand the information provided or the uses of the product
- Confirm the user has the knowledge needed to perform activities or use products
- Establish the role users play in a process

These aspects affect if individuals can understand what they need to do as well as use products or content to achieve a healthcare objective in a context of care. Per L-PXD, effective comprehension involves addressing the following factors (St.Amant, 2017a):

Recognition of Items: Individuals must identify/recognize an item in order to use it. Because varying experiences can affect recognition, product developers, content creators, and UX professionals must therefore identify:

- The items individuals use to access content in a context of care
- The materials individuals expect to use for healthcare activities in that setting
- The designs individuals expect and rely on to identify items in that location

The resulting information can help in designing products and creating content patients can recognize and use per their experiences-related expectations.

Literacy of User: In healthcare context, literacy often includes:

- *Ability to Use Modes of Communication:* This element involves if individuals have the literacy (procedural knowledge) needed to access information in certain formats or modes. These dynamics can include literacy levels associated with reading texts, technology literacy for accessing digital information, or visual literacy for interpreting graphical elements. The objective is to determine such elements of audience literacy in order to deliver products or information via modes patients can use.

- *Ability to Understand Information Presented:* This factor encompasses style and vocabulary used, when to explain ideas vs. assume knowledge of a concept, and selecting examples to illustrate processes. Such factors can affect if patients can use products or content because they understand what to do, what to use, and how. Addressing these factors requires collaboration with patients to identify their knowledge of a topic in order to create comprehensible and usable materials for them.

Background of Actors: Just because individuals understand words and concepts or know what a product is does not mean they can use products or content to perform activities. For example, the fact I understand texts describing a surgical process does not mean I can perform that surgery any more than my ability to recognize a scalpel means I can use it to perform surgery. Rather, certain experience and training are often essential to undertaking various healthcare tasks and using related items. These factors affect if individuals can use products or content to perform certain processes. Product designers, content creators, and UX professionals must therefore determine:

- what training or background individuals in a context of care have,
- what healthcare activities individuals can perform based on this background,
- and create products or content that meets related patient backgrounds, abilities, and expectations.

Roles of Participants: In healthcare contexts, comprehension also means establishing who will perform different tasks in terms of:

- *Activity:* The individual responsible for performing certain activities in a process. Is one, for example, the sole actor who performs all caregiving activities or one actor who collaborates with others to provide care? Knowledges or such roles and related expectations is essential to providing information and creating products that allow individuals to perform activities in a context of care.
- *Items:* Individuals must often use certain items to perform a care-related process associated with their role in a context of care. The key is to determine what these individuals expect to use and what they know about using these items to provide care. Equally important is determining if individuals should bring such materials (e.g., products or content) to a setting or if those items will be there for individuals to use. Knowing such factors is central to creating products and content individuals can use based upon whey they expect to do in contexts of care.

Identifying these dynamics can help in developing products and content that meet patient usability expectations in healthcare settings.

Acceptability

The final usability element is if individuals *want* to use items. This acceptability factor involves if patients consider products or content legitimate and credible in relation to the healthcare activities performed in a context of care (St.Amant, 2015, 2017a). Essentially, acceptable materials will be considered and used; unacceptable ones will not.

According to L-PXD (St.Amant, 2017a), acceptability involves three factors:

1. *Processes to Perform:* Audiences can have different expectations of what constitutes a credible healthcare process or associated credible healthcare item (e.g., product or document) worth using. These factors can affect if individuals accept and use certain processes—and related products or content—to achieve healthcare goals. Some audiences, for example, consider acupuncture a credible treatment for high blood pressure; it is viewed with skepticism by others. This difference can affect if audiences use—or expect to use—acupuncture-related products and content in a health-related context.
2. *Presentations of Processes:* Healthcare processes often encompass sensitive topics or controversial subjects. The design of content on or products associated with such topics can affect if individuals consider such items acceptable for use or offensive and to be avoided. If certain product features or content factors (e.g., visuals) violate a patient's sense of appropriateness, that person might refuse to use associated products or documentation. Product developers, content creators, and UX professionals therefore need to understand such factors and develop products or content accordingly.
3. *Participants in Processes:* Who is a credible healthcare provider can vary from person to person. Such differences can affect if patients heed the advice of a care provider or even allow individuals to perform care-related activities. Identifying such expectations helps determine the best methods for conveying healthcare information or designing healthcare products. Doing so involves determining:
    - Who patients consider to be legitimate healthcare providers
    - What credentials or criteria patients associate with this credibility
    - How individuals should display this credibility per patient expectations

If patients must consult informational sources during a process, one must also determine what those patients associate with credible sources and provide content that meet these expectations.

The complexities of acceptability make it challenging, but addressing such factors is often essential to patients using healthcare products or content. The better individuals understand such aspects, the more effectively they can create content and products patients will use in a context of care.

Researching User Expectations

L-PXD makes patients central collaborators in the development and design of healthcare products and content by working with patients to identify their access, comprehension, and acceptability expectations. The first step involves determining which patient groups to collaborate with based on their experiences accessing and receiving healthcare (see St.Amant, 2017a, 2017b, 2019). This first step is particularly important per addressing issues of inclusion and equity in healthcare as the exclusion of different groups and communities has historically led to healthcare disparities across communities, societies, and regions (Braveman, 2014). Next, individuals need to employ certain methods to identify usability expectations via interactions with patient collaborators. L-PXD facilitates such activities by engaging with patients to identify their context of care expectations.

Engaging in such interactions requires individuals recognize the patient information they collect often covers a variety of personal and sensitive topics. Such factors could affect if patients agree to participate in such collaborations, the answers they provide to questions (see "Interviews and Focus Groups" sections), and their willingness to participate in follow-up activities (see "Task Assessment and User Testing" section). Individuals doing such research must therefore begin such collaborations by:

- Obtaining related permission (e.g., IRB approval) from their organization or institution prior to conducting this research
- Confirming the collection of patient data follows legal statues (e.g., HIPPA) and ethical codes (AMA Code of Ethics)
- Providing prospective patient collaborators with clear explanations of what the research process will entail, what data will be collected from them, how that data will be organized (e.g., identified or de-identified), stored, and used as well as for how long that data will be kept and how it will be disposed of
- Offering prospective patient collaborators the opportunity to opt out of (i.e., exclude themselves from) the research process at any point in time as well as the opportunity to request their data be removed/not considered at a later point in time per patient prerogative
- Explaining what control patient collaborators have over their data in terms of rights to access, review, amend, or remove such information during and after the research process is complete
- Following best research practices of the researcher's discipline or field in interacting with patient collaborators during and after the overall research process

Such factors provide patient collaborators with the means for understanding related processes and the agency essential to maintaining control over their personal information throughout such activities. These factors also help the individuals conducting such research collaborate with patients in ways that respect the patients' integrity as a collaborator as well as conform to best practices for engaging in human subjects research.

Interviews and Focus Groups

Interviews are one-on-one interactions where product developers, content creators, and UX researchers can ask patient collaborators questions on their context-of-care expectations. Resulting responses can provide insights on individual perspectives associated with different healthcare processes (InterQ, 2020; Schwab, 2020). Focus groups involve asking the same questions to a gathering of three to eight patient collaborators to obtain that group's perspective on such factors (InterQ, n.d.?; Schwab, 2020). Combining these methods allows one to compare individual and group perspectives in order to identify the healthcare expectations for a particular patient group.

Access

Access factors are the first context of care aspect to identify, and individuals can use the following interviews/focus group questions to research such expectations:

- Do you do [healthcare process] yourself or have someone else do it for you?
- When do you perform this process?
- Where do you perform [healthcare process]?
- What do you (or others) use to access information when you perform this process?
- What do you (or others) use (or expect others to use) to perform this process?
- How do you (or others) contact individuals with questions or updates or obtain needed items during this process?

The responses can provide patient perspectives on access expectations in healthcare contexts.

Comprehension

Next, individuals need to expand their questioning to address the comprehension expectations of patient collaborators. This involves augmenting interview and focus group questions as follows:

- Do you do [healthcare process] yourself or have someone else do it for you?

- When do you perform this process?
- Where do you perform [healthcare process]?
  - *Can you describe this location to me? What is in that location?*
- What do you (or others) use to access information when you perform this process?
  - *Can you describe that item to me? What does it look like, feel like, and sound like?*
- What do you (or others) use (or expect others to use) to perform this process?
  - *Can you describe these items to me? What do they look like, feel like, and sound like?*
- How do you (or others) contact individuals with questions or updates or obtain needed items during this process?
  - *What do you use? Can you describe it/them to me?*

The questions in italic prompt patient collaborators to note the features they use to recognize and use products and content for the related healthcare process. Individuals should compare resulting responses to identify the items (e.g., tools, technologies, and documentation) patients associate with such situations and the features patients use to recognize those items.

Acceptability

Interviews and focus groups can also identify patient expectations of acceptable healthcare products, content, or processes. Doing so involves asking patient collaborators the following questions:

- Can you describe the process to me from the beginning to the end? What are the different steps in this process?
- Who performs each step?
- (If not the patient) How do you identify this person? Can you describe that person to me?
- What do you use to do this step?/What does that other person use to do this step?
- Can you describe that item (those items) to me?
- Can you describe how you use that item (those items) to perform this process?/Can you describe how that other person uses that item (those items) to perform this process?
- Do you consult anything—a manual, a website, some other source—for information during or after this process?
- (If yes) Can you describe that item/those items to me?
- Where did you get that item/those items?

- If you have to obtain answers or information or obtain needed items during or after this process, what would you do? Who would you contact or what would you use? Can you describe this process to me? Can you describe the item(s) you use to me?
- How do you know that source (or what source) is trustworthy for such information?
- Can you describe that trustworthy source to me? What makes it trustworthy?

These questions help identify factors patient collaborators associate with credible processes, individuals, items, and content involved in healthcare activities. They also help identify what patients consider credible sources of information for these activities. Individuals can then use this information to identify the mental models patient collaborators rely on when assessing usability in such contexts.

Observational Methods

What patients say they do and what they actually do can differ (Eyal, 2014). Individuals researching patient expectations should therefore collect certain information beyond responses to questions noted here. L-PXD advocates using observations to compare if words and actions align per patient behaviors in contexts of care. Doing so involves observing patient collaborators as they perform a healthcare process in a context of care. (Note: Researching such behaviors involves following the guidelines for patient awareness and data collection noted at the start of this overall section.) Such practices could take one of two forms: non-participant observation and think-aloud protocols.

Non-participant observation involves visiting the setting patients identified as where a caregiving activity occurs and silently (without interacting with patients) observing how individuals perform health-related processes there (Crossman, 2019). During these observations, one would note:

- What products or content patients use when performing healthcare activities there
- What patients use to perform such processes and
  - If these items are already in that setting at that time
  or
  - If someone brings these items to that setting—if so, who and how
- What patients use to access outside information or items as well as to share information with individuals outside of that immediate context

Observers/researchers would review information from multiple observations to identify how patient collaborators perform healthcare processes in that setting. (The number and length of visits would depend on available time and resources.)

While this approach provides information on what patients do in a context of care, the lack of interaction means observers/researchers:

- Are dependent on their observational skills to note factors involved in such processes.
- Cannot determine (other than guess) why individuals engage in behaviors or use items.

Additionally, patient awareness of being observed—as well as the venues where observations occur—might affect how they perform activities (Crossman, 2019).

Think-aloud protocols involve interacting with patient collaborators during a process (Nielsen, 2012). Such interactions allow observers to ask questions about why patents engage in certain behaviors and use certain items during a process in order to determine both what patients do and why when performing an activity (Nielsen, 2012). The resulting information could be used in in combination with data from non-participant observations to understand patient behaviors.

During think-aloud protocols, observers/researchers could ask patient collaborators to explain what they are doing and why as they perform a particular activity in a context of care. Such an approach can help:

- Clarify actions (e.g., "What are you doing now? Can you describe this process or show it to me?")
- Identify items involved in actions ("What are you using to perform that task? Can you show me or describe it to me?")
- Determine underlying reasons for such behaviors ("Why did you decide to do that? Why did you use that item for that task?")

Ideally, researchers would collect data from as many patient collaborators as possible to identify common actions and uses of items in a context of care. When combined with interview and focus group data, the resulting information could help identify patient usability expectations for contexts of care.

▪ Developing and Testing Designs

Researchers would review the data collected via the methods noted previously to identify patterns in how patients access, understand, and evaluate the acceptability of products and content used in a context of care. Researchers could use the resulting information to create the following resources to guide product development and content creation:

- A *checklist of features* to include or items to address when designing products or content patients can access, comprehend, consider acceptable, and use in a context of care.

- A *sample design (e.g., a sketch) of a context of care* based on and including features and items from the design checklist.
- *Draft materials*—documentation, online informational products, or devices—for individuals to use in a context of care (St.Amant, 2017a, 2017b).

These initial resources are not final products. Rather, they require testing with patient collaborators to evaluate how effectively the meet patient usability expectations as well as address:

- Inaccurate information collected during interviews and focus groups.
- Limited ability of observers to note certain factors during observations.
- Lack of patient comments on a particular item during think-aloud sessions.

Testing these draft resources allows one to collect additional patient input and revise these items to better parallel patients' usability expectations. As such processes involves collecting information from patients, researchers need to follow the guidelines for data-collection noted at the start of the "Researching User Expectations" section when collaborating with patients to do such testing.

Interviews and Focus Groups

When evaluating draft resources, researchers can use interviews and focus groups to collect patient perspectives and reactions. Such interactions could involve asking patient collaborators to review draft resources and respond to the following questions:

For draft representations of context of care or draft items created for such contexts:

- Where is this? (for locations/contexts)

Or

- What is this? (for items/objects)

If individuals correctly identify a location:

- How do you know?
- Would you modify the design of this location? How? Why would you modify it that way?
- Can you identify the items in this location?

As individuals identify items:

- What is it (item) used for?
- Who uses it?
- How do you (or they) use it? Describe this process for me.
- Would you modify the design of this item? How? Why would you modify it that way?

If individuals cannot identify the location:

- How would you modify this representation to make it resemble a [context of care]?
- What would you add?
- What existing features would you modify? How?
- Would you remove anything? (If yes) Why would you remove it?

If individuals cannot identify draft items or items in a draft context of care representation:

- How would you modify [item] to make it better resemble a [kind of item]?
- What would you add?
- What existing features would you modify? How?
- Would you remove anything? (If yes) Why would you remove it?

Researchers can use the resulting answers to modify the related draft resources to better reflect patient expectations for healthcare activities and related contexts of care (St.Amant, 2017a, 2017b).

Task Assessment and User Testing

Recognition and acceptability represent some aspects affecting usability. The additional aspect to assess is comprehension—do individuals understand how to use an item to perform a healthcare activity in a location. Evaluating comprehension involves patient collaborators using draft items to perform care-related activities in a context of care.

For such evaluations, researchers would bring patient collaborators to or meet them in the location where they engage in a healthcare activity. Researchers would then present patient collaborators with a draft item—a draft document, beta version of an app, or a prototype of a product—and ask those collaborators to use the item to perform a specific healthcare activity in that setting (St.Amant, 2017, 2018). Patient collaborators would be instructed to talk out loud during such processes and to note:

- What they are doing and why.
- What aspects are particularly effective or ineffective.
- What makes such aspects effective or ineffective.
- How to modify ineffective items to be more effective.

Researchers would record these activities and comments as well as note:

- How long it takes patient collaborators to use a draft item to perform a process.
- How many individuals successfully complete the process.
- If activities were done correctly.

Researchers would also note when (and, ideally, why) a process seemed to break down or an unexpected pattern of use emerged.

After patient collaborators complete a process, researchers would ask individuals:

- Do you think you completed the activity effectively? (If no, why not?)
- Do you think you completed the activity in a reasonable amount of time? (If no, why not?)

If patient collaborators did not complete the assigned task, researchers would ask them:

- At what point did you notice the process was not going well?
- What happened then that affected the process?
- What would you suggest as a solution to avoid this problem in the future?

All participants would then be asked:

- What aspects of the process did you think went well? Why?
- What aspects of the product [item they used] did you think were effective? Why?
- What aspects of the process did not go well? Why? Do you have any suggestions for how to improve such items?
- What aspects of the product [item they used] did not work well? Why? What suggestions do you have for how to fix such factors?
- Do you have any additional suggestions or comments on the process you performed or on the items you used?

The resulting answers could help identify additional areas where revisions are needed to better meet the usability and context-of-care expectations of patient collaborators.

Applying Results and Assessing Revisions

Researchers could use testing results to modify draft materials and related design resources/checklists. Ideally, they would test these revised items with new patient collaborators representing the same audience. Such testing would involve similar methods, questions, and assigned tasks to evaluate the usability of revised designs (St.Amant, 2017a, 2017b).

The results of this second round of assessment could help determine if additional revisions are needed to meet the usability expectations of patient collaborators. If additional revisions are needed, researchers would again revise sample items and corresponding resources and then re-test these revised items with patient collaborators representing the same audience. This iterative process of test, review data, revise, and test revision would continue until testing indicated a usable design was achieved or the time and resources for these processes are exhausted (St.Amant, 2017a, 2017b). Ideally, this iterative process would allow researchers to create the product development/content creation resources and associated items that meet the usability expectations of the intended patient audience.

▌ Implications for Readers

While this chapter examines collaborations related to healthcare contexts, readers can apply the ideas covered in the chapter to developing usable materials for almost any situation. The core ideas of access, comprehensibility, and acceptability are central ones to address when creating usable designs in general. Moreover, the cognitive factors described and the methods used to identify them are not restrictive to healthcare contexts. Rather, they are relatively easy-to-implement approaches for identifying common cognitive processes.

These factors mean readers can use the methodology described in the chapter to collaborate with audiences associated with almost any product. This is because the cognitive processes the chapter described affect usability expectations in general. Moreover, by using the research approach described here, individuals can effectively collaborate with different partners to identify the usability expectations for different groups. The researchers and their collaborators can then use the resulting information to develop usable designs and products based on the testing and assessment processes the chapter describes. So, while the chapter focuses on health-related situations, readers can apply these same approaches and ideas across different collaborative situations to help develop usable designs.

▌ Thoughts

The usability of an item reflects how well it meets the expectations of the individuals who use it. By understanding the cognitive models affecting such processes, product developers, content creators, and UX professionals can conduct the research needed to identify such expectations. Doing so requires collaborating with the intended patient audience throughout the content/product development process. Localized Patient Experience Design (L-PXD) facilitates such collaborations to created products and content patients consider usable in healthcare settings.

By guiding collaborative interactions to focus on understanding patient expectations, L-PXD fosters effective interactions with patient collaborators throughout product design and content development processes. Through collaborative methods for collecting information and testing draft designs, L-PXD enhances understanding of the usability expectations of specific patient audiences. Through guided interactions with patients, L-PXD can help product developers and content creators address the cognitive models that guide how patients use materials in contexts of care.

■ References

Aitchison, J. (1994). Bad birds and better birds: Prototype theory. In V. P. Clark, P. A. Eschholz & A. F. Rosa (Eds.), *Language: Introductory readings* (4th ed., pp. 445–459). St. Martin's Press.

Baah, F. O., Teitelman, A. M. & Riegel, B. (2019). Marginalization: Conceptualizing patient vulnerabilities in the framework of social determinants of health: An integrative review. *Nursing Inquiry, 26*(1), e12268. https://doi.org/10.1111/nin.12268.

Braveman, P. (2014). What are health disparities and health equity? We need to be clear. *Public Health Reports, 129*(1, Suppl. 2), 5–8. https://doi.org/10.1177/00333549141291S203.

Bryant, M. (2017). Patients and doctors both agree: Visits are too short. *HealthcareDive*. https://tinyurl.com/yey98h75.

Clark, E. & Israelski, E. (2012). Total recall: The consequences of ignoring medical device usability. *User Experience Magazine*. https://uxpamagazine.org/total-recall/.

Crossman, A. (2019). What is participant observation research? *Thought Co*. https://www.thoughtco.com/participant-observation-research-3026557.

Das, R. (2019, February 4). Top five digital health technologies in 2019. *Forbes*. https://tinyurl.com/4mthu3cf.

Duhigg, C. (2012). *The power of habit: Why we do what we do in life and business*. Random House.

Dunn, A. (2017). Digital health: Current state & future growth 2017–2025. *Health Standards*. https://tinyurl.com/48m6shvr.

Eyal, N. (2014). *Hooked: How to build habit-forming products*. Portfolio/Penguin Books.

Fortune Business Insights. (2020, January 27). mHealth market to reach USD 293.29 billion by 2026; increasing smartphone penetration to contribute healthy growth, states *Fortune Business Insights*. *PR Newswire*. https://tinyurl.com/y4zkfkwx.

Frakt, A. (2016, January 4). The hidden financial incentives behind your shorter hospital stay. *The New York Times*. https://tinyurl.com/rhp9e25b.

Gittel, J. H. (2009). *High performance healthcare: Using the power of relationships to achieve quality, efficiency, and resilience*. McGraw-Hill.

Gouge, C. C. (2016). Improving patient discharge communication. *Journal of Technical Writing and Communication, 47*(4), 419–439. https://doi.org/10.1177/0047281616646749.

Heath, S. (2016). Patient portals, mHealth top 2016 patient engagement trends. *Patient Engagement HIT*. https://tinyurl.com/5vz2a6xn.

InterQ. (n.d.). Focus groups versus in-depth interviews. https://interq-research.com/focus-groups-versus-in-depth-interviews/.

Lindstrom, M. (2010). *Buyology: Truth and lies about why we buy*. Broadway Books.

Linzer, M., Bitton, A., Tu, S., Plews-Ogan, M., Horowitz, K. R. & Schwartz, M. D. (2015). The end of the 15–20 minute primary care visit. *Journal of General Internal Medicine, 30*(11), 1584–1586. https://doi.org/10.1007/s11606-015-3341-3.

Melonçon, L. (2016). Patient experience design: Technical communication's role in patient health information and education. *Intercom, 62*(2), 12–16.

Melonçon, L. (2017). Patient experience design: Expanding usability methodologies for healthcare. *Communication Design Quarterly, 5*(2), 19–28.

Morley, L. & Cashell, A. (2017). Collaboration in health care. *Journal of Medical Imaging and Radiation Sciences, 48*(2), 207–216. https://doi.org/10.1016/j.jmir.2017.02.071.

Nielsen, J. (2012). Thinking aloud: The #1 usability tool. *Nielsen Norman Group.* https://www.nngroup.com/articles/thinking-aloud-the-1-usability-tool/.

Pacey, A. (1996). *The culture of technology.* MIT Press.

Phaneuf, A. (2020, January 11). Latest trends in medical monitoring devices and wearable health technology. *Business Insider.* https://www.businessinsider.com/wearable-technology-healthcare-medical-devices?op=1.

Ratey, J. J. (2002). *A user's guide to the brain: Perception, attention, and the four theaters of the brain.* Vintage.

Resnick, R. (2019, 17 July). What are the pros and cons of mHealth? Cureatr. https://tinyurl.com/5aauabbw.

Rosch, E. (1978). Principles of categorization. In E. Rosch & B. L Lloyd (Eds.), *Cognition and categorization* (pp. 27–48). Lawrence Erlbaum.

St.Amant, K. (2015). Culture and the contextualization of care: A prototype-based approach to developing health and medical visuals for international audiences. *Communication Design Quarterly, 3*(2), 38–47.

St.Amant, K. (2017a). The cultural context of care in international communication design: A heuristic for addressing usability in international health and medical communication. *Communication Design Quarterly, 5*(2), 62–70.

St.Amant, K. (2017b). Of scripts and prototypes: A two-part approach to user experience design for international contexts. *Technical Communication, 64*(2), 113–125.

St.Amant, K. (2018). Reflexes, reactions, and usability: Examining how prototypes of place can enhance UXD practices. *Communication Design Quarterly, 6*(1), 45–53.

St.Amant, K. (2019). The cultural context for communicating care. *Journal of Technical Writing and Communication, 49*(4), 367–382. https://doi.org/10.1177/0047281619871213.

St.Amant, K. (2020, November 28). Usability for contexts of care: Medical usability. *UXNess.* http://www.uxness.in/2020/03/ux-for-contexts-of-care-medical.html.

Schwab, P. N. (2016, May 19). Pros and cons of focus groups vs. interviews: an in-depth review. *Into the Minds.* https://www.intotheminds.com/blog/en/focus-groups-vs-interviews-pros-and-cons/.

Sevelius, J. M., Gutierrez-Mock, L., Zamudio-Haas, S., McCree, B., Ngo, A., Jackson, A., Clynes, C., Venegas, L., Salinas, A., Herrera, C., Stein, E., Operario, D. & Gamarel, K. (2020). Research with marginalized communities: Challenges to continuity during the COVID-19 pandemic. *AIDS and behavior, 24*(7), 2009–2012. https://doi.org/10.1007/s10461-020-02920-3.

Sun, H. (2012). *Cross-cultural technology design: Creating culture-sensitive technology for local users.* Oxford University Press.

Tomkins, S. S. (1978). Script theory: Differential magnification of affects. *Nebraska Symposium on Motivation, 26,* 201–236.

Tomkins, S. S. (1987). Script theory. In J. Arnoff, A. I. Rabin & R. A. Zucker (Eds.), *The emergence of personality* (pp. 147–216). Springer.

Woods, B. (2019, April 9). America's $103 billion home health-care system is in crisis as worker shortage worsens. *CNBC.* https://tinyurl.com/2vepucby.

Zhang, J., Johnson, T. R., Patel, L. V., Paige, D. L. & Kubose, T. (2003). Using usability heuristics to evaluate patient safety of medical devices. *Journal of Biomedical Informatics, 36,* 23–30. https://doi.org/10.1016/s1532-0464(03)00060-1.

16. Feature Flow Analysis: Collaborate More Deliberately with Your Users

Lane T Lynn, Matthew R Miller, and Holly Lussenden
NORTHROP GRUMMAN CORPORATION[1]

Joy Robinson
GOOGLE

Abstract. Feature flow analysis is a method for collaborating with users to improve designs. It is a quick and easy way to get feedback on specific features of your designs. This method can be used early in the design process to get feedback on ideas, or later in the process to validate designs. Feature Flow Analysis helps UX teams work more closely with SMEs and expert users to facilitate co-design and creation processes.

Our UX team works on various projects with external customers to help improve the workflows, navigation, and ultimately the complex interfaces of the software and hardware we develop for them. To accomplish many of these tasks, we rely on users to provide quality feedback through multisite and multi-user usability testing. Below we describe how Feature Flow Analysis began as a result of a set of unique circumstances and then describe a use case for the method.

It began in January of 2020.

Upon return from a user touchpoint, extensive usability testing on our software application revealed a number of issues that would need to be addressed in an upcoming software redesign. Users were struggling with the navigation and terminology, as well as understanding some of the feature workflows. The team concluded that improvements were needed to streamline a number of workflows, improve major systems information architecture, and clarify navigation, labeling, and system feedback. As one user commented "A user would have to know what they are looking for" in order to use the new software.

Our site visit provided a long list of issues. Given the limited time needed for the redesign (nine months) a series of site visits were planned. Site visits were to begin in March and occur approximately every six weeks and would include four site visits. Each visit would help our team to verify application redesigns which we would use to inform development. Our next site visit was planned for late March 2020.

We began by ordering the issues from most-to-least important and most-to-least troublesome for the user, as well as areas that affected the largest

---

[1]. Approved for Public Release; Distribution is Unlimited; #21–1163; Dated 09/09/21

DOI: https://doi.org/10.37514/TPC-B.2025.2517.2.16

proportion of our users. With input from project's project owner and visibility into the backlog, we were able to prioritize 19 items that would need to be addressed across the next few incremental releases leading up to the beta release in November 2020. With our plans in hand, we began with the highest priority item: navigation.

Users of the earlier version of the software were used to adding layers of information onto a map using a series of modal boxes. In the test version of the software (shown to users during usability testing at our first site visit), we had already modernized the navigation using a navigation rail with a retractable tray. In the redesigned version, the old layers were represented as cards. As a user added data to the map, a card representing a layer would collect in the tray. To make the navigation easier to use, we wanted to introduce a favorite's tray that would include the users' most used layers. We needed to know if this new navigation feature, the grouping of the users' most frequently used layers—would resonate with users.

As March neared, it was clear that our jobs and site visits were in jeopardy due to Covid-19. In late March, our entire team, and the majority of our 70,000+ company, was sent to work from home. All travel was canceled. Without user site visits, we were in the dark.

We needed a new plan. How could we answer our questions? How did we proceed without visiting our users? We thought back to our resources. Our user touchpoint was a wealth of resources in many ways. It provided an extensive list of issues to address and priorities to consider, but it also provided us with a long list of power users eager to assist us with this redesign. More than one power user commented that we could contact them anytime for ideas and opinions, and they would be willing and ready to assist.

That week after our travel was canceled, and we were set up at home, we made our first conference call. We contacted User1,[2] our power user, at a prearranged time. The day before the meeting, we had emailed her our design ideas (our facilities didn't at that time permit screen sharing via video conferencing). During the meeting, we walked through the designs page-by-page asking about her impressions of the new favorite's tray. We asked and answered questions along the way, collaborating on the best ways to make the workflow, well . . . work for her. She understood the concept, had reviewed the designs, and thought it might work well.

Two days later, we were on conference call with User2. She had similar feedback; we collaborated to make a few tweaks here and there. Add another layer to the favorites. Add a button to clear all layers. We used checkboxes to turn on and off the layers (indicate which layers were added to the tray). We used options and the eye icon to toggle the visibility of the layers. The resulting changes were

---

2. The identification of the participants have been altered to protect the privacy of the participants.

reviewed and worked well for the power users. We collaborated with a few more power users. By the end of the week, we were ready to demo the finalized designs and have them added to the backlog for future development.

From there, we were off to the next feature, and the next, and so on. And yes, there were snags along the way. The emailing of designs was a major issue. It was very difficult to collaborate without being able to control the flow of the visuals, ask and answer questions about them while remaining in sync. Sometimes, the files never arrived, taking up much of our power users' precious time waiting for tardy files to show up. Finally, by June we had resolved the majority of our connectivity issues between us and the users' community and were able to use video conferencing effectively.

After that, we established a cadence of meeting with users two or more times per week to collaborate on complex workflow designs. Using this process which was later named—Feature Flow Analysis, we were able to systematically source guidance and input from our expert user community to help improve our designs, saving hundreds of wasted hours. From there, we verified and completed hi-fi designs with remote usability testing among a myriad of user groups.

Figure 16.1 shows a general review of this process enveloped in a traditional UX workflow.

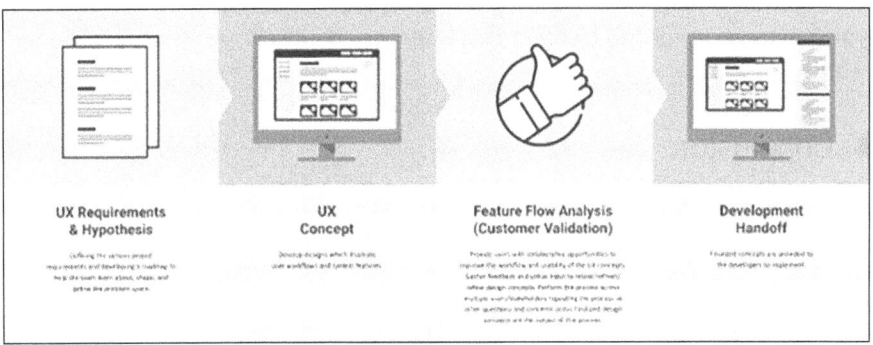

Figure 16.1. Traditional UX workflow.

■ Benefits

Feature Flow Analysis gives a team the ability to quickly collaborate with users to improve designs. The process enables a feature-by-feature review and validation of a design. Unlike a cognitive walkthrough or usability testing, where larger parts of the system or process are often considered, Feature Flow Analysis doesn't require a specific research question or a part of the system to be ready for evaluation. Instead, it is a collaborative process where the user, for a brief part of time, is a part of the design team, helping to source ideas, consider, and select them. Leveraging the knowledge of SMEs for the expertise they possess can help improve the quality of experiences for all levels of users.

▪ Cons

Users must be intermediate to expert users. Beginners can't help with complex design questions. The collaboration efforts would collapse. Additionally, the process calls for reasonable fidelity in the designs requiring either developers or designers or both to spend time creating mid-fi designs that can communicate workflow options well enough for conversation. Finally, some projects might necessitate obtaining expert users from multiple user groups in order to equality balanced design input—a process that might be time consuming and potentially costly.

▪ Feature Flow Analysis: A Simple Idea

While Feature Flow Analysis began as a simple idea, it grew into something much more powerful. In a nutshell, we would, for one feature/idea, brainstorm and build designs demonstrating potential workflows. From there, we would meet with power users (familiar with the specific features/areas of the app) for as little as 20 minutes via phone or video conference. At the meeting, we would exchange ideas about the designs: collaborate on what needs to change, discuss what workflows were working, figure out which ones need more work, decide which ones we needed to toss. For that brief period of time, we would collaborate as a design team.

▪ Conclusion

At the time of writing this chapter, we have been using the Feature Flow Analysis method for most of the year. There is a vaccine being distributed and the future looks a bit brighter. Our small team of four have completed over 20 feature designs using this method and accumulated 35+ hours of talking with users in doing so. A colleague commented just after we wrote this chapter, "Calling up users and talking to them about a design, that's not a method." To which I said, a method is simply a process that someone follows in the same way each time so that it may yield similar results. Yes, I replied, this method is one possibly many teams may have practiced. But my research showed no articles about a similar method among the short history of UX, HCI or related areas. Yes, there is likely a similar method in another field, but that doesn't stop our field from discussing, naming, and benefiting from it. UX, meet Feature Flow Analysis.

▪ Overview of Feature Flow Analysis (TL;DR)

What

An evaluation method in which people review a design of a feature/workflow and collaborate about the efficacy of the new design as they consider it.

Why

To get quick feedback on whether or not a workflow will be workable/suitable for a specific user group who is familiar with the system. This method is suitable for improving user experience at any stage in the production process, but it is predicated on using real users or SMEs.

Frequency

Consider obtaining at least two to three SMEs input depending on the feature/project/user groups.

Process

1. Identify specific features of concern for specific categories of users of a design solution.
2. Develop a set of workflow designs that solve the specific issues identified by the user groups. Transfer the workflows to a form that can be reviewed by users.
3. Source Subject Matter Expert (SME) users and set up the meeting. (Remote meetings work well if the system is software.)
4. Before the meeting send the SMEs the designs and any questions you have.
5. During the meeting, discuss the designs with SMEs and record the interaction.
6. Ask questions as objectively as possible. Allow SMEs to provide their opinions freely
7. As they go, ask what they would attempt to do next or how they might modify the workflow to suit their needs. Ask participants, if your assumptions are incorrect or anything we need to reevaluate?
8. After the meeting, review the results and make changes to the designs using the SME input. Make more workflow choices if required.
9. Move to the next SME. Rinse. Repeat.

17. Empathy, Access, and Engineering: Empathy Maps in a Disability Studies Course for STEM Students

Sarah Summers
FRANKLIN COLLEGE

Renee D. Rogge
ROSE-HULMAN INSTITUTE OF TECHNOLOGY

Abstract. In this chapter, the authors describe an empathy map assignment in a cross-disciplinary introduction to disability studies course. The course, co-taught by a professor of English and a professor of biomedical engineering, asked students to integrate engineering design skills with human-centered approaches. The chapter includes three lessons about using empathy maps in the classroom: keep maps simple and focused on accessibility, embrace digital communication as a way to interact with users, and emphasize opportunities for enhanced team and cross-disciplinary communication.

Empathy is hard work, but it is a skill well-suited to the classroom. As empathy researcher Brené Brown (2018) argues, "if we can't be learners, we cannot be empathetic" because empathy is intimately linked with curiosity and the ability to make connections (p. 145). In this chapter, we describe three lessons learned by using empathy mapping to teach human-centered design skills in an introduction to disability studies course for STEM students.

Often, STEM students compartmentalize their educational experience, focusing on technical knowledge and design in their major area courses and "soft skills" in their required arts, humanities, and social sciences courses. As Graham Pullin (2011) notes, this separation often extends into design for disability "where teams still tend to come exclusively from clinical and engineering backgrounds, [and] the dominant culture is one of solving problems."

Our introduction to disability studies course, co-taught by a professor of English and a professor of biomedical engineering, asked students to integrate their engineering design skills with human-centered design by focusing on empathy research. This approach allowed the instructors to emphasize the human dimensions of engineering design and highlight the integration of the liberal arts and engineering for which human-centered design is known. For the final project of the course, we asked multidisciplinary teams of students to design and develop a conceptual prototype of a new product for a person with a disability, focused on encouraging full participation in life. We wanted to move students from solving a problem (e.g., designing a tool to make it easier for someone with a tremor to put on jewelry) to playfully reimagining an experience. Thus, the design project reinforced a foundational concept of the course—people with disabilities deserve to have full, fun, enjoyable lives.

We introduced students to concepts of design thinking, focused on the role of empathy in the design process (Hess, 2016; Schmitt, 2016). As part of the project, students were required to make empathy maps—a UX tool that encourages a focus on user needs and perception—by talking to real stakeholders and listening to their experiences (Figure 17.1). Students had to talk to at least two potential users of their product as well as other stakeholders, including community organizations and our institution's accessibility coordinator. This research alerted students to challenges like cost, comfort, and the desire for some users to blend in with friends that students might not have otherwise considered.

In designing and refining this assignment, we've learned three lessons about using empathy maps in disability studies and with STEM students more broadly.

1. Keep Empathy Maps Simple and Focused on Accessibility

A Google image search will return several different templates for empathy maps. Some of the most popular examples, including innovation coach Dave Gray's (Gray, Brown, and Macanufo, 2010) original design (Figure 17.2), include sensory experiences that don't make empathy maps accessible for all potential research subjects. For example, categories for "see," "hear," and "say," assert these abilities as the norm and do not align with a disability studies framework.

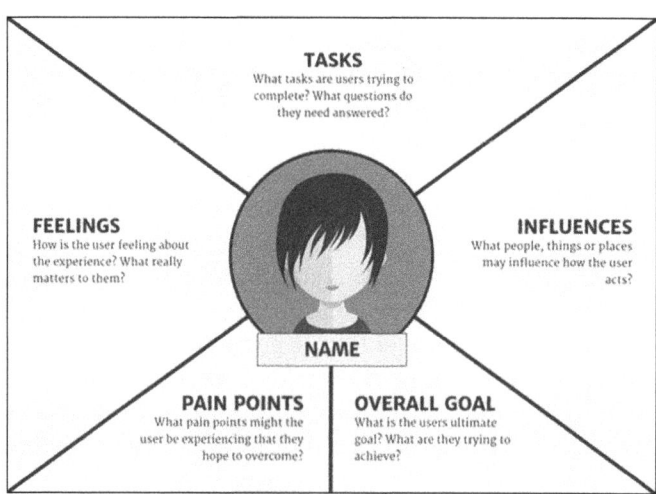

Figure 17.1. Empathy Map Template: Students began with this online template (Smyk, 2017) and added information based on interviews and secondary research. In the completed maps, each section included at least three statements with a superscript that corresponded to a reference list of interview subjects and sources.

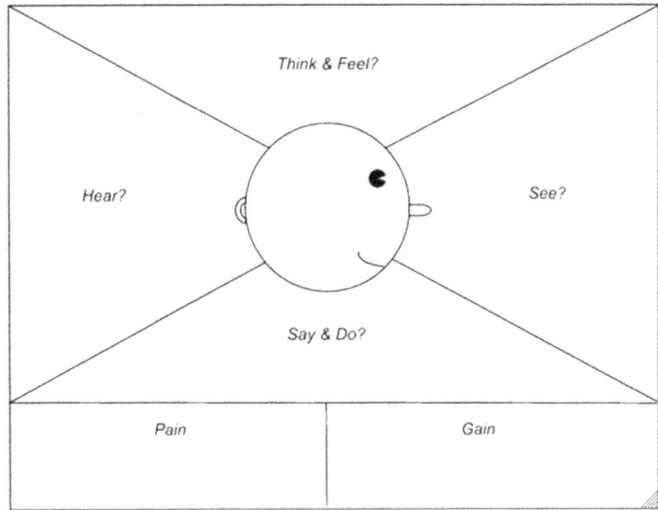

Figure 17.2. Traditional empathy map template that does not account for disability. Note. This empathy map template assumes sensory experiences like sight and hearing are universal and thus was adapted to reflect all potential users. Image from Solutions IQ.

Our students used and modified UX consultant Paul Boag's updated empathy map. Boag (2015) adjusted the original map because he felt it was too generic, not to account for accessibility. However, because Boag's adapted version removes sensory experiences, it is a better starting place for students focused on addressing the needs of diverse users.

We asked students to create empathy maps with three to four categories focused on user goals, perceptions, and challenges. To keep the map focused on user experiences, as opposed to stereotypes or their own assumptions, students used superscripts to link each experience to its source on a separate reference page. Later, when students wrote a rationale for their design, they were required to link every decision to one or more points on their empathy map.

2. Embrace Digital Communication as a Way to Connect with Users

Many students didn't have immediate and personal access to the target audience for their product. On top of that, for many college-age students the idea of calling someone on the phone is just as bad as the idea of not completing an assignment. Student teams turned to resources like podcasts and documentaries to get additional perspectives, but that didn't allow them to fulfill the requirements of speaking to two potential users of their design. The most creative teams used digital communication to meet this challenge. For example, the team that created the empathy map in Figure 17.1 was designing for rock climbers without upper limbs. They joined online forums for climbers with disabilities and chatted with potential users in those forums. They gained valuable insight from these users that was reflected in their maps. In particular, they learned the importance of haptic feedback to users to help them feel safe using the device. In the rationale that accompanied their final design, they described the safety mechanism that locks the climbing hook to the prosthetic:

> The purpose of this mechanism is to provide rotary articulation and locking capabilities, however, as we have learned from our research, these features must give physical feedback to the user in order to be truly functional. The locking mechanism as well as the rotation socket will both "click" when used. With these functions we hope to achieve dynamic adjustment while climbing, which was an issue brought to our attention by [name of climber they spoke to during empathy research].

As this excerpt demonstrates, students were able to connect their empathy research directly to design choices meant to improve the user experience.

3. Empathy Maps Provide a Connection to a User's Experience that Enhances Team Communication, which is Useful Across Disciplines

The empathy map was a simple, easy-to-develop, and easy-to-understand visual that helped novice designers in the disabilities studies course understand and communicate the needs of the audience for their product. Specifically, the empathy maps emerged as an effective way for students to share with the group the research that they had conducted individually. The empathy maps also helped instructors communicate design feedback to students. For example, the empathy map content was populated with short phrases such as "lack of dexterity" or "limited sensory feedback" which could prompt deeper discussions about how a team's design concept addressed the issue. After seeing the direct benefits of improved team communication and linking design requirements to specific empathy map content, empathy maps were introduced as a requirement in a first-year student design course in biomedical engineering. The empathy maps were used to establish common ground among the team members, prioritize user needs, and align design priorities to address the pain points for a team's proposed product. Medical school professionals have also identified empathy maps as framework to improve the communication and empathy levels of medical students (Cairns et al., 2021).

■ Conclusion

The students in the disabilities studies course received formal instruction on how to develop and incorporate an empathy map into a design project. Most design courses in engineering emphasize the importance of correctly identifying "user needs," but struggle to teach students a coherent framework for capturing and communicating information that sets aside their own assumptions so that they might develop insight beyond a user's "needs" that includes perceptions, emotions, and feelings. The framework presented here introduced and reinforced best practices by treating empathy mapping as an ongoing activity where a successful team must revisit the empathy map as their understanding (of the project and the person) grows and evolves. Once students leave the controlled environment of higher education, they may work on larger cross-functional teams where it is not practical or possible for every member of a team to interact with every potential user. The success of the team working on a human-centered design will depend on the ability of a team to communicate and describe user personas. The empathy map framework will serve as a solid foundation for those conversations. Because they help students design with a user in mind, empathy maps can augment any authentic assessment that students create for an audience. From writing assignments to community action assignments, empathy maps encourage students to think beyond their own experiences and problem solve with a larger context in mind. Students can then create more useful projects and learn how to integrate others' values and experiences into their work.

■ References

Boag, P. (2015, November 3). Adapting empathy maps for UX design. *BoagWorld*. https://boagworld.com/usability/adapting-empathy-maps-for-ux-design/.

Brown, B. (2018). *Dare to lead*. Random House.

Cairns P., Pinker I., Ward A., Watson E. & Laidlaw, A. (2021). Empathy maps in communication skills training. *The Clinical Teacher, 18*, 142–146. https://doi.org/10.1111/tct.13270.

Gray, D., Brown, S. & Macanufo, J. (2010). *Gamestorming: A playbook for innovators, rulebreakers, and changemakers*. O'Reilly Media.

Hess, J. (2016, June 26–29). The development and growth of empathy among engineering students [Conference presentation]. *American Society for Engineering Education 123rd ASEE Annual Conference and Exposition*. New Orleans, LA, United States.

Pullin, G. (2011). *Design meets disability*. MIT Press.

Schmitt, E. (2016, June 26–29). The importance of incorporating designer empathy in senior capstone design courses [Conference Presentation]. *American Society for Engineering Education 123rd ASEE Annual Conference and Exposition*. New Orleans, LA, United States.

Smyk, A. (2017, March 10). How to design empathy maps to better understand your users. *Adobe Blog*. https://blog.adobe.com/en/publish/2017/03/10/how-to-design-empathy-maps-to-better-understand-your-users.

18. Crafting the Story: Engaging Stakeholders in UX Research

Ginnifer Mastarone
UNAFFILIATED

Abstract. Strong methods and reporting are only a part of the UX research process. Communication, UX evangelism, and stakeholder buy-in are just as important to deploying impactful research programs. This chapter describes strategic and logistical lessons that I have learned throughout my career as a user experience researcher. Throughout, I provide insight into what is top-of-mind as I think about research projects. I also present practical approaches to communication and interactions with stakeholders at different parts of the research process.

Stakeholders are key partners during the UX Research process, and throughout my career I have learned to work with many who occupy different roles and are responsible for different aspects of product development.[1] Some of these roles are close to my background as a researcher, such as data scientists, other researchers and analysts. Others may be more technical or represent strategic functions, such as engineers, product managers, and other business leaders. For each stakeholder type, I ultimately needed to craft a story throughout the research process that resonated with them, including why I was proposing certain research questions and approaches. I also needed to ensure that my research design and delivery were compelling enough to impact product decisions. Without impact, the research was just an exercise in doing research.

In this chapter, I describe principles and behaviors that I have learned in order to plan and deliver impactful research. Impact has different criteria based on where the product is in its lifecycle as well as people problems and business problems. For example, impact could take the form of evangelism as a stakeholder comes to understand how research informs product decision-making. Or, impact could be aligning different stakeholder perspectives into a cohesive research objective. When I think about impact, I ask myself: how would the product (or understanding of the product) be different if research was not a part of this project? To that end, below are strategic and logistic principles that I have adopted to drive impact with stakeholders:

1. Define and share with stakeholders how research impacts product strategically and tactically. In order to support this objective, I suggest that

---

1. The opinions within this chapter are my own, and represent lessons learned from my own experiences throughout my career.

DOI: https://doi.org/10.37514/TPC-B.2025.2517.2.18

user experience researchers (UXRs) need to be visible to many types of stakeholders. Sometimes this requires carving a space to have a seat at the table. Additionally, researchers may need to step out of their comfort zone and initiate communication with other functions (e.g., engineering, product leaders)
2. Build into your roadmaps milestones, planning sessions and syncs with stakeholders. This lesson is more procedural. The objective here is to manage stakeholder expectations through constant, clear communication.

I discuss each in the following sections.

Lesson 1: Define and Share with Stakeholders How Research Impacts Product Strategically and Tactically

There are two types of research that UXRs might engage in depending on their organization's structure (i.e., the logistical way that research is completed, including the role and scope of research). The first category is strategic research. This research looks forward and uncovers foundational principles or patterns in user thinking or behaviors. These insights inform product strategic visions because they help us understand what our users are like, what motivates them, what challenges they face, and what larger objectives they have (e.g., business objectives). The second category of research is tactical. One objective of tactical research is to uncover or fix problems within the current product (e.g., usability testing). Other objectives might include testing concepts or benchmarking designs. Tactical research is typically iterative, and is framed by how the product is expected to change over some timeframe (e.g., three or six months).

Most academic programs teach how to plan and conduct tactical research. Students learn to do usability testing, heuristic evaluations, concept testing, wireframing, focus groups, and many other methods that evaluate product features in relation to expected user tasks. However, what I found to be an area of personal growth was to think beyond current product features to shape what a product could be in the future. In order to make this leap, it was important to hear other perspectives outside of research.

Ask to Attend Meetings, Sprints, and Brainstorms Where Stakeholders are Thinking About Future Directions

These conversations are where future vision comes into focus. They help me (as a UXR) to understand the vision for the software, and position research in the strategic space with different types of stakeholders. For example, product managers might drive the overall arc of the product because of their interactions with leadership. Engineers and data scientists might be responsible for analyzing behavioral data (who, how, and where). In my experience, the superpower of UX

Research is providing insights into user mental models, beliefs, needs, concerns, and experiences (who, how, why, and what). The goal is to understand business needs and see how they align with user needs. One method to carve out space in these meetings is to provide lightweight input in the moment that affirms, challenges or raises questions with regards to user needs. By providing feedback in the moment, stakeholders can see the contribution of the researcher without having to wait for reports or larger research studies.

Lesson 2: Build into Your Roadmaps Milestones, Planning Sessions and Syncs with Stakeholders

Research is a blocker is a phrase that I actively strategize against through careful planning and clear, constant communication with stakeholders. A blocker during a project is a pain point that stops forward movement. For example, the inability to recruit for a study is a blocker; you can't do interviews without participants. I have used my meetings with stakeholders to understand their mental model for a blocker and empathize with their position, such as the need to implement product changes. Most often, the concern was that research would slow things down. Less mature UX environments might even see researchers as those people who only raise problems without providing actionable solutions. Qualitative research, in particular, has been accused of taking too much time to complete while the findings are not generalizable. Therefore, product teams and stakeholders might gravitate to quantitative research because it fits into their mental model regarding metrics, key product indicators or key quality indicators. And, depending on the industry/culture of the organization there might be a review process (e.g., IRB) before research can launch.

There are times when I have felt behind the ball with staying in step with product teams and stakeholder demands. My solution has been proactive communication in my roadmaps about the scope of the work I am planning, the timelines for this work, and documenting shifting priorities. This process has looked different across my career (e.g., charters, mural boards, roadmaps), but one practice has been consistent: create milestones for each stage of research. With regards to impact, research output takes center stage. My next suggestion is:

Be Clear About What stakeholders can expect at the end of research

Output for research can take several forms, such as formal reports, research papers, slide decks, executive summaries of findings and recommendations, or even thought pieces that synthesize and contextualize a larger body of research. Regardless, prime stakeholders by being clear about what your plans are. In the roadmap, build in time to get feedback on the output. Be clear about how you expect the output (e.g., recommendations) to impact your team's goals.

Be Strategic About Which Stakeholders You Engage with the Most on a Project by Project Basis

Identify which stakeholders are the most important for a given project in relation to research. Then, plan regular meetings with these stakeholders. My argument is simple: there is only so much time to meet with people when a researcher also has to plan and execute research. Maximize your impact by speaking with the right people who make key decisions during development. For some projects, you might need an experimental environment because the product is in the experimental stage, so a regular check-in with engineering is essential to sync about their findings and decisions from these experiments. For a tactical project, the output might be usability findings or concept testing insights. Therefore, a regular sync with design is advantageous to understand their perspective. Or perhaps, a new process or product is being developed. In this respect, it might be necessary to sync with data science, subject matter experts (e.g., managers), or other leaders. I suggest to use these meetings to get updates about any changes to business or product objectives. Use this information to prioritize (or de-prioritize) proposed and on-going projects.

Use Syncs and Other Milestones to Educate Stakeholders About UX Research Over Time

Throughout my career, I have worked with stakeholders who know about UX Research and are excited to have us on the Team. I have also worked with stakeholders who didn't know what a UXR does, but wanted to learn. And, I have also worked with resistant stakeholders who did not think that research was valuable. So, I have adopted the practice of educating stakeholders about UX Research in bite-sized chunks over time. This reduces their cognitive load, and allows me to point to recent examples of how UX Research was valuable or explain the research process in real-time.

Now, some researchers might argue that our job is to plan, execute, and report out on research. Why should we have to "defend" or "educate" others about our research? Who has time for that? Over time, I have learned to evangelize research while empathizing with my stakeholders. My argument is that research can seem like a mysterious process. We are knowledgeable about a wide array of methods that have strengths and weaknesses. We strategically decide how to execute research in a way that maximizes resources without compromising data integrity. We have our own jargon and come from many different academic disciples. We have insight into our process, but why would product teams know our culture and understand our decision-making unless we invite them in?

I have learned to invite stakeholders behind the curtain over time through a three-part approach: provide rationales, seek alignment, and demonstrate research. My goal is to reinforce that research is a partner to product, and to build authentic relationships with stakeholders. I discuss each part in turn.

1. **Provide rationale.** Create documents or reserve a few minutes during regular meetings with key stakeholders to answer questions about methodological decisions. I have found that a detailed research plan provides stakeholders with insight into why the research is being done with a particular sample, and why certain questions are being asked (or not). Throughout the research process, the research plan can be referenced during meetings. A more difficult story to explain is why one method (or type of data) is better to answer research questions. In these situations, I have presented a table to stakeholders that breaks down each research question, the pros and cons of using a given method to answer those questions, and what type of data we can reasonably expect to collect using each method. For example, if we decide to collect interview data to answer a research question, then we can reasonably expect data that is detailed and answers why and how users are interacting with a product. But, if the stakeholders require more large-scale insights to feel confident with changing directions, then we need to choose another approach to get data to support that decision. Similar to a research brief, the table becomes a tool to facilitate conversations at different phases of the research project.

2. **Consistently seek and confirm alignment.** The primary technique that I have found to quickly ensure alignment is a kick-off meeting where the research brief is presented to key stakeholders. The goal of the kick-off is to carve out a space to communicate the proposed value of the research, to be transparent about methods and timelines, and to clarify the role of each stakeholder in the process. Additionally, I might ask stakeholders for any relevant milestones in their roadmap that might impact product direction over the course of the research project so that I can check-in and confirm that there are no major changes that could impact the value of the research.

3. **Demonstrate research.** I have learned that some stakeholders better understand what research can do once they see it in action. My primary approach is to invite stakeholders to research sessions with users as well as pilot sessions that I might hold with other researchers. After these sessions, we all debrief about what we saw. During the course of the research and in future interactions, I can refer back to what the stakeholders saw and experienced in order to illustrate key datapoints or to provide context to a story that I am telling. An additional benefit of inviting stakeholders to pilot sessions is that it provides a contextualized view into how we administer sessions. One of my fondest memories is

when a product manager told me that they had no idea about everything that goes into planning and executing research. They continued that they didn't realize, for example, how I actively planned for worst-case scenarios to ensure that we got meaningful data. This PM became one of the most vocal champions of UX Research.

■ Conclusion

This chapter describes strategic and logistic approaches to building stakeholder relationships over time in order to maximize the impact of research programs. As researchers, we are methodological experts. But equally important to impacting product direction are persuasion, communication and stakeholder education. The approaches that I have detailed have worked for me, but I acknowledge that each researcher works within different organizational cultures. I encourage each researcher to approach these principles as inspiration, and apply the ones that resonate to their teaching and research practice.

Contributors

Tatiana Batova is Associate Professor at the Darden School of Business in the University of Virginia where she teaches leadership communication, user experience, and storytelling with data. Her research interests focus on cross-cultural data visualization, user experience methodologies, content strategy, and global communication in business and healthcare.

Amelia Chesley is Assistant Professor of Professional Writing at Embry-Riddle Aeronautical University in Prescott, Arizona, where she teaches in the department of Humanities and Communication. Her research engages with multimedia access, transdisciplinarity, and digital rhetorics, as well as communities of participatory knowledge-making and creative, crowdsourced projects. She helps coordinate the student-run podcast *What's the Word? Eagle Alumni Spotlights*, serves as a faculty sponsor and co-editor of The Black Box, Embry-Riddle's creative arts magazine, and records audiobooks with LibriVox when she can.

Felicia Chong is a senior content strategist with UX experience in both industry and academic settings, as well as government agencies. She received the 2022 Nell Ann Pickett Award for her co-authored article, "Student Recruitment in Technical and Professional Communication Programs," in *Technical Communication Quarterly*. She is also the co-author of Interpersonal Skills for Group Collaboration.

Richard Douglas Divine earned his PhD in human centered design and engineering at the University of Washington. His research focuses on technology-assisted reflection and workplace communication. He is a user-centered analyst, researcher, and data enthusiast with over twenty years of experience leading programs in operations, analytics, and product development. He currently serves as a principal analyst managing finance IT governance for the City of Tacoma in Washington state.

Jeffrey M. Gerding is Assistant Professor of English at Xavier University in Cincinnati, Ohio. His research and teaching focus on technical communication, the rhetoric of civic engagement, service learning, and digital rhetoric. His work has appeared in *Technical Communication, Journal of Business and Technical Communication, IEEE Transactions on Professional Communication*, and the *Journal of Interactive Technology and Pedagogy*. He received his PhD in English from the rhetoric and composition program at Purdue University in 2018. He is available at gerdingj1@xavier.edu.

Laura Gonzáles researches, teaches, and practices UX, translation, and community engagement. She is Vice President of the Association of Teachers of Technical Writing (ATTW) and editor-in-chief of *Reflections: A Journal of Community-Engaged Writing and Rhetoric*.

Keith Instone's thirty-year career has been divided in three periods of about 10 years each: human-computer interaction researcher, industry practitioner (IBM), and user experience consultant. His newest role is industry analyst.

Jennifer Ismirle is a user experience researcher and technical writer with over seven years experience conducting qualitative research and evaluations for industry, nonprofits, government, and academic departments or institutions. She collaborates with cross-functional teams and stakeholders to design, plan, and conduct strategic UX research and provide clear and actionable insights for improving the experiences of their products. She has three degrees from Michigan State University: an M.A. in digital rhetoric and professional writing, a B.A. in professional writing, and a B.A. in English.

Billy Kangas is Executive Director of the Pope Francis Center in Detroit, a nonprofit organization that provides services and support to the homeless and marginalized. He is also a writer and teacher who explores the intersection of spiritual practice and creating effective and compassionate teams. He has successfully led teams for the past twenty years to have a significant impact on serving people in need. He holds a PhD in theology from the Catholic University of America.

Rita Koris is Associate Professor in the Department Human Resource Development at Budapest University of Economics and Business (Hungary) where she teaches courses in business and management in the EMI program of the university. Her research interests lie primarily in innovative teaching practices of business education, internationalization of HE, collaborative online international learning (COIL), transversal skills development and teachers' academic development.

Lane T Lynn is a user-centered design leader at Northrop Grumman with sixteen years of experience in digital design, process improvement, and communications. She specializes in scaling UX practices, experience measurement, and applying human psychology to complex system-of-systems product development. Her work has been featured in internal industry publications, including *Women Designing a Digital Path Forward* and *10 Ways Digital Transformation is Changing How We Work*, highlighting her contributions to digital transformation, Agile integration, and enterprise knowledge sharing.

Benjamin Lauren is Associate Professor and Chair of the Department of Writing Studies at the University of Miami. He also serves as Director of Innovation and Society, a co-major that infuses design thinking and data science in support of sustainable futures. His scholarly work intersects songwriting, user experience, design (thinking), rhetorical theory, and community-led and institutional change.

Holly Lussenden is a user experience researcher with Northrop Grumman Corporation. Her work has spanned across several different fields including Air Force Weather and America's intercontinental ballistic missile defense programs where she's been able to conduct extensive user research and ultimately impact user interfaces. She received her M.A. in Geography from East Carolina University and her B.S. in Atmospheric Sciences from the University of Nebraska-Lincoln.

Ginnifer Mastarone is a user experience researcher with more than ten years of experience creating impactful user experiences. Her career has spanned across the academic, healthcare, government and technology sectors. She earned a PhD in communication at the University of Illinois at Chicago where she specialized in health communication and survey research.

Casey McArdle is Assistant Professor in the Department of Writing, Rhetoric, and Cultures at Michigan State University. He is the Director of the Experience Architecture Program and has several publications and conference presentations that focus on online interaction via academic, professional, and social spaces. His research examines experience architecture, learning experience design, generative artificial intelligence, online writing instruction, leadership, web development, user experience research, user experience design, and rhetorical theory.

Matthew R. Miller is a senior principal UX designer at Northrop Grumman, leading the design of mission-critical systems that drive key DoD programs. He specializes in visual and interaction design, information architecture, and user centered research across multiple platforms. Using methods like in-person interviews, contextual inquiry, and A/B testing, he uncovers user insights to create intuitive, high-impact design solutions. His mobile application designs have been classified as a Northrop Grumman trade secret, underscoring their strategic importance to the organization.

Sushil K. Oswal is Professor of Human-Centered Design and HCI at the University of Washington and research faculty in the Center for Research on Education and Accessible Technology and Experiences. Sushil's sociotechnical research focuses on overlooked accessibility issues in human-computer interaction design spaces such as the ecology of medical device design, mobile platforms embedded in such devices, user interfaces of computer hardware, contexts of use in web applications, and web experience architectures of learning systems. His COIL courses translate some of this design knowledge for distributed learning spaces.

Zsuzsanna B. Palmer is Associate Professor in the Department of Writing at Grand Valley State University in Michigan where she teaches professional writing, UX writing, and document design. Her research interests include intercultural communication, virtual exchange projects, visual rhetoric, website accessibility, and translingual writing. Her articles have been published in *Journal of Technical Writing and Communication*, *Journal of Business and Technical Communication*, and *Business and Professional Communication Quarterly*. She has also contributed chapters to edited collections about translingual pedagogy and citizenship and advocacy in technical communication and has published articles about website accessibility.

Ashley Patriarca is Associate Professor of English at West Chester University of Pennsylvania, where she teaches courses in professional and technical writing and directs the first-year writing program. Her research can be found in *Journal of Business and Technical Communication*, *Assembling Critical Components: A Framework for Sustaining Technical and Professional Communication*, and other publications.

Liza Potts is Professor in the Department of Writing, Rhetoric, and Cultures at Michigan State University where she leads WIDE Research and is a co-founder of the Experience Architecture program. Her research interests include networked participatory culture, social user experience, and digital rhetoric. Her professional experience includes working for technology startups, Microsoft, and design consultancies.

Chalice Randazzo researches the intersection of practical and critical-cultural technical and professional communication, especially silence and missing voices. She is Associate Professor of Professional Writing at Utah Tech University.

Cody Reimer is Associate Professor of English at the University of Wisconsin-Stout, where he teaches courses in the Professional Communication and Emerging Media program. His research examines the intersection of technical writing and game studies, specifically user experience research and documentation. He also works as the rules writer for Paverson Games' award-winning board games and co-hosts the podcast *Game Studies Review*.

Joseph W. Robertshaw. As a first generation academic from a working-class family, Dr. Robertshaw (rhetoric and writing, Bowling Green State University) also holds an M.S. of Ed (curriculum and instruction) and an M.A. in English from Youngstown State University. He currently loves teaching students in the Business and Technical Writing Program at the University of Alabama in Huntsville and conducts research in the field of rhetoric, writing, and composition. He also enjoys writing fiction, gardening, and fishing.

Joy Robinson is a Senior UX Researcher on the ChromeOS team at Google, where she delivers insights that shape the Chromebook user experience. Her journey includes roles as a UX Manager for Northrop Grumman and Assistant Professor at University of Alabama in Huntsville (UAH) specializing in UX. At UAH she taught UX and technical writing courses, founded and ran the university's only UX lab. Joy earned her PhD from the Illinois Institute of Technology (IIT) in technical writing. She also holds M.S. and B.S. degrees in engineering from IIT and Rensselaer Polytechnic Institute, respectively.

Renee D. Rogge earned her bachelor's and doctoral degrees in biomedical engineering from Tulane University and the University of Iowa, respectively. She is Dean of Faculty and Professor of Biomedical Engineering at Rose-Hulman Institute of Technology where she co-developed a capstone design sequence that emphasizes assistive technology development. Over 100 undergraduate capstone teams have participated in the program, which has previously received support from the National Science Foundation as part of the Research to Aid Persons with Disabilities program.

Missie Smith researches how technology use affects human perception, performance, and preferences. She is currently Assistant Professor of Industrial and Systems Engineering at Auburn University. Prior to that, she spent four years as a Research Scientist at Reality Labs and two years as Assistant Professor of Industrial and Systems Engineering at Oakland University. She received her PhD in Industrial and Systems Engineering at Virginia Tech and her M.S. and B.S. degrees in Industrial Engineering at Mississippi State University.

John M. Spartz is a reformed Associate Professor from the University of Wisconsin-Stout English and Philosophy Department now working as a Senior

UX Researcher at Edward Jones. As a member of a SAFe enterprise software development team, he leads the strategic design and execution of UX and usability research to help inform product decisions. He has previously published in *Journal of Business and Technical Communication, IEEE Transactions in Professional Communication*, and *Programmatic Perspectives* around UX and entrepreneurship.

Kirk St.Amant is Professor and Eunice C. Williamson Chair in Technical Communication at Louisiana Tech University where he serves as the Director of Louisiana Tech's Center for Health and Medical Communication. He is also an Adjunct Professor of Health and Medical Communication with the University of Limerick in Ireland and a Research Fellow in User Experience Design with the University of Strasbourg in France. His research focuses on usability in international health and medical contexts, global health literacy, and developing health and medical products patients in different cultures can use easily and effectively.

Sarah Summers earned her bachelor's and doctoral degrees in English from DePauw University and Penn State, respectively. She is Associate Dean for Academic Affairs at Franklin College where she oversees faculty development, engaged learning, academic advising, and first-year seminars. Her scholarly work focuses on faculty development and writing pedagogy and includes articles in *Writing Center Journal, Computers and Composition*, and *Insight: A Journal of Scholarly Teaching*.

Heather Noel Turner is Assistant Professor and Director of Internships in the Department of English at Santa Clara University (SCU). Her research interests include user experience (UX), pedagogy, design methodologies, and rhetorical approaches for data visualization. At SCU, Dr. Turner serves as founder and director of the User Experience Research and Writing Lab.

Ryan Weber is Associate Professor of English, Director of Business and Technical Communication, and Director of UX Programs at the University of Alabama in Huntsville. His work has appeared in publications including *Communication Designed Quarterly, Technical Communication Quarterly*, and *Journal of Technical Writing and Communication*. He hosts the podcast *10-Minute Tech Comm*.

Kristin Williams is the human resources coordinator for Avalign Technologies. Before joining Avalign, she was a web team writer for West Chester University of Pennsylvania and previously worked in digital marketing.

Eric J. York is Associate Professor of English at Iowa State University where he teaches courses in rhetoric and in UX design and development and studies the social and pedagogical implications of emerging technologies. He's also a practicing fullstack web developer.

Mark Zachry is Professor of Human Centered Design & Engineering at the University of Washington where he directs the Communicative Practices in Virtual Workspaces Laboratory. His research areas include intelligent interfaces to support virtual interactions and social behavior in computational systems. He is an STC Associate Fellow and Fellow in the Association of Teachers of Technical Writing (ATTW).

www.ingramcontent.com/pod-product-compliance
Ingram Content Group UK Ltd.
Pitfield, Milton Keynes, MK11 3LW, UK
UKHW021850210426
53221PUK00022B/576